DIVIDED IN UNITY

DIVIDED IN UNITY

IDENTITY,

GERMANY,

AND THE

BERLIN POLICE

ANDREAS GLAESER

The University of Chicago Press
Chicago and London

HV
8210
.B4
G56
2000

Andreas Glaeser is assistant professor of sociology at the University of Chicago.

The University of Chicago Press, Chicago 60637
The University of Chicago Press, Ltd., London
© 2000 by The University of Chicago
All rights reserved. Published 2000

09 08 07 06 05 04 03 02 01 00   5 4 3 2 1

ISBN (cloth): 0-226-29783-7

Library of Congress Cataloging-in-Publication Data

Glaeser, Andreas.
    Divided in unity : identity, Germany, and the Berlin police / Andreas Glaeser.
      p.   cm.
    Includes bibliographical references and index.
    ISBN 0-226-29783-7 (cloth : alk. paper)
    1. Police—Germany—Berlin—History. 2. German reunification question (1949–1990) 3. Identity (Psychology)—Germany. I. Title.
    HV8210.B4G56   2000
    363.2′0943′155—dc21   99-32698
                                                                   CIP

Meinen Eltern
Hildegard und Horst Glaeser

CONTENTS

PREFACE

Divided in Unity has a double agenda. On a substantive level it aims to understand why Germans feel deeply divided along east-west lines in spite of the fact that they have come together again under the roof of one state. On a theoretical level it develops an analytical theory of identity formation processes that is centered around the notion of acts of identification. From both the substantive and the theoretical angles, *Divided in Unity* is concerned with the ways in which selves and lives are made meaningful. It pursues this question by following eastern and western police officers on their daily patrols through the once-divided city of Berlin. Through their experiences of space and time, through their expectations and hopes, their attitudes towards work, their understandings of democracy, and their moral quarrels this book analyzes how the experiences of otherness and sameness between east and west are constructed and played out.

The challenge of postunification Germany as a field for the study of identity lies in the fact that its interpretation—its very description—eschews the categorizations which have been the mainstay of identity research in the social sciences during the past decades. In other words, the sense of otherness between east and west Germans cannot primarily be understood in terms of gender, sexual preference, class, race, ethnicity, or nation. This need for an adequate conceptual framework in the scientific discourse is mirrored by a similar need in common discourses. While elsewhere the experience of otherness may be quickly and easily explained by invoking regional or national differences, Germans on both sides of the former iron curtain, and especially Berliners, cannot resort to the color coding of the mental maps of regions and nations. Worse, perhaps, the very concept of *nation* seems to add to the confusion rather than to dissolve it: seeing their experiences of otherness in terms of nationality creates a morally ambiguous situation because the foreignness between easterners and westerners is illicit within the stipulated intimacy of shared nationality. To flag their differences, then, east and west Germans have resorted to the makeshift categories of "Ossi" (nickname for easterner) and "Wessi" (nickname for westerner) while wondering about the roots of their experience of otherness, attempting to understand what is referred to in a widely used metaphor as the "walls in the heads of people."

For the social scientist studying identity, the interest of the experience of otherness between east and west Germans does not lie, therefore, in viewing it as yet another act in the ongoing drama of continuous definitions and redefinitions of German nationhood. Other social arenas—such as the debates about the physical reconstruction of Berlin—are much more fruitful in this respect. Nor does it lie in a deconstruction of the ontological pretensions of nationalism, as tempting as this might be given the ironies of the situation. Rather, the present German context offers an excellent opportunity to gain a processual understanding of identity formation and change. The question is, then, What exactly is it that people do to align themselves with some fellow humans rather than others? What leads them to identify themselves and others in particular ways with places, times, values, beliefs, capabilities, power, and knowledge. Tracing the actual interactions of eastern and western police officers has produced interesting insights into what matters most to them in their stipulations of who and what they are and who and what their respective other is. These perspectives on roles played in identity formation processes by organizational frames, space, time, work, morality, and the public-private divide lend structure to this book. Taken together, they offer a perspective on the roots of the experience of otherness between east and west Germans.

Throughout this book I have tried to intertwine theory and ethnographic investigation. Each chapter addresses theoretical as well as substantive issues. The introductory chapter opens with an exposition of the mood-swing from the joyous celebration of the fall of the Berlin Wall to the mutual mistrust after the actual political unification of the two parts of Germany. Thus, the central substantive question of this study is introduced: What is it that divides eastern and western Germans in spite of political unification? Subsequently, I discuss the fundamentals of the analytical theory of identity construction, which I will develop step by step as the book progresses. Central to this theory is the proposal to study the processes of identity formation in terms of acts of identification as *modus operandi* rather than in terms of identities as *opus operatum*. The introduction also contains a basic outline of the field methodology, which tries to be equally responsive to theoretical and substantive issues. The introduction concludes with a sketch of the two field sites where most of the ethnographic work underpinning this study was done.

East and west are spatial categories. In chapter 1, "Viewing Each Other through Space," I show how officers from both sides of the former iron curtain experience spaces as eastern and western and how they use these spaces, the layout of streets, and the color, shape, and odor of houses to identify themselves and others. I show how easterners and westerners construct their identities by reading and writing spaces as well as by tying each other to places. In this chapter I also intend to show that identities are not just mental constructs, open only to intellectual reflection, but that they are open to sensual exploration. The theoretical center of the first chapter is the development of a theory of modes of identification in terms of basic tropes and emplotment structures.

Chapter 2, "The Political Organization of Identification," revolves around the idea that identifications are not only deployed in face-to-face interactions but are also very much a feature of policies, administrative practices, and laws. Thus chapter 2 traces the kinds of identifications of easterners and westerners that have been inherent in the rhetoric and practice of the relations between the Federal Republic of Germany (FRG) and the German Democratic Republic (GDR) since 1949, the actual political organization of German unification in the form of accession, and finally the incorporation of eastern officers into the (West) Berlin Police. Subsequent chapters will make clear not only the extent to which the historical relations between the two German states and the actual organization of the unification of country and police build a rather coherent whole, but the degree to which they inform face-to-face interactions.

Temporal identifications are the focus of chapter 3, "Times Ajar." East and west Germans perceive each other frequently as living in different times. Yet, as this chapter shows, temporal displacement is also a formidable instrument of "othering," effectively undermining any meaningful east-west dialogue by not granting the other equal status as a partner. Especially for east Germans, the revolution of 1989 has raised many issues concerning the connection between time and identity. Their life trajectories suddenly became very uncertain, and it was not clear anymore how they should integrate their own pasts into their present lives. Chapter 3 addresses, therefore, the question of how easterners experience the discontinuity of revolution and how they try to create a sense of continuity in spite of it. Theoretically, the linchpin of this chapter is the notion of narrative, which provides a formidable means of making identifications in time.

The issue of work ethic is one of the most hotly contested topics between easterners and westerners. They accuse each other of not knowing how to work well, of not having the right (German) attitude toward work. I trace this issue in chapter 4, "Performing Work," along with the question of how uniformed police officers can actually derive a sense of self from their work even though their work often has no tangible results. The analytical theory of identity formation is expanded in this chapter by the notion of performance—the fact that identifications are just as inherent in actions as in verbal utterances—and by the idea that style and skill are highly self-identifying, contributing immensely to a sense of personal difference.

The final three chapters deal with the relationship between moral discourses and processes of identity construction. The ways in which sincerity as the key criterion for moral evaluation informs the negotiation of identities between eastern and western officers is the dominant theme of chapter 5, "Challenging Sincerity." As I show in this chapter, the valuation of sincerity as a core moral tenet has ironically led many eastern officers, both in the former GDR and after unification, to identify themselves in contradictory ways, thus creating painful double-bind situations. Another interesting finding of this chapter is that even when easterners and westerners share a commitment to the same values, thus sharing what is usually considered a fundamental aspect of culture, their differential placement in the process of unification and their different histories can still prove to be divisive.

Chapter 6, "Individual Rights and the Morality of States," foregrounds the question of how officers can identify with the state as a whole while maintaining a differentiated moral evaluation of its constituent parts. I show in particular that moral discourses relying on sincerity made it much more difficult for officers in the GDR to criticize individual aspects of the state than for western officers, who used a language of individual rights. The empirical bases of these investigations are the moral identifications and counteridentifications in discourses about two subjects of central moral importance to the police officers: (1) the role of the secret police, Stasi, in the former GDR, including the mostly voluntary assistance provided by many GDR citizens to the Stasi, and (2) the deadly,

'high-security' border regime at the Berlin Wall and along the border between both German states.

In chapter 7 I attempt to show how for both easterners and westerners,
"Building, Shifting, and Transgressing the Public-Private Divide" is an
effective way to create identifications. I will map out how the boundary
between the public and the private was differently handled in the People's
Police and in the Berlin Police, and I will explain why former People's
Police officers experienced the movement from one regime to the other
as a loss of meaning. Central to this chapter is the idea that intimate
human bonds are created by a dance of revelations and counterrevelations of private matters that produce intimacy and trust, and which allow
for more sensitive and also more critical identifications of self and other.
Following a social event which is thought to facilitate the production of
intimacy, I will try to shed light on the question of why Germans from
the eastern and western parts of the country find it so difficult to befriend
each other.

I conclude this study by reflecting on what the divisions between east
and west Germans are about, and what it is that stabilizes them. By summarizing the ways in which I have found officers to be active in building
self-transcendence from one social situation to the next and across time,
I critically evaluate postmodern theories of the non-self. Inspired by the
late Wittgenstein's private-language argument, I proceed to summarize
the analytical theory of identity construction in a metaphor which relates
single acts of identification to the notion of identity. Since this theory is
eminently social, I also summarize the relationship between culture and
identity as it has emerged from my field observations. Finally, on the basis
of the complete theory of identity construction, I provide something like
a contingency map for an answer to the question of how long Germans
of the east and west will continue to live divided in unity.

ACKNOWLEDGMENTS

This book would be unthinkable without the extremely friendly reception I received at the two field sites where the bulk of the research was done: Police Precinct 66 (Köpenick) of the Berlin State Police, and the Potsdam Police Station, including its Babelsberg Substation of the Brandenburg State Police. I would like to express my deep gratitude to the officers and civil employees at both locations for welcoming me into their ranks, for sharing their thoughts and their feelings, their worries and their hopes so freely with me. In more than just one sense, I owe this study to them.

I would also like to thank the following offices and institutions of the Berlin and the Brandenburg State Police for extensive interview time and for making valuable documents available to me: the Union Representatives and the Administration of Police District 6 in Friedrichshain; the former and present members of the President's Office, the Central Administration, the Central Investigative Unit for the Persecution of Government Crime, the Central Library, and especially the Berlin Police Museum in Tempelhof; the Police Academy in Spandau; the president and the Office of the President of Police in Potsdam; and finally, former and present members of the Department C III of the Ministry of the Interior of Berlin in Willmersdorf. I would also like to express my gratitude to the numerous former officers of the GDR's People's Police who are no longer on active duty, the former Presidents of Police of East and West Berlin, and the former Minister of the Interior of West Berlin at the time of unification for sharing their views with me.

The fieldwork for this study was made possible by a greatly appreciated fellowship from the Program for the Study of Germany and Europe, Center for European Studies, Harvard University, for the academic year

1994–95. An earlier version of chapter 3 was published as "Placed Selves: The Spatial Hermaneutics of Self and Other in the Postunification Berlin Police," in *Social Identities* 4, no. 1 (Spring 1998): 7–38, and is reprinted by permission of Carfax Publishing Limited, PO Box 25, Abingdon, Oxfordshire, OX14 3UE, United Kingdom.

This book grew out of a dissertation, and I have benefited enormously from the support granted to me by the members of the Department of Anthropology and the Department of Sociology at Harvard University. I would like to thank first and foremost Sally Falk Moore for her unwavering guidance, constructive criticism, and wonderful moral support. I could not have wished for better counsel throughout the project. I would like to express my gratitude to Theda Skocpol, not only for being a great role model in rigorous scientific pursuits, but also for not losing confidence in a project that is quite removed from her own research interests. I would like to thank Michael Herzfeld for many spirited insights into the study of culture which I would certainly not have had without him, and I would like to thank Orlando Patterson for his insightful reading of the entire manuscript. Werner Sollors first suggested the police as an interesting venue for studying Germany's east-west problematic. While visiting Harvard, Fredrik Barth provided valuable comments on two chapter drafts. Outside of Harvard, Robert Bellah has offered not only encouragement and support, but his critique of the whole manuscript contributed greatly to its revision. I owe many thanks to Douglas Mitchell at the University of Chicago Press for the truly heartwarming support and his highly professional guidance of the manuscript through the editorial process. John van Maanen's review of the manuscript was not only a veritable well-spring of ideas for improvements but also in its very style of writing a much appreciated gift for a first-time author. Hans Joas has saved the manuscript from a number of shortcomings, for which I owe him many thanks.

Finally, I would like to thank my friends, fellow sociologists, and anthropologists Chris Tennent, Michael Biggs, Ann Frechette, Levent Soysal, Don Seeman, Komatra Chuengsatansup, and Thomas Malaby for their enormously helpful comments on earlier drafts of selected chapters. To thank Fowzia Khan, my wife, would simply understate her influence: no single thought in this book remains untouched by her reflection.

INTRODUCTION

At first I was simply euphoric about unification. But today? Now there are these deep gorges dividing east and west. It is awful. And I don't know how to get out of that either. . . . The people here [in eastern Germany] have just been programmed differently, and we [the westerners] have been programmed too, and these programs do not harmonize yet. As long as these programs don't harmonize, Germany will remain divided. Only once we will all work from the same basic programming will there be a feeling of unity.

West German police officer working in east Germany

German unification poses a puzzle which is almost a paradox: its completion has divided the country. How this is so, why unification has created a near paradoxical situation, is the topic of this study. The nature of the puzzle of unification is perhaps best captured by juxtaposing the enormous mood swing in both mass media coverage and popular sentiment between early winter 1989, right after the fall of the Berlin Wall, and summer 1991, just a few months into actual unification, when talk emerged about the "walls in the heads of people."

Two Walls

The pictures of the fall of the Berlin Wall have circled the globe. But despite their much repeated showing in the mass media, they have lost very little of their original impact. Even after the passage of almost a decade since they were taken on and after 9 November 1989, they still have the power to move. They have captured a rare moment of emotional intensity which is even rarer on public display in adult life: deep joy, mixed with utter incomprehension at the good luck of the moment, and all that thousands of times over. These pictures seem to show human beings for whom a dream has come true. But not just an ordinary dream, something that can be achieved with a good bit of perseverance and stamina, but a dream that has for a long time been relegated to the status of a utopia. "I didn't think that this would ever happen in the course of my lifetime" and "it was sheer madness" are among the helpless phrases I have heard over and over again in attempts to lend shape to the sea of emotions connected to the opening of the Wall. These pictures have two main themes, but only one topic. One set shows easterners overcome by tears, pouring through the cracks in the Wall, embracing each other but also falling into the open arms of waiting westerners.[1] The other set shows easterners and westerners, mostly young people, united, sitting on top of the Wall, as if on the back of a slain monster, cheering, singing, drinking, meditating, beginning to pry pieces out of the concrete as one might pull the fangs of the beast to prove final victory. What one seems to witness is human communitas at its best, a oneness in joy. In the weeks after the fall of the Wall the media were filled with celebratory reports of Eastern-ers visiting the West. The apparently never-ending queues of East Ger-man Trabant cars,[2] with their widely visible and widely smellable exhaust fumes, lining up to cross the border between the two Germanies became *the* image of German rapprochement after the Cold War.[3] Each Monday in those days the papers in West Germany cheered to ever-growing num-bers of Easterners visiting the West on the preceding weekend. More was always better; it was a sign of improvement, a sign of success. These times are remembered in stories about spontaneous solidarity between East Germans and West Germans. The feeling conveyed by the mass media was in general that of an ongoing party. These images produced right after the opening of the Wall looked then and still look today as if the Cold War rhetoric about one nation living in two states and longing for nothing more than to be united again was actually founded in the thoughts and feelings of ordinary people.

The unification process itself went head over heels. From the opening of the Berlin Wall on 9 November 1989 to the conclusion of political unity on 3 October 1990, barely eleven months elapsed. This was possible only because it was carried through under the presupposition of an *essential* unity of the German people, which therefore did not require substantial negotiation. Essentialist presuppositions have a remarkable history in the relations between the two Germanies. In 1949 the Constitutional

1. Indeed at this time the holes in the wall weren't anything but cracks: nobody knew whether they adumbrated the final downfall of this monstrous monument of inhumanity or whether they would be repaired soon.

2. The Trabant was the standard East German car. Its plastic body, two-stroke engine, and its sheer size make it stand out in marked contrast to the standard models of West Germany, the Volkswagen or Opel, not to mention higher-end cars like the Mercedes or BMW.

3. In 1994 the German Postal Services commemorated the event with a stamp showing just this scene: a line of "Trabbis" moving west, cheered upon arrival.

Figure 1. Celebration of the fall of the Berlin Wall in front of the Brandenburg Gate (November 1989). Courtesy of German Information Center and JN Press.

Figure 2. Celebration of political unification in front of the Reichstag building. The riot police in the background were not only there to protect the keynote speakers but to prevent possible right-wing demonstrations (3 October 1990). Courtesy of German Information Center and JN Press.

Assembly working in Bonn on the Basic Law of the Federal Republic of Germany assumed to be speaking for *all* Germans; in 1955 the government of the FRG insisted in what came to be known as the Hallstein Doctrine that it was the only legitimate government of Germany. In 1990, almost half a century later, and despite the progress made by the government of the GDR in winning the recognition not only of the world but also of the FRG, it looked as if *the people of the GDR retrospectively warranted the mandate assumed by the FRG.* Two facts in particular seemed to support the notion that East Germans wanted to be West Germans: the mass exodus of Easterners into West Germany, and the surprising 18 March 1990 election victory of the Christian Democrats who, in contrast to the Social Democrats and the GDR civil rights movement, campaigned on a platform of unification by accession to the FRG.[4] It looked as if West Germany was *the one* Germany after all, not only by Western presumption but by East Germans' public consent. In view of this embrace, it just seemed logical to unite Germany not by calling upon east and west Germans to work hand in hand in a new constitutional assembly to negotiate the structure of their common home, but by the accession of five refounded states on the territory of the former GDR to the FRG.[5]

The feeling of oneness did not last. Barely a few months after the political unification of the two Germanies on 3 October 1990, the mass media started to report extensively on what has ever since been depicted as a profound *dis*unity between east and west Germans. The feelings and thoughts that easterners and westerners express about each other in the media are characterized predominantly by mutual disappointment, incomprehension, even alienation. This experience is captured well in a metaphor which enjoys widespread currency in the public discourse on east-west relations in united Germany. The Berlin Wall that once geographically and politically divided country and nation is said *not* to have been destroyed once and for all, but merely to have been *replaced* by what is now described as "the wall in the heads of people" that mentally and culturally divides the country, perhaps even more effectively than the original wall cast in concrete. Article after article has appeared on east-west differences, about east-west disappointment and disillusion. There are reports of western students, intellectuals, businessmen, and administrators withdrawing in frustration from their involvements in the east because they did not manage to find a common basis of understanding with easterners. There are also stories about easterners failed by the merciless mechanics of the western socioeconomic system, stories about the debilitating effects of long-term unemployment or about frustrated hopes

4. This initial election victory of the Christian Democrats was later reconfirmed in the first general election after unification on 2 December 1990.

5. This does not mean, of course, that no one urged caution regarding the speed of unification, pointing to the possible negative consequences of a hasty currency union and unification by accession. Basically the entire civil rights movement in East Germany, as well as the Greens and large parts of the Social Democrats, and intellectuals such as Jürgen Habermas in the West thought that way. Neither does it mean that no one suggested that unification was a bad thing altogether because of the fear—expressed, for example, by the prominent writer Günter Grass—of the resurgence of aggressive German nationalism. However, these more critical or cautious voices were swept aside and drowned out by the desire for rapid unification.

after failed entrepreneurial experiments. These in turn are contrasted with reports of easterners reveling in GDR nostalgia, exemplified by the revival and success of eastern brands of consumer goods, the perseverance of the reformed communist party, the Party of Democratic Socialism (PDS), in eastern elections, and the foundation of museums dedicated to the preservation of the material culture of the GDR. Easterners are also reported to be disgruntled by westerners' incessant rebukes for engaging in one kind of behavior or another and their air of arrogance, suggesting that they know everything better.[6] They are also said to be deeply disappointed by the western market economy-cum-democracy, especially because it seems unable to solve the persistent problem of unemployment in the east.[7] Westerners are said to wonder what has become of the hundreds of billions of marks they have transferred to the east, frequently thinking of easterners as very ungrateful. Westerners are also reported to wonder whether easterners even have the capacity to help themselves. Finally, many public figures worriedly ask, in the wake of persistent election successes of the PDS in the east, whether something like a distinct East German culture or an East German identity might exist that could ultimately thwart hopes for complete unification. Thus, if one describes the celebration of the fall of the Wall and the subsequent unification of the two Germanies as a party, one might describe the present mutual disillusionment as a hangover. But is this metaphor well chosen? Is the image of the hangover really appropriate in its insinuation of merely temporal problems, or is what is going on in postunification Germany much more fundamental than that?

The Substantive and Theoretical Lines of Inquiry

In this study I pursue two different sets of questions. The first deals directly with the empirical subject matter; the second concerns more general issues of sociological theory.

---

6. The term for this arrogant, know-it-all westerner coined in the east is *Besserwessi*, rolling well off the tongue by virtue of its sharp, double *s* alliteration. It is a composite term derived from the German word for "know-it-all" *(Besserwisser)* and the colloquial term used for westerner *(Wessi)*.

7. As of fall 1996, the unemployment rate in eastern Germany had reached 15 percent. This figure did not include all those who were still undergoing retraining financed by the Federal Labor Office.

Mental Walls, Understandings,
and Misunderstandings

On a substantive level I intend to explain the significance of the "wall in the heads of people," which the public discourse posits as the cause for the experience of otherness between east and west Germans. In doing so, I analyze the kinds of lived experiences and preconceived notions which amplify or at least sustain the idea of a marked difference between easterners and westerners; but I look also at the commonalties presumed and experienced. Since we cannot fully understand one without the other, I attempt to analyze the complex interplay between *experiences* of and *assumptions* about differences and commonalties. Thus my goal is to outline the obstacles to and possibilities for a better understanding between east and west Germans.

It will become clear in the course of the analysis that this cannot be done without also thinking about the perception of German history and the concrete politics of unification. The questions here concern the extent to which easterners' and westerners' views of each other are informed by the experience of more than forty years of the Cold War, with its distinct discourses about the other, and—what is perhaps even more interesting—by the perception of Germany's Nazi past. I also investigate the extent to which the concrete organizational process of German unification—its political projection, its concrete laws and regulations—influence the perception of self and other in everyday life. In other words, I intend to shed some light on the way in which east and west Germans try to make sense of themselves and each other within the concrete sociopolitical context in which they live while they have recourse to traditionally formed frameworks of understanding. Ultimately, I address the possibility of a separate, self-sustaining East German identity and culture, suggesting an answer to the question of whether they actually do exist now or under what conditions they might emerge.

Inscribed in German unification is a fundamental asymmetry. Because of the particular way in which unification was organized, virtually all adjustments had to be made by easterners. Thus, for east Germans, unification was a "twilight of the gods." Their old world was breaking down with enormous speed while a new world was emerging which most of them knew only from hearsay. Not only did the state in which they lived change, but their economy was turned upside down, and their material culture changed down to the very bread they were eating and the detergent they were using to clean their apartments. Accordingly, I pay particular attention to the self-interpretations of easterners in this study. I try to understand how their identity did change not only through conversation with fellow easterners and westerners but in reaction to the general changes in the world surrounding them. However, the question of how easterners make sense of the new situation into which they have been hurled and the question of how easterners see themselves as well as their new western compatriots as persons are closely intertwined. In most cases it is difficult to separate these two issues because, as I hope to show, easterners take what they see as the western world and western persons as proxies for each other (as westerners frequently take what they see as the eastern world for the easterners they encounter). Persons and worlds are linked by all sorts of interesting connections, which I explore in the following chapters. Thus, although this study is an ethnography among police officers, it is not a police ethnography in the traditional sense. In other words, I am not concerned here primarily with the practice of policing (for which I would have set up the study in an entirely different fashion) but with the problems of German unification. For excellent studies of policing in the Anglo-Saxon world, see Bittner (1990), Manning (1977), Rubinstein (1973), Reiner (1992), Smith (1983), Young (1991).

Identities Identified:
A Framework for the Processual Study of Identity

Since the experience of otherness among east and west Germans does not neatly fall into the categories which have dominated the social science literature on identity in the last two decades—race, ethnicity, sexual preference, gender, class, and nation—an alternative analytical framework needs to be developed. One fascinating aspect of the interaction between easterners and westerners is that they themselves bring to the foreground issues of identity.[8] This concern with interpretations of self and other is amplified among the police by a strong emphasis on mutual dependability in times of crisis. Easterners and westerners both value this quality; as one easterner put it, "If it's getting serious, I need to know that I can rely on the other." In addition, German unification took place in a morally highly charged atmosphere, which has led officers—especially easterners but increasingly also westerners—into situations that

---

8. See the subsequent section on the ethnographic adequacy of identity as theoretical focus.

challenge their long-held self-understandings.[9] The interactions between easterners and westerners therefore offer excellent opportunities to observe identity negotiation and formation processes at work and thus provide an opportunity not only to expand the substantive focus of identity studies beyond the traditional master concepts but to shift the focus to the *process* of identity formation itself.[10]

In close dialogue with the ethnographic field material, I have developed an analytical framework for the study of processes of identity formation and change. I present the basic orientation of this framework here, refining and extending it in all subsequent chapters. Prompted by the officers' own formulations of their identity concerns in terms of understanding and misunderstanding, I have chosen to take my departure from the hermeneutics of existential phenomenology (e.g., Heidegger 1986). Thus, I define identity as the meaning of self to itself or to another. My identity to me is what I mean to myself; my identity to you is what I mean to you. I assume that human beings constantly interpret self and others, especially if an unknown other suddenly assumes importance in interactions, or if their own self-understandings are challenged. The production of meaning, in turn, can be understood as a hermeneutic process which works principally by contextualization, that is, by making connections. The meaning of self (i.e., identity) is produced by identifying (i.e., connecting) self with itself at other points in time; with other persons; with beliefs, ideas, and values; with the world in the widest sense. Identifications are, then, the building blocks of the hermeneutic process called identity formation.[11] If identifications are repeated and reconfirmed by others

9. Easterners have been systematically suspected by westerners as participants in authoritarian suppression in the GDR, while westerners face increasing reproaches by easterners for being smug about their own "democratic attitudes." These issues are discussed at length in chapters 5 and 6.

10. On a similar note, Appiah and Gates (1995, 1) remark, "In the 1990s, however, 'race,' 'class,' and 'gender' threaten to become the regnant clichés of our critical discourse. Our object in this book is to help disrupt the cliché-ridden discourse of identity by exploring the formation of identities and the problem of subjectivity."

11. Although the term *identification* has been used in the sense advocated here by symbolic interactionists (e.g., Becker 1977, chaps. 12–14), it has not been developed into an overall analytical framework of identity formation. The way I use the term (in alliance with everyday usage) should not be confused with the psychoanalytic concept of "identification" (Freud 1960b, 183–88; 1974a, 98–103). Freud contrasts "identification" *(Identifizierung)* and "object cathexis" *(Objektbesetzung)* as the two principle libidinous forms of relation of a subject to the world. "Identification" for Freud is a wish to be like that object (as in a daughter who wants to be like her mother, or a student who wants to be like a teacher); "object cathexis," in contrast,

and thus stabilized, they congeal into parts of identities. Identities are thus like snapshots, the provisional results of an ongoing process of interpretation of selves, one's own as well as others'.

The crux of identity is meaning. Perhaps the common denominator of almost all recent theories of meaning is to understand meaning as a result of contextualization.[12] Making identifications as the medium of contextualization central to the analysis of identity constitutes a shift in focus from the whole to its parts as well as from product to process. This shift has a set of clear-cut advantages. Most important, identifications are much more easily observable in daily interactions than identities, because identities are enacted in identifications. They occur frequently, not only in face-to-face interactions of all kinds, but also in many political, legal, and administrative procedures. While the larger part of this study traces the ways in which eastern and western police officers identify themselves and each other in everyday situations, I also show how public representations of history, the legal and organizational frameworks of German unification and the unification of the Berlin Police have identified easterners and westerners in specific ways.

Immediately linked to the observability of identifications are two more advantages. First, the principal dimensions of the content of identity-formation processes are open. Rather than presupposing the relevant sub-

---

denotes the wish to possess a particular object (as in sexual love, or as in the desire to own consumer goods).

12. This is as true for philosophical hermeneutics, where contextualization is the synthetic element of the hermeneutic circle (e.g., Gadamer 1993) in understanding a part of the text in view of the text as a whole, as it is for structuralist linguistics and semiotics (e.g., Saussure 1959; Benveniste 1971; Eco 1979), where the meaning of a word is inherent in its relations to all other words in the text, or the meaning of a sign is a function of its relations to all other elements of a sign system. Contextualization is also at the core of narrative analysis (Barthes 1977; Ricoeur 1984, 1991, 1992; Danto 1985; Linde 1993; Somers 1994), where a single action or episode, or even a historical epoch can be understood only in its relation to the plot of a story, or even to the course of history at large. Contextualization is also the linchpin of Wittgenstein's (1984) use-theory of meaning, as he argues that the meaning of an utterance must be understood in terms of the interactional pattern in which it is embedded. Finally, contextualization is the hallmark of pragmatist and neopragmatist theories of meaning, such as symbolic interactionism (Mead 1962; Blumer 1969; cf. Joas 1985), where meaning emerges from the interplay of communicative action and reaction, and even of analytic approaches to the philosophy of history (Danto 1985). In all of these cases, contextualization is achieved by making connections: along the syntagmatic (diachronic) chain of words and the paradigmatic (synchronous) level of themes in structural analysis, or by inclusion into patterns and sequences of action in pragmatist thought.

stantive dimensions of identities, one can allow a broader set of themes of identifications to emerge from the field. This study reveals, for example, how aspects of space, time, work, and morality are significant poles of identity-formation processes for eastern and western police officers. Listening and watching for identifications is thus also a safeguard against the social scientific reification of prescriptive identity narratives in hegemonic as well as subversive discourses (cf. Butler 1990; Herzfeld 1997).

Second, the analytical focus on identifications makes it possible to pose important questions regarding the unity or fragmentation of identities as empirically researchable problems. Postmodern theories of the nonself (e.g., Jameson 1991; Gergen 1991; Baudrillard 1990; Lasch 1984) have described contemporary selves as depthless and fragmented, as formless, or as arbitrary collages of ever-shifting images. They celebrate their descriptions of the fragmented self as liberation from modernist theories which stress the internal coherence and unity as well as the predominantly rational character of the self in spite of its inevitable degeneration into states of alienation, anomie, bureaucratic rigidity, neurosis, and inauthenticity.[13] While these postmodern critiques form a necessary corrective to often rigid and frequently sterile modernist understandings of the self, they are—at least in the generality aimed at in theories of the nonself— overstating the fluidity and playfulness of the self. Again, rather than postulating the self as fragmented or unified, empirical studies focusing on identifications can thematize the durability or mutability of identifications across time and across social situations. I therefore explore in more detail how east German officers in particular deal with the radical break they have experienced in their lives due to the complete disintegration of the sociopolitical and economic system in which they have lived, as they cherish and acknowledge discontinuities in some respects while weaving continuities in others.

13. One of the dominant characteristics of modernist theories of the self is that they describe degenerated versions of the self in the face of a vision of what the whole self is about. They imagine modern selves as beautiful but broken vases. Alas, some of them think that they have a glue, like Marx (1973, 1974), who believes that the course of history itself will cure alienation through revolution, or Freud (especially 1972), who recommends therapy as a means to strengthen the ego against the neurosis triggered by impingements of the id or the superego. Others, like Durkheim (1973, 1930), almost despair over not having a glue to mend the vase broken by anomie, or feel helpless, like Weber (1988), who has nothing to recommend against the power of the iron cage. Postmodern theorists in their most radical form (Baudrillard 1990) would contend that there never was a vase to begin with, and that, moreover, all potential descriptions and prescriptions of vases are potentially suppressive ideologies.

The analytical framework developed in the course of this study may prove to be useful in other research contexts. If identity is supposed to be a meaningful sociological concept, then all forms of identity discussed in the literature should share certain key elements of their development as well as certain key elements of their consequences for human beings and for society. What seems to be desirable in the face of an almost overwhelming literature which at times alludes to the concept of identity in a very diffuse manner is a framework that is, on the one hand, maximally open to the empirical investigation of identity-formation processes and that can serve, on the other hand, as the basis for comparisons among different studies on identity. I also hope that the framework developed in this study can help to bridge the gap created by the common analytical distinction between social and individual (or personal) identities, and the ensuing division of labor between sociological and psychological approaches to identity. From yet another angle, one could also say that the framework proposed here will have to prove its usefulness as an analytical concept not only in terms of identity-formation processes in face-to-face encounters but also for attempts to understand how these processes are embedded in larger social and historical contexts.

Research Design and Method:
Analytic Ethnography

Following Weber, I consider the dialogical parallelization of theoretical and empirical inquiry as the cornerstone of every successful scientific pursuit. It avoids the epistemological naïveté of a blind inductivism as well as the world-weariness of sheer deductivism. Since the social sciences as sciences of the human *as* human cannot be nomological, a further problem is added: that of the tension between the particular and the *relatively* general. Most social occurrences are not simply the instantiation of some sort of local regularity. They cannot be fully interpreted in the light of contingent generalities; certain aspects always differentiate any particular occurrence from others. It is just as true, however, that many similarities do indeed exist among various social occurrences, even if this *similarity* is never *sameness,* ultimately retaining a metaphorical quality (cf. Vico 1968). Moreover, only the possibility of identifying meaningful similarities makes the social a possible subject of rational inquiry. Social occurrences, then, are as interesting for their unique specificities as for their similarities with others.

Weber was more aware than others of this tension between the particular and the general, and he found a unique way to deal with it, developing what he called his method of "ideal types" (Weber 1980, 9–10; 1988, 536–37). Ideal types are self-consciously rational constructs developed in dialogue with empirical case material. They serve as *heuristic* devices facilitating the interpretation not only of the cases from which they are derived, but of others which have not yet been analyzed. Using generalizations as ideal types means that one must be aware of the metaphorical character of these generalizations. I understand the theoretical framework and the concepts I develop in this study as ideal-typical in this Weberian sense.

The full potential of ideal types is only revealed in comparative work. Although this study is not comparative in the usual sociological sense of the term,[14] it does involve extensive comparisons. It may be helpful to differentiate between internal and external comparisons (see Barth 1997). External comparisons involve different historical processes that are distinct in space and time. Internal comparisons are made within the same historical process. Within this study, I make extensive use of internal comparison in contrasting easterners and westerners, in comparing different westerners and different easterners with each other and at various levels of several hierarchies, in juxtaposing dimensions of identity-formation processes (e.g., temporal and spatial aspects), and by looking at two different field sites. Only on the basis of these internal comparisons could I develop the ideal-typical framework used here for the study of identity formation processes, and only on this basis can it find some corroboration.

These deliberations about the importance of comparison for the building of concepts lead straight into considerations about method. If what I have said about meaning making as a process of contextualization is taken seriously, if the goal of a study on identity as meaning making *qua* identification is to grasp the meaning of the identity conflicts of easterners and westerners, then their identifications need to be contextualized. This contextualization can be achieved in two complementary ways: by watching and listening for these identifications in everyday life, in other words through ethnographic fieldwork, or by integrating these identifications into the life histories of the officers and into the histories of the organizations in which they have worked, and the places and countries in which

14. This means it is not comparative in the same sense that, for example, Barrington Moore (1966), Skocpol (1979), or Patterson (1991) may be called comparative (cf. Skocpol 1984).

they have lived.[15] Thus, while mostly relying on ethnographic fieldwork undertaken during eleven consecutive months in 1994–95, and again in the summer of 1996, I have also tried to integrate the fieldwork experience with the history of the unification of the Berlin Police and the history of German unification, as well as the relationship between East and West Germany since 1949.

If the theoretical and the substantive interests are to be pursued through ethnography, the choice of field site and the choice of theoretical framework must be carefully adjusted to each other. The best defense an ethnographer can put forth to a challenge of conceptual choice is to point out its ethnographic adequacy. Ethnographic adequacy is usually talked about by asserting that the theoretical framework in question does not do any "violence" to the field data or, in positive terms, that it "flows" from the field observations or "captures" the scene. What this means also is that the ethnographer is open to the specific opportunities that a particular field setting provides.[16] As the very term *opportunity* suggests, however, the reasoning must also proceed the other way round—a point frequently forgotten. The choice of any particular theoretical framework and any intention to develop it on the basis of ethnographic observations requires strategic deliberation about the theoretical adequacy of the empirical basis. Taken together, both directions of argument take the form of a dialectic. What is at stake, then, is an *adaequatio intellectus et rei,* understood in its old Thomasian form as a hermeneutic process (rather than in its more modern, positivistic guise as a static mapping; cf. Gadamer 1990, 270).

Typically, the rhetoric of ethnography emphasizes the choice of theory vis-à-vis a location, which is presented as a datum, rather than the choice of location vis-à-vis theory. I would argue, however, that a great deal of ethnography could be made theoretically more yielding if the reasoning proceeded in both directions, that is, if the choice of site and theoretical focus would mutually inform each other. This is especially true in circum-

15. One could formulate this still slightly differently. If identity is the provisional result of the hermeneutics of self and other, then the sociologist's task is first to grasp this process at a descriptive level, and then to interpret it at a theoretical level or metalevel. Sociology in this sense is a reflection on the hermeneutics of the everyday; we might also call it a (theoretical) hermeneutics of the (practical) hermeneutics of everyday life.

16. Ethnographic adequacy is a thus a rather vague concept. It is more an invitation to argue for a particular approach to interpretation than a set of criteria which can be checked one by one. In this sense it is also, of course, part of the rhetoric of any ethnographic study.

stances where the standardization of languages makes such a choice viable. I suggest that ethnographic endeavors which explicitly proceed in this way be called *analytical*. I begin, then, by arguing for the ethnographic adequacy of the choice of identity as a theoretical focus before I evaluate the theoretical adequacy of my chosen field site, thus presenting this study as an exercise in analytical ethnography.[17]

The Ethnographic Adequacy of Identity as Theoretical Focus

The choice of identity as the theoretical focus of this study requires justification. Following the logic of this study, using an ethnographic account as a window into a larger historical process, the ethnographic adequacy of identity as a theoretical focus must be demonstrated as plausible on two different levels. First, identity must be shown to be a prevailing theme in the historical process called (with the benefit of hindsight) German unification.[18] The simple fact is that without the presumption of shared identity between East Germans and West Germans, unification would not have been undertaken at all. East Germans and West Germans were assumed to belong together in one state. The preunification preamble of the Basic Law (Grundgesetz) of the FRG makes unity a declared goal of the state on the ground of "the unbreakable unity of the German people" (die unverbrüchliche Einheit des deutschen Volkes).[19] In the absence of an idea of shared nationhood, the relationship between the FRG and the GDR would in all likelihood be quite similar to that between the FRG and Poland or the Czech Republic today. The present experience of a substantial rift between easterners and westerners therefore challenges this presumption of an essentialist identity, thus thematizing the question of identity in the public discourse.[20]

17. This is not to argue, of course, that there is no great social theorizing on the basis of ethnographic work. However, few ethnographers justify the choice of a site or a topic with a theoretical interest. Analytic ethnography shares with Michael Burowoy's (1998) "extended case method" the explicit goal to develop theory through ethnographic work. Burawoy also clearly chooses sites in accordance with his theoretical agenda (e.g. 1979, 1992).

18. I argue this extensively in chapter 2, "The Political Organization of Identification."

19. The difference in reasoning in the new preamble is remarkable. Now the unity of Europe is the declared state goal. However, this goal is not based on the identity of Europe but on the concern for peace in the world.

20. This can again be made plausible by a counterfactual proposition. It is quite inconceivable that Germany and Poland would have decided to create a common

Second, identity must be shown to be an issue for the police officers themselves. As I have mentioned, officers frequently explained the alienation they have experienced in encounters with Germans from the respective other side in terms of their inability to understand who their counterparts really are. One western officer, for example, while finishing an evaluation of an eastern colleague, exclaimed in exasperation, "After four years I still don't know who they really are; I still have the feeling I don't know them." In a late-night conversation in a patrol car in the midst of musings about the difficulty, perhaps the impossibility, of sustaining friendships between easterners and westerners, an eastern officer described his western colleagues as "slippery as an eel" *(aalglatt)*, which referred not only to the presupposed ability of westerners to twist themselves out of trouble, but also obviously connoted his inability to "grasp" them, for he added, "They never seem to drop their masks." Concern with understanding or misunderstanding self and other, and disputes about the proper interpretation of self and other are pervasive, as illustrated by the following snippets from interviews about first encounters between easterners and westerners:

It was awful, they just came in here and thought they could do whatever they pleased.

I didn't know who they were, but I did know that we had been enemies for decades.

I was a communist then, and I still believe in it as a good idea.

I wanted to show them that I also was somebody, that I knew something too.

We had to show them what good police work is about.

They treated us as if we were lepers.

I just didn't want to work with them for what they had done in the past.

They were everything, we were nothing.

We intensely mistrusted each other and stuck pretty much to ourselves.

I didn't know whether it would be possible to work with each other, they weren't just colleagues yet.

---

state after the end of the Cold War, and it is utterly inconceivable that their unification would have taken the actual form of German unification, that is, the form of an accession. If they had, however, nobody would be surprised at the degree of difference and alienation that seems to bedazzle Germans about each other today.

Despite everything, we had to work with each other; thus we had to get to know each other better.

These excerpts raise issues of authority, competency, knowledge, trust, hierarchy, recognition, character, and history, and tie them to the theme of identity. Also, police officers like to point out how important it is in their profession "to be able to rely on each other" (sich aufeinander verlassen können), to trust each other blindly, especially in difficult situations. But the issues between easterners and westerners cannot be resolved simply by the development of trust that the other will have the right reactions at moments when they are dearly needed. The issue for westerners in the initial phase of the unification of the two police forces was not just trust, but the very trust*worthiness* of the easterners.

Easterners had a different set of concerns. They were outraged by the ease with which westerners assumed a commanding position while simultaneously devaluing every aspect of the People's Police without ever having known it. Moreover, easterners were also very concerned about their own future; they didn't know what would become of them. Yet it was communicated clearly to them that their future as officers in the Berlin Police hinged on two factors: the very trustworthiness that was so vocal a concern among their western colleagues (epitomized in the question of secret-police connections) on the one hand, and the effectiveness of their performance as police officers on the other. Thus the primary concern of eastern officers in their relation with western colleagues was and had to be recognition.

This brief exposition of ethnographic adequacy is only a beginning. In the course of this study it will become even clearer that identity is indeed an adequate lens for an analysis of the interplay between eastern and western police officers, and of the relation between east Germans and west Germans in general.

The Theoretical Adequacy of the Field Site

For several reasons, I deliberately chose police officers as the subjects of my investigation. German unification is about the dissolution of one state and its assimilation into another, and in many ways, the police epitomize the state. This is true as much in the public imagination—as the People's Police officers realized after the fall of the old regime in the GDR, when they were publicly scorned as its representatives—as in the minds of the officers themselves, who are quite aware that they do indeed represent the state (cf. Manning 1977, 4ff.). I assumed that the unification of Germany (in all cases where police officers were directly affected by it) posed particularly interesting and more pronounced identity problems for them than for the majority of the population.[21] The special relationship between the police officers and the state is emphasized through the use of paraphernalia such as uniforms, badges, coats of arms, flags, and weapons. For eastern officers, the dissolution of the German Democratic Republic also meant the dissolution of the police organization for which they worked, the People's Police (Volkspolizei) of the former GDR. Effective with unification on 3 October 1990, all officers not eligible for early retirement were integrated into the police forces of the five newly founded (or refounded) states and the now unified state of Berlin.[22] In this way they became police officers within the bureaucracy of a state that was not so long ago their declared enemy. Likewise, I assumed that western officers serving in the east were also particularly aware of their identities, because both the eastern population and their new eastern colleagues might perceive them as representatives of the new regime.

Berlin as the location for a field site also has particular relevance. Berlin and the Wall that divided it were the ultimate icons of the division of Germany and of Europe. As a result of making Berlin first the formal capital and then, after a heated debate, the seat of government too, Berlin also became the symbol of German unification.[23] Moreover, Berlin is the

21. While all former East German police officers were affected by unification, officers in western states who did not opt to move temporarily or permanently to any of the five states could remain relatively unaffected by it.

22. Germany, much like the United States, has a federal structure of government, but the division of power among the various levels of government is different in the two countries. Thus, terms literally translated may not have the same meanings. Translators therefore face the problem of whether or not to translate the names of institutions. Since I believe translation improves readability for those who do not understand German, I have opted to translate them as follows. The level of the federation in German is the *Bund,* which can be used alone, but it also appears as a prefix. I will translate all uses of *Bund* as "federation," and I will render its use as a prefix by the adjective "federal." The organizational units after the level of the federation in the hierarchy are called *Länder.* Following the American usage, I have translated *Länder* as "states." In general, German states are less autonomous than American ones (e.g., they may not enact their own penal codes). The responsibility for all police functions (with few exceptions, such as border controls—and here again the state of Bavaria is an exception) rests with the states.

23. Although the Unification Treaty declared Berlin as the formal capital of united Germany, it left the question of the seat of government open for decision by the first jointly elected Bundestag. In 1991, after a long and controversial public debate which emphasized the symbolism of the move alongside its cost, the Bundestag

only state in Germany which actively blended east and west—the only state which had to create integrated east-west administrative structures. Also, the Berlin police force has managed the organization of unification in a particularly interesting way. Upon political unification, about half of the remaining eastern officers were sent west, and a similar number of western officers were sent east. Thus, the typical situation in Berlin after unification was that patrol cars, for example, were staffed with one eastern and one western officer. By mixing police officers from both parts of the city, the Berlin police force became one of the few organizations in which westerners and easterners had to cooperate across the same level of hierarchy and not just up and down the hierarchical ladder, which is by far the more common situation. While most police forces in the five new states employ westerners in higher positions, the rank and file consist almost exclusively of former People's Police officers. This unique situation in Berlin gave me an opportunity to observe countless face-to-face encounters between easterners and westerners.

The actual precinct in which I did my fieldwork was chosen not by me, but by the Berlin Police. I had asked for permission to do fieldwork in an east Berlin precinct, because overall I was more interested in how easterners would make sense of the novel situation on their own turf, and as a westerner I was more curious to learn something about the east. I was granted permission to do my fieldwork in Precinct 66 (i.e., the sixth precinct of the sixth district), which comprises the southern half of the borough of Köpenick.[24] The officers of Precinct 66 frequently honor Köpenick by referring to it as a spa *(Bad)* alluding to the fact that their precinct is known for its relative quietness, that is, for crime rates (and hence work intensity) much lower than those of such notorious boroughs as Kreuzberg, Neukölln, or Friedrichshain. This may well have been the reason for its being chosen as a good field site for me. And although this choice might have been a severe drawback for the purpose of writing an ethnography concentrating on the police *qua* police, it was actually an

---

voted by a narrow margin in favor of Berlin. What is widely believed to have swayed undecided members of Parliament to cast their votes in favor of the old Prussian— and from 1871 to 1945 also German—capital is that after organizing unification by accession, a strong symbol for a new beginning was needed. Although the President of the Federation (Bundespräsident) already resides in Berlin, the Bundestag will move only in 1999. Most of the ministries will have moved to Berlin by 2000.

24. The state of Berlin (Berlin is, with Hamburg and Bremen, one of the three city-states in Germany) is subdivided into twenty-three different "boroughs" *(Bezirke):* twelve in the east with roughly 1.5 million inhabitants and eleven in the west with approximately 1.9 million inhabitants.

asset for focusing on east-west identifications because the officers had a lot more time to spare for conversations with each other and for interviews with me.

Yet the advantages of Berlin as a field site are also its disadvantages. The situation in Berlin is in many ways so special that I felt the need to supplement my fieldwork in Berlin with work at a secondary site in one of the five new states. I was lucky to get permission to do fieldwork in Potsdam, the capital of the state of Brandenburg, which is in easy reach of the Berlin commuter rail system (S-Bahn). I worked there in both the city station and the more suburban Babelsberg substation.

As I quickly realized, the second field site not only gave me a chance to develop another perspective on my Berlin field data, giving me some initial insight about the degree to which I could generalize my findings, but opened up a very interesting possibility for comparison. What made the Berlin site so attractive to me was the opportunity to observe daily, *face-to-face* interaction between westerners and easterners. This face-to-face interaction was almost completely absent at the two Potsdam locations. At the time of my fieldwork, only four western officers worked in Potsdam city station, three of them in more advanced positions, and at the Babelsberg station everybody was an easterner. The question that thus arose was whether the former People's Police officers of Potsdam and east Berlin differed in their understanding of westerners and of their own lives in unified Germany. In other words, would I find any marked difference between identity-formation processes among eastern police officers who had a relatively high rate of direct interaction with westerners as opposed to those who learned about western attitudes towards easterners only through occasional encounters, renarrations, and the mass media?

In both locations, I focused on four distinct kinds of police practices: the patrol car shift, the neighborhood-beat patrol, the case administration, and the precinct administration and leadership. I chose these four practices not only because they constitute the bread-and-butter business of a precinct, but also because this was the best way to get in contact with officers of different ages, genders, and ranks.[25] I followed officers on most of their daily routines; that is, I spent many days and nights in the back of patrol cars observing officers recording accidents, calming marital quarrels, picking up drunken persons, and dashing to the sites of

---

25. Officers on patrol car shifts tend to be younger than officers in neighborhood beat patrol, which are ordinarily a refuge for officers beyond the age of forty-five. While there are very few women in the operative services of the police (less than 5 percent), more than half of the administrative positions are held by women.

possible break-ins; I walked with officers on neighborhood beat patrols, watching them give tickets, withdraw licenses, serve as liaison with local businesses, and check the consistency of traffic signs; I lounged around in the administrative offices and in the offices of the precinct leaders, seeing them handle vacation requests, write orders, read telefaxes, and evaluate officers; I was part of routine conferences, of operational briefings and debriefings. Finally, I also took part in the social life of the precinct, in get-togethers during work time as well as after hours, and finally also in the regular festivities of the precinct or sections of the precinct.

In both locations I asked those officers whom I got to know during participant observation for an open-ended, tape-recorded, biographical interview. These interviews lasted anywhere from two to six hours, and they were conducted frequently in several installments (e.g., in the dead of night between two and five A.M. when there was nothing else to do). While I used a standard guideline for these interviews to make sure that I would get a fair number of narrations of the same event or at least of comparable experiences, such as the opening of the Wall, the first visit to the respective other half of the city, or the first day with the new colleagues, the interviews were open to following the narrative interest of the interviewee.[26] Since the People's Police was no longer in existence, I used these interviews also to learn as much as I could about everyday life in the People's Police.[27]

The identity-construction processes in everyday interaction, as fundamental as they are, cannot be fully understood without an appreciation of the larger organizational contexts in which they are embedded. Con-

26. Accordingly, some of these interviews follow more or less a biographical time line; others shift, on the basis of momentary associations, from one period of life to another. There are sixteen taped interviews with easterners in Köpenick, including three with former members of the People's Police district of Köpenick, of whom two no longer work for the police, and one was transferred to a western precinct. These interviews also include three with Köpenick officers who have been dismissed for collaboration with the former secret police. There are six formal interviews with westerners who have been in the Köpenick precinct since unification. I also conducted eight taped interviews with Potsdam officers, six of them with easterners and two of them with westerners working for the Brandenburg police.

27. I have also studied published sources to learn something about the People's Police. Unfortunately all of them are official, edited by the Ministry of the Interior of the former GDR (e.g., MdI 1987) or by the office of the president of the People's Police Berlin. While these sources are interesting as documents on the projection of a self-image of the People's Police, they are all very trite instruments of heroization with little information about daily life.

versations between easterners and westerners are, for example, strained by the fact that easterners receive a salary lower than that of their western colleagues (at the time of my fieldwork, 62 percent of western pay); that some of their qualifications are acknowledged, while others are not; that easterners had to undergo extensive retraining; that the police organizations reserve the right to investigate and dismiss officers for collaboration with the Stasi, the former secret police of the GDR; and so on. This is to say that the ways in which the state in general and the police organizations in particular treat eastern officers on the basis of laws and regulations are as important to the identity-formation processes as direct contact. They constitute what has been called the politics of identity.

An essential aim of this study, therefore, is to understand as clearly as possible how the unification of the formerly independent Berlin police organizations was planned and then actually carried out, or how exactly—from another perspective—the former People's Police in the territory that today constitutes Brandenburg was transformed into the Brandenburg State Police. Furthermore, it is also important to see how the unification of the Berlin Police and the transformation of the Brandenburg Police were embedded in the process of German unification as a whole. In other words, I needed some way to make a connection between face-to-face interaction and the larger social and political context.[28]

The basic method I employ to establish a link between the face-to-face interactions of the officers and the political context of unification is to use a series of organizational linkages,[29] mostly those within one formal organization (the [West] Berlin Police) as an "elevator" between these two levels of analysis.[30] Therefore, I conducted several interviews with high-ranking Berlin police officers who were instrumental in planning the unification of the two police forces. The interviewees include the former minister of the interior of the state of Berlin,[31] the two former presidents of police in Berlin at the time of unification, and the staff officers who

28. Since I was unable to attain sufficiently good data in this respect on Brandenburg, I had to focus as far as the details are concerned on Berlin. Thus, the following discussion deals only with Berlin.

29. I present a drastically simplified picture here, which disregards many cross-linkages across organizational boundaries, as well as the interaction between an organization and a much more broadly defined environment.

30. In chapter 2 I explain how I think this "elevator" works and clarify the justification for focusing exclusively on the West Berlin police organization rather than the People's Police.

31. The last interior minister of the GDR, who was appointed after the elections of 18 March 1990, did not give me an interview.

planned the selection and retraining efforts for former members of the People's Police corps. With the help of these staff officers, I also obtained access to important files which document the processes of decision making leading to the choice of the particular form in which the unification of the Berlin Police was carried out.

Since eastern officers had to submit to substantial retraining, and since this effort at reeducation and socialization sheds an interesting light on how the Berlin police viewed eastern officers, I also conducted a series of interviews with teachers at the Berlin police school who were involved in designing and conducting these retraining programs. Through the police college I could study documents which give an overview about the schedule of retraining, the teaching materials used, and the organization and rationale of the training program. Finally, I also met several times with union representatives responsible for the sixth district, to learn more about the relationship between the police officers and the organization from a vantage point different from that of the officers immediately involved. In Germany union representatives in the public service are an especially interesting source of information, since they participate in most personnel decisions, such as promotions, transfers, disciplinary measures, and dismissals.[32]

A sideline of my fieldwork focused on a branch of the Berlin Police which is responsible for the criminal investigation of "government crime" *(Regierungskriminalität)* of the former GDR.[33] Thus, one part of the police organization is directly concerned with Germany's efforts to process her own past (the German term for this is forcefully substantivized: *Vergangenheitsbewältigung*), in particular with the history and experience of life in the GDR. In a sense, this agency too is part and parcel of identity-formation processes in present-day Germany, through the information it provides for some of the widely publicized major trials against former leading members of the GDR government and the Communist

32. This means, for example, that union representatives always participate in the decisions about dismissals for collaboration with the secret police.

33. The full name of the office is Central Investigative Unit for Government and Unification Crime (Zentrale Ermittlungsstelle Regierungs- und Vereinigungskriminalität [ZERV]). Government crime includes human rights violations by GDR authorities, the cases of 538 people killed and 757 injured (Der Polizeipräsident in Berlin 1994, 8) at the border of West Berlin and the FRG while fleeing from the GDR, perversions of justice, and the misappropriation of funds by GDR authorities. Unification crime includes illegal handling of the property of the GDR at the time of unification, such as attempts to move the wealth of the Communist Party out of the country, and so on.

Party. Although staffed with criminal investigators from the entire republic, the agency is organizationally attached to the Berlin Police. Here, too, I was mostly interested to find out what the former GDR meant to the officers working there and what their image of former GDR citizens was.

In sum then, this study is based on several distinct sources of data gathered between fall 1994 and summer 1996. The most substantial set of data is derived from participant observations at the two field locations in Berlin and Potsdam, collected between September 1994 and July 1995. The second set is derived from tape-recorded biographical interviews. The third part originates from conversations (partly tape-recorded) with members of the Berlin police organization on several layers of the hierarchy, all the way up to the former minister of the interior. Archival data include unpublished files of the police and the interior ministry of Berlin and training material for eastern officers, as well as memoirs, speeches, and discussion papers by high-ranking officers. I have also made use of laws and regulations, ranging from the provisions of the German constitution, the Basic Law, and the Union Treaty (Einigungsvertrag) to police regulations about conduct with citizens and proper wearing of uniforms in the Berlin Police, the Brandenburg Police, and the former People's Police.

The Field Sites

The interactions I describe and analyze in this study take place in particular geographical and social contexts; they are embedded in the lives of police officers as police officers in Köpenick and in Potsdam, and they have to be seen in relation to particular police practices. Though I aim at larger contexts—even theory—most of what I have to say in this study has grown out of this interactional environment. Here, then, I want to set the stage for the following chapters.

Köpenick

Until the creation of "greater Berlin" in 1920, Köpenick was an independent township. Thus, Köpenick still has much of the flair of a small city. It has its own center, with town hall and market, shops of all kinds, a full range of schools, public libraries, a theater, movies, restaurants, hospitals, and a range of businesses from small-scale crafts and the professions to large factories, subsidiaries of multinational corporations. To live a decent life, one would not have to leave Köpenick for a single day. One could be properly born there, properly schooled and apprenticed; one could work there as well as enjoy one's pastimes, be married and buried comme il faut.

Köpenick constitutes the southeastern margins of the city and the state of Berlin, where the already much-tamed metropolis gives way to the lovely landscape of lakes, forests, and fields of the surrounding Mark Brandenburg. Köpenick is easily Berlin's most spacious borough, but only its sixteenth most populous, with little more than a hundred thousand inhabitants. Half of Köpenick is covered with fir woods and another seventh by the waters of the Spree and Dahme rivers, as well as Berlin's largest lake, the Müggelsee. This setting makes Köpenick one of Berlin's most popular weekend hangouts during the summer: good for a swim, cruising with a sailboat, or simply taking a walk, or even a hike in the footsteps of the poetical *genius loci*, Theodor Fontane, his famous *Hikes Across the Mark Brandenburg* in hand. The flood of recreationists causes severe traffic congestion across the handful of bridges that connect the sandy shores of Köpenick waters with the trunk of the city. And once they have arrived, there is barely enough parking space—all problems for the police.

Precinct 66 covers the southern part of the borough, which is, as the officers in Köpenick are eager to point out, certainly the more beautiful half. It includes not only the old city, but also most of the landscape attractions. Accordingly, it comprises the more fancy neighborhoods with a good stock of attractive old villas lining the water. One of these fancy neighborhoods is Karolinenhof, which was famous in GDR times for housing a fair number of well-known generals, party officials, and ministers. Among them were Friedrich Dickel, minister of the interior of the GDR (and thus also chief of the People's Police from 1963 to 1989), and Markus Wolf, East Germany's notorious spy chief. Parts of Karolinenhof were off-limits not only for the population at large but for the People's Police, who were replaced there by the Stasi, the secret police. Another prominent inhabitant of one of Köpenick's fancier neighborhoods is Stefan Heym, one of the best-known novelists of the GDR, part dissident and part public showpiece of the GDR intelligentsia. As a celebrity candidate of the reformed communist party (PDS), Stefan Heym became a member of the first jointly elected Bundestag.

But Köpenick is not all villas and lakes; it has its share of the neighborhoods that resulted from the rapid urban expansion of the 1960s and 1970s. In the GDR, as in the FRG, urban expansion was synonymous with functionalist, high-rise apartment blocks often built far away from the old city centers. Frequently, they became little cities within cities, though often without the amenities of the old towns. Both west Berlin and east Berlin have extensive areas of such urban expansion: what the Märkisches Viertel and Gropius Stadt are to the west, Marzahn and Hellersdorf are to the east. But while these new suburbs were quickly decried in the west as the death of urbanity and eschewed by renters if they could afford to live elsewhere, they have remained sought-after living space in the east. The reason for the relative attractiveness of these buildings in East Germany was that (in the absence of urban redevelopment) they were the only apartments available that had central heating and private bathrooms with running hot water.[34] These blocks were built in a distinctive style that was common to all of socialist Europe. Walls and facades were composed of a few modular forms of highly standardized, prefabricated panels, which allowed for quick and cheap assembly. For edifices constructed in this style, westerners have introduced the term "panel-buildings" *(Plattenbauten)* and for settlements composed of such buildings, the term "panel building settlements" *(Plattenbausiedlungen)*. While these words are used more and more universally in a pejorative manner, Easterners, for the reasons just outlined, used to refer to them simply as "new buildings" *(Neubauten)*. The biggest such new settlement in Precinct 66 is the Allende Quarter, named after Chilean president Salvador Allende, which houses more than ten thousand people. Many of these urban-expansion settlements are facing serious demographic problems. As these apartments were all rented out at the same time, to families with the same socio-demographic characteristics, the renters have all aged as a group: some of the playgrounds are deserted already, or they are more occupied by unemployed youths than by playing children.

Precinct 66

Precinct 66 is located on a one-way side street off one of the major thoroughfares of Köpenick. The buildings surrounding it are mostly residential, but there are a few small businesses, such as retail stores, a garage, and a roofer's shop, and there is also a school just around the corner. From the precinct it is a mere five-minute walk to the center of the old town, with its little shops and banks; thus, errands can be conveniently

34. The GDR invested very little in the renovation and modernization of old buildings, giving preference to much cheaper new construction.

Figure 3. Precinct 66 in Berlin-Köpenick. Courtesy of A-Shift, Precinct 66.

run from the precinct. Most of the shops around, like many of those elsewhere in east Berlin, have only opened gradually after unification, and their number still seems to be growing. But a few establishments predate unification. The bakery one block down from the precinct, which is very popular with the officers, existed as an independently owned enterprise even in GDR times. The precinct building was constructed in 1988 for the People's Police and is therefore also a typical, "new," four-story building visually structured by three layers of equally cut but differently finished panels. To the right of the building is an inconspicuous iron gate cutting off the driveway, which leads to the courtyard behind the building, so that usually not even the patrol cars are visible from the street. Except for the three flagpoles in front of it and a plaque with the coat of arms of the Berlin Police right next to the entrance, the structure hardly betrays its official function.

The interior of the precinct appears somewhat confining due to the relatively low ceilings (calculated for heating efficiency), which allow hardly more than six feet of clearance for a door. Any person entering through the front door steps into a narrow hall with a reception window at the far end. Chairs left and right increase the feeling of narrowness.

Any further progress is hampered by three milky glass doors which must be buzzed open from within the guardroom, except for the days and hours when the registry of inhabitants on the fourth floor of this building is open to the public.[35] At those times, anyone can roam freely through most parts of the building. The officer on duty can be called by a bell right next to the reception window. Visitors are usually not permitted to go any further on the ground floor, which is dedicated to the guard area, housing the patrol car shift on duty, the plainclothes patrol, and the detention cell.

The center of the guardroom proper is formed by three desks pushed together, two headways and one sideways. The desk closest to the back wall of the room is occupied by the shift leader, who can overlook from this "commanding" position not only the entire room, but also parts of the adjacent courtyard, so that he can see incoming and outgoing patrol cars. The other two desks are taken by the deputy shift leader, who serves as the administrator of the shift, keeping a log-book of patrol car activities, planning the roster, and so on, and the officer in charge of the radios. Deputy and radio officer both face the shift leader with the open room at their backs. Although this is the formal arrangement, people usually ignore it and sit facing the counter. The counter separates the area of these three desks from the space through which everybody enters or leaves the guardroom. It functions as a rest—for pen and paper used in quickly filling in a form—but it serves most importantly as a rest for countless elbows, supporting the many chats that take place across it. Other important features of the guardroom are the five telephones gathered on the three central desks in such a way that it is hard at times to tell which one is ringing, the 4-m radio through which communication is maintained between the patrol cars and the precinct, the coffeemaker, which runs almost incessantly under the attentive supervision of the radio officer, and finally a TV set, which is frequently the focus of attention during night shifts and on boring weekends.

Right next to the guardroom proper is the perpetually smoke-filled lounge. Here too the center is formed by an arrangement of three tables. In this lounge, officers sit to eat food brought from home, fast food pur-

35. In the GDR, the registry of inhabitants was a branch of the People's Police, hence its accommodation in the same building as the police station. In the FRG, the registry of inhabitants *(Einwohnermeldeamt)* is a branch of the city administration. By law, all Germans must be registered in the community in which they live. Through registration, every citizen automatically becomes a voter in this community and the state in which it is located, thereby losing voting rights at any former residence.

Figure 4. The Köpenick guard room, center of the patrol car shift (1995).
Author's photo.

chased on the streets, or meals prepared in the precinct's own kitchen just across the hall. During the day shift, officers regularly arrange for breakfast sandwiches. Occasionally on weekends or during night shifts one officer takes the initiative to prepare a hot meal for his colleagues. Also, each of the four shifts has its *own* properly padlocked refrigerator in the kitchen (police officers are human too), which is stocked with non-alcoholic beverages (alcohol consumption is forbidden during service), and snacks of all sorts. For all commonly arranged food, the expenses are paid out of a common cashbox, where officers leave money to pay for what they consume.[36] The lounge is also the place where officers may sit down on one of the donated sofas lining the wall, taking a rest, smoking a cigarette, having a chat with others, or reading one of the papers (mostly tabloids) brought along by the one or the other officer and left lying on the table.

Then there are the writing rooms where the officers hammer out their reports on old mechanical typewriters, most of them still from the stocks of the former People's Police. Almost none of the Köpenick officers have

36. Prices are a little higher than cost, and the slight profit which accumulates during the year is regularly spent on a common Christmas party.

Figure 5. The Köpenick lounge (1995). Courtesy of A-Shift, Precinct 66.

ever learned to touch-type, despite their daily use of typewriters. When more than two people are working on their reports, which usually happens toward the end of a day shift, sometime after 5:00 P.M., the noise produced by the typewriters mixed with the voices of officers loudly discussing a case can raise the sound level in the room to mind-boggling proportions. Usually officers try to avoid writing up a day's work all at once, because this might easily imply several hours of paperwork, which might also entail staying on way beyond the official end of the shift at six o'clock.[37] The preferred way to go about report writing is to come in intermittently during the shift; thus there is a continuous flow of officers writing. One room is reserved for the computer, known mostly by its acronym, ISVB, or *Informationssystem-Verbrechensbekämpfung* (infor-

37. The Berlin police is working under a dual twelve-hour-shift regime. While the official shift change in Berlin is 7 A.M. and 7 P.M., the Köpenick officers have decided to change at 6 in an attempt to preempt rush hour traffic. This was a particular concern for most western officers whose way from and to work has been considerably extended. I don't know whether western precincts have made similar arrangements to accommodate eastern officers' identical problem.

mation system for fight against crime). All criminal reports must be entered into this computer by using a coding system. This means that not all officers can actually enter their own reports, because they may not have passed the obligatory training program (this is Germany after all) which would allow them to do so. Thus, several reports are usually bundled up after they have been approved by the shift leader and entered together by someone who is licensed to use the computers.

Arguably the most important room for patrol car officers is the patrol car itself. The Berlin Police exclusively uses spacious Volkswagen Wagons as regular patrol cars, of which Precinct 66 has four on twenty-four-hour duty.[38] The advantage of this car—as the officers like to point out—is the little table in the back around which four people can sit quite comfortably. This feature of the car is mostly used to interrogate witnesses and record their statements; for most practical purposes, this means that it is used for the questioning and paperwork involved in car accidents. Since every patrol car in Berlin is staffed with two officers, eight members of each shift are occupied in patrolling the streets. The more senior officer serves as the patrol leader, usually operating the radio, while the other officer is driving the car.

The cars leave the precinct with two different types of orders: either they go out with a specific assignment to accomplish a particular task, or they simply go out to patrol the streets, where they are either called via radio to a task or themselves encounter a problem that may require police attention. In principle the patrol cars take care of any kind of issue that requires police attention in the most general sense; in the categories of the police law this means anything that either constitutes a crime or poses a threat to life or limb of a person or to public safety and order. The typical tasks facing police officers during an ordinary day are traffic accidents; helpless persons who need assistance (often little more than a euphemism for drunken people); vehicles under suspicion of being stolen; unregistered, apparently dumped vehicles; suicide threats; traffic impediments such as broken water pipes; garbage cans on fire; deceased persons with unclear cause of death; and so on.

How does one go about patrolling? Mostly by just going to places which have impinged themselves on the officer in some ways as trouble spots, the places of some previous action. Yet the patrolling agenda is not solely set by the officers themselves. Sometimes they receive official

38. There is one other car, the "team car," which is at the disposition of the shift leader. For special purposes, more cars or different vehicles (e.g., buses) can be ordered from the district.

directions concerning chosen areas of particular attention, such as commuter rail stations, or the areas around particular buildings, or neighborhoods where people are known to drive without licenses. These factors can make patrolling repetitive; it seems as if the same streets, the same areas are continuously screened, while others are completely ignored. But then patrolling is also about taking arbitrary turns, at least once in a while, especially when boredom looms large in the car, and the day or (more commonly) the night has passed without any exciting occurrences. The arbitrary turns are taken when the usual routes are unproductive and the desire for something to happen is intense, which is not always the case. Patrolling is therefore not only about the search for action; it is also about "fucking off" *(sich verpissen)*, about getting away from the superior in the precinct with whom one might just happen to live in conflict; it is about taking a break, enjoying the sunshine for a while at a nice spot in the forest. "Fucking off" is a way of asserting one's own agency in the face of attempts at control which are experienced as too rigid.

The life of the patrol car shift is suspended between the street and the guardroom area on the first floor. Only on rare occasions does an ordinary patrol officer venture up the stairs to the second floor of the precinct. The patrol officers call the second floor the "carpet story" *(die Teppichetage)*, and on those metaphorical carpets the leadership of the precinct holds office and the administrators spend their workdays. But that floor is not homogenous either, even if it might look that way from "below." The invisible boundaries that take effort or special reason to overcome structure the building not only vertically but also horizontally.

First, there are the quarters of the precinct leader (Abschnittsleiter). He has two rooms to himself—a little conference room and his office proper—completely furnished with sofa, armchairs, and coffee table, all remnants of the GDR past of the building. Since everybody refers to him (there are no females in this position yet) simply as "the chief" *(der Chef)*, I will henceforth adopt this nomenclature. The chief is usually the only staff officer in the precinct. Immediately adjacent to his offices are those of the chief of operations (Leiter Einsatz) and his crew. The chief of operations is ex officio also the deputy leader of the precinct; hence, I will simply call him "deputy." Usually he (again, there are no women in this position yet) is an older, experienced police captain who often knows the precinct better than the chief, if only because his is a final career position, while that of the chief has the potential to be a career springboard. The main responsibilities of the deputy are patrol car services and the plainclothes patrol.[39] The next man in line is the main administrator of operations (Hauptsachbearbeiter Einsatz). His main operative responsibility is the neighborhood-beat patrol, which I discuss in the context of the third floor. Both are supported by an assistant, who is a uniformed officer.

The morning in the operations area begins at 7:00 A.M. with a review of the reports written at night. This is simply a way to stay informed about the occurrences in the precinct. Then the telexes are digested; these are still the main way in which the different branches of the Berlin Police keep each other informed about important developments. Finally, the main work of the day can begin, which might involve writing a particular order for a bigger event (such as security measures for a fair); considering personnel issues, promotions, transfers, or an evaluation for an officer; or addressing the formal complaint of a citizen.

Right across from the operations area is the precinct's administrative office. Here two persons work, the administrator (Geschäftsführer), who as of January 1995 is no longer a uniformed police officer, and her (!) assistant.[40] Here, all the records pertaining to the precinct proper are kept: finances, personnel, equipment, building, payroll. All the information about officers who have called in sick or gone on holidays come together in this office; if there is some repair to be done on the building, the craftsmen are called from here and they call in here when they want to begin their work. Thus, there is a constant coming and going in the administrative office. The precinct administrators know everybody, because once in a while, everybody has some business with them. From the precinct administrator one can find out the total number of employees in the precinct: the answer I got as of November 1994 was 149, but this number changes weekly.

39. I did not do any participant observation with the plainclothes patrol, since in Köpenick it does not include any easterners. The plainclothes patrol is a part of the uniformed police *(Schutzpolizei)* investigating all sorts of petty crimes such as shoplifting, break-ins into garden cottages, and so on. They are not to be confused with criminal investigators *(Kriminalpolizei)*, who belong to a completely different branch of the police. Needless to say, there are rivalries between the uniformed police and criminal investigators.

40. Although the civil employees of the precinct are not, properly speaking, police officers, I will refer to them throughout the manuscript as officers; otherwise, because there are so few of them, they might easily be identifiable. This convention is justifiable, moreover, since many of the eastern civil employees were actually uniformed officers in the People's Police and because in Köpenick most civil employees do work which is also done by uniformed officers.

The rest of the second floor is taken up by the case administration *(Vorgangsbearbeitung)*. Not only are the reports written by patrol car officers and neighborhood-beat patrol officers processed here (i.e., they are recorded and sent further along), but the case administration also takes reports from persons who walk into the precinct during the day. A person whose bicycle had been stolen could ring the officer on duty to be buzzed in and to wind her way up the stairs to the second floor to report the theft there during regular office hours between 7:00 A.M. and 4:30 P.M. At all other times, reports from walk-ins are handled by the patrol car shift. In a separate subdepartment, the case administration also deals with traffic issues. Detours for construction sites are checked here for their viability, the signing at construction sites is checked for its conformity with the law, and here the officers try to make sure that the regular traffic signs make sense—that they do not contradict each other left and right.

The refuge of the neighborhood-beat patrol officers *(Kontaktbereichsbeamte* or *KoBBs)* is on the third floor. Hardly anybody comes up here except for the beat patrol officers themselves; if there is some business with the administration or with operations, they go down—the others do not come up. The reason for this is simple. It is hard to guess whether a particular beat patrol officer is in or whether he (there are no female beat patrol officers in Köpenick) is out somewhere patrolling his neighborhood. Also, since their regular hours may be anytime between 6:00 A.M. and 10:00 P.M. and since they are also supposed to be in on Saturdays and Sundays at least once every month and are thus eligible to take off regular weekdays, one does not even know whether a particular officer is on duty without looking at the roster. Thus, the third floor is quite calm compared to the first or second floors; it is less public than the other two.

The Köpenick beat patrol officers are divided into three groups with six officers and one shared office each. In every group two officers form a tandem, which is to be taken almost literally, because their desks usually face each other. The rationale for this arrangement is to create a system of substitution, a team of officers who are so well acquainted with each other's work that they can replace each other in cases of longer periods of absence. The tandems also have their particular unification history, because they were originally composed of a westerner who served as a master to an apprenticed easterner.

The beat patrol officer is an invention of the police reform of 1974, which abandoned the smaller neighborhood police stations in favor of larger precincts. The beat patrol officer was then meant to bring the distant precinct closer again to the various neighborhoods. The beat patrol officer is supposed to know his milieu well, and he ought to be known personally to the major institutions of his precinct, such as schools or businesses. Ideally, the beat patrol officer would have plenty of time to chat with the people in his neighborhood in order to gain an intimate knowledge of what is going on there and also to give the inhabitants of the neighborhood the feeling that the police are present and caring. To increase their visibility, beat patrol officers are asked to walk through their neighborhoods, rather than just driving from one place to another. The Berlin police are very concerned with "getting more green onto the streets" (mehr Grün auf die Straße bringen), green being the color of German police officer's cloth jackets, anoraks, and regular caps.

Often, however, the beat patrol officers have their pile of cases to work through, which means that they don't get around to what they are purportedly supposed to do. Their caseload is varied and might involve anything from extending an identity card for a handicapped or elderly person to invalidating a license plate, withdrawing a license, or just finding out somebody's actual current address. Much of the work of beat patrol officers is assistance to other state authorities who do not have their own means of enforcement. But beat patrol officers also pay attention to the parking in their neighborhoods, and they might be busily writing tickets until the parking patterns take acceptable forms. Thus, the task of a beat patrol officer involves a certain tension between the role of "the friendly policeman" and that of the officer who is most perceptibly enforcing laws and regulations.

Potsdam and the Babelsberg Police Station

Potsdam is a place steeped in mythology. As the summer residence of the kings of Prussia, it is known for its many palaces and gardens, most notably Sanssouci, the favorite repose of Frederic the Great, Prussia's most revered king. Potsdam was also one of Prussia's most important garrisons, and as such it has become an icon of Prussian militarism. The teamed-up spirits of king and military made Potsdam the ideal stage for symbolic performances of power. Two which have taken place in this century deserve mention here. In 1933 Hitler used the scenery of Potsdam for his theatrical, quite successful bid to win the allegiance of the traditionalist right wing in Germany in the "Day of Potsdam" (Tag von Potsdam). After Germany's defeat in 1945 the Allied Powers picked up on the symbolic significance of Potsdam and staged the Potsdam Conference in the Cecilienhof palace.

Needless to say, the government of the GDR was also highly aware of Potsdam as symbol to which it reacted in a rather ambiguous fashion. The GDR government chose not to reconstruct at least two key edifices in the city center, which was damaged by one night of heavy Allied bombardment in April 1945. the ruins of both the Garnisonskirche (the Church of the Garrison) and the Stadtschloß (City Palace) were finally blown up in 1962 to make way for a wide, four-lane city highway, a "socialist throughway" *(sozialistische Magistrale)* meant to furnish Potsdam with a decidedly socialist face. However, after the GDR had abolished the five historical states on its territory in 1952 to replace them with fourteen administrative provinces *(Bezirke),* Potsdam became the capital of the province with the same name. Even more in keeping with its military tradition, Potsdam also became the seat of the University of the Secret Police (Hochschule des Ministeriums für Staatssicherheit). Today Potsdam, with roughly one hundred and forty thousand inhabitants, is the largest city as well as the capital of the state of Brandenburg.[41]

In some ways, the landscape in and around Potsdam bears many similarities to Köpenick's. The Havel river flowing through Potsdam forms, much like the Spree and the Dahme in Köpenick, a set of pretty lakes before it enters the city and right after it leaves it. Thus Potsdam too is surrounded by water, and there too the villas lining its shores are considered to have the potential to become preferred living space for rich Berliners. The landscape in Potsdam, however, is highly sculptured and has very little of the rural tartness of southern Köpenick. The nineteenth-century garden architect Lenné has created a very unique park-lake landscape in which it is possible to lose oneself, walking for hours from one palace's park to the next, traveling thus from Pfaueninsel and Glienicke in southwestern Berlin to Babelsberg, Cecilienhof, and Sanssouci in Potsdam.

All these attractions of architecture, landscape, and history make Potsdam a prime tourist attraction as much for ordinary people as for foreign guests of state. I mention this not only because Potsdam's attractions are a source of pride for its police officers, but because all these features give

41. An attempted fusion of the states of Berlin and Brandenburg, which would have made Potsdam the capital of this united state, was turned down by popular referendum only last year. The negative result was mostly due to the rejection of the proposal by the citizens of Brandenburg.

police work a particular flavor. I have mentioned traffic flow and parking problems already while discussing Köpenick. If anything, both are even worse in Potsdam. The additional problems in Potsdam's city station derive from the high visibility of *all* police actions (not just the spectacular ones). Also, inaction seems more apparent here than in the quieter backwaters. This visibility is due to what might be called the two sides of the "limelight factor." On the one hand, Potsdam plays the role of a showcase for the state of Brandenburg. On the other hand, the high density of public officials, politicians, and high-ranking bureaucrats leads to more intensive scrutiny of police action and more effective complaints about police negligence because these public officials are versed in feeding their complaints into the right channels.

No matter how and no matter from which direction one approaches the Potsdam city station, one must cross or come along Potsdam's "socialist throughway." And although it sports some of Potsdam's real architectural treasures, it rather passes them by in the domineering presence of panel-style, "progressive" architecture. Thus it is a surprise to find oneself, just a few yards further down a side street, suddenly in front of a large building complex with an interestingly strict baroque facade, which even more surprisingly indeed houses the city police station *(Hauptwache)*. Unfortunately, as so often happens in war-ridden Germany, the beauty of the facade is not carried into the interior of the building, nor does it inspire the adjacent ensemble, which is built in a hodgepodge of styles. Yet, with several rather quiet courtyards, some areas exude a whiff of monastic life nonetheless. The complex as a whole is home not only to the city police station, but also to the administration of the Potsdam security area, the administrative headquarters of the police district of Potsdam, and the ministry of the interior of the state of Brandenburg.

The organizational structure and the nomenclature of the Brandenburg Police differ markedly from those of the Berlin Police. The reason for this is not so much the stark contrast in the geography of both states, the one Germany's only metropolis, the other one of Germany's most rural states,[42] but much more that the state of Northrhine Westphalia in north-

---

42. Berlin, with a population of 3.4 million, is twice as populous as Hamburg, Germany's second largest city. Brandenburg, in contrast, with 2.5 million inhabitants in an area which makes it easily the largest of the five new states, has a population density which is barely undercut by the even more rural Mecklenburg-Vorpommern at the Baltic seashore. Historically, Brandenburg is the classical hinterland.

western Germany was a partner to Brandenburg in helping it to build up its administrative structures.[43] Thus, the Brandenburg police force is organizationally a much smaller clone of the Northrhine Westphalian police force, sharing its basic structure, its police laws and regulations, its terminology, and in many ways also its choice of equipment.[44] The state of Brandenburg is divided into five police districts *(Polizeipräsidien)*, each headed by a president of police (Polizeipräsident). Each district is in turn divided into several security areas *(Schutzbereiche)*, which are divided into several police stations, which are ultimately differentiated by size into main stations *(Hauptwachen)* and branch stations *(Neben-wachen)*.[45]

At the time of my fieldwork, the city station *(Hauptwache)* was under major reconstruction. The main parts of the guardroom area on the first floor were already thoroughly renovated and "technologically updated" *(auf den neuesten Stand gebracht)*. Novelty and modernity seemed to be highlighted by the clean white of the walls and the technical grey of the wall-to-wall carpeting. In contrast, the administrative offices on the second floor were dominated by the yellow and brownish tones of smoked walls and linoleum floors, exuding an almost timeless old age. On the second floor, very little seemed to have changed since the bygone days of the People's Police.

I limited my fieldwork in the city station to the leadership of the security area located on the second floor. At the time of my fieldwork, the leader of the security area *(Schutzbereichsleiter)* was an east German officer, while his deputy and chief of staff *(Leiter der Führungsstelle)* was a westerner who had transferred from Northrhine Westphalia to the Brandenburg Police. The day in the Potsdam security area leadership begins with a 7:00 A.M. morning conference of the various departmental

43. The five new states in eastern Germany all had partners in the west who were supposed to provide assistance in the creation of a working state administration. Thus, Saxony was assisted by Bavaria and Baden-Württemberg, Thuringia by Hesse, and so on.

44. Historically, this is quite ironic. While Prussia annexed Westphalia and the Rhinelands after the Congress of Vienna, imposing its rule and its administration on this non-Prussian territory, the arrow of influence seems to have been reversed a century and a half later.

45. Thus, a station is usually smaller than a precinct in Berlin, but a Berlin precinct is not as large as a Brandenburg security area; many Berlin districts, however, are larger than the ones in Brandenburg. Especially the positions of president of police are not comparable. The president of the Potsdam district heads an organization with roughly twenty-five hundred employees. The president of the Berlin police heads an organization with more than thirty thousand employees.

heads, who report important occurrences in their areas during the last twenty-four hours. This is also the time to elicit support from other departments or to coordinate activities across administrative boundaries. The morning conference in Potsdam testifies to the most important difference between the Brandenburg and the Berlin Police. While nobody in the leadership of the Köpenick precinct was an easterner, the only western participant in the morning conference in Potsdam was the deputy.

For cineasts, the name Babelsberg probably still rings a bell resonating with places like Cinecittà and Hollywood. As the site of the Ufa-Studios, it became world famous in the late 1920s and early 1930s as Germany's hub of film production. Babelsbergers are proud to point out that the careers of star actors such as Marlene Dietrich or directors such as von Sternheim had their beginnings here. Seen this way, Babelsberg and Potsdam seem to make strange bedfellows indeed. But the recollection of the smoothly functioning propaganda machinery of the Nazis and the skill with which they used film for their own purposes quickly establishes a connection: Leni Riefenstahl and the "Day of Potsdam" share something of the same spirit.

The Babelsberg police station is tucked away on a quiet side street a good ten to fifteen minutes' walk from the center of town. It is easily recognizable by the green-and-white patrol cars lined up in front of it. The station building is a composite of a flat side wing serving as the guardroom area and a four-story apartment house in which the flats on the first and second stories are taken up by the police, while the rest of the building is inhabited by families. The Babelsberg station welcomes its visitors in a quite different way from the Köpenick precinct. A decisive pull at the modern glass door quickly leads to the insight that somewhere there must be a bell to ring. But instead of an immediate buzzer response that opens the door, the officer inside requests through an intercom the reason for the visit. Any answer brings an invitation to have a seat in the waiting room furnished with chairs and a table. The posters on the wall suggest that a career in the Brandenburg Police might be an adventurous pursuit, and brochures on the tables tell how one could go about protecting one's house more efficiently from burglary. As soon as an officer inside decides that he or she has time to attend to the visitor, the intercom sounds again, asking the visitor to proceed through another modern glass door into the guardroom, where progress is stopped at a counter. The Babelsberg officers explain later that the electrically locked glass doors that shield off the waiting area function as a floodgate. To their dismay, Brandenburg patrol car officers are working eight-hour shifts (early shift: 6:00 A.M. to 2:00 P.M.; late shift: 2:00 P.M. to 10:00 P.M.; night shift: 10:00 P.M. to 6:00 A.M.). The disadvantages of the eight-hour shift for the officers are more frequent journeys from home to work and back, and shorter total absences from work. At the time of my field-work, they were trying to exert pressure through the trade unions to move back to the old twelve-hour shift system they were used to in the People's Police.

The entire Babelsberg station is freshly renovated, shining in the same white and grey as the city station's guardroom area. In both stations in Brandenburg, officers can work with personal computers (PCs) to write out their forms, but they can also choose from a set of electrical or me-chanical typewriters. (The more modern, frequently brand-new equip-ment of the Brandenburg Police creates much envy in Berlin.) The leader of the station and the beat patrol officers *(Revierpolizisten, or Repos)*[46] have their rooms on the second floor of the apartment building in two apartments, giving these offices a rather homey atmosphere.

* * *

Precinct 66 in Berlin and the Babelsberg station of the Potsdam Police form the stage for the encounters between eastern and western officers which are the basis of the following chapters. These spaces are not merely background for the officers; they are deeply imbued with meaning for their own lives, and they are an important resource for understanding others, as well as institutions and even political systems.

---

46. I have used the same English term, *neighborhood beat patrol,* to denote equiv-alent police functions in Berlin and Brandenburg, although they are known under different names in German. A *Kontaktbereichsbeamter,* or *KoBB,* in Berlin is a *Re-vierpolizist,* or *Repo,* in Brandenburg.

ONE

Viewing Each Other through Space

During a long interview with a western officer late in May 1995 I asked
one of those vague, open-ended questions meant to stimulate a long, un-
interrupted narration of experience: "So how do you see Germany after
unification?" I asked somewhat awkwardly. He responded that he was
doubtful that unification had actually happened and that what he saw
was a clash of very different cultures. To illustrate his point, he fetched
a set of photographs, telling me that he had recently purchased a house
in a development where easterners and westerners were living right next
to each other. He proudly showed me the pictures of the development
and of his house, including an aerial view. As he explained the differences
to me, he created an interesting metaphor of internal German diversity
in spite of external similarity through shared nationhood:

> From the outside, they all look the same, red roofs, neatly whitewashed
> from the outside. But you should go into the houses where western
> people live and where eastern people live. A fundamental difference!
> You see it as you pass through the door. I don't know whether that
> has anything to do with money, but it certainly has something to do
> with taste. When I visit a western house, I see wall-to-wall carpeting
> nicely skirted on all sides. When I visit an eastern house, the wall-to-
> wall carpet is unevenly cut; at places it creeps up at the corners, and
> there is no skirting. Then there is this old-fashioned oak furniture. In
> the front yard they have jammed in plastic fences, while the westerners
> have neatly trimmed hedges; the easterners place their satellite dishes
> on the front walls of their houses; westerners try to tuck them away
> on their garages.

Even before easterners and westerners have encountered each other in person, each group typically has experienced the space in which the other lives; and from this experience of each other's space they have formed an initial understanding of who the other is. Easterners and westerners interpret differences in space as differences between people and cultures, between institutions and political and economic systems. The preceding excerpt illustrates nicely how police officers in Berlin and in Potsdam connect space—for example, the condition, shape, odor, and color of houses, or the layout, size, condition, and uses of roads—to the state, society, or organization which has produced or sanctioned the production of these houses and roads. They also connect these spatial features in manifold ways with their own selves and those of their fellow human beings. In other words, police officers—by identifying each other with spatial features—experience their own identity as well as the identities of their fellow human beings.

I will show in this chapter that processes of identity formation can have an important spatial component, that identity is constructed not only in dialogue with other people, but also in response to the physical environment in which people live. Due to its prominent role in phenomenological writing (e.g., Heidegger 1986; Schütz and Luckmann 1979), time has been of considerable significance in theorizing identity, in recent times most notably in the literature on narrative (e.g., Czarniawska 1997; Somers 1994; Linde 1993; Ricoeur 1992; Bruner 1990; McIntyre 1984). Spatial aspects of identity, however, have traditionally played at best a minor role in works on regional or national identities, and have only recently received wider attention.[1] In this chapter, I characterize three important processes through which the experience of space influences identity formation. I call these three processes *reading space, writing space,* and *placement.* I use these three concepts to understand the role of space in the identifications of east and west Germans. With the help of Mikhail Bakhtin's (1981) concept of chronotope, I then begin to outline the important connections between time and space in their relation to identity.

It should be noted that police officers have a special, professional rela-

1. While Giddens (1984, chap. 3) could still claim in the mid-eighties that space had remained an altogether marginal field for social theory, the situation has fundamentally changed at the beginning of the 1990s. Critical Marxist geography has stirred up intensive interest in the social production of space (Harvey 1989; Soja 1989; Zukin 1991). However, the literature does not directly address processes of identity construction in relation to space.

tionship to space, because policing itself is essentially a spatial practice. Policing is the operational conjunction of three of Weber's definitional characteristics of the state: territory, legitimacy, and the claim of monopoly on physical violence (Weber 1980, 29). The police are organized along spatial principles into neighborhood precincts and districts within the boundaries of a state.[2] Thus, every police officer has a clear sense of territorial responsibility, of rights and duties tied to space. Within their territory, police officers must enforce the law of the state, on the state's behalf. The police usually act primarily in the service of the legal system, but they also assist other state agencies that lack their own capacity to enforce state rule in a given territory. In this sense, therefore, policing *is* the state in action, and police officers are a synecdoche for the state.

In the next section I want to show how Berlin and Potsdam police officers read the space in which they work and live, in an attempt to understand themselves, their new compatriots from the respective other side of the former iron curtain, and the social world in which they live. What follows is therefore my reading of their reading of spaces, my meta-interpretation of their primary interpretation of the connection between space and identity.

Reading Space

The fall of the Wall on 9 November 1989 was for Berliners on both sides a virtual explosion of possibilities to move in space. Since GDR citizens of working age were not allowed to visit the West,[3] most of them had not been to the other side of the Wall since 1961, the year it was erected. Many younger Easterners had never seen the West with their own eyes, knowing everything they knew about it from hearsay or from the media. Although West Germans could in principle travel to the GDR, arduous border controls, costly forced currency exchanges, visa requirements, and

2. In Germany, responsibility for the police rests principally with the states, not the federation. The highest authorities are therefore state ministries of the interior and not the federal ministry of the interior. (There are exceptions, but they are irrelevant here.) The point is this: much as a German police officer has no jurisdiction in France (although this is changing!), a Berlin officer has no jurisdiction in the state of Brandenburg.

3. Special permits could be obtained for funerals of close relatives and similar events; otherwise, travel was restricted to "travel cadres" *(Reisekader),* a select echelon of party members and officials.

other travel restrictions made visits to the East rather cumbersome. In addition, many Westerners entertained the notion that not much of interest was to be discovered on the other side of the Iron Curtain anyway. Both administrative hassles and a generally negative attitude to the East kept Westerners from visiting East Germany on a regular basis, except for those who had close relatives living in East Germany.[4] Thus, to East and West Berliners alike, the other side was a virtual terra incognita, which they eagerly went out to explore once the opportunity was there. By Christmas 1989, barely six weeks after the opening of the Wall, approximately 2.5 million East Germans had visited the West, and about 1 million West Germans had visited the East (Diemer and Kuhrt 1994, 139). While Easterners first ventured to the glitzy shopping centers in the West, Westerners flocked to the countryside for recreation. For both sides this was the fulfillment of long-held dreams: "shopping according to desire rather than to availability," as one eastern officer put it, and "taking week-end trips in reasonable driving distance from home just like any other normal big-city-dweller in Europe," as one western officer expressed it.

This encounter with alien space, as much as it was desired, also came as a shock to many Berliners. They experienced it as threatening, especially since they were asked, through political unification, to take that other space on as their own, to consider that other side as a part of *their* Berlin, *their* Germany too. After the frenzied party celebrating the demolition of the Wall, Berliners withdrew into their respective halves, claiming that they "just didn't feel right" or "didn't feel at home" in the other part of the city.[5] Shopping was moved back to the east at the same rate that stores of all kinds opened there, thus rendering trips to the west unnecessary, and many west Berliners rerouted their weekend vacations back to their favorite places in northern Bavaria and eastern Lower Saxony, that is, to places within the borders of the old Federal Republic which lie within the shortest driving distance from Berlin. Both easterners and westerners have described extensive stays in the respective other half of the city as thoroughly depressing experiences. While easterners mainly

4. On a regular basis only Easterners past the age of sixty-five were allowed visits to Western relatives. Westerners had to convert 25 DM for 25 Marks of the GDR per capita and day for journeys into the GDR. The border controls are a lively source of gruesome stories for many West Berliners; for decades they constituted the only personal contact most Westerners had with Easterners.

5. Still today, Berliners of both sides continue to talk about the "true Berlin" and "the false Berlin."

complained about the pace of life in the west, westerners experienced the east as polluted, at times even complaining about symptoms of disease, such as rashes and nausea after more extended visits to the east.[6] Yet for some Berliners, such as many of the police officers I encountered, longer stays on the other side of Berlin became inevitable, as they were assigned to precincts beyond the former Iron Curtain.

In addition to the enormous extension into unknown territory, the urban landscape of Berlin has been transformed rapidly. The face of east Berlin has undergone comprehensive westernization as countless shops, banks, and branches of western franchises, have opened their doors, while many buildings and roads have been demolished and reconstructed or renovated in western styles. Moreover, the entire city has become a construction site as whole quarters such as Potsdamer Platz and Leipziger Platz are rebuilt to close the gap axed through the heart of the city by the erection of the Wall. Finally, the decision to move the government from Bonn to Berlin has triggered a construction megalomania geared not only to accommodating bureaucrats and institutions but also to representing united Germany in architecture new and old.[7]

Eastern and western Berliners are therefore continually confronted with new spatial arrangements, be it by visiting the other half of the city, voluntarily or involuntarily, or by seeing their immediate neighborhood change its character before their eyes. From the perspective of the phenomenology of lifeworlds, then, it is not surprising to find east and west Berliners particularly engaged in interpreting and reinterpreting the spaces in which they live. Temporal and spatial arrangements are the aspects of lifeworlds that are perhaps most taken for granted, constituting the deepest core of the "unquestionably given" (Schütz and Luckmann 1979). Thus, spaces are not usually read; rather, they are literally overlooked. But spaces are read—that is, they give rise to interpretative activity, once spatial features stand out from the smooth surfaces of everyday assumptions, thwarting expectations and challenging the habitual vista.

6. While some of these complaints were certainly self-serving in the sense that western officers working in the east had to drive much farther to their new workplaces, and thus sought reasons for reassignment to the west, there seems to have been much more to these complaints than rational calculus.

7. The meaning of Berlin as capital of united Germany and the meaning of Germany in a uniting Europe is fervently fought out in Berlin over architectural designs. It is as if Germans participating in these debates tried to inscribe an interpretation— their vision of Germany's past and future—into steel, stone, and glass. For a well-written review of major architectural conflicts in Berlin and their connection to interpretations of Germany's past and future, see Ladd 1997 and Wise 1998.

Construction sites, repainted buildings, suddenly closed-off thorough-fares cannot fail to be noticed.

The most intensive reading of space is likely to occur, however, if human beings are entering a world which is quite different from the one they know. Space then becomes relevant (Schütz and Luckmann 1979, 224–90), that is, an object of interpretative activity, principally in two different ways. For one, the spatial structure of this different world—the elements of which it is composed as well as the way in which these elements are linked together—is known only in part or not at all.[8] One must learn what the new structures are by closely observing and monitoring them. Ordinary language captures this by expressions like "trying to find one's way around." One officer has pointed out to me, for example, how embarrassing it was for him not to know where to find a public toilet and, once he found one, not to know how to operate the flushing system. Yet space can become relevant in a much more general sense. The world entered may be so different as a whole that people search desperately for any signs by which to make sense of it. Under such circumstances, people may attempt to interpret features of the novel world which are not primarily thought of as spatial (such as the quality of a government) in terms of space. Space can facilitate such interpretations (as every archeologist knows) because it is a formidable repository of signs created by the simple fact that much of human activity leaves traces in space. Moreover, upon entering a novel world, visitors experience its space *before* they encounter its inhabitants. Thus, for better or worse, the experience of space can become the metaphoric source code for the interpretation of a new world as a whole.

Accordingly, I distinguish two different kinds of spatial readings. The first interest in reading these spaces is often (but of course by no means exclusively) pragmatic, literally concerned with the space as space: *finding* the supermarket nearby, *locating* the nearest post office, *orienting* oneself in order to find a way home. In what follows, I call these readings of space as space "literal." Spaces are also intensively read, for example, when people plan to make a space their everyday habitat. Before deciding on such a move, people frequently try to assess the "fit" between the spaces they have seen and themselves, trying to gauge whether they would feel comfortable in a particular environment. These intensive spatial encounters give rise to readings beyond space itself; they are concerned with more than orientation in order to find one's way. These readings are preoc-

8. In the most extreme case this is like encountering a new language, of which neither the vocabulary nor the grammar is known. The listener then desperately listens for recognizable elements that provide some clues for understanding.

cupied with atmosphere, beauty, social relations, wealth, power, and so on. I call these readings, for reasons I will elucidate below, "rhetorical." After people have "settled in," and especially after they "know their turf," home spaces will be consciously read only after longer periods of absence. The return home will be noted as immersion in familiarity, no matter whether this familiarity is evaluated positively as comforting and reaffirming, or negatively as stifling, suffocating, or just plain boring.

Rhetorical Readings of Space

Literal readings of space simply point to a knowledge deficit. Rhetorical readings, however, open a fascinating realm of interpretative activity. The readings of space which captured my special interest in the field employ spatial features to point to something beyond space itself.[9] The beyond that interests me here is, of course, an identification of self or other. I found the everyday life of Berlin police officers replete with spatial readings used to make statements about the quality of self or the character of others. The violation of a lifeworld assumption or a literal reading of space is frequently just the occasion for such a rhetorical reading. For example, the question of a western police officer regarding the whereabouts of his new precinct on his first trip to his new workplace in east Berlin was not simply put to rest by finding it (literal reading). Upon his arrival the location triggered a comment replete with identifications of self and other. The officer remembered saying to a western colleague that in the West the precinct building would never have been built in such a ridiculous place. He recalled arguing that it was completely foolish to construct a police precinct at a location without easy access to traffic in all directions, but that this was precisely what was to be expected of such

9. There are a few highly interesting sociological studies in which space is also read in an attempt to understand something else, and sociological interpretation is fundamentally a rhetorical reading of space. Benjamin (1983) begins his analysis of an entire epoch, the nineteenth century, with an interpretation of the shopping arcades of Paris, which he takes to epitomize the important features of the city of Paris, which is taken in turn to summarize life in the nineteenth century in general. Thus, Benjamin reads the arcades of Paris in a *pars pro toto* fashion; in the language of rhetoric, he reads a very limited space as a synecdoche for an entire historical period. In a similar fashion Norbert Elias (1983) has provided a brilliant analysis of the architectural structure of seventeenth- and eighteenth-century palaces as a means to understanding court life in baroque France. Lately poststructural critics have provided readings of space in order to analyze the "late-capitalist" condition (for example, Jameson 1991; Soja 1989; Zukin 1991).

a state as the GDR. This comment, made to another western officer, was not only an invitation to identify with the postulated good sense of the western police organization as well as one's own sharing in it, but it also suggested fraternization against the supposed stupidity of a system that was still found to linger in the police officers who were trained and employed by it.

Space is thus not read only as space, and in this sense readings like the one in the preceding example are not literal. Instead, the reading of space identifies spatial features with something beyond space—with institutions, politics, and selves. In the introduction, I presented identifications as the building blocks of identity-formation processes, which contextualize self and thus make it meaningful, connecting it with particular aspects of the world at large. All identifications thus have to overcome the difference between a self and aspects of the world by some form of equalization, by making the same what remains different. According to Burke (1969b, 22), it is precisely the function of rhetoric to create identifications between two elements so that these elements fuse, in a sense, while remaining separate at the same time. Identifications and a fortiori rhetoric, according to Burke, create what he calls "consubstantialities" between two elements.[10] For Burke (1969b, 21) consubstantiality is, quite literally following the etymology of the term, the creation of a common ground to stand on.[11] In this sense, any kind of human interaction insofar as it presumes a shared understanding of the world is based on rhetoric. Collective action seen from this vantage point is also based on rhetoric, because in order to pursue a common goal human beings need to fuse in their identification with this goal. Thus, Burke stresses the strategic and therefore immensely political aspect of rhetoric, its intention to bestow or to deny value, to create allegiances, to promise, to form alliances to exclude and to include (cf. Fernandez 1986, 8ff.). In general, then, identifications of selves can be understood as an exercise in the "rhetorics of

10. Burke (1969b, 20ff.) emphasizes the ambiguity created by identification: "A is not identical with his colleague, B. But insofar as their interests are joined, A is *identified* with B. Or he may *identify himself* with B even when their interests are not joined, if he assumes that they are, or is persuaded to believe so. Here are ambiguities of substance. In being identified with B, A is 'substantially one' with a person other than himself. Yet at the same time he remains unique, an individual locus of motives. Thus, he is both joined and separate, at once a distinct substance and consubstantial with another."

11. In a Burkian sense, then, rhetoric overlaps considerably with the phenomenological and symbolic interactionist approaches in the social sciences. Historically speaking, rhetoric is thus a precursor of the culturally oriented social sciences.

self-making" (Battaglia 1995a). Identifications between space and something else can then be called "rhetorical readings" of space.[12]

Before I can dissect the preceding example of a rhetorical reading of space, however, I must extend Burke's analysis of identifications by developing a clearer understanding of how, in which *modes,* identifications are cast. Surprisingly, Burke does not carry his argument that rhetoric is fundamentally concerned with the creation of consubstantiality over into a discussion of basic figures of speech. Yet the standard tropes of the Ramist tradition—metaphor, metonymy, and synecdoche—do precisely that:[13] they connect the different in very distinct ways and create thereby specific forms of sameness. Metaphors connect by way of suggesting similarity. Metonymies connect by way of making two elements contiguous to each other, most commonly by treating them as elements of an encompassing category. Synecdoches connect by integrating parts into wholes, suggesting an organic relationship.[14]

These tropic modes lend specific character to identifications, insinuating different relationships between the identified elements. Thus their use has different effects on the social interaction in which they are employed; they make claims of a very different kind and accordingly provoke different reactions. Metaphoric identifications remain cognizant of the fundamental separateness and independence between the elements, suggesting a limited sameness which is thus more a similarity or comparability.[15] The extent of the similarity suggested by metaphors is, due to their nonconventional character, basically open to negotiation. Metonymies by contrast stress a basic equality, but also often an interchangeability in the sameness imposed by a unifying category which obliterates remaining differences among the elements of the category. Synecdoches, finally, emphasize hierarchy but also mutual interdependence in the juxtaposition

12. Rhetoric is frequently misunderstood in the sense that "plain speech" is thought to relate to "rhetoric" as the "real" relates to the "fake." Rhetoric as Burke understands it, and as I use it in this study, is not defined as the production of appearances, but it is about the creation of some form of sameness, which may be warranted in some way or which may be completely illusionary. Therefore, to convince or to persuade are both equally rhetorical activities.

13. Traditionally, irony is included in this list. I will discuss irony, however, as a form of emplotment (see below).

14. Seen in this way, tropes are a fundamental aspect of human cognitive activity (cf. Lakoff and Johnson 1980).

15. In order to emphasize this dynamic, nonreductionistic aspect of metaphor, which always has a surprise element contradicting expectations as long as it "lives," Ricoeur (1975) defines metaphor as "impertinent predication."

of part and whole. Thus, synecdoches suggest a much stronger, necessary relationship between the identified elements than between constituent elements of a category in a metonymy or the elements compared in a metaphor.

The most important difference for the context of this study, however, is that metaphors do not lend themselves as easily to totalizing identifications as do synecdoches and metonymies. Metonymies built on the principle of a category can transport identifications from a particular element to the category at large. The western superior who is visibly unhappy about a report written by an eastern officer and says, "This is vintage Lehmann [last name changed], really just the kind of crap you get from former People's Police officers" not only identifies officer Lehmann but with him all former People's Police officers at the same time. It should be noted, however, that the identification of an element does not necessarily identify the category. In terms of the example, the western officer might have chosen to identify Lehmann and Lehmann only. Conversely, metonymies carry identifications of the category to all elements. No individual officer escapes the biting comment on the quality of Peoples' Police report writing. Synecdoches carry identifications from the part to the whole or vice versa. In contrast to metonymies, the relationship of transference in synecdoches is, because of its implied organicism, necessarily symmetrical. The eastern officer who complains about the misleading formulations in an advertisement, insinuating that this is what the capitalist system is about, has inevitably transported the identification of the part to the whole, as advertisement is to him an essential part of capitalism. Yet he could just as well have identified the whole of capitalism as a license to cheat, thus a fortiori identifying advertisement—an integral part of capitalism—as likely to be misleading as well. While the carryover effect in metonymic and synecdochical identifications poses as fact, metaphoric identifications self-consciously introduce an element of artifice. They bring a link into play which is obviously aiming at comprehension, while admitting that the similarity suggested is inevitably one of degree. An example of this openness and indeterminacy of metaphor is the image created by an East Berlin officer who rendered his impression of West Berliners after his first visit as a "cluster of startled chickens fluttering to and fro."

The use of tropes in the example of the officer's reading of the relative location of the precinct building can be analyzed now in the following way. The placement of the precinct building in relation to several access roads is read as a metonymy for its supposed creator, East Germany's People's Police. The People's Police is thus identified as rather careless in placing its buildings in the context of the space it was supposed to police, thereby reducing its effectiveness. The peculiar location of the precinct is also used as a synecdoche for the whole of the sociopolitical system of state socialism. Its failure is understood in terms of the mindlessness evident in the parts which make up the whole. By yet another synecdoche, the failure of the organization is bestowed on its constituent parts, the individual police officers. Both the organization and its officers are thus identified in a derogatory way. In symmetrical fashion, a synecdoche is used to extend the foresight of the (West) Berlin police organization to the speaker. Finally, by still another metonymy, the addressee of the words is gracefully included in the self-identifying praise. Thus, a few sentences about the reading of space spin a whole complex web of identifications of persons and institutions.

It is not always easy to decide in which mode any particular identification is cast—that is, whether it has the character of a metonymy, a synecdoche, or a metaphor. Research into the *use* of tropes (Fernandez 1986, 1991b) has revealed the inherent instability of any trope in action. On the one hand, metaphors shade at their margins into metonymies by the sheer act of establishing consubstantiality in comparison. If the impertinent character of predication is lost, metaphors run the risk of getting dissolved (Ricoeur 1985). On the other hand, metonymies can be transposed into metaphors. In the example above, the metonymic identifications of spaces and their organizational creators could function as metaphors if the emphasis was shifted from a totalizing identification to the discussion of particular, limited similarities. The consideration of context is therefore extremely important in analyzing how a particular tropic identification functions within social interaction. In the preceding example, the totalizing juxtaposition of east and west and the satiric tone in which the identifications are put forward make clear, for example, that these identifications do not function as metaphors.

Any attempt, therefore, to reify a trope in actual use for analytical purposes can be highly misleading. Moreover, the fixation on one trope might silence interesting connotative identifications, as is clear from the simultaneity of metonymy and synecdoche for the same link between institutions and space in the preceding example. A more complete understanding of the actual identifications implied in the use of tropes requires an openness to the appreciation of what has been aptly called "the

play of tropes" (Fernandez 1991).[16] This awareness of the potential indeterminacy of identification in the use of tropes in speech and performance (Turner 1991) is also important because it highlights how built-
in ambiguities in the use of tropic structures open the possibility for
reinterpretation and change. It also emphasizes that the identifications,
even at this basic, fundamental level, are unstable, thus requiring stabilizing, ambiguity-reducing activity.[17]

Eastern and Western Rhetorical Readings

Easterners and westerners put different emphasis on their rhetorical readings of space, as the following examples illustrate. I begin by presenting
two more western readings and shift subsequently to typical eastern identifications between space and selves.

Against the background of decades of Cold War rhetoric, with its totalizing juxtapositions of capitalism and socialism, peace and war, slav-
ery and humanism, it is understandable that synecdochical readings of
space, in which spatial features are read as microcosms of a social system, enjoy considerable popularity with both east and west Germans.
During my first visit at my field site in east Berlin, a western officer accompanied me back through the front door of the building. Thus, we
passed through the reception area, which he described as a vital interface
between the police and the public. Apparently slightly embarrassed, he
pointed out the unfriendly, unwelcoming setup of the entrance area, begging me not to mistake it for the way in which a western precinct is laid
out. Directing my attention to the long, narrow aisle at the end of which
there was just a small window through which all inquiries had to be made
to the officer on duty (fig. 6), he described the entrance area in a typical

16. Since it is impossible, however, to trace verbatim all the connections/identifi-
cations insinuated by a trope, I will often resort to naming the trope by the connection
which seems most salient in the context. Thus I do not hesitate to call a verbal utterance simply "a metaphor" or "a synecdoche"; the reader is invited to play through
the possible dynamics and ambiguities.

17. One of the main concerns of the literature on tropes is to investigate the precise
relationship between them, to find a sensible system of classification (e.g., Ricoeur 1975;
Friedrich 1991). Especially the relationship between metaphor and metonymy has received much attention, at one time promoting metonymy and at another time preferring
metaphor as anchor of the classificatory system. In a truly Wittgensteinian spirit, understanding meaning from context, Fernandez's (1991a) notion of a play of tropes relativ-
izes this concern with a precise or even true classification.

Figure 6. Window to the Köpenick guard room, interface between
public and police (1995). Author's photo.

western precinct as totally different, namely, wide and open, so that police officers and citizens were separated only by a counter at which people
could write comfortably if they needed to. He insisted that both setups
reflected the relationship between the state and its citizenry: authoritarian in the East and service-oriented in the West. One of his colleagues
later pointed out exactly the same features, adding that the infamous
window was deliberately placed too low, so that everyone had to bow
down to the state. Again, the situation is densely packed with identifications and self-identifications, which involve at least three different
levels: a metonymic reading of the space as characteristic of the institution that built the space, leading to a comparison of the characteristics of
the police-citizen relationship in East and West; a synecdochical reading
comparing aspects of both political systems; and another metonymic
reading that involved personally owning and disowning spatial arrangements.

In almost the same vein, western officers point to the security features
of the People's Police buildings and grounds. The electric fence around
the courtyard, the barred windows, and the alarm systems are read as
synecdoches for a paranoid state that mistrusted its own citizens to such
a degree that it needed to entrench itself behind "fortifications." These
security measures are also read by westerners as metaphors for the aloofness of the state from the population and its concerns. The combination
of this synecdochical reading, hinting at a paranoid system, and the metaphor for aloofness lead some western officers to the conclusion that
the police in East Germany must have been a closed society, almost a
caste. This interpretation is then supported in the eyes of many westerners by the fact that many People's Police officers lived together in apartment blocks, where they had very little contact with other people.[18] The
soundproofing of some of the walls within the building and the seals at
the doors to some rooms are read by westerners as synecdoches for an
organization that was quite suspicious about the trustworthiness of its
own members. While some easterners today agree with their western colleagues in this reading of security measures in an ordinary police precinct,
others defend these "precautions" as signs of the legitimate interest of
the state in defending itself. This is again a synecdochical reading of a

18. While this may or may not have been intended by the government, at least
one other reason for this pooling is that a significant part of housing was distributed
via workplaces; larger factories and agricultural cooperatives followed this practice
just as much as did the police.

political system which is perceived as precarious, certainly in need of defense from its enemies.[19]

Thematically, westerners and easterners pursue different interests in their spatial readings. While westerners typically read eastern spaces for their differences from the west to find traces of authoritarian politics or economic mismanagement, easterners frequently read the transformation of their familiar environments as mirrors of deep changes in their own lives, including their situation in a new state in which westerners have the say. The following two examples of eastern spatial readings exemplify this thematic difference.

On a neighborhood patrol in the outskirts of Potsdam during which we were talking about the differences between life and careers in the People's Police and the Brandenburg Police, as well as about the role of the state in managing or facilitating work life, an eastern officer was pointing to a huge pile of rubble. He explained that this was until recently a wonderful day care center, adding that people in the GDR were proud of the social accomplishment of their state. Again, space, in this case the demolition of a building with a special social service function, is used as a convenient synecdoche for the state, which is identified as much less caring than the state it replaced (day care being an acute problem in the FRG, while the GDR did have a fairly comprehensive day care system). However, this instance of spatial reading is also used as a metaphor for the way in which an east German and, by metonymic extension, all east Germans feel treated by their new government: they see their pride destroyed, and what they thought they had worked for (another metonymy) in shambles. This includes, of course, the progress of their own careers, which in most cases came to an abrupt halt after unification. Most eastern officers who were taken into the unified police organizations were demoted by several ranks. In this contextual juxtaposition of work, state, and building, the officer managed to establish the demolished building as a metaphor for his own life. He thus identified himself as victim, while pointing to the ruthlessness of his victimizers.

In another incident, east German officers were poking fun at the temporary aluminum structure that housed a municipal theater company, which was erected after demolition of the edifice that had been planned and was still under construction at the time the GDR was dissolved. The

---

19. Both models of reading follow official examples and are inspired by the debate about the Wall; see chapter 6.

new authorities deemed the GDR building too ugly to be completed. The police officers not only expressed the view that the temporary structure was just as ugly as the demolished one, but they expected that the new building would probably be no more beautiful than the admittedly ugly GDR project. Again, the reading of space provides the basis for a handy metaphor that rejects western pretensions of making everything better (metonymic identification) and thus also of *being* better.[20]

There is one important type of reading spaces in which eastern and western officers concur. This is the metaphoric use of an inside/outside distinction. Since virtually everybody uses it, and since it occurs in narrations of events in the former People's Police as well as in stories about the West Berlin Police, I assume that this distinction is highly scripted and an active part of the culture of both organizations. The inside/outside distinction gives rise to identifications across hierarchies rather than across the otherwise omnipresent east/west divide. A patrol car team leaving the precinct usually announces this by telling the shift leader and the radio control center that they are driving *out*. "Outside" is accordingly the place where the action is, where a self-respecting police officer is supposed to "stand his man." The "outside" is "the real life," in which a man can prove himself. "Inside," by comparison, is the locale of boring paperwork. "Inside" is also the place of hierarchy, the place of supervision, whereas "outside" is the place of freedom and agency, where actions are undertaken at the discretion of the police officers themselves. Therefore "inside" is the place of "vain theory," the place of those who do not know what is really going on "outside," which is police practice in touch with life. "Going in" does not only imply a return to the precinct; the phrase is also used to denote a talk with a superior. However, the inside/outside metaphor is not as unambiguous in expressing evaluative preferences as it sounds at first. "Inside" is also the place where there is food and coffee, TV and company; "inside" is a place of relaxation when there is no paperwork to do. Moreover, superiors do have an interest in sending people out on patrol duty, in which case trying to stay in is an act of resistance against the demands of superiors. Finally, advancement in the hierarchy, something almost everyone strives for, inevitably means more and more time inside. Elders have the right to stay inside. In fact, every level of hierarchy uses the same inside/outside dichotomizations in speaking about the next higher level, including the president of police

20. To save space, I do not give a detailed interpretation of this instance; the reader, after the example of the two previous ones, should be able to construct one.

himself, who characterizes the political leadership in this way. The inside/ outside distinction is also the basis for fraternization on the same level of hierarchy, fueled by derogation along hierarchical lines.

A whole genre of spatial readings makes considerable use of ellipsis and hyperbole, two tropes which are not part of the classical canon. They are useful, however, in understanding other modes of identification.[21] Ellipsis and hyperbole form opposite poles in a reading of presences and absences and thus play on affirmation and negation. While ellipsis draws attention to what is missed in presence, hyperbole amplifies what is there. Stories about vacations spent at other places account for a substantial portion of all narrative performances among the police officers I have observed.[22] While these stories definitely make use of metaphoric readings of space (invoking ideal lifestyles, *savoir vivre*, etc.), and also employ synecdoche and metonymy in interesting ways, they direct attention to reading spaces as ellipsis; for what seems at times to matter more than what is present in any vacation space is what is absent. In other words, the vacation space is read for the comforts or the threats of home. The flip side of this elliptical reading of the vacation space is the hyperbolic reading of home: Space which is usually scarcely noticed is suddenly read as the epitome of everything one has ever hoped for, or as that which couldn't be worse, or any mixture thereof. Both ellipsis and hyperbole are the basis for strong affirmations of a particular self which seems to gain in discernability through a simple change of places and intensive spatial reading.

Emplotting Readings of Space

Before I can offer a further refinement in understanding eastern and western officer's readings of space, I have to introduce an additional dimension to the emerging theory of modes of identification: the art of creating alliances between speakers and listeners by emplotting an utterance. I have shown already that tropes (e.g., by metonymic inclusion) can provide valuable clues about how the hearers of an utterance can be

21. Note that both the reading of the location of the precinct as well as the reading of the demolished day care center have elliptical elements in them, which I did not discuss above.

22. Vacation stories are in fact so vigorously exchanged that I could not help but think at times that the generation of story material is one of the important aims of vacationing. This is in keeping with a German saying which may be freely translated as, "Whoever takes a journey can come home to tell a tale" (Wer immer eine Reise tut, der kann etwas erzählen).

included in the identifications of the speakers even though the utterances are, strictly speaking, not about them. However, tropes only secondarily capture the dynamics of alliance-building in social interaction. The theory of emplotment developed by the literary critic Northrop Frye (1957) offers a congenial starting point to develop an understanding of how speakers invite listeners to identify with them.[23] For the present study, I would like to emphasize the following aspect of emplotment: Literature has developed in the course of its history various types of conventional narrative structures—modes of speech—which invoke a particular relationship among authors (or speakers), the components of narrative utterances, especially characters and themes, and listeners.[24] Typically, emplotments aim at generating an agreement between speakers and listeners to take a particular cognitive and emotional stance with regard to objects, characters, and themes of the narrative utterance.[25] The best known of these structures (and therefore the ones which are most easily communicated) are comedy, tragedy, romance, satire, and irony. All of them invoke a specific, complex set of attitudes which contextualize and thus qualify the identifications made within the narrative.[26] In other words, they build a frame of reference which facilitates the interpretation of interactions by managing their polysemy.

In a rough approximation, the five forms of emplotment mentioned can be positioned in the following way:[27] *Comedy* aims to bond speakers and listeners through sympathy for the characters and pleasure in their reconciliation with the world;[28] *tragedy* intends to unify speakers and listeners by invoking empathy for failed characters and relief that one

23. The work of Frye has enjoyed limited influence in the social sciences through the works of Hayden White (1973) in history, and more recently in anthropology through John Borneman (1992).

24. The focus on the relationship triangle between speakers, characters of a narrative, and audience is crucial for my work on identifications in interactional contexts. White (1973) focuses in his use of the concept of emplotment on the attitude of historians toward what they might have seen as the nature of history. Borneman (1992) is mostly interested in the configuration of experience by standard cultural forms.

25. Goffman (1955) has analyzed a similar tendency to create agreement between speakers and listeners as "face-work."

26. A better term than *attitudes* would be *sets* (*Einstellungen;* cf. Schütz and Luckmann 1979) because it addresses both emotional and cognitive aspects.

27. These views are informed predominantly by Frye (1957). The characterization of irony is more informed by Rorty (1989).

28. The attitudes invoked primarily pertain to characters, but they can also extend to objects, places, and ideas, which then become the "real" characters of the narrative. As shorthand, I refer in the rest of the paragraph to characters only.

is not among them, although one might have been; *romance* insinuates partnership by advocating the adoption of a common goal epitomized in the characters' quest; *satire* aims at cohesion by deformation and derogation of the main characters; finally, *irony* proposes a common ground between narrator and audience through the self-distancing of the narrated characters. Thus, even more than tropes, emplotments add a decisive emotional tone to identifications.

* * *

In the spatial readings discussed above, an analysis of their emplotment shows the stance the speakers take toward the connections they have created between spaces, institutions, ideas, and selves. These examples also reveal interesting differences between western and eastern emplotment strategies. In the first instance of spatial reading, in which a western officer comments on the location of the precinct building in relation to major access roads, the satiric undertones can scarcely be overheard. According to Frye (1957, 34, 223), one of the primary characteristics of satire is the identification of the principal character of the satire as irretrievably below the capacities of speaker and audience. Therefore, as Frye points out, in satire there can be no reconciliation between the characters and the world. Thus it is not surprising that western officers most frequently use emplotment in terms of satire in their readings of eastern spaces and in their identifications of east German institutions. Western readers typically deny any kind of equality or equivalence between eastern and western institutions.[29] The tropic reading of the entrance hall of the Köpenick precinct is a case in point. With the help of satirical emplotment, western officers stress an unbridgeable gap between western and eastern institutions. Eastern institutions are cast as beyond repair; remedy is only to be found in their complete replacement. Western officers thereby also express the need for radical change and acquisition of western ways by their eastern counterparts. Contrary to political rhetoric, western officers rarely engage in romantic readings of eastern spaces. Tragic emplotments are used almost exclusively in descriptions of the decrepit state of westerner's former eastern home spaces, and comic or ironic emplotments of western readings of eastern spaces are completely absent.

Easterners' readings of space show a much wider variability in emplotment, reflecting a much more multifaceted attitude toward the various

---

29. The next two chapters trace the history and the present status of the western transformation narrative for the East.

spaces they encounter. Especially right after the opening of the Berlin Wall, readings of western spaces had—and at times still have—the ring of romance. Romances, according to Frye (1957, 186ff.), are stories of positive transformation in the direction of an affirmed telos. In this sense, many aspects of western space are accepted as positive, imitable "repro-topia" (rather than what they were before, unattainable u-topia). At the same time, eastern spaces are frequently given a tragic reading. Tragedy is characterized by a dramatic loss of agency (Frye 1957, 207ff.), which many easterners suggest they have experienced twice in their own life-times: first in the difficulty of creating spaces which could compete with the admired western models because of their forced participation in the Soviet realm of centrally planned economies, and second in the destruc-tion of many eastern buildings by the new western authorities—buildings that had, for a variety of reasons, become dear to easterners. The reading of the torn-down day care center has a tragic plot structure; its author at least partly takes the blame for the failure of the GDR and the unques-tioned adoption of the western model.[30]

Finally, as the example of the makeshift structure housing the Potsdam theater makes clear, easterners have also started to use comic emplotment. The outstanding characteristic of comedy is the rejection of presumed supe-riority, while allowing for reconciliation between conflicting parties (Frye 1957, 165). This comic reading betrays the cunning of the reader vis-à-vis those who have the privilege, in de Certeau's (1984) terms, of strategic command over space.[31] In the end, "the big ones will do whatever they want regardless of what the little man thinks," as one officer said in this context,

30. Many persons who had actively held a stake in the GDR, believing in the superiority of socialism, blamed themselves after the breakup of the GDR for restraining their criticism for so long, for not trying to speak up more vigorously. Moreover, many see the vote for the Christian Democrats by a sizable majority of the GDR voters in the first free East German elections on 18 March 1990 and again in the first elections to a common Bundestag in a unified Germany as a hasty but ultimately voluntary sellout of GDR accomplishments.

31. De Certeau (1984) distinguishes between two different kinds of agency: strat-egies and tactics. Strategies are actions which are autonomous, that is, free of con-straint within a particular, designated domain. In terms of space, the planning and building of houses or whole city quarters may be considered strategic. For de Certeau, strategic action is a sign of power. Tactics are actions without a proper domain of autonomy. Their freedom is entirely derived from the clever manipulation of given structures within a domain. Tactics are grafted, as it were, on the existing strategies of others. Thus, tactics for de Certeau are the weapons of the weak in the face of the power of others. In terms of space, typical examples for tactics are unforeseen uses of space, such as jaywalking, the appropriation of railway stations as dormitories by the homeless, or the tapping of public power supplies by slum dwellers.

and here lies the criticism of the easterners: in situations like this one, they insinuate that there is no difference between the sociopolitical regimes of capitalism and socialism, despite the claims of either to represent the common human being. And here also lies an invitation to reconciliation from the common human being of the east to the common human being of the west—an invitation that westerners usually reject in eager identification with the advantages of their own system.

So far comedy is only initiated by easterners; westerners remain adamantly satiric. Worse, westerners sometimes suggest that they are comic when in fact they are satiric. The fine line between the two is the difference in power created by the inequality of the unification process itself, and this is the reason why a derogatory phrase about a western building by an easterner has a different effect than the same phrase applied by a westerner to an eastern building. Because of the imbalance of power, westerners can initiate comedy only in response to their own buildings, which would require a humility that is indeed still very rare.

Since speakers use emplotment structures to bond with listeners, fieldworkers as professional listeners should feel their force in particular ways. My attention was drawn to emplotment structures in the first place because I felt the need to analyze a set of situations which invariably left me uncomfortable. Especially at the beginning of my fieldwork, when I was still very concerned with building rapport, the following type of situation occurred several times. Officers from either side emplotted the identifications inherent in their stories in such a way that an officer from the other side would be prone to feel resentment if he overheard the story in passing. Thus I found myself in a situation where I did not want to accept the invitation to concur with the attitudes espoused in the emplotment because the passer-by, in no more than ephemeral contact, might have carried away an impression of me which I by no means wanted to convey—yet it was nearly impossible for me to disregard or refuse the invitation with face-saving grace. Later, if officers I got to know chanced to overhear a narrative I was told by an officer from the other side while disagreeing with the invitation inherent in its emplotment, they typically tried to undermine the credibility of the other officer's emplotment in some form. While easterners would frequently find me after the officer whose emplotment they were concerned with had left the scene to present their corrective views, westerners often chose to break into the ongoing conversation. One day I was involved in a chat with an eastern officer in which she described her experiences with the GDR day care system in glowing colors, leading us to agree on the desirability of a comprehensive, state-sponsored day care system. This officer used romance as a form of emplotment for narrating her own experience, effectively inviting me to bond with her in agreement over shared values. A western officer who had overheard our conversation jumped in and addressed us smilingly, "Sounds like a fairy tale, doesn't it?" intending to reduce the possible effect of her romantic emplotment by satirizing it. He then turned to me, saying, "Don't get yourself lulled into these stories."

Within the conflicted social field of relations between easterners and westerners, both sides tried to convince me of the validity of their positions, in effect asking me to side with them. With an intense interest in not losing my credibility with either side, I felt that I had to be careful not to give in too easily to the carefully emplotted invitation to identify with the speaker. A good example for this tension is the emplotment of the entrance-hall scene. The officer who led me back through the front door was apparently embarrassed about the entrance area to the precinct. I was a newcomer, an outsider, and he might have been afraid that I would read the setup as a metonymy of the Berlin Police, an identification which he tried to undermine with his satiric reading of that very space, disowning it through his reading. Yet his satiric reading implicated me as a coconspirator in his plot, urging me to side with him, through sharing in his laughter. This of course left me embarrassed, because I neither wanted to be unfriendly to him, nor did I want to be seen by easterners laughing with the western officer about the eastern building.

In sum, then, police officers in Köpenick and in Potsdam proved to be avid readers of space. Sennet (1990) has argued that inhabitants of modern cities, unlike those of ancient Greek or medieval cities, cannot read their cultures by moving through space. The reason for this, according to Sennet, is a rigid division in the modern world between public and private which is deeply inscribed in spatial arrangements. On the basis of my fieldwork material, however, I believe Sennet's argument requires qualification. Especially in comparing spaces, a possibility enhanced by global mass tourism, people come to understand complex aspects of societies by experiencing space today as they did two thousand years ago. Of course, the codes have changed, and what one might have to look for today is not what one might have had to look for in classical Athens.

Reading Texts and Reading Space

Using the metaphor of reading suggests a text to be read, thus creating a potential analogy between text and space. Since this analogy almost suggests itself, while adumbrating a set of unwanted extensions, I must point out where I see the differences between reading a text and reading space. If *text* is taken to mean a clearly bounded system of signs referring mainly to each other, then reading space is clearly not like reading a text. To begin with, spaces are much less definitively bounded than texts. Spatial readings can be restricted to the minutest detail of a room at one moment, and may encompass the entire neighborhood in the next. In contrast to texts, many spaces are also continuously in the making, if only because the spatial practices of those living in a space are part and parcel of the very fabric of the space. And it is precisely this flux, the continuous making and remaking of space, which is of special interest to the spatial reader. The reading of space is also much more fragmentary and selective than the text analogy would imply. In other words, space is not read in linear fashion like a book, starting with the first word in the first line on page 1 and ending with the last word in the last line on the last page; its reading may start anywhere and jump virtually to anywhere else. That is to say that, in contrast to reading texts, there is no conventional idea about the direction of reading spaces; there are simply no first and last lines. Finally, spaces rarely have a single author, but a shifting number of authors who play different roles in making a particular space. Clearly some spatial readings are closer to the model of reading a text, like architectural criticism, and others are relatively far from it, like reading a prevailing Nazi grandiosity into the reconstruction of Potsdamer Platz at one moment and then understanding the same set of buildings as a harbinger of an exciting big-city rhythm in the next.

The degree to which signs are conventionally defined in reading space and reading texts is perhaps the most important difference between them. What is to be taken as a signifier in space rests much more on cultural, historical, personal, and situational factors and therefore changes much more quickly than what is usually considered to be a signifier in a text. The signified, too, may change rapidly and is thus much more ephemeral than in texts: codes for spatial reading are considerably more fluid, varying from relatively strong fixation in the case of stylistic codes of architecture to an almost spontaneous, improvised production of code by a flaneur or the itinerant reader in general. The text to be read, one could argue, must first be produced.[32]

I am fully aware that the definitional aspects I have used here to

32. In this sense readers of space have a strong similarity with ethnographers as Crapanzano (1992, 43) describes them: "The ethnographer does not, however, translate texts the way the translator does. He must first produce them."

characterize a text have been heavily criticized by contemporary streams of literary theory such as reception-aesthetics (Iser 1976; Eco 1984) and deconstruction (Derrida 1976; Culler 1982). Yet, while it might be an illuminating strategic move for literary theory to transgress the traditional understanding of what constitutes a text, it is equally important for the social sciences to be aware of the metaphoric nature of concepts such as "texts" and "reading." Here, more traditional understandings of "text" are a useful backdrop for other forms of interpretative actions. There is only limited usefulness in calling everything interpretable a text, especially after this has been done for a while. Moreover, it is productive to understand the differences between various kinds of interpretative action, between the seeming extremes of a technical semiotics of signs (Eco 1979) and a literary hermeneutics.

The fluidity of signifiers and signified becomes apparent when it is considered that the very way in which easterners *look* at space has, in many cases, undergone a considerable transformation. Some of my informants have pointed out that they see space today as if with different eyes, meaning both that they see things today they would not have perceived before and that they read today a different meaning into the same spatial features. Buildings they had seen in the GDR as signs of progress are reported to be seen suddenly in a changed light. On a neighborhood beat patrol in Köpenick, an eastern officer pointed to what he perceived now as clearly visible flaws in the construction and design of the panel buildings which are part of his area. He explained to me that the panels were frequently joined in a very sloppy way and dramatized his criticism by putting his arm into the next best panel joint we passed, nodding to me, "This is what I mean." The same officer also began to question the aesthetic wisdom of these panel buildings by saying, "In the GDR it never would have occurred to me to consider these buildings here as ugly. But now, with the beautifully restored buildings of the old city in front of my eyes, things are different."

A Potsdam officer reported in a chat about his hobbies that he only started to *perceive* churches after the fall of the Wall, and that his interest in visiting them clearly postdated unification. "In GDR times," he said, "I never set foot into a church. I didn't even know their names; they simply didn't exist for me." Since unification, however, he had not only begun to visit churches regularly, but he went on family weekend outings to churches and long-defunct monasteries in the surroundings. What he started to discover in these churches is what he took to be *his own* history. In other words, he began to produce identifications with space which were markedly different from those he had made in the GDR. Thus, on the basis of experience and the use of space, his identity has started to shift.

Writing Space

Some of the spatial readings I have presented above invoke a product-producer relationship. Space is seen as the product of an institution, a whole social system, or even an epoch. There is a keen awareness of the fact that space is socially produced, that shaping the form of space is a matter of power. As the satiric reading of the temporary structure housing the theater illustrates, police officers know that writing space in any big way is beyond their purview. Still they are ardent critics of those who do have the power to write larger chunks of space: the government and big companies. Their criticism of these spaces written by others informs their deviant spatial practices, thus helping them to preserve a degree of agency in a situation in which they have very little power.[33] Thus, the police officers I encountered take routes homeward that city planners did not envision, or they choose their shopping places not in accordance with the hopes of these suppliers of goods and services, en bloc and close to home, but in keeping with their own idiosyncratic preferences, even if this entails considerable detours from the usual routes traveled.

Conversely, much of police work involves enforcing the use of space envisioned by the designers of public roads and places. Police officers must try to thwart illicit uses of roads which are in conflict with the official rules. Thus they are busy ticketing shortcuts involving still-prohibited left turns, creative albeit unlawful parking, speeding, and so on. As far as the traffic flow is concerned, individual police officers may have a limited influence on the setting of rules by addressing and sometimes even arguing with the officials who are responsible for traffic regulations. In some instances, police officers even side with those who make imaginative use of the street against the regulators of space; they may use their legal discretion in isolated cases, or they may systematically turn a blind eye on certain violations by pointing to possible contradictions in the rules.[34]

33. I am following here again de Certeau (1984).
34. In Berlin, police officers may choose whether or not to follow up on a violation of rules *(Ordnungswidrigkeit)*; they have no discretion, however, as far as criminal offenses *(Straftaten)* are concerned. Failure to report a criminal offense is a criminal offense in itself.

The agency of the police officers with respect to space is, however, not restricted to the creative use of space essentially produced by others. Most of the police officers I got to know see themselves as writers of space on a smaller scale. Many of them aspire to build or to buy a house sooner or later, and almost all of them are passionate "renovators" of the spaces they inhabit. A fair number of them also own or rent little weekend or summer cottages in one of the many cottage colonies in and around Berlin.[35] Actually, stories about buying new furniture, about wallpapering, painting, or repairing some feature of the apartment, house, or cottage are probably even more frequent than vacation tales. The police officers are not only involved in the "beautification" *(Verschönerung)* of their own private spaces; some of them also tried to "improve the appearance" *(das Aussehen verbessern)* of their offices. Privately arranged-for *(organisierte)* furniture in designer black or chic mahogany is used instead of the trite, officially provided steel furniture in uniform gray;[36] plants are set up, posters hung, lamps exchanged, floor mats and tablecloths placed, and shelves moved around to embellish the work space.

Such writing of space is not confined only to setting up the office; it also involves more work-related activities. The patrol cars are correctly lined up in the courtyard, documents are filed in a particular way, the supplies of forms and other material are organized neatly in shelves, keys are kept at particular places. Any disruption of this orderliness will be

35. In the west these cottages are called *Lauben* (pergolas) or *Hütten* (huts). In the east they are called *Datsche* (from the Russian word for "cottage"). Actually, they are frequently veritable little houses with running hot and cold water, telephone, electricity, and mail delivery. They are located in what is called a *Garten* (garden plot) which is part of a *Schrebergartenkolonie* ("garden colonies" named after their founder, Mr. Schreber). These colonies are organized by clubs, often running their own little pub or restaurant. These clubs, depending on how active they are, may also organize social activities catering especially to the elderly and to the young. From spring to fall many families spend the weekends in their cottages; occasionally, people move completely to their gardens during summer. Roughly 10 percent of the territory of Berlin is covered with Schrebergärten. There are about eighty-five thousand individual plots, which are in great demand, frequently not even showing up on the free market, but sold and bought within networks of friends and relatives.

36. "To arrange for" *(organisieren)* is an important phrase here, used by the police officers themselves. The point is that they do not want to buy anything to embellish their offices. They use things that are becoming superfluous elsewhere, due to renovations at home, at relatives' or friends' places, or at other workplaces they would know of. *Organisieren* connotes "to make do" or "to improvise"; it also always implies getting something without paying for it, or at least not paying the full market price, or getting it by mobilizing personal contacts.

Figure 7. The head administrator in her beautified office (summer 1995). Author's photo.

immediately recognized and complained about. Nothing is more of an embarrassment than a supposedly filed form that cannot be found, because this shatters the self-understanding of bureaucracy, which is partly inscribed in orderly spatial practices of record keeping.[37] One day, the armorer of the Berlin precinct showed me his magazine. Pistols, rifles, and submachine guns, sticks, shields, tear gas containers, masks, and ammunition were all neatly paraded in orderly rows, minutely spaced, almost measured, on immaculately clean shelves. Even the workbench top was kept in fastidious order, the wiping cloth draped right next to the vice. He told me that he would know immediately if somebody had been in the magazine without his knowledge—he would just be able to tell. He said that he was an orderly person, and that this was just what made a good armorer. After all, he was accountable for every single piece of equipment, every single bullet.

37. With computerization, these practices will lose their spatial character almost entirely.

Figure 8. The chief of operations in his newly refurbished
office (1995). Author's photo.

The motivations that the officers give for their writing of space point
to a close association between their own selves and the space which they
transform into a desirable shape. "I just didn't feel at home here. I
couldn't stand this desk of mine; it just wasn't me." Another frequently
used expression justifying the embellishment of offices makes use of the

term *gemütlich* (cozy): "Well, we also want it a little bit cozy in here." Expressions of this kind point to a particular state of being they want to achieve in the spaces they inhabit: they are striving to achieve a fit between themselves and their space. If this fit is achieved in a very good way (which the officers say is rarely the case in offices; it is said most frequently to be achieved in their garden plots and cottages), both eastern and western officers use an expression which is taken by them to be a good old, hearty Berlin idiom: "Here you can let your soul freely swing" ("Hier kannste de Seele so richtig baumeln lassen").

Thus I found the police officers in Köpenick and Potsdam busily involved in writing their home and work spaces. This writing is done with much care and attention. Renovations at home and rearrangements in the offices are serious projects which are thoroughly discussed in advance with friends and relatives; they involve weighing alternatives, studying catalogues, visiting vendors, and so on. The metaphor of writing is appropriate here, because a reading of these spaces is invited. At home or in the garden, friends and relatives are shown around and improvements pointed out, or else the visitors are expected to be perceptive enough to realize for themselves that the composition of the space has changed. These invited readings in the form of in-house sightseeing tours are usually accompanied by comments like, "I had to do something about it; the old wallpaper really started to bug me." Compliments about neatness are received with comments like, "Well, I am an orderly person." Renovations are often motivated by the possible readings of the spaces by others: "It was about time to repaint the bathroom, or else—What would people think about me?"

The expected readings of these spaces are therefore metonymic: the space is taken to represent its writer. Police officers read the spaces they know as created by a particular person more precisely even as extensions of this person. Conversely, they identify persons by reading the space known to be written by these persons. In the same vein, they write their spaces to ensure that others will identify these spaces—and therefore them—in a particular way.[38] In all cases in which the writing of space was narrated to me, a visit to that space was taken as an opportunity to give me a grand tour of it. People do have or are assumed to have some agency in the writing of their spaces. At the same time, the writing of space is highly valued and generally considered as one of the most signifi-

38. A variation on that theme is the reading of bookshelves by more intellectually inclined people.

cant activities that one can undertake. People who have lost agency for the writing of spaces they would normally be assumed to have written will try to avoid outside reading of these spaces in order to escape unwanted, "misleading" interpretations of themselves. People would, for example, try to eschew potential misreadings of their home spaces by not inviting the potential misreader. Eastern police officers gave this as a reason why, at least at the beginning, they did not welcome westerners into their homes. They feared that westerners would do to their homes what they had watched them do to their old offices and to public spaces in the east in general: derogate them as manifestations of an inferior political system.

The writing of office space, since it is much more restrained (because there is less agency), has an additional quality: it displays the inhabitant's capacity to "make do" *(organisieren)*, that is, his or her ability to improvise with limited resources. Particularly far-reaching forms of beautification can also demonstrate an officer's willingness to go against the directives of the organization; that is, they involve an element of daring, a readiness to test limits. There is another aspect to the work-related writing of space that I should mention here. Keeping order in filing documents or storing equipment conforms to the scripted ideal of a bureaucrat or armorer. The metonymic writing and invited metonymic reading, therefore, set up a three-way relationship: the written space conforms to the ideal of its writing, which in turn reflects on its actual writer. Thus, through the writing of space, writers try to present themselves also as good role models.

The significance of writing home spaces is further emphasized by the amounts of time and financial resources put into it. Home development is perhaps the foremost material goal in the lives of both eastern and western police officers. Few things stir up such violent negative emotions about the former GDR in the east German officers I got to know as the shortage in building supplies and furniture. Some tell long stories about the pains involved in getting bricks, tiles, or cement, and stories about the connections that were needed to get anything at all. In the end, despite all the effort, things frequently didn't match—tiling, wallpaper, wall-to-wall carpet, and furniture didn't add up to an aesthetically pleasing whole. One officer commented on the patchwork of tiles adorning his kitchen wall, which had been completed, after much trouble, just before the fall of the Wall: "When I look at it today, I get so furious that I could just tear it down. Nothing matches. And today I just need to drive to the next lumber yard to buy whatever I want."[39] Most eastern officers, therefore, began thorough renovations of their apartments, room after room as money permitted, soon after unification.

Just as the police officers are quite conscious of their writing of space, so is the government. Every single project for which (especially federal) government money is used—reconstruction or renovation of roads, railway links, telephone switches, administrative buildings and so on—is used as an opportunity for self-advertisement of the government's role in remodeling the former GDR. At all of these sites huge billboards announce what exactly the government is building here for the people. Public relations managers have invented zippy campaign slogans for these construction efforts. One such series is heralded as "Booming East,"[40] while all sorts of improvements on traffic infrastructure are marketed as "Traffic Projects German Unity" (Verkehrsprojekte Deutsche Einheit). In television advertising clips, the government uses cranes crowding the Berlin airspace to insinuate metaphoric readings of construction sites, likening them to change, renewal, and economic boom. People have their own readings, though. The crane touting the imminent opening of yet another shopping center was by one officer by no means read as a sign of progress. He remembered that it was erected on the site of a former factory for locomotives. To him, the comparative loss of jobs in conjunction with an invitation to consume sounded like a bad joke.

In sum, the writing of home space in particular must be understood, to extend what Goffman had to say about space as the background setting of performances (Goffman 1959), as a formidable self-performance in its own right. That is, the written space is not only a stage *for* performance; it *is* performance itself (cf. Herzfeld 1991). Nothing makes that clearer than the construction-site tourism that has developed in Berlin to celebrate the reconstruction of the city. Not only do Berliners go construction sightseeing on the weekends, but major sites such as the "heart" of prewar Berlin, the Potsdamer Platz, has become a must-stop for all visitors too. The glaringly red "Infobox," housing exhibits on the past and future of Potsdamer Platz, has easily become one of Berlin's most visited

39. Of course, this also bespeaks frustration at the futility of the effort in the first place. What was quite difficult then, quite an achievement within the framework of the GDR, is relatively easy today, rendering old efforts, substantial as they were, worthless from the perspective of unlimited availability of materials.

40. In German, *Aufschwung Ost*, in which the upward slope of the *A* is used to support a strong, skyward-pointing arrow in the national colors: black, red, and gold.

Figure 9. The government broadly advertises its reconstruction efforts in east Germany (here, railway construction in Potsdam) (spring 1995). Author's photo.

tourist attractions. Much more than with the purchase of durable consumer goods, where only the choice of the product (and occasionally innovative use) reflect agency, the writing of space is a process which involves many more degrees of freedom and thus involves a considerable level of agency, reflecting taste and lifestyle and leading to something like the inscription of self in space.

Placing Self

The identifications between spaces and selves that I have discussed in the section on reading space are indirect. For the spatial reader, the experience of space is more or less the occasion and sometimes also the source of metaphors to identify self and other with the world at large. Spatial

Figure 10. In countless exhibitions, Berliners and tourists are shown models of what Berlin will or might look like. Here, a view onto the city center with rebuilt Hohenzollern castle on the site of the still-standing Palast der Republik (spring 1995). Author's photo.

writing, by comparison, creates a direct link between self and space by establishing metonymic identifications. For most people, however, writing is a technique of limited scope: the places that can be written, or partially written by an individual person are normally small, even though extremely important. In other words, writing is not the technique by which a self can be linked to a street, neighborhood, city, region, or a whole country.[41] Direct identifications between selves and spaces which these selves cannot be assumed to have written I call "placements."

One important type of placement is the synecdochical identification of self as a part of a spatial whole. "I am a Berliner" is an example of such a synecdochical connection between self and space. The most exclusive level for which this form of placement is in use is the street, and the most inclusive level is the world; it is most frequently employed, however, at the level of the city, the state, and the nation.[42] Which level is chosen in discourse is highly contingent on the placement of the interlocutor as well as on the issue being discussed. Street placement, for example, only makes sense vis-à-vis an interlocutor who has intimate knowledge of the neighborhood (which is typically the case for police officers), and it is chosen in instances in which the street can be meaningfully addressed as a whole, bounded in some respect, as in the case of a socioeconomic milieu. Placement at one level not only preempts placement at another location on the same level (e.g., "I am a Berliner" implies that the speaker is not a Hamburgian or a Frankfurter),[43] but it can also imply rejection of placement at a higher or lower level. As one officer once said, "We are all Berlin police officers now," rejecting any placement as eastern or western. Another officer said with the same intention, "We are all Germans." Thus placement stresses the level of local identification which is deemed relevant.

Placement may also take on the character of a synecdoche which identifies self as an integral part of an organic whole.[44] As self-identification, this occurs, for example, in the expression "I am a real Berlin plant" ("Ich

41. Writing city quarters or even whole cities is the prerogative of princes, governments, and big corporations, along with city planners of the stature of Corbusier, Haussman, or Pombal.

42. This form of placement lends itself to segmentary identifications: for example, the residents of two streets within a borough may be opposed to each other but they unite to support their borough against another borough.

43. "Hamburgian" (German: *Hamburger*) or "Frankfurter" (German: *Frankfurter*) might sound contrived in English; however, the German grammatical form of city + suffix *-er*, indicating being of that city, is much stronger as a form of placement than the use of the preposition "from" (German: *aus*). In German, the *-er* suffix is invariably used to emphasize synecdochical, part-whole identification with a place. The use of the preposition *aus* is much more metonymic in character and need not indicate more than residence. If even less of an identification is claimed, a German speaker is likely to use the form, "I live in" (*ich lebe in*) + city.

44. This can of course also be read as a metonymy (if a producer-product relationship or the subsumption under a common category is insinuated) rather than an organism-biotope one. See the comments on the "play of tropes" dealing with the context-dependent character of the modes of identification further above.

bin eine echte berliner Pflanze"),[45] or in "I am a real Potsdam grown" ("Ich bin ein echtes Potsdamer Gewächs"), where the metaphor of a plant is used to describe a self as a product and constituent part of a particular environment, heightened by the self-authentication in the use of the word "real," which also suggests long-standing presence, usually from birth. This kind of synecdochical relationship of self to space is often part of an entire rhetorical web of relations in a verbal performance which may also illustrate the interaction between readings of space and placement. The placement "I have just grown up here" is used frequently as an explanation of feelings attached to one or the other aspect of the former GDR. In a conversation about GDR nostalgia, for example, one officer added "I have just grown up here" to an expression of strong attachment to the "Palast der Republik," the highly controversial parliament building–cum–sociocultural center of the GDR, which many westerners deem too ugly to preserve, given its conspicuous position in the center of the city. In the context of this conversation the speaker thus anchors a whole field of identifications between self, space, and the state with the placement "I have just grown up here." There is a metonymy between space and self as producer and product, a synecdoche between space and state, another one between self and emotions, and an important metonymy between the state and the phase of life marked out as sentimentalized. The attachment to the building is also a metaphor for the attachment to the state and, by implication, a metonymy between the GDR and the emotions of the individual is invoked.

Police work itself is rife with placements along these lines. The entire area to be policed is mentally and often statistically broken up into "problem-zones." One neighborhood beat patrol officer once explained to me that the incidence of crimes and violations in a given area is reciprocal to the average intelligence quotient in that area. More specifically, some areas are known to be frequented by illegal cigarette vendors, or to have more than their fair share of car thefts, and still others are notorious for parking violations. Since all precincts seem to have their "problem-children" (individuals who come into contact with the police again and again), and since these "preferred customers," as they are also known, frequently inhabit the same neighborhood, a new, previously unknown "client" might be introduced as "just another of these lads from So-and-So Street."

The elliptic reading of alien spaces and the subsequent hyperbolic reading of the home space find their counterparts in an elliptic identifica-

45. *Berliner Pflanze* has the character of an idiom.

tion of self, more commonly called homesickness (its negative form could perhaps be called "home-loathing"), and a hyperbolic identification of self's well-being (in the negative form, despair) as forms of placement. In this way spatial reading and placement mutually reinforce each other to the degree that a distinction becomes difficult: self and space are on the verge of fusing. From the many narrations of vacation trips that I heard, I gathered that they typically followed as a general plot scheme this elliptic reading/identification of alien space/self and the consecutive hyperbolic reading/identification of home/self. In a way, narratives of holiday trips seem to suggest that reaffirmation of home placement is, if not the prime reason for vacationing, certainly one of the more important side effects of a trip away from home. A frequent summarizing comment is that people like being at a vacation spot for a while, but that under no circumstance would they want to live there. This is true for east and west Germans alike. It is, however, after decades of highly restricted travel in the GDR followed by the almost frenzied traveling activity of east Germans after the fall of the Wall, a particularly interesting result for easterners, because it raises the interesting (albeit ultimately unanswerable) question of whether the GDR government could have allowed its people, under certain conditions, to travel freely without risking that too many of them might not return to their work (for this is what mattered). Put differently, the regime might have deprived itself needlessly of the benefits of this reaffirmation of home.

Still the overriding interest in placement in the east Berlin police precinct is to differentiate between easterners and westerners. In order to place themselves, people make use of a wide variety of codes. The police officers I worked with were always busy finding new, reliable signs that would permit placement of their own selves and those of others. During the time immediately following unification, clothes, shopping bags, posture, and of course cars were mentioned as signifiers allowing easy placement. As time passed, and easterners replaced their clothes and cars with western brands, these signs lost at least their unambiguous placing power. Paying attention to dialects is a very effective way of placing selves. Speakers of dialects are invariably placed by hearers, which is a great asset for those who can shift back and forth between dialect and high German, thereby manipulating their own placement by others. For those who cannot easily shift modes, dialect is a giveaway.[46] Since the

46. In the context of German unification this is especially true for people from the Saxon- and Thuringian-speaking parts of the former GDR. Since these dialects are not represented in the West, as are the Berlin dialect or the idioms of the Baltic

vocabularies of the FRG and the GDR have drifted apart, certain words are also easy markers. An east German who uses a west German term is making a statement, and so is a west German who uses an east German one. Substantial differences exist between much of the organizational and technical vocabulary of the People's Police and that of the (West) Berlin Police. An east German using People's Police terminology is surely inviting placement (unwittingly or purposefully). Also license plates are used everywhere to place easterners and westerners.[47] West Germans working in East Germany employ them as convenient self-identifying placements: they simply fail to register the car at their new work location, thus keeping their old plates with their easily identifiable *K*s for Cologne (Köln) or *F*s for Frankfurt. Berlin police officers have even found ways to tell east and west Berlin drivers apart, whose plates all begin with a *B,* by scrutinizing the second set of letters in their registration number. The fact that it takes some effort to acquire this knowledge, which is not readily available, seems to betray a deep-seated need for placement.

Placement is, however, not only usable as a technique. In some ways it just happens, since life itself has a clandestine and therefore all the more effective power to place selves. Living and working in a space creates a wealth of stories, which make up the biography of a person. The memories of these stories are always placed.[48] During my fieldwork officers frequently followed up on narratives they had told me by showing me the locale in which they had actually taken place. This happened not only in passing, that is, by accidentally traveling past the locale of the story ("Oh, by the way, this is the spot where . . ."), but also quite deliberately by making detours to reach the locale of a story; sometimes a trip was undertaken for the sole purpose of seeing the locale of narrated action.

---

seashore, Saxon and Thuringian epitomize the GDR dialect. This impression is exacerbated by the fact that they are the two largest dialect groups in the former GDR, so that many former officials in the GDR had Saxon or Thuringian accents. Unlike Berliners, Saxons also did not usually have relatives in the West, making them sought-after personnel for border controls. Many westerners therefore associate negative border-control experiences with officers speaking with heavy Saxon accents.

47. German license plates (i.e., the former West German and now all-German plates) are composed of three blocks. The first indicates, using one to three letters, the county or city in which a car is registered (e.g., Berlin plates all start with a *B;* Potsdam plates all start with a *P*). The location block is followed by a hyphen and then a set of letters (usually one or two), which serve to multiply the number of possible registrations in conjunction with the third block, consisting of numbers of up to four digits.

48. Bachelard (1964) argues that space takes precedence over time in anchoring memories.

Being there often gave rise to a renarration, this time with more attention to circumstantial detail, and sometimes even to partial enactment, so that the narrator would partially relive what at times had happened decades ago. These sightseeing tours of memory are not necessarily sentimental journeys undertaken out of nostalgia (although these do occur as well). The places shown to me were also imbued with bad, uncomfortable memories of unhappy childhoods or times of hardship. And far from involving only personal experiences, a good number of them were work-related—journeys to sites of spectacular police action, both successes and failures. Police officers would also quite frequently travel during slack time to places that figured in the narrative of some colleague just days ago.

Two kinds of places carry special significance in this respect: homes, and workplaces (including schools). Bachelard (1964) is right when he points out that places can collapse whole sections of a biography,[49] and the places that are usually chosen to denote whole phases of life are homes and workplaces. Some of the police officers in Köpenick and Potsdam made sure to guide me past all the houses they had lived in. Space does in this sense almost take the role of external memory, and locations of stories are cherished as gateways to the past. The loss of these locations, due to destruction and reconstruction of buildings, streets, and other places is therefore always also a loss of memory, a loss of a piece of one's own past.

Ultimately, placement is one of the reasons why the restitution of expropriated buildings, especially private homes, stirs up very deep emotions among west Germans and east Germans alike.[50] Those who have lost property not only want it back, but also their memories, the *places* of their *selves*. Usually those who get their property back are appalled at what others have done to it; they bemoan any changes. Those who lose the right to reside in the spaces they have often inhabited for decades feel, in the true sense of the word, displaced. Few things made Potsdam police officers more angry than the restitution of real estate to a group of heirs rather than to the former owners, who would have been expected

49. Bachelard exhibits a Freudian leaning in emphasizing the overall importance of the first house in which a person has lived. He is especially interested in the refuges this first house has offered for daydreaming, because he links these primordial experiences with later reading and writing of poetry.

50. In many ways, the restitution of expropriated property has proven to be one of the biggest burdens of the unification process. Since the outcome is by no means clear, it is one of the greatest sources of legal uncertainties for investors, because there is always some risk that real estate transactions undertaken in the East will finally be declared void.

to come back and live again in the house that had been so dear to them. Heirs without personal ties to the property are assumed to use it "merely as an object for speculation." The very fact that this was possible after unification betrayed to easterners the venality of the capitalist system.[51]

This conflict over the rights to space as rights to memory, about who has the prerogative to place themselves in real, experienceable space, is by no means restricted to private homes. Some West Germans who were born in the former GDR, having fled in the early postwar period, and who returned after unification often for the first time since leaving, are frequently appalled by "what the communists have done to their cities." They scorn the GDR for not having invested in the restoration of the city as they knew it; they scorn it for having erected new structures instead of restoring the old ones. Now they frequently demand the demolition of these GDR buildings, overlooking the fact that other memories are attached to the buildings they want torn down.[52] The restitution of street names that were changed after 1943 is likewise a hotly contested issue.

That life itself uncannily connects human beings to locations was most acutely felt by some western officers, who spoke with quite ambiguous feelings about their own "easternization."[53] The common terminology of "Wessis" for westerners and "Ossis" for easterners was enriched by a hybridization of the two, "Wossis," applied to all those who had in some way taken to the other side. Western police officers whom I asked whether they felt at home in east Berlin, whether the east was now also their Berlin, answered regularly with a decisive no, but many of them added quickly that they had to exempt the precinct in which they were working. Asked why, one of them said, "So much of my life has happened here, you know; the last five years were very exciting."

In a world divided neatly into zones of competence, zones of authority,

51. This is in fact a synecdochical reading of spatial practices.

52. Since the GDR regime has been delegitimized, the decisions of the regime in changing the layout of spaces are by metonymic extension also delegitimized, and changes can be demanded. The most prominent debates in this respect are those about plans to raze the Palast der Republik, the GDR parliament building, and to construct a replica of the Hohenzollern castle over the ruins on which the parliament was built. Police officers in the precinct are clearly divided along east-west lines on this conflict: westerners favor the destruction of the parliament building, if not necessarily the reconstruction of the castle, while most easterners find the idea of destroying the parliament building highly disturbing.

53. The term they have used in German is *Verostung,* which sounds somewhat more negative than *Veröstlichung,* the literal translation of "easternization."

zones of knowledge, zones of mentalities, wherever spatial distributions are used as the organizing principle of a human ontology, placement is a powerful technique to decide who is who and what is what. Modern discourses make a wide use of human ontologies based on spatial distribution. There is the North-South conflict (the global one as well as the American, Italian, German, . . . ones), there is orientalism (Said 1978), there is nationalism, there is a kind of "continentalism," and of course there was the East-West of the Cold War, which has neatly translated into a German east-west. The German east-west ontology is also one of "purity and danger," of spoiled and unspoiled lineage (Douglas 1966), the power of which may be illustrated by a concluding example.

An eastern officer told me the following story in order to show me how deeply distrusting westerners are of everything that comes from the east, how everything that is identifiable (placeable) as eastern is viewed as "spoilt" *(verdorben)*. A western officer had handwritten an evaluation that included something like a grade report for some patrol officer, which he gave to the eastern officer who was relating this story to me, to have it typed. Once she had finished her job, she returned the material to the westerner, who just minutes later came back steaming into her office saying, "If I continue with a capital letter after a colon, then I mean it," and pointing to his original version and her correction. She recalls having responded, "But it is wrong," to which he is said to have answered, "It can't be: that's how we have learnt it at school." Thus, she fetched the *Duden* (Germany's ultimate authority on spelling), proving him wrong. He then simply looked at the book, identified it as an "eastern" *Duden*, and added triumphantly that he just could not accept that as an authority. Thereupon she ran to get a "western" *Duden* from a colleague, showing that the rule of spelling in east and west was just the same, that both versions even had the same illustrative example.

Chronotopes of Eastern and Western Life

Time and space are closely intertwined with each other. Every action is simultaneously in time and in space. Moreover, most lives are structured in a fundamental way by an interesting, regularly recurring overlap between times and spaces. Following the rhythm of the shift, police officers leave home at certain times go to the precinct, spend the time together there, and return to their homes. As they move up the hierarchical ladder and as they marry, the locations of both their homes and their workplaces will change, and so will the times during the day when they go to work and come home. Many police officers find it desirable, for example, to drop out of the shift and pursue regular day work as they become older. There is also with increasing age a tendency to prefer bureaucratic work in the precinct to work "in the street."[54]

Hägerstrand (1975) has pioneered the use of a simple way to plot the movement of persons through a three-dimensional time/space,[55] revealing not only the recurrent patterns of a single individual's movement through space, but also the bundling of several individuals' paths at certain spots at certain times (cf. Giddens 1984; Harvey 1989). Hägerstrand's time/space condensations translate, if narrated and thus endowed with meaning, into what Bakhtin (1981) has called "chronotopes." Bakhtin's units of analysis are primarily literary novels, but the concept is easily extendable to narrative in general, as he demonstrates himself by analyzing eulogies in ancient Greece. Chronotopes are significant time/space intersections, and Bakhtin defines their function in narrative as follows: "They are the organizing centers for fundamental narrative events of the novel. The chronotope is the place where the knots of narrative are tied and untied. It can be said without qualification that to them belongs the meaning that shapes narratives" (250). Bakhtin uses the term *chronotope* in two distinctly different ways. On the one hand, it denotes single, recurrent time/location couplings which ground a narrative, making time and space experienceable: "Thus the chronotope, functioning as the primary means of materializing time in space, emerges as a center for concretizing representation, as a force giving body to the entire novel" (250). Chronotopes in this sense are the salon in the nineteenth-century realist novel, the castle in the English "Gothic" novel, or the open road as a meeting point for human beings of quite different social strata, a chronotope spanning many genres and epochs. Chronotopes are, therefore, concrete, spatiotemporal microelements of a novel. The spatial element is at this material level dominant; time is almost collapsed into space. On the other hand, Bakhtin uses chronotope also to denote the spatiotemporal plot-structure of narratives at large—a whole novel, let's say, or even a whole genre.[56] In this sense he can speak of the chronotope of the Greek Ro-

54. Compare the metaphorical use of the inner/outer distinctions in the section titled "Reading Space."

55. Space as the two horizontal axes and time as the vertical axis.

56. For Bakhtin, it is precisely chronotope which defines genre.

mance or of the Rabelaisian chronotope. In order to differentiate between these two uses, I will call the former "concrete chronotopes" and the latter "plot-chronotopes."

Bakhtin's concept of chronotope can be usefully employed to understand the differences as well as the similarities between east and west German processes of identity formation in time and space. The stories told by the police officers in the precincts in Berlin and Potsdam center around a handful of concrete chronotopes. The most important ones are stories about work, which can be further broken down into stories of the street and stories of the precinct; they are stories about home (apartment/house and garden/cottage), which can be differentiated into stories about the writing of home space and narratives of events that take place at home (birthday parties, marital conflict, the adventures of children); they are stories of the road from work to home and back; and finally, they are stories about vacations. While the locales of these stories are the same for easterners and westerners—home and cottage, road to work, workplace, and vacation spot—the ways in which these places are worked out as concrete chronotopes, and especially the ways in which they are woven together into a plot-chronotope, are different for narrations about easterners' former lives in the GDR and westerners' lives in the FRG.[57]

In order to bring to the fore the differences between the linkages of a concrete chronotope to a plot-chronotope in eastern and western narratives, I will focus on the differences between the GDR model and the FRG one. This follows the narrative strategies of my eastern informants, who explained features of the GDR reality as deviations from presently conceived conditions.[58] Stories about life in the former GDR reveal almost in unison that the workplace was a much more encompassing anchor for life in general than it was in the West. This becomes immediately apparent

57. The descriptions presented here are reconstructions of the GDR past, and descriptions and experiences of the past and present of the FRG.

58. Of course, this bespeaks already a normalization of the western model, which has not only been adopted as a strategy to communicate effectively with westerners, but is also (as far as I can tell from overheard conversations) a strategy used among easterners. It would be interesting (although extremely difficult) to find out exactly when the change from normalizing practice, that is, describing the new as a deviation from GDR practice, to describing GDR life as a deviation from present practice, took place. Certain situations still invoke a GDR-perspective description. The question then would be, Under which circumstances is one or the other perspective chosen?

when it is considered that vacation places and apartments were chiefly distributed through the workplace. The typical People's Police vacation was spent somewhere in the GDR in a camp—at the Baltic seashore or in the Ore Mountains—that was owned and run by the Ministry of the Interior. If the family was lucky or the officer of higher rank or well connected, the vacation was spent, thanks to exchange programs with "socialist brother-countries," in a similar institution somewhere in Eastern Europe, preferably in the sunny Balkans. The People's Police was also much more involved in keeping contact with retirees than the (West) Berlin Police.[59] The workplace served too as the location for meetings of the various groupings of the Socialist Unity Party (Sozialistische Einheitspartei Deutschlands, SED), for several voluntary (or quasi-voluntary) organizations such as the Society for German-Soviet Friendship and the sports club "Dynamo," and thus it was the location for many social and almost all political activities of the police officers.[60] In this sense, the workplace superseded in the GDR the territorial principle of organization which characterizes most West German voluntary associations.[61] Most West German police officers are members of voluntary associations like sports clubs and political parties which have strong local (i.e., for all practical purposes: residential) roots, even though the local connection is vanishing as people move from one part of the city to another.

Similarly, home for eastern police officers encompassed more than just the apartment in which they lived. The "house-community" (*Hausgemeinschaft*), usually comprising all inhabitants of all flats centering on the same stairwell in an apartment block, was an important aspect of social life too.[62] In so-called Subotniks, volunteer actions, house-communities got together to do the necessary gardening around the house, to

59. About the importance of the workplace for life in general in the GDR, compare Martin Kohli (1994), who characterizes the GDR as *Arbeitsgesellschaft* (work-centered society) because the workplace was, according to Kohli, the single most important socializing institution in the lives of GDR citizens.

60. Party membership and membership in the two voluntary organizations mentioned was expected of all police officers in the GDR. Party membership was mandatory for all commissioned officers.

61. By *territorial* I mean "organization within the limits of a city, a borough of a city, or any further subdivisions based on spatial contiguity."

62. House-communities *(Hausgemeinschaften)* were formally organized, including an elected leadership with several offices: the leader, the house-bookkeeper, and sometimes also a safety inspector. Official figures mention approximately thirty-two thousand house–communities in 1986, and also mention efforts to increase this number substantially by 1990 (Herbst, Ranke, and Winkler 1994, 398).

repaint common areas such as hallways and basements, or to repair or construct playgrounds.[63] Frequently, these Subotniks were also followed by a social gathering after the work. Some house-communities had for this purpose a party room, which was itself the product of a common effort. The previously mentioned fact that employees of the GDR Ministry of the Interior were pooled in buildings or parts of buildings implies also that the house-communities into which many eastern police officers were integrated were dominated by other members of the People's Police; thus, there was an immediate connection between home and workplace and a host of common topics that people could discuss. While most east German officers seem not to have minded this proximity to other police families, some experienced this intertwining as quite limiting. Despite the many unwanted and sometimes even despised forms of control allowed by the intensive social contact at home and in the workplace, many former East German police officers remember the socializing quite fondly, and they actually miss social activities organized through work or in the house-communities which made it easy to become acquainted with other people. Finally, a home was for most citizens of the former GDR not a matter of choice, but a matter of luck and connections. The severe housing shortage in the GDR, made it next to impossible, above all in Berlin, for most people to choose a neighborhood or even a borough in which they wanted to live. Also, the size of the apartment was not so much a matter of taste, or willingness or capacity to pay the rent, but a matter of availability, officially assessed need, and appropriate connections.

In addition, traveling to and from work was a quite different experience for the members of the former People's Police and the (West) Berlin Police. While most officers of the Berlin Police change from plain clothes to uniforms only after they reach the precinct, People's Police officers had to travel from home to work and vice versa wearing their uniforms. Since many eastern officers in the GDR did not own cars, or because public transportation was free for police officers in the GDR, and gasoline was very expensive, they traveled on buses, streetcars, and commuter trains

63. The house-communities were also used as a means of control: not only did visitors have to be registered, especially those from abroad, but the leadership of the house-community might also watch over regular participation in elections and other political activities. The system of house-communities was not comprehensive; it characterized especially life in big, "new" apartment blocks, the most common form of housing for police officers, especially in Berlin.

to work, while most western officers used their cars. Thus, People's Police officers were recognizable as such on the way to and from work, and many of them tell stories about the reactions of fellow citizens to their presence in uniform. They were asked questions or used as sounding boards for all sorts of concerns, and at times they were also abused as public symbols—scolded or spat on—to show disapproval of the regime.[64] This also meant that the officers felt compelled to intervene as police officers when something called for their attention. Thus, their work was only over once they actually reached home. In contrast, the ride to and from work is a completely private matter for the majority of western officers: they travel in plain clothes, in their own private cars, listening to their favorite radio stations, and their obligation to intervene in anything happening on the road is restricted to that of the common citizen. They also avoid any negative comment inspired by public response to their uniforms.

The meanings of the concrete chronotopes of workplace, road to work, and home, therefore, were quite different for members of the People's Police and for officers of the (West) Berlin Police. Eastern officers perceive this shift in meaning frequently as a *loss* of meaning. They see, for example, wearing plain clothes on the road to work as a backing out of the responsibilities of a police officer; in extreme cases they interpret it even as apparent shame of *being* a police officer, suggesting that their western counterparts are *acting a role*. Western officers see this much more as a positive affirmation of their right to a private life free of the impingement of work.[65]

While these differences in the ways in which the various concrete chronotopes are connected with each other are already quite significant, they become even more pronounced once plot chronotopes are fully taken into account and divergences in biographic development are acknowledged. While easterners entered the police usually with much more experience in other ranges of work—according to the requirements, with at least an apprenticeship in some trade—most younger westerners entered the police directly after school, so that they had a significantly longer training period in police work (one year of basic training in the east, three years of basic training in the west) with the status of an apprenticeship in its

64. According to many eastern officers, negative reactions were increasing markedly during the last few years of the GDR.
65. This differentiation plays into different notions of the boundaries of the private and the public, which will be discussed in chapter 7.

own right.[66] Police work in the west is, at least in the generations below the age of forty-five, seen as a profession, whereas easterners describe it more frequently in terms of a calling.[67]

The notion of calling *(Beruf, Berufung)* does have, however, a strong rhetorical tinge to it, since it is used in a very formulaic way, mostly left unexplored and mostly employed in situations of confrontation. Directly asked, most east Germans offer very clear career goals as reasons for entering the police: either they found themselves stuck in a particular company without much hope of financial or career advancement, or they found themselves stranded in a particular location, a move being possible only on the basis of a career change. In the West employment security was a frequently mentioned pragmatic goal for entering the police. Another feature of the career process is perhaps even more striking. The initial suggestion for joining the police is described by easterners as a suggestion coming from the outside, as an idea advanced by a friend's father or by an uncle. Westerners, by contrast, insist that it was their own initiative, that they saw an advertisement of the police and responded to it. This pattern repeats itself in terms of internal schooling and therefore advancement within the police. The majority of easterners, for example, described their entry into the police academy to become commissioned officers as induced by superiors. Frequently they insist that at first they did not even want to attend school but were partly coerced into it by the combined efforts of direct superiors and party officials, after which they would agree that it had been a good idea. Accordingly, narratives of thwarted careers are rather scarce. Westerners reverse the relationship between superiors and subordinates. They highlight their own agency in applying for further schooling, actively trying to enlist the support of their superiors for such a move. It is not surprising, then, that they tell many stories in which superiors are described as causes of interrupted or unsuccessful careers. The plot-chronotope of easterners' life narratives is

66. In Germany, a trade is established formally by arranging for a three-year apprenticeship, usually followed by opportunities for further training in master-schools. Therefore, treating police training as apprenticeship professionalizes it in West German minds.

67. This is, of course, Max Weber's cherished distinction between *Beruf* (profession) and *Berufung* (calling), which has found its way into German popular culture. Members of the older generation of western policemen are, in this respect, much more similar to their eastern counterparts: they frequently complain about the "job mentality" *(Job-Mentalität,* leaving the English "job" intact, which has in comparison to *Beruf* a very flimsy, ephemeral connotation). Certain conflicts are not just East-West matters but clearly generational as well.

therefore much more often one of accidental encounters with persons and circumstances, and a frequent interjection in life narratives is, "How life just plays with you."[68] Its overall emplotment scheme is thus satire.[69] The life narratives of westerners are more frequently cast in terms of the pursuit of a career goal; therefore, depending on their success, they resemble the emplotment scheme of a romance or a tragedy. It is noteworthy, however, that for both easterners and westerners the likelihood of casting career as pursuit rather than as accident increases with the achieved rank; that is, it is much more common among staff officers than among noncommissioned officers.

In sum, then, the ways in which easterners combine space and time in their biographical tales of life in the former GDR are quite different from the techniques used in the narratives of their western colleagues. The spaces in which East Germans lived were used in different ways and therefore carried other meanings for their lives. It would be easy to conclude that from travel destinations to home locations space was much more determined for East Germans than for West Germans (cf. Borneman 1998, 98–103). This conclusion would be hasty, however, for determination only appears as such against the background of perceived possibilities. Thus, what might appear to the western observer as fate was not necessarily perceived in this way by the easterners themselves, because choice was frequently not even thematized—it was culturally out of the question.

Summary and Conclusions

I have discussed four different ways by which selves are identified with and through space, and thereby endowed with meaning. On the basis of fieldwork material, I have analyzed the rhetorical reading of space, the writing of space, the placement of self, and the narrative interweaving of time and space in chronotopes as four types of microprocesses of identity construction. All four processes reveal that selves are connected through a complex, multilayered web of identifications with space and therefore with a fundamental expression of material culture. Spaces are searched for answers to large questions, such as the nature of political sys-

68. German: Wie das Leben eben so spielt. As an idiom, it is not restricted to eastern Germany.
69. The narrations of East Germans about their lives in unified Germany do, if anything, rather exacerbate the tendency to satirize biography.

tems, the relationship between governments and their citizens, the character of organizations and persons. Spaces are also searched for support
in confirming one's own identity. Spaces may cause existential angst,
and they may give life-affirming comfort. Through space, people experience their own agency, and in space they realize their own creativity;
but through space, people may also experience their own powerlessness.
People see spaces as their mirrors, and they understand themselves as
mirrors of space. Spaces ground human activity as well as narratives
about that activity. Social interaction and the construction of identity are
therefore not only to be understood as two-way relationships between
self and other, but as three-way exchanges between self, other, and all
sorts of spatial contexts.

The recognition that identities have a spatial dimension opens up the
view that identities are not only knowable, but that they can be experienced. Even more, the spatial dimension of identity makes clear that identities may only be partly known, because in part they must be felt. Perhaps
the experience of identity is the ultimate secret of traveling. The encounter
of unknown spaces highlights the existing as well as nonexisting ties of
self to the world by making us feel what is missed and what is not, by
making us feel what is appreciated and what is not. The appeal of travel
may lie precisely in the fact that it reveals identifications to self in a completely nonintellectualized form.

Writing the spaces of their homes, their gardens, and (to some extent)
of their offices is an individuating social practice for police officers in
both parts of Berlin. Writing these spaces as an expression of self is one
of the most significant life projects of the officers I spoke with. There is
clearly a poetics of writing home spaces, as much as there is a poetics of
public spaces, which I could unfortunately not explore here in more detail. As Herzfeld (1991) has shown, much can be learned about the relationship between convention and invention in human society from an
investigation of the poetics of space, from the ways in which publicly
available cultural forms (e.g., the notion of a party room, a garden cottage, styles of furniture, or the notions of a square, or a downtown, etc.)
are interpreted and adjusted to individual needs. Reading space is in many
ways the necessary complement to writing it. While writing remains for
most officers restricted to their intimate environments, reading larger
spaces leads to the identification of whole societies or states.

Following the lead of Kenneth Burke, I have also introduced the notion
that identifications can be understood as a matter of rhetoric. Expanding
on Burke, I have begun to introduce a heuristic framework to analyze

identifications, and thus the ways in which selves are made meaningful. I have argued that even brief verbal utterances can quickly spin a whole web of such identifications. The intricate structure of this web, and thus the complexity of the meaning of self implied, can be illuminated by analyzing identifications in terms of tropes and emplotments. I have argued that an analysis in terms of tropes can reveal the underlying cognitive principles, the ways or modes in which a self is thought to be connected to the world. It makes a difference whether the relation between a self and aspects of a world is seen as an organic link between a part and a whole (synecdoche), as a membership in a set of equal, exchangeable elements (metonymy), or in terms of a playful, uncertain similarity (metaphor). Thus thinking through identifications in terms of tropes helps to reveal the kind, intensity, validity, and reach of the suggested connections. An analysis in terms of emplotments can contribute moreover to an understanding of how speakers invite listeners to identify with them over a shared attitude towards characters, objects, and events of narrative utterances. Interpreting identifications in terms of emplotments thus helps to unravel the dynamics of interpersonal links and their meaning for selves. Paying attention to emplotments also helps to understand the emotional charge inherent in identifications. Analyzing identifications in terms of particular tropes and emplotment structures works to the degree that they are relevant cultural models pervasive in the everyday communications of the people whose identity-construction processes are under scrutiny.

***

As spaces in eastern Germany are reshaped according to West German templates, as efforts continue to eradicate the spatial writings of the socialist regime in the GDR, Germans on both sides of the former Iron Curtain will find that spaces in east and west look more and more alike. Accordingly, their feelings of alienation will markedly decline as they visit or even move to places on the respective other side. This is possible because of a gigantic destruction/investment program in the east. The more familiar these spaces become, the less they will ripple the smooth surface of everyday life and hence will give little cause for spatial reading and active attempts at placement along the lines of an east-west dichotomy. The molding of former GDR spaces on western patterns must be understood as a form of identity politics, as the deconstruction/reconstruction programs remove or alter beyond recognition the physical anchors of memories and thus the possibilities for self-placement of easterners as easterners. On the one hand this active attempt to close access to memories will lead to further conflicts, as easterners fight for ways to integrate their past and their present. On the other hand, however, some east Germans willingly and happily collaborate in this partial eradication of their past, because they have always found some of the spaces created in the GDR to be deficient, dreaded as much today as then as signs of a shortage economy. Needless to say, not all memories of the GDR are fond memories worth preserving. Thus the western models and the possibilities at writing home spaces are eagerly taken up because they cater to long-held desires.

The relationship of east Germans to their changing spaces is, then, fundamentally ambivalent. How this ambivalence comes about, and how and why east Germans become coconspirators in the destruction of their own spaces and their reconstruction on western models is part of chapter 3, "Times Ajar." Since the core argument of that chapter revolves around West Germans' attempt to displace easterners in time, more precisely into their own past, chapter 2 provides a general historical overview of relations between East and West Germany, and the unification of Germany and the Berlin Police.

TWO

The Political Organization of Identification

Politics and Precinct:
Two Different Sources of Identifications

The identifications discussed in the last chapter arise from the minutest situations of the everyday. They are made en passant on the occasion of admiring a building, during interactions between officers and citizens while recording an accident, in using a piece of equipment that is either identified as eastern or western, in the context of a chat with a colleague during a coffee break. All of these identifications are interactional in character; they are embedded in some kind of ongoing exchange between people. Even if they take place between a superior and a subordinate, it is still possible to respond in some way, even if only through a grin or through eyes narrowed in anger. Also, in situations involving the identification of a third person, the identified third person may hear about it, perhaps from a loyal friend, and thus be able to answer it directly or by disseminating gossip. In other words, these identifications are embedded in networks of face-to-face encounters. Therefore the metaphor of *negotiation* seems appropriate to characterize these exchanges of identifications, even if obvious power differences exist between the people involved in them.

But not all identifications take place within networks of face-to-face encounters. Many identifications arise from situations in which the identified person has almost no opportunity to react, where it is next to impossible to communicate with the source of the identification. For such identifications, the negotiation metaphor seems wholly inappropriate, because there is virtually no exchange between the source of identification and the persons identified.

Non-negotiated identifications are typically inscribed in policies, rules, regulations, and of course the law, but also in customs and traditions. In short, they are embedded in forms of action which are depersonalized or institutionalized. The administrative decision of the Berlin Police to exhaust the provisions of the Unification Treaty to check every single former People's Police officer for personal and professional qualifications as a precondition for continued employment is such an identification. And so is the decision of the governments of the GDR and the FRG to carry out the unification of Germany under the provisions of Article 23 of the Basic Law (the constitution of the FRG), allowing for the accession of "other territories" to the FRG.[1] Non-negotiated identifications are also embedded in widely disseminated discourses in politics, the mass media and, to a lesser extent, the arts and sciences. Thus they are inherent in principally unidirectional mass communication. The various publicized discourses about the when and how of German unification in the spring and summer of 1990 and the ongoing debates about the meaning of Stasi collaboration fall into this category.

Analytically it is helpful, therefore, to differentiate among identifications along at least three interlocking dimensions: their effective dissemination, their structural power, and the response strategies they necessitate. Although these dimensions are clearly a continuum with many shades and gradations, for simplicity's sake I will differentiate only between two levels: institutional identifications and local identifications. (1) Identifications are characterized by very different degrees of effective dissemination in space and time. While institutional identifications can have perceptible impact on thousands or even millions of people, local identifications typically affect only a small group or a single person. The effective dissemination of an identification is not the same then, as the number of people implied in it. In a conversation, for example, one person may identify another while implying a whole category of persons through metonymic extension. The reach of this identification is, however, in all likelihood limited to that particular person or a small group of interlocutors.[2] (2) Institutional and local identifications exert themselves in very

1. I discuss the identifications inherent in both of these procedures at some length below.

2. Of course one could imagine that such an interactional identification might have juridical relevance because it meets, for example, the criteria of libel. Then, one might surmise, a lawsuit could entail, which could perhaps even bring the attention

different ways. Institutional identifications are typically backed up by formal organizations that ensure their effectiveness, while local identifications rely more heavily on interpersonal skills. This does not mean, however, that the impact of local identifications on individuals is any less significant than the impact of institutional identifications. (3) The differences in effective dissemination as well as in the way power is exerted necessitate different response strategies for institutional and local identifications. To counteract institutional identifications, other institutions need to be mobilized, which typically requires resources. Local identifications can frequently be responded to immediately, or they can be counteracted by manipulating the reputation of people in face-to-face networks.

For the purposes of this study, and by yet another leap of simplification, the levels of local and institutional identification can be mapped onto the actual field site of the precinct on the one hand and the organizational and political context in which the precinct is embedded on the other. How, then, do the political and the precinct levels connect with each other? How do political or organizational identifications come into play in the exchange of identifications in the face-to-face encounters in the police precincts of Köpenick and Potsdam? The basic method underlying my attempt to establish a connection between the political level and the precinct level is to use a series of organizational linkages,[3] primarily those within one organization (i.e., the [West] Berlin Police), as an "elevator" (cf. DiMaggio 1991). In other words, I propose to connect precinct and politics through a chain of what Moore (1978, 57) has called "semiautonomous social fields."[4]

Concretely this means an attempt to trace east-west identifications through the hierarchical levels of organization, from the police precinct to state and national governments. In the case of government agencies such as the police, this approach probably works better than it would, for example, in private corporations, since the organizational linkages

---

of the media. Thus an interactional identification can be converted into an institutional one. The lure of such a conversion and the power it lends to a person's ability to identify self and others may well have inspired some of the more widely publicized lawsuits in the United States in recent times. Likewise, celebrities or persons who interact with celebrities might want to institutionalize their identifications by going public (e.g., giving interviews, writing books).

3. I present a drastically simplified picture here, which disregards many linkages across organizational boundaries, as well as the interaction between an organization and a much more broadly defined environment.

4. Another important elevator between the local and institutional level is provided by the mass media (see Hannerz 1992).

may be mapped out more easily (at least formally). The police force connects its smallest organizational units, the precincts, through three increasingly integrative hierarchical levels with the minister of the interior, thus tying it to the government and the legislature of the state of Berlin.[5] All interior ministers of the FRG maintain a coordinating committee, the conference of ministers of the interior *(Innenministerkonferenz)*,[6] thus tying all states to the federal level of government. Since Berlin, until unification, enjoyed a special status, I should mention also that the four Allied commanders ultimately held power over the Berlin Police: the Americans, the British, and the French in West Berlin, and the Soviets in East Berlin. The status of Berlin prior to unification and the simple fact that without major changes on the international level unification would not have been possible at all indicate that it is important to consider international relations as one more important level of analysis.

A somewhat similar hierarchy can be constructed for laws and directives. Thus, different levels of organizational linkages nest within each other like Russian puppets. Every level has some leeway in decision making that affects subsequent levels with regard to the provision of resources, laws, directives, or in the case of the police also in terms of orders. Lower levels, in contrast, influence higher levels mostly through performance, that is, by the consequences of their everyday activities. The feedback loop is established within these organizational layers through the responsibility of the higher levels for the performance of the lower ones. Each level in the hierarchy must act toward subsequent levels in such a way that the outcomes produced on these lower levels reflect favorably on the higher levels.

Looking at this chain of semiautonomous social fields, two main processes which have become sources of identifications emerge. The more comprehensive, overarching one is the political unification of Germany, which itself is informed by the ways in which the two Germanies have related to each other in the forty years of their existence. The second

5. These levels are as follows. Between four and eight precincts *(Abschnitte)* compose one district *(Direktion)*. There are seven police districts in Berlin, which comprise between two and five boroughs of the city. All districts together form the Department of Public Security *(Landesschutzpolizeiamt)*. Together with other branches of the police (e.g., criminal investigation units), they are headed by the president of police *(Polizeipräsident)*, who in Berlin reports to the minister of the interior (Senator für Inneres) but is elected by the State Parliament *(Abgeordnetenhaus)*, according to Article 44 of the Berlin constitution.

6. The federal minister of the interior participates in this conference, but he does not chair it.

process, which is by no means the less important one for the police officers, is the political-organizational unification of the Berlin Police. I will
discuss both of these processes, beginning with German unification as a
whole.

The Political Organization of German Unification

Unification by Westernization

The actual *form* of the German unification of 1990 as the peaceful accession of one independent state to another, is quite unique, seen from a
world-historical perspective. The complete incorporation of one independent state by another typically proceeds by military conquest or coloniza-
tion and annexation. Otherwise, the integration of formerly sovereign
territories is honored by the foundation of a set of new, overarching institutions, or at least by reserving special rights for the acceding territories.[7]
By contrast, the accession of the GDR to the FRG did not even involve
much negotiation for special rights, exceptions, or a special status: it was
based on almost complete self-dissolution of the GDR and wholesale
adoption of the West as a model.[8] This process not only left the Basic
Law (Grundgesetz), the constitution (and with it the Federal Law) of the
FRG, intact while expanding its jurisdiction,[9] but also allowed for the
transfer of basically the entire political, judicial, and administrative system of the FRG to the territory of the former GDR. Even the foundation

7. In this respect, the German unification of 1990 opens up the possibility of a
whole series of interesting comparisons with the foundation of the North German
League (Norddeutscher Bund) in 1866 and the subsequent German unification of
1871, in which Bismarck succeeded only by waging war against France. Moreover,
although these events proceeded under the hegemony of Prussia, they were only possible with a strong federal structure allowing the preservation of regional differences.
More recently, even the reintegration of Hong Kong into China was negotiated under
the reservation of special rights for Hong Kong.

8. The Unification Treaty provides for transitory regulations, ranging from pay
scales and rents to such important policy issues as abortion (the abortion laws of the
GDR were much more liberal than those of the FRG). Hence east German women
were allowed to proceed under the rules of the old GDR law until a jointly elected
Bundestag could promulgate a new, all-German abortion law). None of these provisions, however, amount to the permanent retention of special rights for east German states.

9. The only changes in the constitution in the context of unification pertain to
those parts which explicitly address the German unification as such (see Maunz,
Dürig, Günter et al. 1963–, commentaries on the preamble and Articles 23 and 146
of the constitution; Hesse 1991, 35–41).

of the five new states in the GDR proceeded with the close assistance of western federal and state authorities following western templates suitable to the existing western federal structure. The laws drafted for these new states were more or less copies of western models. One officer in the state of Brandenburg recalls this adoption process thus: "When we got the new laws and regulations you could virtually see that they had often just over-typed 'Northrhine Westfalia' (the western state that principally assisted the eastern state of Brandenburg) with 'Brandenburg.'" He went on to explain that today the shortcomings of this procedure have become more and more apparent since "their [the Northrhine Westfalian] structures just don't fit us."[10] German unification did lead in this sense to a thorough institutional westernization of eastern Germany.

On the basis of this wholesale transfer of West German institutions to the former GDR and against the background of its historical peculiarity, it is perhaps not surprising that eastern officers sometimes feel as if their country has been occupied by their old-time foe from Cold War days. One retired east German officer, narrating his experience in a long biographical interview, expressed his feelings thus: "They have won the Cold War. I must say they have been rather nice. I don't know if we would have been as nice, but still they behave like an occupying force. The trials against former government officials of the GDR are sheer victor's justice; they just take revenge now that they have a chance." While this statement is certainly extreme in the sense that it is not shared in its full force by most eastern officers, the use of the military imagery of wars lost and won to describe the relation between both parts of Germany is rather common. Clearly easterners, especially when they feel mistreated, use this imagery more often than westerners, since it is a forceful tool to delegitimize the west. Yet, westerners also make use of it. Describing his experience of driving for the first time across the former boundary in uniform and with a patrol car, one western officer said, "Suddenly I knew how they must have felt in 1940 in Paris," thus likening the beginning of his service in east Berlin to the German occupation of the French capital in World War II.

The historical peculiarities of the German unification process are also reflected in interesting ways in terminological choices and the difficulties that come with them. The official name of what used to be West Germany, the Federal Republic of Germany (FRG), is now applied to Ger-

10. Northrhine Westfalia is the most populous state of the federation, densely populated and, with the Rhine-Ruhr valleys as heartlands, heavily industrialized. Brandenburg, by contrast is Germany's second most rural state.

many as a whole. The use of this official name is therefore ambiguous with respect to its referent, which may be West Germany from 1949 through 1990, or unified Germany since 1990, or both. In order to avoid possible confusion, speakers sometimes feel compelled to add an "old" or a "new" to the phrase "Federal Republic."[11] Similar problems were encountered in denoting the new territories of the new/old state FRG. The use of "former GDR" (*ehemalige* DDR) was quickly considered odious, since it seemed to preserve something that many users, western politicians above all, aspired to overcome. Thus, new inventions popped up after unification on 3 October 1990. The two most common ones are "accession area" (*Beitrittsgebiet*) and "the new states" (*die neuen Länder*), of which the latter has become the most widely accepted term. Yet from a longer, historical perspective, this expression is awkward too. A "new state" like Saxony was not only already a state within the Reich of 1871, but an independent kingdom before that. It is in fact much older than the "old state" of Northrhine Westfalia, which was established after World War II. The problem of historically ambiguous referents of proper names arises for all institutions that were in place before unification, including the Berlin Police, which of course used to be the West Berlin Police.[12]

These naming practices, especially the consistent retention of the western terminology, highlight, I would argue, two interesting effects. On the one hand, they annihilate the GDR symbolically after it has already been made to disappear institutionally without a trace in the abyss of history. On the other hand, they normalize the FRG as a model for the former

11. That unification is supposedly a new beginning is also underscored by some speakers who employ the phrase "Bonn Republic" (Bonner Republik) for the FRG from 1949 to 1990. This expression is of course formed by analogy with "Weimar Republic." The Weimar Republic was so named because the National Assembly (Nationalversammlung) drafting the constitution for the post–World War I German republic sat in Weimar. Since the Parliamentarian Council (Parlamentarischer Rat) drafting the constitution of the FRG sat in Bonn, this analogy seems justified at first. Yet that constitution is not history yet; it is still the basis of united Germany. In this sense the Bonn Republic is still alive.

12. For this study I have adopted the following convention: Whenever precision is necessary, I will use capital letters (e.g., East Germany/Berlin or West Germany/ Berlin) for the two states/cities in existence between 1949 and 1990. I will use lowercase (e.g., west Germany or east Germany/Berlin) for the formerly separate parts in now unified Germany. Of course the ambiguity created by the accession can not be overcome by any stylistic convention. Sometimes, in order to make the history of the development (and hence the ambiguity) more visible, I use parentheses, as in (West) Berlin Police, in order to emphasize that the institution is basically the old West German one.

GDR. The names themselves signify that the FRG has been set as the standard to be emulated. The eastern police officers in Köpenick and Potsdam are quite aware of these effects of naming. Many of them have pointed out to me that they wish that at least the name of the country had been changed from Federal Republic of Germany to something else. Some favored "just Germany" (*einfach nur* Deutschland); others offered "German Republic (Deutsche Republik), because it is a mixture of both and yet different." Thus many eastern officers would have liked a new name that signaled a new beginning for both Germanies, something that would have stated that the new is a composite of two and not just an extension of one.[13]

Some officers put more emphasis on the symbolism of names than on the actual character of institutions. One officer, for example, said on a day commemorating the bombardment of Potsdam on 14 April 1945, a day full of events, rife with speeches on German history: "I fully stand behind the Basic Law [i.e., the (western) constitution], I think it is a very good constitution. But the name of the country should have been changed." However, many easterners go farther than that, especially in the context of conversations highlighting the failure of western institutions to deal with, for example, unemployment or juvenile delinquency. Then they suggest that some Eastern institutions they have experienced as positive should have been retained for the benefit of Germany at large. "Not everything in the GDR was bad; one should have retained the one thing or the other," runs the almost formulaic answer of many east Germans to my question whether, with the benefit of hindsight, unification should have proceeded differently.

How, then, was it possible that unification proceeded organizationally the way it did, identifying westerners unquestionably as leaders and easterners as followers, thus establishing willy-nilly a hierarchical relationship between them?

Historical Identifications of the Other Germany

The actual form taken by German unification is utterly incomprehensible without embedding it in the history of relations between both German

13. This question of symbolic changes resurfaced with full force in 1991 in the discussion of whether or not the institutions of government should be moved from Bonn to Berlin. (The Unification Treaty declared Berlin the capital of united Germany, yet left it open to parliamentarian decision whether this choice of capital should also imply that the government should move to Berlin.)

states since their foundation in 1949. Thus we need to analyze in more detail how the two German states and their citizens have identified each other since 1949. Since the West German state and the East German population have played the leading roles in the unification process, it is especially important to show how the West German government has identified East Germany (and by metonymic or synecdochical extension all East Germans), and how the East German population has identified West Germany (and West Germans). I will differentiate between two main phases governed by drastically different West German policies with regard to the East, referring to them as "the claim to sole representation" and "Ostpolitik."

THE WESTERN CLAIM TO SOLE REPRESENTATION. The fact that both the FRG and the GDR formed part of the same country before 1945 is of course at best a partial explanation for why accession rather than reconstitution was chosen as a solution for Germany. After all, both states were only created in 1949 in an air of Cold War confrontation between the western Allied Powers and the Soviet Union. Thus the GDR was not previously part of the FRG; both were integral parts of a common predecessor state, the German Reich (Deutsches Reich). The political and administrative institutions of the FRG were as new as those of the GDR, and both in their own way were not only reactions to Germany's recent Nazi past but were also influenced in characteristic ways by the respective occupational powers: the United States, Britain, and France in the West, and the Soviet Union in the East (Grosser 1974; Leonhard 1981; Weber 1991). Seen in this light, the total absorption of the GDR into the institutional framework provided by the FRG is indeed remarkable.

From the beginning, the FRG projected itself as the true, the real Germany, presenting itself as the sole power that could represent the German people as a whole (this is the so-called claim to sole representation [Alleinvertretungsanspruch]). This claim is manifest in several political choices which are frequently also reflected in key legal positions. To begin with, the FRG, not the GDR, insisted on being the juridical successor of the Deutsches Reich. In fact, the FRG claimed that the Deutsches Reich had never ceased to exist, that it was indeed identical with it, if not in territory, then at least as a corporate entity (Maunz, Dürig, Günter et al. 1963–; Frowein 1983, 34–37).[14] Beyond the pragmatic advantages this

14. Deutsches Reich (German Reich) was the official name of Germany from 1871 to 1945. Of course, the notion of a radical break with the past resonated more

claim may have offered (such as the continuity of international treaties, judicial decisions, ownership of property, etc.), this position has great symbolic significance, and the FRG has put much effort into maintaining it in international treaties, in memoranda of the foreign office, and through high court decisions.[15] For the GDR, which insisted that the Deutsches Reich was defunct, the FRG's insistence on legal identity with the Deutsches Reich has always been a welcome reason to identify it as thoroughly fascist.[16]

Part of the FRG's claim to represent the whole lies in the symbolism of places and names for the institutions of the new republic. The claim to sole representation embedded in the assertion of legal continuity could not, however, always be successfully staked out by direct identification with the Reich. Several facts must be taken into account here. For one, the latest form of the Deutsches Reich, the Nazi dictatorship, could serve only as an antimodel. Full-fledged identification with the Reich was prone to produce undesirable ambiguities which would not have been tolerated by the Allied Powers, nor would they have been wanted by the majority of the architects of the FRG. For another, Germany was under the administration of four powers which by 1948 had developed thoroughly hostile relationships. These hostilities were effectively dramatized in the blockade of Berlin by the Soviet Union and the airlift organized by the United States in response to it. Finally, certain perhaps desirable positions, such as making Berlin the seat of government for the FRG, were not feasible because of the division of Germany.

---

easily with the revolutionary rhetoric of the GDR than with the bourgeois concern for legal continuity in the FRG.

15. This seeming pragmatic advantage also entails a never-ending series of embarrassments to the more liberal-minded, if perhaps not for the ultraconservative, especially those in the juridical profession itself, which was a stronghold of former Nazis who almost seamlessly continued to serve under the FRG. The insistence on legal continuity ensured that not only the judgments regarding "normal" (i.e., conforming to the law and legal procedure of the Weimar Republic) civil and criminal procedures remained in effect, but also all judgments proclaimed by the Nazi high court, the Volksgerichtshof. The consequence of this legal position is that verdicts against the few Nazi resistance fighters that Germany can marshal are still in effect. They need to be rehabilitated singly (as there is currently a movement to rehabilitate Dietrich Bonhoefer). It also means, for example, that deserters from the German army in World War II are to this very day treated as criminals.

16. Ironically, in the FRG, the names of the railway and the postal services were changed to Federal Mail (Bundespost) and Federal Railway (Bundesbahn), while the GDR has maintained the pre–World War II names, Reichspost and Reichsbahn, for the government-owned and government-run postal services and railway respectively.

Therefore, the leading politicians had to choose carefully by what means to emphasize their claim to representation of Germany as a whole. They did so mostly by highlighting the provisional and transitory character of the FRG. This self-identification was achieved with a rather effective rhetorical device which might be called "negative hyperbole." Institutions were made significant for Germany as a whole by consistently choosing names and places with *no* historical connotations. Thus the congregation drafting the constitution for the FRG called itself Parliamentarian Council (Parlamentarischer Rat) instead of National Assembly (Nationalversammlung); it was nominated by the state parliaments, rather than elected directly; it sat in Bonn, which was historically only mildly significant, rather than in Frankfurt, the convention place of Germany's first democratically elected parliament and the coronation place of German emperors since the Middle Ages. For the same reason of conspicuous inconspicuousness, Bonn was chosen as the capital of the FRG. Finally, the constitution was called (almost in spite of itself) Basic Law (Grundgesetz; Maunz, Dürig, Günter et al. 1963–; Schmid 1979).

The Basic Law and its interpretation in legal commentaries and high court decisions is a rich source of identifications of East Germany and West Germany, of East Germans and West Germans. The Preamble of the Basic Law contains a commitment of the German people (as represented by the Parliamentarian Council) to "preserve its national and political unity" (seine nationale und staatliche Einheit zu wahren) as well as an appeal to each one of the German people to "complete the unity and freedom of Germany in free self-determination" (in freier Selbstbestimmung die Einheit und Freiheit Deutschlands zu vollenden).[17] Moreover, the council, drawn exclusively from the American, British, and French occupational zones, professed "to have also acted for those Germans, for whom it was made impossible to participate" (hat auch für jene Deutschen gehandelt, denen mitzuwirken versagt war).[18]

Since the mandate assumed by the Parliamentarian Council in this proclamation is not based on democratic procedure (those who could not participate by definition did not have any elected members in the assem-

17. It of course no longer does so, but it contains the following phrase: "The Germans in the states of [list] have in free self-determination completed the unity and freedom of Germany."

18. According to Maunz, Dürig, Günter et al. (1963–), the leading commentary on the constitution of the FRG, those "for whom it was made impossible to participate" refers to two groups: the Germans of the Saar area (the territory was then still annexed by France), and the Germans living in the Soviet-occupied zone, that is, the people of the later GDR.

bly), it must be based on something else. The only interpretation that seems plausible is the assumption of an *essentialistically* conceived German nationhood. This nationhood is thus not derived from participation in a political, primordial act of state creation by contractual consensus (as in the act of drafting and promulgating a constitution), but by membership in the same ethnic group, "the German People" (*das Deutsche Volk;* cf. Brubaker 1992, esp. 165–178; Greenfeld 1992, chap. 4).[19] To assume a mandate in this way presupposes that the eventual result of the negotiations would not have been significantly different if those who were excluded had participated. This maneuver works along the lines of a synecdochical identification of part and whole, and a metonymic interchangeability of the parts for the representation of the whole, provided that there is no distorting outside influence on one of the parts. Precisely this, however, was assumed to be the case for that part of Germany which lived under Soviet occupation; thus, it must be the "free Germany" that can represent the whole. The emplotment structure of this move is tragic in the vividly portrayed choicelessness of the situation, and it is romantic in its aspiration: the "unity of Germany in freedom." Freedom, in turn, is where West Germany already is, but where the East under Soviet occupation must first go.

Other measures also supported West Germany's claim to represent all of Germany. One of them was the citizenship law of the FRG (Brubaker 1992). Since the FRG never recognized the GDR fully as an independent state, it did not recognize independent GDR citizenship either. For that matter, from the perspective of the FRG, there has never been FRG citizenship either. In keeping with the fiction of legal continuity, the only citizenship category that was used by FRG authorities was "German" (Deutsch), which was thought to pertain to West Germans and East Germans alike. Thus citizens of the GDR (and of course by international law there was such a thing as GDR citizenship) could simply go to any town hall in West Germany to collect their identity cards or passports. For those living in the GDR who wanted to flee, this provision meant that they would not have to trade their citizenship for the precarious status of refugees.

Citizenship law was not the only means to claim overall representation. Several other points highlight how the FRG identified the GDR after the foundation of both states. After attaining (for most practical purposes) de facto sovereignty in 1955, the FRG proclaimed the Hallstein

19. This is also supported by the peculiar description of unity as a—by no means necessary—conjunction between the nation' and a set of political institutions in the Preamble (see above).

Doctrine, threatening to discontinue diplomatic relations with any state that recognized the GDR. Even after both countries joined the United Nations in 1973, and long after the Hallstein Doctrine had been revoked factually[20] and even West Germany's closest friends had recognized the GDR, the FRG still did not officially recognize the GDR as a foreign country. For this reason, relations with the GDR have never been labeled foreign policy, and the offices established by both governments in each other's capital to foster "good-neighborly relations" *(gut nachbarliche Beziehungen)* were not called embassies, but Permanent Representative Offices (Ständige Vertretungen). Relations with the GDR were discussed in the FRG under the rubric of "intra-German relations" *(innerdeutsche Beziehungen)*, and the boundary between the FRG and the GDR was therefore not considered to be an international boundary at all but was called the "intra-German boundary" *(innerdeutsche Grenze)*. Accordingly, relations between the FRG and the GDR were not the responsibility of the foreign office but were handled either by a special ministry for inner-German affairs, or by a special department of the Chancellor's Office.

The two governments adhered to very different principles of legitimization. Like the three western Allied Powers occupying western Germany, the government of the FRG derived its legitimacy from the formal rationale of liberal democratic procedure and the rule of law. Following the model of the Soviet Union, the government of the GDR derived its legitimacy from the substantive rationale of its assumed role as the vanguard representative of the German class of workers and farmers as well as from its lived and proclaimed antifascism (Meuschel 1992). Thus the governments vigorously disputed each other's legitimacy on the basis of different ideologies marked by different concepts of rationality. Yet the formal symmetry between these legitimizing claims and counterclaims neither translated into symmetrical approaches to German-German relations, nor to equal positions of power with respect to the other side. In the first two decades of their existence, both governments initiated several attempts to solve the "German question" *(Deutsche Frage)*, to overcome the division of Germany. All initiatives launched by the FRG aimed at free elections with equal and secret ballots coupled with demands for immediate freedom of coalition and freedom of speech as preconditions for any closer cooperation or unification. In contrast, the initiatives of the GDR tended to demand mutual recognition as a precondition for

20. The Hallstein Doctrine was abandoned in 1967 by the FRG itself in establishing diplomatic relations with Romania.

further negotiations. Neither government considered the other's propos-
als in earnest, usually rejecting them as unfounded rhetoric (Diemer and
Kuhrt 1994; Weber 1991). Typically, the government of the FRG dismissed the initiatives of the GDR out of hand as cheap attempts to attain
equal status. The government of the GDR regularly "debunked" Western
advances as only thinly veiled revanchism aimed at obliterating the advances made in liberating workers and farmers.[21]

For the FRG, the policy of nonrecognition barely involved any cost—
quite to the contrary. For the GDR, however, nonrecognition tended to
undermine political and economic stability, and for a very simple reason:
the ease with which refugees from the GDR could obtain West German
citizenship. The GDR would have benefited from recognition, because
the acknowledgement of separate citizenship might have helped to contain the movement of refugees from East Germany to the West. During
the period between 1949 and 1961 an average of almost a quarter of a
million people fled the GDR annually, amounting to a total of 2.7 million
by 1961 (Diemer and Kuhrt 1994, 238).[22] Undoubtedly, this enormous
influx of mostly skilled and highly skilled labor fueled rapid economic
growth in the West, while at worst straining the already tight western
housing market. At the same time, however, the refugee movement created severe labor shortages in the East. The erection of the Wall was an
attempt by the GDR government, supported by the Soviet Union, to stem
this flood of refugees (Weber 1991, 93ff.).[23]

---

21. The Cold War rhetoric between the two Germanies about recognition also
involved conflict over the use of proper names. While the GDR quickly reverted to
the use of acronyms for both states, calling itself "DDR" (GDR) and the West "BRD"
(FRG), the West referred to itself exclusively by the full official name, though frequently shortened to just "Bundesrepublik" (Federal Republic), while consistently
using the acronym for the GDR. In an attempt to relativize the Eastern self-identification as "democratic," some Westerners even insisted on putting DDR in quotation
marks (most notably the newspapers published by Axel Springer, among them [West]
Germany's biggest tabloid, *Bild*). In a paranoid attempt at control, the FRG even
banned the acronym BRD from official use. Likewise, the GDR tried to set off West
Berlin as a separate entity, naming it in an unhyphenated version "Westberlin,"
while East Berlin was always referred to as "Berlin, Hauptstadt der DDR" (Berlin,
capital of the GDR). The FRG insisted on calling West Berlin "Berlin" or, if necessary for clarity, "West-Berlin" or "Berlin (West)," considering "Westberlin" an af-
front.
    22. If it is taken into account that the GDR had at unification roughly sixteen
million inhabitants, the dimensions of this refugee movement become apparent.
    23. In chapter 6 I discuss extensively how eastern and western police officers
think about the construction and dissolution of the Berlin Wall.

OSTPOLITIK. Paradoxical as it may seem at first, the creation of the Berlin Wall and the nearly complete closure of the border between the two Germanies in August 1961 initiated a slow shift in the policy focus of the FRG towards the GDR, which developed by the end of the 1960 into what has come to be known as *Ostpolitik* (Garton Ash 1993). The Wall suddenly and drastically separated not only many Easterners from their workplaces in the West, but it made contact across the now truly impermeable Iron Curtain extremely difficult. For many Germans on both sides of the divide, this meant that they were unable to visit even their closest kin. For many eastern police officers I got to know, the erection of the Wall amounted to a total breakdown of all contacts with their western relatives. Since People's Police officers did not have permission to entertain "contacts with the West" *(West-Kontakte)*, and the erection of the Wall afforded easy means to control East-West communication, many officers didn't see their relatives again until November 1989. In addition, the situation of West Berlin had de facto become that of a hermetically sealed-off island, leading to a state of mind described by most western officers as "island-fit" *(Inselkoller)*. What became apparent under these drastically altered circumstances was the need to alleviate the immediate personal pains of millions of Germans created by the building of the Berlin Wall. Thus, one of the immediate goals of policy became the creation of "human alleviations" *(menschliche Erleichterungen)*.

The formula that the Social Democratic government that came into power in 1969 under the charismatic leadership of Willy Brandt developed in order to achieve this goal was "change through rapprochement" *(Wandel durch Annäherung)*. The idea of Ostpolitik was to overcome the polarizing rhetoric of the Cold War, first by taking the tensions out of East-West relations through establishing trust and then effecting change in the East by getting involved in closer interaction at all levels (see Garton Ash 1993). Substantively, the heart of Ostpolitik was the negotiation of a considerable network of treaties regulating the communication between both countries by the exchange of emissaries for the governments, and by land traffic, telephone, and mail for ordinary people. The overall aim of this treaty network was to "normalize" the relationship between both countries for the benefit of the people. In this way, Ostpolitik led indeed to a progressive de facto, if not de jure, recognition of the GDR by the FRG.

While Ostpolitik was initiated by the Social Democrats, it was continued seamlessly by the conservative government that came into power in 1982 under the leadership of Chancellor Helmut Kohl. Continuity pre-

vailed despite the fact that the conservative opposition had fiercely opposed Ostpolitik at its instigation in the early seventies, and even though
the conservative CDU (Christlich Demokratische Union) under the leadership of its founding father, Konrad Adenauer, had originally engineered
the policy of sole representation. The biggest diplomatic successes of the
GDR in its relations with the FRG occurred in the era of conservative
government: the arrangement for credit worth 1 billion marks, which was
granted to the GDR by the FRG in 1984, and the full-fledged state reception accorded to the leader of the GDR, Erich Honecker, who was received in Bonn in the fall of 1987.

One of the GDR's reactions to western initiation of détente, was to
present herself as a completely self-contained, socialist state, no longer
requiring any allusions to Germany as a whole, however conceived. For
the GDR, German-German relations did not have any special character,
they were in fact to be treated just like any other foreign relations. In
1976, the Ninth Party Congress revoked all references to German unity
in official documents ranging from the constitution of the GDR to the
national anthem and the party statutes (Weber 1991, 139). Meanwhile,
Ostpolitik did yield "human alleviations," for example, in relaxation of
travel restrictions. It also eased the lives of West Berliners considerably by
improving, for example, the transit traffic from West Germany to Berlin
through the GDR. But the GDR also managed to make the West pay
for it, whether in the form of infrastructure investments, or by selling
off political prisoners, by substantial guaranteed credits, or by forced
currency exchanges. The most visible improvement yielded by Ostpolitik
as far as "human alleviation" is concerned was the marked increase of
western visitors to the East after 1969, especially those of West Berliners.
Eastern visits to the West, however, increased very slowly, showing a
large increase only after 1986.

It is hard to gauge accurately what effect the increased stream of visitors, first in one direction and then also in the other, had on the development of the GDR, and harder to determine whether it might even have
contributed to some extent to its downfall.[24] From my fieldwork I know,

24. Garton Ash (1993) raises doubts about the success of Ostpolitik in terms of
the goals that it set for itself. Especially the formula "change by rapprochement"
(Wandel durch Annähung) seems not to have worked insofar as an internal liberalization of the GDR is concerned. Garton Ash is quite right to point out that, contrary
to its proclaimed goals, Ostpolitik not only did not correspond with a liberalization
of the GDR, but relative to other countries in eastern Europe, the GDR became even
more pronouncedly conservative.

however, that contact with the West meant a lot to those officers who dared to maintain them even though they were forbidden for all officers of the "Armed Agencies" (Bewaffneten Organe), of which the People's Police was a part. Such contacts not only ensured a supply of desirable consumer goods, which were either very expensive in the GDR or could only be obtained with great difficulty, but eastern officers with regular western contacts did have, generally, a more critical attitude to the regime of the GDR. Visitors from the West undoubtedly played a major part in forming the image that easterners developed of the West.

The effects of western television, receivable via antenna in most parts of the GDR, are frequently overestimated in their impact on the production of Easterners' ideas about life in the West. It is usually assumed that what Western media showed was taken for the truth by Eastern viewers, thus providing a corrective to Eastern mass media. This is not true, however, at least not in an unqualified sense. Critical about their own television, many eastern officers did not necessarily trust the western media much more than the eastern ones. Both were seen as presenting a view blurred by government propaganda. In this context, visitors from the West added a *tangible* component to East-West comparisons. They supplied a third, mediating information channel that clarified the contradictions among the other two in favor of Western TV. According to my observations in the field, only the double encounter with both Western TV and visitors from the West made a difference. Western television alone did not, because it was tangled up in the contradictions of two sources of information.

The ability of Westerners not only to visit the GDR (while this was almost impossible for Easterners of working age), but to come in cars that were superior to their Eastern counterparts, and to bring valued consumer goods which were unavailable or far too costly in the GDR clearly helped to produce, or at least to reinforce, an image of a superior West, which must sometimes have appeared to many easterners as a country of bounty. In this sense Ostpolitik, by putting the relationship between the two German governments on a more equal footing, helped to highlight the actual differences between both German states in the experience of hundreds of thousands of people. Ostpolitik allowed East Germans and West Germans alike to *experience* the West as superior to the East, to feel that the West was *desirable* and the East was not.[25]

25. Seen in this light, Garton Ash's (1993) critique of Ostpolitik as stabilizing the Eastern regime must be qualified. Ostpolitik might not have affected the GDR elites and their attitudes. Yet through the alleviation of travel restrictions, it almost cer-

The 1980s added another dimension to the relationship between the two German states which constitutes a qualitative step beyond the negotiation of humanitarian alleviation in East-West relations. As the Cold War was revived, triggered by a new arms race in medium-range missiles, the Soviet invasion of Afghanistan, and the election of Ronald Reagan as president of the United States, several leading Social Democratic politicians, vital members of the peace movement in the FRG, tried to revive détente by an intensified dialogue with leading GDR politicians (Garton Ash 1993, 312–42). The underlying idea of this dialogue was to counter the seemingly irrational behavior of the superpowers with rational, peace-oriented activities by both German states. This dialogue aimed at building a "security partnership" *(Sicherheitspartnerschaft)* between the FRG and the GDR or, more inclusively, between western and eastern Europe (SPD 1987). This exchange of ideas (for more it has not been) between prominent members of the ruling elite of the GDR and representatives of the Social Democratic Party of the FRG signaled a new quality of recognition, which had not previously been an element of GDR and FRG relations. This "second Ostpolitik" (Garton Ash 1993) took place just before the eve of the developments that would eventually lead to unification.

In sum, the history of the relations between the two German states can be divided into two different phases, roughly coextensive with the first two and the last two decades of German-German relations. Each phase is characterized by a particular model of interaction between the two states. In the first phase, or first model of interaction, the FRG and the GDR are not only pitted against each other in Cold War confrontation, but the FRG refuses to recognize the existence of the GDR as an equal partner. This is the model of the claim to "sole representation" *(Alleinvertretungsanspruch)*. The government of the FRG felt vindicated in its policy of sole representation by the massive flight from the East to the West. The second phase, ironically triggered by the extraordinarily aggressive position of the GDR in holding both West Berlin and its own population hostage, is one of increasingly closer cooperation, in which the two German states consider each other increasingly as de facto equal

---

tainly did have a considerable impact on the views of the GDR citizenry. My hypothesis could be quite easily tested by finding out how many of the people who chose to flee the GDR had relatives in the West with whom they maintained regular contact, and to what extent this contact was constitutive for their image of the West. These refugees could then be compared to those Easterners who not only remained in the GDR but also severed ties with their Western relatives (this procedure could control for what might be called the "nesting factor," the added ease of a decision to flee made in the knowledge that friendly, personal helpers awaited on the other side.

partners. This is the model of Ostpolitik. Ironically, this model too not only made it possible for a sizable number of easterners and westerners to experience the difference between both states but supported the hierarchical identification of the states as superior and inferior along the lines of the old model of sole representation. Both models can be seen as cultural forms, institutionalized and stored in different ways, ready to be retrieved and acted upon in novel circumstances. Such circumstances arose in 1989.

The Disintegration of the GDR
and German Unification

In contrast to the regimes in Poland and Hungary, the East German regime did not seize upon the opportunities for internal liberalization created by Mikhail Gorbachev's policies of glasnost and perestroika (Lewin 1991; Hosking 1990). Just as if the thaw in the Soviet Union was not happening at all, the GDR continued to crack down on every sign of protest, on every demand for liberalization. As before, after Stalin's death, the GDR tried to isolate itself from the thaw taking place elsewhere in Eastern Europe (Weber 1991, 183–85). To the utter consternation of many people in the GDR (several of the police officers I got to know in Potsdam and in Köpenick included), the GDR regime took this policy of isolation so far as to restrict travel to Poland and Hungary as well as to suppress the circulation of the organ of the Soviet Komzomol (youth organization), the *Sputnik*.

In the face of this increasing discrepancy between what happened in the world around the GDR and what happened in the GDR itself, it is not surprising that the destabilization of the GDR and its eventual dissolution began with yet another mass exodus (see Maier 1997, 120ff.). Those willing and ready to flee chose two different avenues. In late summer of 1989, several thousand people sought refuge in the embassies of the FRG in Budapest, Warsaw, and Prague as well as in the Permanent Representative Office in East Berlin; in the course of events in the fall, most of them were granted permission to leave for the FRG. By far the largest number, however, took advantage of the dismantling of the Iron Curtain by the Hungarian government on 9 September 1989. In September 1989 alone more than twenty-five thousand people left the GDR for the FRG by way of the Austro-Hungarian border (Weber 1991, 343).

The police officers in Köpenick and in Potsdam remember having very mixed feelings about the flight of thousands of people in the late summer

of 1989. Some of them say today that then they simply could not understand why so many people wanted to leave the GDR. Others say that
they felt rather disquieted by the refugees, that somehow the flight of so
many people epitomized for them a general feeling of crisis. It was a crisis
about which they had already collected many pieces of evidence (such as
increasing information about economic problems) which, until then, had
not added up to a fully conscious picture. Some of them also remember
today that they were then quite disappointed by the government's reaction to the massive flight. The moral disparagement of the refugees by
the government sounded unconvincing to many officers for the simple
reason that there were so many of them.

At the same time, the civil rights movement in the GDR stepped up
its protest. Opposition groupings started to demand public recognition
and roundtable discussions with the government. New organizations
were founded, and their protest activities received rapidly increasing public support. After arrests in the context of a prayer for peace on 11 September in Leipzig, an increasing number of people gathered there every
Monday to demand political reform and the release of those who had
been arrested (the famous Monday Demonstrations). The fortieth anniversary celebrations commemorating the foundation of the GDR on 7
October were accompanied in many cities by protests. Clashes with the
police occurred in several cities, and more than one thousand demonstrators were arrested. The following Monday roughly seventy thousand
people gathered in Leipzig to protest the arrests in the context of the
anniversary celebrations, renewing their demand for democratic reforms.
Banners at these Monday demonstrations read, "We are the people" *(Wir
sind das Volk),* which became an anchoring motto for the protest movement. Barely ten days later, in the midst of ever-increasing tensions, Erich
Honecker, the GDR leader for almost two decades, was replaced by Egon
Krenz, his long-standing heir apparent.

On 4 November about one million people gathered on East Berlin's
Alexanderplatz in the largest demonstration in the history of the GDR.
Members of the civil rights movement spoke on this day alongside well-
known intellectuals and leading members of the Socialist Unity Party
(Sozialistische Einheitspartei Duetschlands; SED). Almost all speakers
demanded democratic reforms in the GDR, and many of them (and by
no means just the representatives of the government) invoked "socialism
with a human face" as the guiding idea for a new beginning in the GDR.
It is worth mentioning that in this demonstration, just as much as in the
previous ones in Leipzig, German unification was not an issue.

On 9 November much to everyone's surprise, the Berlin Wall fell, leading to spontaneous celebrations in Berlin.[26] By the end of the first weekend after the general opening of the border, three million citizens of the GDR had visited West Berlin or West Germany. From then on, weekend after weekend, citizens of the GDR virtually poured into the West. Barely ten days after the opening of the borders, the prime minister of the GDR, Hans Modrow, vaguely brought German unification into play by suggesting that the "community of responsibility" *(Verantwortungsgemeinschaft)* between both German states, a term echoing the second Ostpolitik, be changed into a "treaty community" *(Vertragsgemeinschaft)*. Subsequently, on Leipzig's by now institutionalized Monday Demonstrations, the first banners emerged changing the slogan of protest "We are the people" to "We are *one* people" *(Wir sind ein Volk)*. Thus, by the end of November, after many Easterners had had firsthand experience of the West, the first popular demands for unification occurred. Also, the new leader of the GDR, Egon Krenz, no longer excluded a German confederation as a form of cooperation between the two German states, on the conditions that the GDR could remain a socialist country, and that both NATO and the Warsaw Pact would be dissolved. In response to these advances from the East, Chancellor Kohl of the FRG suggested in his "Ten-Point Program" (see Diemer and Kuhrt 1994, 230–36) that cooperation between the German states be intensified by the creation of "confederative structures." Kohl made it clear, however, that these confederative structures would demand the introduction of liberal democratic and economic institutions in the GDR. With respect to unity, Kohl said in his Ten-Point Program: "Nobody knows today what a unified Germany will look like in the end. I am certain, however, that unity will come, if the people in Germany want it" (233).[27]

To maintain some kind of legitimacy, the Socialist Unity Party desperately tried to fight an uphill battle by reinventing itself in late November and December. To this end, it followed the chorus of the protesters by revoking its special status as a vanguard party, correcting the constitution accordingly. Former leading members were excluded from the party, among them Erich Honecker; some of the former grandees were also put under house arrest, and others were arraigned. The government began regular consultations with civil rights groups (following the Hungarian

26. See the section "Viewing the Wall" in chapter 6 for a more detailed account of how the Wall was perceived on each side before and after its fall, and how its fall was experienced.

27. My translation from the German original.

and Polish examples by calling them "roundtables"). Finally, even Egon Krenz, who had assumed the leadership of party and government only late in October, had to make way as party leader for a much younger candidate, Gregor Gysi, who was free of immediate associations with the old regime.[28] The Socialist Unity Party finally apologized for the abyss into which it had lead the country and signaled its intended self-purification by appending to its name the title Party of Democratic Socialism (Partei des Demokratischen Sozialismus).

Shortly before Christmas, Kohl met with Prime Minister Modrow of the GDR in the East German city of Dresden for consultations about a possible confederation or treaty community of both states. He was welcomed at the airport by cheering crowds displaying a sea of federal flags and masses of "We are *one* people" banners. Kohl (1996) has described this visit to Dresden and his perception there of what the people of the GDR wanted as decisive for his attempts to spurn German unification (cf. Zelikow and Rice 1996, 147). Kohl (1996) remembers today that walking down the gangway, he said then to his chief of staff, "It [implying German unification] is a done deal."

By the beginning of the new year, the topic of German unification had assumed center stage in the public debate in both Germanies. At the same time, East Germany was rapidly disintegrating politically because the roundtables proved to be a rather unwieldy instrument of government. The debate about unification was further fueled by an unabating number of people leaving the GDR with the intention to settle in the FRG.[29] The high number of refugees was portrayed in the Western media in metaphors of unmanageable water masses: as "floods," "bursting dams," and so on.[30] Faced with such large numbers of refugees, Western politicians also started to beseech East Germans to "stay home" *(Bleibt*

28. Gysi still leads the Party of Democratic Socialism as of this writing. He has been a member of the Bundestag since the elections of 2 December 1990, the first all-German elections. As a witty critic of the conservative government under Kohl, he was able to gain popularity far beyond the electorate of the PDS.

29. The total number for 1989 was 343,854 (the comparable figure for 1988 was 39,832), of which by far the largest part came in the last months of the year. The political changes in the GDR seemed not to influence the number of refugees at all. In January 1990, 58,043 people moved from the GDR to the FRG. This means that the GDR was losing its population at a rate of one third of a percent per month (Weber 1991: 347–48).

30. For example, see Robert Leicht, "Wenn deutsche Schleusen brechen: Der Ausgleich zwischen der Bundesrepublik und der DDR läßt sich nicht aufhalten," *Die Zeit,* 1 February 1990.

daheim).[31] This movement of refugees was quickly understood in terms of a flight to the German mark. Thus, an economic and social union with the GDR was debated from very early on in the year as a possible means to convince the citizens of the GDR to stay where they were. Accordingly, the political pressure in East Germany started to increase to hold general elections as fast as possible, and by the end of January, it was agreed to hold them on 18 March 1990.

The impending election in the GDR caused the Western parties to seek sister parties in the East. These parties were then usually furnished with extensive Western "support," which frequently meant nothing less than remodeling them in the image of their Western counterparts. At the same time two different blueprints for German unification (which was no longer in doubt) were debated intensively. The first plan proposed unification in accordance with Article 146 of the Basic Law,[32] implying the joint election of a national assembly that would sit to draft a new constitution for Germany as a whole. This plan was advocated especially by liberals in West Germany, left-leaning Social Democrats, some Free Democrats, and the Greens, together with the majority of the civil rights activists in East Germany. The advocates of unification via Article 146 pointed to the shortcomings of both countries, the GDR and the FRG, and insinuated that unification offered a chance to reform, which could draw on the experiences of both states (cf. SPD 1989). Supporters of Article 146 unification also pointed out that it would be the more constructive way to deal with the GDR past, that it allowed for a much more dignified process that didn't smack of easy abandonment and fast adaptation, if not submission, to new authority.[33] In this sense, the suggestion to unify

31. One example is the FDP (Freie Demokratische Partei) politician Wolfgang Mischnick, himself originally from eastern Germany. The quotation is from Garton Ash (1993, 347).

32. Article 146 of the constitution stated simply that the Basic Law would lose its validity on the day on which the German people produced, in free self-determination, a new constitution. It has always been understood as a possible avenue to unification (Maunz, Dürig, Günter et al. 1963–).

33. See, for example, Joachim Nawrocki, "Ein Andersdenkender: Wolfgang Templin sieht sich bereits wieder an den Rand gedrängt," *Die Zeit*, 9 March 1990; Helga Hirsch, "Der Neubeginn als Selbstaufgabe: Warum sich die Menschen in der DDR wieder so schnell der Obhut eines Stärkeren anvertrauen wollen," *Die Zeit*, 16 March 1990. Most well-known intellectuals in the GDR favored unification via Article 146. In the West, Jürgen Habermas (1990) was a well-known advocate of a new constitutional assembly, for he feared that unification by accession would constitute unified Germany as defined by its economy rather than by an act of political will.

Germany under the provisions of Article 146 was very much in keeping with the spirit of Ostpolitik as a model for the relationship between both countries.

The second proposed plan was to unify Germany in accordance with Article 23 of the Basic Law. Article 23 specified that "other territories" could accede to the jurisdiction of the Basic Law (Maunz, Dürig, Günter et al. 1963–).[34] This meant basically that all the political, juridical, and administrative institutions of the FRG would expand into the territory of the GDR. Since the FRG is a federal country, unification by Article 23 implied also that the GDR had to recreate states. It was suggested that the five historical states that had existed on its territory until 1952, when they were replaced by fourteen ahistorically defined administrative districts, could be reinstated. Unification under the provisions of Article 23 was espoused most notably by the conservative arch of the political spectrum of the FRG and also by the former bloc parties in the GDR. These bloc parties had happily lived in the procrustean bed of SED domination for much of their history (Suckut 1994), and they were now revived and relegitimized under the tutelage of their chosen western counterparts.[35] Unification by Article 23 is fully compatible with, indeed an almost logical extension of, the principle of sole representation, which governed FRG policy towards the GDR for the first twenty years of their existence. There were two principle arguments put forth in favor of Article 23 unification. First, the political institutions of the FRG were tried and had proven to be capable of sustaining a viable democracy—the first stable democracy ever on German soil—coupled with unprecedented

34. In 1957, Article 23 had been already employed to integrate the Saarland into the territory of the FRG. The accession of the Saarland was therefore seen as a model case for unification. See, for example, Robert Leicht, "Deutsches Haus: Einheit durch Beitritt," *Die Zeit,* 22 February 1990, and "Königsweg zur Einheit: Das Saarland als Beispiel," *Die Zeit,* 1 March 1990.

35. In 1946 the Social Democrats (SPD) in the Soviet-occupied zone in Germany (the later GDR) were forced into a union with the Communist Party (Kommunistische Partei Deutschlands, KPD). This new socialist vanguard party was called Socialist Unity Party (SED). Thus, unlike the conservative CDU, or the liberal FDP, the SPD in the FRG did not have a well-established partner in the GDR, because it seemed illicit to cooperate with the successor organization of the SED, the Party of Democratic Socialism (PDS). It is of course highly ironic that conservative parties in the FRG had no qualms about cooperating with former bloc parties, thus inheriting their party machinery. Instead, the SPD cooperated and later absorbed the Social Democratic Party (Sozialdemokratische Partei, SDP), which was only founded in 1989 as part of the civil rights movement, and which had no significant party organization in East Germany.

wealth. Many people argued that it would be outright foolish to abandon it for something new, increasing uncertainty in a time when some security would be welcome. Second, in view of a rather unpredictable, but presently favorable international environment and in consideration of the persisting movement of people from the GDR to the FRG (which was frequently also taken as voting by feet), many thought it a considerable advantage that unification under the provisions of Article 23 would be much faster.

As the general elections were scheduled in the GDR for 18 March 1990, the various parties, partially grouped into alliances, entered the campaigns on platforms espousing the one or the other plan for unification. Most political commentators, relying for their forecasts in part on an analysis of election behavior in the early 1930s, predicted a victory for the Social Democrats.[36] Instead, the conservative Alliance for Germany (Allianz für Deutschland) under the leadership of the CDU, which had been for decades a reliable ally of the SED (Weber 1991, 231), routed all other parties, especially the Social Democrats and the civil rights movement, which suffered a crushing defeat.[37] This election result was widely interpreted as a plebiscite for fast unification under the provisions of Article 23 of the Basic Law.

The rest of the story follows from here. The four victorious powers of World War II, which still held rights over Germany as a whole, needed to be convinced that German unification was a good thing, which basically meant they had to be persuaded that a united Germany would not pose a threat to its neighbors. This was accomplished by means of the so-called 2+4 talks (Zelikow and Rice 1995; Maier 1997, 244ff.). While the Bush administration in the United States fully supported Kohl in his

---

36. This exercise amounts to a very interesting projection of identity over generations and through the most diverse political and economic circumstances. Of course this perspective also suggests that the forty years of GDR history were believed not to matter at all. The analysis of the final election results by region and by class revealed that few of the historical voting patterns held true for the GDR. Especially the variable conjunction of being traditionally a Protestant part of Germany and having a high proportion of blue collar workers proved to be a poor predictor for the turnout of social democratic votes (see Maier 1997, 212).

37. The election results were as follows (Weber 1991, 232): The conservative "Alliance for Germany" as a whole won 48.1 percent of the vote (CDU alone: 40.8 percent); the Social Democrats were thoroughly defeated with a total of 21.9 percent, and the reformed communist party, which by then had completely dropped its old name SED in favor of the phrase appended in December (PDS), won 16.4 percent. The civil rights movement (allied in "Confederation 90") won a mere 2.9 percent of the vote, thus suffering a particularly bitter defeat.

drive for German unity, some reservations had to be overcome in Mitter-
rand's France, which were finally dissipated by Kohl's convincing thrust
for improved European cooperation, and Thatcher's Britain. Understandably the greatest concerns arose in the Soviet Union, but they too were
finally assuaged by skilled diplomacy, a package of mostly military assur-
ances and reassurances, and a hefty package of financial aid. On 19 April
the newly constituted government of the GDR declared its intention to
accede to the FRG in accordance with Article 23 of the Basic Law. At
the same time negotiations about a unification treaty began. Following a
tried script from the immediate postwar period and decades of successful
European integration, the economic and social union of Germany preceded political union. Economic and social union (mostly visible as a
currency union) took effect on 1 July 1990 on the basis of a very generous conversion rate. The GDR reintroduced five states on its territory
by the end of July, and finally, on 23 August 1990, the parliament of the
GDR voted almost unanimously, except for the PDS, for accession to the
FRG under the provisions of Article 23 of the Basic Law, effective 3 October 1990.

EXCURSION: EXPERIENCES, MORAL DISCOURSES, AND THE ORGANIZA-
TION OF UNITY. What remains puzzling after this short account is why
sole representation ultimately provided the blueprint for German unification and not Ostpolitik or, to say it more bluntly, why nonrecognition
prevailed over partnership. What is it that made unification by accession
(the provisions of Article 23) a more convincing solution to politically
relevant actors than unification by reconstitution (the provisions of Article 146)? I begin my sketch of an answer to this question by first enumer-
ating three important factors which probably made accession the preferred solution for the West German elites. I then explain why unification
by accession might have been more palatable to the East German electorate. Finally I direct attention to the relationship between the salient moral
discourses of the time and the two suggested paths for German unification.

   From the perspective of West German political, administrative, and
economic elites, three factors probably contributed significantly to the
persuasiveness of unification by accession. In the history of the FRG a
broad consensus had evolved that considered the Basic Law a congenial
constitution for (West) Germany. The phrase that had won widespread
acceptance in describing this attitude towards the Basic Law in the FRG
was "constitutional patriotism" *(Verfassungspatriotismus)*. In reaction to

the Weimar experience, "loyalty to the Basic Law" *(Verfassungstreue)* had become the cornerstone of political acceptability in West Germany.[38] Furthermore, it must be remembered that civil servants in the West stood to gain immensely from unification by accession, since their skills would be in great demand.[39] Finally, it is probably safe to assume that it was also in the interest of the West German economy to proceed along the lines of Article 23 because it maintained the stability of law, which is essential in order to keep economic transactions predictable.

After the opening of the Wall, East Germans visited the West by the millions. If those who had regular contacts with Westerners had experienced the West already as a superior social system, this perception was amplified and multiplied by these visits. The majority of Easterners experienced the West as the place that had effectively solved all the problems the GDR seems to have had. To East Germans who constantly thought in terms of shortages in the supply of consumer goods, the West with its plentiful availability of everything looked like the land of bounty. What was of course less visible to them, especially during the first few months, was that the West did indeed have problems that the East did not have. Easterners tended to overlook these problems because they were not part of the relevance structures of their lifeworlds. Certainly most East Germans did not, in the spring of 1990, foresee the radical consequences of accession to the FRG, such as the thorough devaluation of their social and cultural capital. What seemed to matter more then was to find an escape from the excruciating uncertainty created by a disintegrating state (particularly if it is appreciated that one feature of the GDR was a high degree of social security).

Beyond the importance of all these factors, another perspective can reveal yet another facet of a probable explanation for why unification by accession was preferred to reconstitution. The argument I want to make is that the advocacy of accession could focus on salient aspects of the

38. It is no accident that the security agency in (West) Germany which investigates politically motivated crimes is called "Federal Office for the Protection of the Constitution (Bundesamt für Verfassungsschutz)." It is supposed to monitor all possible threats to the political order in Germany. These threats are believed to come from the far right or the far left of the political spectrum, and they are therefore called "left-wing radicalism" *(Linksradikalismus)* and "right-wing radicalism" *(Rechtsradikalismus)*.

39. To illustrate this beneficial effect of unification on the civil service (I will say more about this in the next section), it may suffice to remember that by the end of the 1980 a huge wave of unemployed law graduates had emerged from West German universities. Unification created employment for virtually all of them.

principal moral discourse of the time or, conversely, that advocacy of unification by reconstitution was seriously impeded by these moral discourses. Put differently, accession offered a way to circumvent pressing moral issues, while reconstitution emphasized these issues. This was a particularly fateful problem for the proponents of reconstitution, since their main argument for reconstitution was fundamentally moral as well: it aimed at equality and symmetry in the treatment of Easterners and Westerners.

A fuller understanding of the moral resonances of both prospective paths to a unified Germany requires another historical flashback. It must be remembered that the two relationship models—sole representation and Ostpolitik—are embedded in a particular moral outlook. Sole representation was staked out in strong moral terms as a commitment to a set of core values grouped around notions of democracy and, perhaps even more fundamentally, freedom. Thus the nonrecognition of the GDR by the FRG was argued on the basis of moral principle. By the end of the 1960, in the wake of the student revolt, the abuse of the values of freedom and democracy by Western powers had become quite apparent, and they were identified by the protesting students and their sympathizers as hollow rhetorical devices in an endless scramble for power. In other words, these values were "debunked" as central pieces of an ideology, or, more precisely, of one of two competing ideologies vying for world hegemony. What appeared as especially appalling to the activists at the end of the 1960s was the justification of extreme violence, possibly even nuclear war, in terms of these values. It seemed absurd that the very existence of humankind should be endangered for the insistence on moral principles which were violated left and right by those who claimed to uphold them. This crisis of values could not be resolved by an equally abstract replacement of the values of freedom and democracy by yet another set of lofty ideas. Put differently, the trappings of one ideology were not to be answered with yet another ideology. The cry of the time was the critique of ideology.[40] What moved to the foreground instead of a set of core values was an interest in the alleviation of human suffering—suffering created by hunger, exploitation and underdevelopment, and by war. The activists of the time argued that these forms of suffering could and should be addressed very concretely. What was identified as the principle cause of human suffering was war, both in its most concrete, literal meaning

40. This does not mean that the debate over ideology was atheoretical, or not also very abstract. I would argue, however, that the point of the student revolt was much more activist than theoretical.

but also in its metaphorical connotation as a model of human interaction in general. Thus the central interest of the movement was peace, more concretely, the *practice* of peace. Ostpolitik grew on the soil of this moral discourse that had decidedly shifted away from a notion of principle to a notion of responsibility.[41] It was geared towards concrete measures for the alleviation of human suffering, and it was geared towards peace: on a large scale as peace among nations or sociopolitical systems, and on a small scale as peace in daily human interaction. In this sense, Ostpolitik was associated with a moral attitude which did not define itself through a set of core values, and which therefore was attacked as amoral by its conservative critics (who defined themselves in terms of a struggle for democracy and freedom).

The peaceful revolutions in Eastern Europe in 1989 reaccentuated the moral discourses. People in East Germany, much as elsewhere in Eastern Europe between Tallinn and Sofia, revolted against their governments because their rulers had treated them as immature beings. They took to the streets for their own liberty.[42] In the course of this upheaval, in the GDR from December on, the full scale of misdeeds of the communist regime became visible. The revelation of one scandal followed another. It became patently clear how little the government had trusted its citizens, and how little the GDR leaders had had faith in each other. It became obvious what an important role the secret police had played, and what odious and violent abuses of human rights it had committed to keep the country in check. Moreover, the whole system of patronage, of granting and denying privileges, was divulged bit by bit. For many of the eastern police officers in Köpenick and in Potsdam these revelations were painful, because most of them did identify with the communist regime at some level. All of a sudden they had reason to feel betrayed, to feel cheated. In the context of explaining his party resignation, one of the Köpenick officers expressed his disappointment as follows:

> First, I stayed in the party because I thought the idea is right, there just need to be different people doing it. . . . But then, when the sleuthing system of the secret police became apparent, something I didn't know before, and all these other revelations about misdeeds, I said to

41. Weber's terminology, developed in "Politics as Profession" (1988b) is helpful here. The underpinnings of the moral discourse shifted from an "ethics of principle" *(Gesinnungsethik)* to an "ethics of responsibility" *(Verantwortungsethik).*

42. This does not, of course, preclude the possibility that they also demonstrated for a better life, a life more along the lines of their fellow (Western) Europeans.

myself that I was abused in good faith by a system, that one never
wanted to be that way. . . . I was very disappointed, not because one
had believed in the wrong thing, but because one was abused so much.
. . . Then, I resigned.

Thus the values of freedom and democracy became again core elements
of the moral discourse, but this time not (at least not initially) as government rhetoric, but as demands of a revolutionary movement. As the an-
cien regime in the former GDR completely lost credibility, its moral bank-
ruptcy cast a shadow on those Westerners who seemed to have bolstered
its international recognition by their overzealous traffic with it. Thus
Ostpolitik and the recognition of the GDR government as a partner in
dialogue became morally dubious, especially since even in the West, the
scope and scale of scandal came as a surprise. The gradual disclosure of
the functioning of a political system built on self-aggrandizing delusions
and paranoid distrust, inviting incompetence and intrigue in conjunction
with the anxious defense of the smallest privileges, seemed to corroborate
in retrospect the views of those who had long been denounced as die-
hard Cold War veterans. Advocates of Ostpolitik looked as if they had
for decades disseminated a false, naive picture of circumstances in the
East. Ironically, the shadow of moral doubt fell thus more on the initia-
tors and proponents of the old and new Ostpolitik and with them on
the proponents of unification by reconsitution than on the conservatives,
who had arguably done much more to proffer the legitimacy of Erich
Honecker and other former GDR grandees. The CDU and its allies managed to be more remembered for their initial opposition to Ostpolitik
than for their later participation in it.

In the face of a renewed stock-taking of the moral state of governance
in East Germany, many Westerners wondered what the East could possibly offer to draft a new common constitution. Moreover, the question
of *who* in the East should play the role of a partner in negotiating a
new constitution became pressing. The old elite had moved within a few
months from sought-after partner to dreaded villain because of its moral
responsibility in what had happened in the GDR. The civil rights movement was at least potentially an attractive partner because of its role in
toppling the old regime; however, the civil rights movement undermined
its own appeal by dreaming about a third way between capitalism and
socialism. Although this idea had much support in the late 1960s, it
sounded flimsy at best at the beginning of the 1990s and strangely out
of tune with the public debates of the time, both in the West, where debate

centered on privatization and flexibility, and in the East, where socialism had just failed so blatantly. For this reason, the civil rights movement looked desirable as a partner in the negotiation of a reformed constitution only to left-leaning Social Democrats and Greens.

This problem of acceptable partners for Westerners translated into a problem of acceptable representatives for Easterners. They could not see themselves represented by members of the old elite or by the civil rights movement, which came across to many Easterners not only as quite unprofessional but also as morally self-righteous. Thus, faute de mieux, it seemed preferable to be represented by Westerners. At least, as one officer in Köpenick put it, "they seemed to know what they were talking about." In this context, unification in accordance with Article 23 of the Basic Law looked to most Westerners and to the majority of Easterners like a way to avoid not only many practical problems but many moral dilemmas as well.[43]

* * *

The actual organization of German unification by accession is a source of east-west identifications whose importance cannot be overstated. This publicly staged drama at the national level sustains and informs countless smaller east-west encounters. In other words, the organizational form of German unification has become the predominant root metaphor (Turner 1974), especially for the ways in which west Germans relate to east Germans. The main characteristic of this root metaphor is the identification of western persons, things, and ways as models to which eastern persons, things, and ways should conform. Unification is thus identified as a unilateral process of assimilation through which easterners are helped to raise themselves to western standards. On the one hand, the pervasiveness of the identifications inherent in the process of unification as root metaphor for east-west relations in united Germany in general arises from its status as all-encompassing national drama, which has occupied center stage in political activity, public discourse, and media coverage since the

43. It is not surprising, therefore, to find a resurgent neoconservatism emerging in Germany after unification, again violently attacking Ostpolitik and the 1968 movement from the same moral perspective. This neoconservatism, whose proponents are thriving on the reaccentuation of the values of freedom and democracy on top of a neoliberal economic platform, is based on the reinstitution of principles as guideposts for differentiating between right and wrong. It also promulgates the thesis that the German nation has paid dearly for the crimes of World War II with forty years of political division, and that it is time now for unified Germany to become a "normal" member of the family of nations.

opening of the Berlin Wall on 9 November 1989 and the conclusion of political unification on 3 October 1990. On the other hand, and perhaps even more important, the process of unification is the predominant root metaphor for east-west relations because it is inscribed in the institutional makeup of unified Germany. In a way, the identifications inherent in the process of unification are dramatized or relived each time an east German encounters formerly Western, now all-German institutions. The identifications implied in unification by accession, echoing the identifications inherent in the model of sole representation, are repeated in the way in which the (West) Berlin Police chose to incorporate the former People's Police officers. The ways in which the (West) Berlin Police identifies its eastern employees on the basis of a cultural form with more than forty years of history is the topic of the next section.

The Unification of the Berlin Police

The opening of the Wall necessitated some form of coordination between the police forces of East and West Berlin. Western officers who came back from these first official encounters frequently condense their feelings and thoughts about the People's Police in a widely used image. One officer recalls:

> "One of my first impressions was that the People's Police had retained many characteristics which are usually attributed to the Wehrmacht [the armed forces of Germany during the Nazi period]. I will furnish you with an example. . . . We faced each other across the table and we were served coffee, not just so, but by a servant in white livery. These things just don't exist in the West anymore. Luckily we have overcome them. . . . And then, when you met them in the hallway, they saluted militarily from five meters away. . . . What I saw there was an embarrassing tendency to preemptive obedience [*vorauseilender Gehorsam*] and a readiness to ingratiate."

This image immediately conveys several important identifications. First, through its sense of hierarchy (livery, salute), the People's Police is metonymically associated with the undemocratic traditions of the pre-1945 German military. Second, since the Wehrmacht was the name for the military in Nazi Germany, two synecdochical relations between a state and its security organs are implied. They amount at least to a metaphori-

Figure 11. In the first few uncertain days after the opening of the Wall, the West Berlin police (cars at the bottom) try to prevent a confrontation between West Berliners and GDR border troops (on top of the Wall; 11 November 1989). Courtesy of Polizeihistorische Sammlung Berlin (photographer: Waize).

cal and perhaps a metonymic relation between both sets; that is, security organs and state in the GDR and Nazi Germany are likened to each other, possibly even equated.[44] Third, the self-identification inherent in this statement is one of self-differentiation from an image which is evaluated in negative terms; that is, what separates self from the characters portrayed is a positive transformation. The point that is powerfully made by this renarration of first encounters with the People's Police is its moral disavowal, which is anchored in its backwardness, in its lack of positive

44. Note that both of these images, a Wehrmacht officer served by a soldier in livery and the heel-clicking subordinate, are also typical clichés of Hollywood movies (e.g., *Casablanca*). They are part of the image inventory of almost every film in which the Wehrmacht has a role.

Figure 12. Cooperation between West Berlin Police and People's Police at border crossings (spring 1990). Courtesy of Polizeihistorische Sammlung Berlin.

transformation.[45] The People's Police is portrayed as deficient and in need of a change akin to the one already undergone by the Western police. In particular it is made clear that the People's Police cannot just be a partner to whom one relates on an equal footing, and it is also assumed that, because of its backwardness, there is nothing to be learned from the People's Police. The intricate identifications inherent in this image, which originated in late 1989, retrospectively adumbrate an agenda for how the West Berlin police would relate to their Eastern counterparts. This image of the People's Police held by western officers also helps to explain why

45. For a detailed analysis of such temporal identification, see the section titled "Temporal Identifications" in chapter 3.

at least the official contacts between the police organizations of East and West Berlin were kept to a minimum.[46]

The People's Police After the Fall of the Wall

As a result of the protests of the civil rights movement against police brutality in arresting and detaining demonstrators during the celebration of the fortieth anniversary of the GDR on 7 October 1989, and due to the establishment of the roundtables in December, the People's Police was forced to reconsider its role in a renewed GDR society (MfIA 1990). In this climate of change and reform, investigations were begun against the responsible officers, and a few leading officers were dismissed, among them the minister, Friedrich Dickel, who had served in this capacity since 1963, and the former president of police in East Berlin. Following the overall changes in the GDR, the People's Police officially repudiated the leading role of the communist party, and officers were no longer obliged to be members of the SED. Once given the opportunity, most officers left the party in what was almost a stampede. As the state began to separate itself from the party, so did the police.

Separation from the party was an incisive experience for the People's Police. A completely new framework for providing guidance in action had to be developed, since the abstract principle of a "class mission" *(Klassenauftrag),* could no longer be legitimately applied, and, more concretely, because the direct orders of the appropriate organs of a vanguard party were no longer available. At the same time, a new framework of orientation had not yet been supplied by a democratically legitimized legislature and government. Thus, from late fall of 1989, an acute sense of disorientation began to beset the entire organization. One high-ranking former Eastern officer has described the situation in the ministry [even before the dismissals] as follows:

> Dickel [the minister] was in a terrible situation. All his life long he was used to getting orders from the central committee of the party. . . . He was desperate, because all of a sudden there was nothing, no orders,

46. Of course, this image too has a much longer history. The theory of totalitarianism and its popularized variants have always insisted on a metonymic relationship between the institutions of Nazi Germany and the GDR. In the case of the armed forces and the police the thesis of an essential similarity of totalitarian institutions seems to have found an easy outward corroboration in some highly visible identical practices (e.g., goose-stepping in parades) and in the similarity of uniforms.

Figure 13. Encounter between West Berlin Police officer (right) and two
People's Police colleagues at East Berlin's Alexanderplatz (spring 1995).
Courtesy of Polizeihistorische Sammlung Berlin (photographer: Eggebrecht).

no orientation, and we were such a centralized organization. . . . One
day I witnessed this situation. I was sitting at the next table in the
cafeteria, and I overheard one of his deputies say to him [the minister],
"We have to tell our people [i.e., the police officers] out there on the
streets what is going to happen, what they are supposed to do," and
then he [the minister] yelled at him, "You don't need to tell me that,
I know that myself, but I don't get any guidance, any help either. I
too have only questions and no answers."

On the one hand this situation led the People's Police into a high degree
of uncertainty, almost to a state of paralysis, which was widely felt outside as a lack of police initiative. First, the People's Police had lost authority through a critique of its role as an executive organ of the communist
party, having exerted too much control and showed too much presence.

Figure 14. West Berlin Police car crossing the border at Checkpoint Charlie. Courtesy of Polizeihistorische Sammlung Berlin (photographer: Eggebrecht).

Then, after the fall of the Wall, it lost even more authority, because it was not only helpless in the face of rapidly rising crime rates, but it seemed unable at times to provide even rudimentary forms of public order, such as the enforcement of traffic rules. Many People's Police officers who actually had to do police work on the streets remember this time with deep dismay. Without proper instructions from superiors, they felt lost; they felt that they no longer knew when, how, or where to intervene, and they were afraid of the anger and perhaps even more of the scorn of the people. During this time they were scolded by the population as "ruffian guard" *(Schlägergarde),* "ruffian-police" *(Schlägerpolizei),* or even as "Stasi [secret police] pigs" *(Stasi-Schweine;* see *Extra* 2: 4).[47]

47. The magazine *Extra,* issued by the Ministry of Interior Affairs of the GDR, is an interesting source for the situation of the People's Police after December 1989. It includes signed, opinionated articles about the future of the People's Police, inter-

On the other hand this time of change was, at least for some high-ranking officers, also an exciting time in which they could think about reforms. It was a time in which the officers themselves could come up with their own ideas about structures and guiding principles for a democratic police force in the GDR (Rektor der HdMI 1990; see also *Extra* 1: 2–4; 3: 3–4; 6: 6; 9: 7). For them, as for many people in the civil rights movement, it was a chance to participate in the writing of history. It was also a time in which many of them sought contact with Western officers in an attempt to collect models that might be worth emulating. Many Western officers who had informal contacts with People's Police officers randomly visiting Western police stations in search of police laws, regulations, and a chat, describe this time as one of friendly exchange and relative openness on both sides. These personal, informal encounters stand in many ways in contrast to the atmosphere of official meetings. By the beginning of July, the West Berlin Police advised all its offices that these unofficial contacts were no longer tolerable. By then, the leadership of the West Berlin Police had also decided how to relate to the People's Police in light of certain unification. High-ranking People's Police officers in particular remember this change in attitude quite vividly as a shift from waiting partnership to open rejection.

The Preparation for Unification

The relationship between both police forces slowly started to take a different turn as people became more aware of the fact that not only was unification going to happen, but it was going to come in the form of accession of the GDR to the FRG under the provisions of Article 23 of the Basic Law. All attempts to reform the GDR on its own terms started to look more and more like vain exercises. There would not be a new GDR, there would not be a reformed People's Police; the East was simply going to be made Western. While this course of events had been quite predictable since the elections of 18 March and the declaration of unification by the new GDR government on 19 April, no serious efforts on either side had been made to plan the actual unification of both police forces until the beginning of July 1990. Then the West Berlin minister of the interior assembled several working committees to work out an action

---

views with ministers and civil rights activists, and reports about the difficulties of police work on the streets.

plan for the unification of both police forces, which was then expected to take place by the end of the year.[48]

Seven working committees were assembled, one to address each different aspect of police work: the uniformed police, criminal investigation, special units, equipment and logistics, law, organization, and personnel.[49] These working committees were composed almost equally of representatives of the West Berlin Police and of the People's Police. The goal for all the working committees was defined in general terms as "development of detailed solutions to dissolve the discrepancies [between the two police organizations]." To this goal, set by the ministry, the chair of the working committee on personnel added the following in the margin: "The West provides the frame of reference. No (or as good as no) changes." Thus no doubt remained that the dissolution of discrepancies meant complete restructuring of the police in East Berlin on the model of the West Berlin Police. The prescribed method was first to produce as good a description as possible of the two police organizations, which could then be compared in a detailed fashion in order to produce recommendations for overcoming the discrepancies, that is, for adjusting the People's Police as rapidly as possible to Western standards.

While the Western leadership of these working committees had thus clearly staked out the direction, participating Eastern officers still hoped that particular elements of the People's Police they thought were superior to those of the Western police could find their way into the unified Berlin Police. At the beginning of the constitutive meeting of the personnel committee, one Eastern officer pointed out in protest that unification in accordance with Article 23 was not yet finally sanctioned by the GDR parliament, and that the goal of these meetings should be "unification [*Vereinigung*] and not taking possession [*Vereinnahmung*]." One former Eastern officer expressed his disappointment about the course and final

48. The slow beginning of this planning process is quite surprising. Asked why the planning for unification started so late, a high-ranking western officer pointed to the particular situation of West Berlin. On the one hand, he explained, West Berlin was governed then by a coalition of Social Democrats and Greens, who favored a unification according to Article 146 of the Basic Law; thus, neither the mayor nor his minister of the interior were talking too much about unification at all. On the other hand, the sovereigns over Berlin were still the Allied powers, and the signals they were transmitting, especially from the French and the British security bureaus, were certainly not in favor of a quick unification. Thus he pointed out that from all the relevant sources the police got signs that there was still considerable time.

49. I had access to the documented proceedings of two of these working committees: uniformed police and personnel and training. All factual information is derived from these documents as well as from interviews with members of these groups.

outcome of the unification of the two Berlin police forces thus: "It still is a big disappointment for me. It is not so much that they weren't keeping anything of ours but that they refused to even think about their own structures, to probe into them to see whether they couldn't be improved." This disappointment arises because Westerners by and large did not accept Easterners as partners in deliberation. Even if they knew that the Berlin Police might have benefited from reforms, these reforms were not to be negotiated with members of the People's Police. It is also interesting to note that when Easterners and Westerners talked about the People's Police, they were at times talking past each other, because they were talking about the same organization but at different points in time. When Easterners spoke of the People's Police in these committee meetings, they were frequently referring to the organization that had already started to reform itself, which—at least to them—was no longer identical with the old GDR's People's Police, the organization that had beaten up peaceful demonstrators on 7 October 1990. Thus they intended to cast themselves as viable partners who had demonstrated their credibility by beginning to correct the errors of the past. When Westerners spoke about the People's Police, they still had in mind an organization that was lead by a Stalinist vanguard party. To them the changes that had been made were rather insignificant, since the People's Police was still basically working with the same personnel. At this point it became clear to most high-ranking People's Police officers that, contrary to their initial hopes, they would probably have no chance of being accepted into the service of the unified Berlin police force.

This tension between the expectations of Eastern and Western officers, signaling increasingly bleak prospects that high-ranking officers of the People's Police would find employment in the united police force, erupted by mid-August into a short skirmish between the police leaderships in the two parts of the city. In a letter to his Western counterpart, East Berlin's president of police expressed deep concern for the future of East Berlin's police officers in a united Berlin police force and found clear words to describe the increasingly depressed atmosphere among People's Police officers: "When in East Berlin police circles, the terms 'occupation' and 'annexation' are increasingly used to describe this [way in which the unification is handled], I have difficulties in finding counterarguments to this description." The reaction of Western officials to this letter bespeaks a considerable degree of irritation. West Berlin's minister of the interior even went so far as to demand the dismissal of East Berlin's president of police. In a patronizing, almost insulting letter to the minister of the interior of the GDR he voiced his concern that "parts of the new government of the GDR apparently care more about finding some hibernating space for former cadres responsible for the old regime than for the difficult lot of the general population tried in suffering."

The Berlin police were indeed quite worried about the possibility that former secret police employees might be hidden as "moles" in the People's Police by sympathetic police leaders. The West Berlin Police therefore made efforts to influence the personnel policy of the People's Police, actually demanding a complete stop to all new hiring and transfers. It also vigorously opposed the intention of the People's Police to establish the functions of press officer and legal advisor, because it feared that these might be prime hideouts for former Stasi employees. Moreover, the West Berlin Police were concerned about the possible destruction of personnel documents that would help them later to uncover possible connections between a particular officer and the Stasi. Thus the West Berlin Police not only assumed leadership in the preparation for unification but tried to influence the People's Police in a ways that betrayed already the future command of the West Berlin police authorities over the People's Police.

The working committees never got beyond step one of their comparative work: they never made any recommendations for the actual organization of the unification process. By the end of August, when the descriptive phase was nearing completion, the groups ceased to meet. It is probably not fortuitous that the end of the sessions coincided with the decision of the parliament of the GDR to accede to the FRG on 23 August and the conclusion of the Unification Treaty on 31 August. Not only had the joint working groups proved to be an unwieldy instrument, but they were no longer necessary: the West Berlin Police could now decide unilaterally, bound only by the Unification Treaty, how to organize unification (Scherz 1995, 48–49). What the West Berlin Police had gained from these working committees is a much more detailed understanding of the internal organization, personnel situation, equipment, buildings, and grounds of the People's Police. What had been achieved from the perspective of the West Berlin Police was a stock-taking of the People's Police (Scherz 1991, 15). This was especially important, since prior to that exercise the Western authorities knew precious little about their counterparts in the GDR. The possession of these data facilitated the actual planning of unification, which began in September, a short four weeks before the actual date for unification.

This does not mean, however, that the ministry of the interior in West Berlin then took decisive steps to plan unification; rather, the initiative came from within the police. Again a working group was formed which debated basically three models of unification (cf. Scherz 1991, 16–23; Scherz 1995, 48–57). The first model suggested was the immediate creation of Western structures in the East. This plan was abandoned quickly because it was deemed impossible to create these structures in the course of four weeks in such a way that they could actually carry out responsible police work. The second model discussed was one in which the existing five Western police districts would simply be pushed eastward in a way that would have divided the work equally among them. This plan was rejected because, in addition to the problem of incorporating the East into the existing police structure, it would also have stirred up the administration of the police in the West. Instead, the West Berlin Police favored a solution by which the three Western police districts bordering East Berlin would simply extend their jurisdiction into the territory of the eastern boroughs of what would then be united Berlin. This procedure had the advantage that established, well-oiled bureaucracies were taking over the responsibility for policing eastern Berlin. Simultaneously, the work of creating administrations for eventually independent eastern police districts was begun.

In order to guarantee that the (Western) law would be effectively enforced in the east, it was furthermore decided to transpose complete western leadership teams into all eastern precincts, backed up by a core of experienced western officers. This transfer of leadership was comprehensive: it ranged from the head of a precinct all the way down to the leaders of the patrol car shifts and their deputies. Higher leadership functions than those at the level of the precinct remained with the districts in the west due to their simple extension of jurisdiction eastward. This meant that at the point of unification, not a single eastern officer had even the smallest leadership role. This comprehensive takeover necessitated a considerable exchange of personnel. Effective with unification, 2,323 western officers were transferred to the east, while 2,700 eastern officers were shifted to the west.[50] The only competency that easterners were recog-

---

50. The unification of the Berlin Police preceded German unification by two days. The rationale behind this maneuver was simply to guarantee a unified, effective police command for the celebrations before and on the day of final unity. The police feared that right-wing demonstrators might spoil the celebrations in Berlin by associating unified Germany with its own ugly Nazi past in front of the cameras of TV networks from all over the world. Nothing would have been more damaging to the image of a newly united Germany. It seemed useful to prepare a strong police presence that would be able to quell any right-wing demonstrations as soon as they emerged.

nized for in these initial days was their intimate knowledge of eastern locations. All eastern officers still serving in the east were effectively reduced to piloting their new western superiors and colleagues through the maze of east Berlin's streets.

The Integration of the People's Police Officers into the (West) Berlin Police

The Unification Treaty between the GDR and the FRG contains provisions for the treatment of the civil servants of the GDR following unification. In particular it asserts the validity of the (West) German civil service laws for the five new states and east Berlin (Art. 20.II). It may be helpful therefore to describe the most salient features of the (West) German civil service system (Maunz, Dürig, Günter et al. 1963, 259–79). The central idea of the system is that sovereign acts of the state (such as arresting somebody or requesting personal identification) require particularly careful and trustworthy execution. Therefore, the state needs special employees, fully tenured civil servants *(Beamte),* who can be entrusted with the execution of sovereign acts of state (Art. 33.IV and V of the Basic Law). These employees owe the state professionalism and special loyalty (e.g., they must swear allegiance to the constitution, they may not go on strike, etc.), while the state answers to this special professional commitment and loyalty by special care (tenure; generous pension and health care plans; comprehensive, fully paid training programs). In addition to the fully tenured civil servant, there are other, untenured employees of the state *(Angestellte* and *Arbeiter)* for whom loyalty and care relations are not as stringent as for fully tenured employees. In principle, they should not perform sovereign state actions. Beyond this partition, the civil service is further divided into three hierarchically connected career paths: the "middle service" *(mittlere Laufbahn),* which for the police is the layer of uncommissioned officers; the "elevated service" *(gehobener Dienst),* which for the police is equivalent to the layer of commissioned officers; and the "higher service" *(höherer Dienst),* which for the police is the layer of staff officers. Each civil service job presupposes particular qualifications, which must be described in terms of tenure requirements, career path, and rank. Within these formal requirements, two kinds of qualifications are considered, personal qualifications and professional qualifications, and both must be satisfied if a candidate is to be considered eligible for a particular position.

Eastern officers' qualifications were checked by the (West) Berlin au-

thorities within these general provisions of the Civil Service Law, guided
by the provisions of the Unification Treaty. The Unification Treaty specifies (Annex 1, chapter 19) the conditions under which former civil servants of the GDR can be given notice of dismissal. Two main cases are
differentiated: regular notice *(ordentliche Kündingung,* which gives the
person dismissed certain rights; e.g., it is not effective immediately) and
immediate notice *(außerordentliche Kündigung).* Since immediate notice
involves the foreclosure of rights, the employee who is to be dismissed
in this way must be proven to be at considerable moral fault. For regular
notice, the treaty lists the following reasons: lacking professional or personal qualification; no need; and the dissolution of the office in which
the employee has worked so far. Reasons given for immediate notice are
all morally charged: violations of "the principles of humanity and the
rule of law" as specified in the universal declaration of human rights and,
furthermore, any activity for the former secret police of the GDR if for
that reason the employer cannot be expected to continue employment.

PERSONNEL SELECTION AFTER UNIFICATION. The (West) Berlin Police has
made extensive use of the provisions of the public service law as well as of
the Unification Treaty.[51] At unification, the Berlin Police had to integrate
roughly eleven thousand former employees of the People's Police into the
existing body of roughly twenty thousand western officers.[52] All former
People's Police officers were funneled through so-called personnel selection committees.[53] The goal of this selection process was stated to all
those who were asked to partake in it as follows:

> The goal of the personnel selection is to make a contribution to the
> creation and the preservation of a police force acting on the basis of
> the rule of law. This police force should be free from connections with
> the former secret police, achievement-oriented, and disinterested; it

51. The presentation in this section is based primarily on a series of documents
made available by the Ministry of the Interior of the state of Berlin (SennInn 1990a).
In addition, it draws on interviews with members of the personnel selection committees and union representatives.

52. The figure for the People's Police already reflects a distinction between police
officers in the more narrow western sense and fire, prison, and registration officers,
which in the GDR were an integral part of the People's Police. In the FRG, firefighting
and registration are handled by city governments, while prisons are a branch of the
state judicial administrations.

53. The procedure was somewhat different for all three career paths.

should have the confidence of the general population, and it should work to the greater benefit of the whole. (SennInn 1990c, 1)

This statement is replete with interesting identifications of the (West) Berlin Police and (by ellipsis) the former People's Police. What comes across is that the Berlin Police assume that the former People's Police officers pose a potential threat to the integrity of the Berlin Police. In this statement, (West) Berlin's Ministry of the Interior asserts what the (West) Berlin Police *is* and what the People's Police *was not:* acting on the rule of law, unconnected to dark powers, achievement-oriented, disinterested, trusted by the population, and working to the greater benefit of the whole.[54]

The personnel selection committees were composed of regular western members of the police, union representatives, and at least one consulting easterner.[55] The committees had to recommend whether or not to give an officer regular or immediate notice (and if so why), and they were also asked to recommend a career path and rank for officers deemed fit for continuing employment. The factual data that they used was gathered in a lengthy (twenty-six pages) questionnaire that all former People's Police officers had to fill out personally, as well as by a digest of the People's Police personnel files. First the committees assessed the professional qualifications of the officers. They were profiled according to the kinds and lengths of training they had received, the kinds of licenses and special permits they held (driving, pyrotechnical, flying, diving, etc.), and the experience, functions, locations where they had served, and ranks held in the People's Police. In order to make an informed recommendation regarding the future rank and function of the officers, training programs in the People's Police and the (West) Berlin Police were closely compared with each other, curriculum hour for curriculum hour (SennInn 1990b). The basis of the comparison was in all cases the (West) Berlin curriculum, and the aim of the comparison was to understand what part of this curriculum was covered by GDR training. Any training of GDR officers that went beyond the Berlin curriculum was deemed irrelevant (e.g., training in weaponry that the (West) Berlin police did not use). The results of this

54. In other parts of this document, which is intended as a guide for the members of the personnel selection committees, the GDR is identified with the same characteristics ascribed here to the People's Police. There is again the play of synecdochical identifications between the GDR as a whole and one of its executive parts, the People's Police.

55. The two main (Western) police unions fully supported the (West) Berlin Police in this personnel selection process.

comparison were predictable: the training of the officers in the People's Police was generally regarded as insufficient for reemployment at the same career-path level (SennInn 1990c, 6–9). Thus Eastern staff officers were considered comparable to Western commissioned officers; Eastern commissioned officers were reckoned on par with Western noncommissioned officers, and Eastern noncommissioned officers were not deemed fit for police service at all, except for those that could balance a lack of training by long-term experience in actual police service, which of course was the case for most of them. The reason why the Eastern training was considered so poor was not only the overall shorter training time, but especially its emphasis on Marxism-Leninism, which took up between 30 percent and 40 percent of the total teaching time. The importance of Marxism-Leninism was taken to correspond with a low emphasis on legal training. Eastern officers with both insufficient training and little or no experience were not offered employment as potentially tenured civil servants, but were instead offered employment as nontenured civil servants. This, however, excluded them automatically from active police duty, since police officers regularly perform sovereign acts of state and therefore have to be tenured employees.

The questionnaires and the personnel file digest focused not only on the *professional* qualifications of eastern officers; the *personal* qualifications were at least as interesting to the Berlin Police. Both questionnaire and digest were intended to provide a picture of the kind and depth of identification that the officers under scrutiny had with GDR state socialism. Any form of membership in socialist organizations (party, youth organizations, sports clubs, etc.) was used as a possible lead for a personal disqualification. What was at issue, however, was not membership per se (a very high percentage of the People's Police officers were members not only of the party but of all sorts of other socialist organizations); anything that could reveal an extraordinary commitment to socialist ideology was deemed of interest (SennInn 1990d, 1990c). Extraordinary commitment was supposed to show itself in activities which went beyond the minimum level ordinarily expected from police officers of particular ranks, such as voluntary service in special positions (serving as party secretary, etc.), or participation in special party training.[56] Special attention was also given to all former People's Police officers who had ever served in special functions thought to be entrusted only to those who had dem-

56. The SED maintained a system of schools offering training that ranged from extended weekend seminars to a full-blown university course.

onstrated the fullest possible commitment to party and state.[57] The most sensitive points, however, were any functions and duties an officer could have had which suggested a possible transgression of human rights. Any connection to the former secret police of the GDR, especially any direct activity for and on behalf of the Stasi, was deemed worth investigating, and all former People's Police officers were asked to reveal their Stasi contacts. As backup for the questionnaires, every member of the personnel selection committees had a list of activities which Berlin's Interior Ministry judged as "typically decisive" for the denial of further employment on active police duty.

The Berlin Police also exercised its right (granted in the Unification Treaty) to screen former People's Police officers for possible connections to the Stasi. This could be done by filing a formal investigation request at the Federal Office for Stasi Documents, the so-called "Gauck Office."[58] The Berlin Police informed all former People's Police officers that they would use their right to file an inquiry with the Gauck Office. Any discrepancies between the answers given by officers to items on the questionnaire and later documentation from the Gauck Office led to immediate dismissal for breach of trust. Many officers whose involvement with Stasi was minor, insufficient at least to be given immediate notice, were ultimately dismissed only because they had lied in their responses to the questions about Stasi contacts on the questionnaire. Others were dismissed in the course of time after inquiries at the Gauck Office launched by other institutions or persons, Stasi victims included, revealed compromising information about them. During my fieldwork in Köpenick alone, four officers were relieved of their duties for Stasi collaboration.[59] Since the files are still open, and many Stasi connections surface only in the context of other cases, still more dismissals may occur.

The Berlin Police has also dismissed every People's Police officer in the

57. These relations become apparent in the annotation to the questionnaire for the members of the personnel selection committees. Such special relations of trust were assumed, for example, for officers with special duties along the Wall, or for officers who had served in the units patrolling the transit routes from the FRG to Berlin.

58. This office is named after the Protestant minister and member of the GDR civil rights movement, Joachim Gauck, who has headed this office since 1990. Inquiries at the Gauck Office are regulated by a special legal code, the Law about Stasi Documents (Stasi-Unterlagen Gesetz).

59. The Berlin Police does not record the reasons why somebody leaves or is made to leave the police; therefore, no official figures about Stasi-related dismissals are available. From unofficial and incomplete figures, my estimate for the time period between 1990 to 1995 is that five hundred immediate notices were issued.

rank of colonel and above. Having held "leading parts . . . [in] the repressive apparatus," they were generally assumed to be personally unfit for further employment in a "democratic police organization based on the principle of the rule of law" (SennInn 1990c, 5). Of the staff officers of the People's Police who held the rank of lieutenant colonel, none is presently working in the Berlin Police in the rank of a staff officer. Regarding positions with command responsibilities, as of summer 1995 twenty-four former People's Police officers were serving as shift leaders (fifteen of them in the western part of the city).

The personnel selection procedures of the Berlin Police in reaction to party affiliations and Stasi contacts show a reasoning which is inclined towards what might be called a comprehensive "contamination model." Certain positions and functions within the organizational structures of the security apparatus of the GDR were identified as morally problematic. Everybody who performed those functions or held those positions, regardless of his actual activities, was at least under suspicion if not under verdict. The judgments of labor courts have over time corrected this procedure in the direction of a more action-oriented and hence more difficult process of proof. It is established by now that the determination of Stasi collaboration in the sense of the Unification Treaty is only made in cases of "conscious and goal-directed" activities for Stasi (cf. decisions of the Federal Court of Labor [Bundesarbeitsgericht] at Kassel, e.g., 8 AZR 656/92, 8 AZR 68/93).[60]

RETRAINING OF FORMER PEOPLE'S POLICE OFFICERS. In July 1990, three months before the official unification of Germany, the Berlin Police started a training program for officers of the People's Police.[61] The target groups of these training programs were then officers in medium and lower leadership positions, who were thought of as apt disseminators of their newly acquired knowledge. These initial training programs, or "basic seminars" *(Grundseminare)* as they became known in the jargon of the Berlin police academy, were designed to acquaint People's Police officers

60. The more specific legal situation has prompted the Ministry of the Interior of the state of Berlin to successively adjust its guidelines (see Senatsverwaltung für Inneres 1991, 1992, 1994).

61. The presentation in this section is based on documents provided by the Berlin police academy. They contain outlines of the courses, curricula, study materials, study guidelines for the former People's Police officers, and documents pertaining to the planning of the logic, the logistics, and the actual execution of these courses. Further data come from interviews with teachers in the courses of the Berlin police academy and from stories told about these courses by participants.

with the basic features of the law of the FRG, especially with state law, constitutional law, and police law. After unification, every former People's Police officer had to go through this seminar, which comprised four weeks of straight lectures.

The retraining efforts of the Berlin Police were (like personnel selection) based on the provisions of the Unification Treaty. The stated rationale for these training courses was the fact that, by the judgment of the Berlin Police, former People's Police officers did not have the necessary legal knowledge to fulfill their function as police officers in a democratic society. The proclaimed goal of the retraining program was, therefore, to bring the knowledge of the former People's Police officers closer to western standards. The Berlin Police hoped that limited theoretical training plus everyday practical experience in real-world circumstances would bring them eventually to the level of their western colleagues. On this basis, the Berlin Police mandated that every former People's Police officer take an additional year of further training, the so-called "one-year course" *(Jahreslehrgang)*.[62] The phrase is somewhat misleading; the course was designed to send the officers through a series of six lecture hours on forty-two days, usually on Friday mornings or afternoons, spread out in various blocs over the year. During the week they were active in regular police service. At the end, each officer had to pass an examination in several subjects. Only those who successfully passed the examination could finally be awarded the status of tenured employees, thus becoming full-fledged Berlin police officers.

* * *

On 3 October 1990 the (West) Berlin Police accepted exactly 10,775 former employees of the People's Police into its ranks.[63] Of these, 9,467 were members (i.e., they had a police rank and uniform), and 1,308 were civil employees. By 12 July 1995 exactly 5,115 of the originally 10,775 were

62. Some officers whose initial training within the GDR had particularly little police-specific content, such as officers serving in riot units of the People's Police, whose training followed basically a military model, were offered a two-year program.

63. This number does not include firefighters or employees of the registration and passport offices, who were part of the People's Police. In the FRG, firefighting and registration were under the auspices of city governments, whereas the police force was organized on the level of the state. This number has already been greatly diminished by dismissals and early retirements which took effect during the reform period of the GDR between November 1989 and the day of unification. The total number of people employed by the People's Police in Berlin is estimated at about twenty thousand.

still working for the Berlin Police—more than half of them had left police service. Of those remaining, 3,319 had become fully tenured civil servants; that is, 1,796 were nontenured employees. I know very little about the 5,660 who left the ranks of the police.[64] Roughly 900 of them took early retirement, probably 500 were discharged for secret police collaboration. This still leaves about 40 percent of the total unaccounted for. Some of them may have gladly left the police as they saw other opportunities; some may have left because they did not want to serve in the police force of their former class enemy; still others might have left because they saw no future in the Berlin Police (e.g., they thought that they would never be eligible for promotions, or would only find employment in inferior positions, or would be preemptively dismissed for Stasi collaboration); still others may have felt daunted by the need to adjust to the new work environment, to go to school again, to learn new ways. In any case, they are witness to the dramatic transformation undergone by eastern Germany after unification, even in relatively well-protected areas such as the civil service.

Conclusions

Identifications do not only take place in everyday encounters; they are also a property of public discourse and of institutionalized action. Some identifications assume the role of cultural forms. As such, they get picked up in one context to be modified and used in another. In this chapter I have described a remarkable similarity among the interactional forms of sole representation, of the unification of Germany by accession under the provisions of Article 23 of the Basic Law, and of the organization of the unification of the Berlin Police. They are similar in that they identify the west as the real Germany, the model, the reference point, the telos of adjustment, while they identify the east as deficient, as needing change and adjustment. The relationships among these three sets of identifications do not follow a simple causal pattern, but they are related metaphorically, produced by countless mimetic processes. There is no necessary link between the three processes of German-German relations seen in the model of sole representation, of national unification under the pro-

64. Many of the former officers I met who were kind enough to grant me an interview were working in financial services; they had become insurance brokers or were working for credit agencies. Others were employed by private security firms. A few had become entrepreneurs, running their own businesses.

visions of Article 23, and in the unification of the two Berlin police forces: All of them could have been at greater variance from each other. Nothing in 1949 predetermined that unification would proceed under the provisions of Article 23 rather than those of Article 146 (for obviously both had been envisioned as possible avenues by members of the Parliamentarian Council), and if history had taken a different course, there might not have been a German unification at all (for a host of possible reasons).[65]

Police unification might also have differed more from the process followed on the national level. That it did not is all the more remarkable if it is taken into account that there was very little immediate influence from the national level on the planning of the unification process of the Berlin Police. At no point were clear political directives issued regarding how to unify the Berlin Police. Western officers planned the unification with very little direct political guidance. At no point was there any contingency planning along the lines of "If the federal government decides to do this, then we must do that with the police." Rather, after the Unification Treaty was published, the unification process continued as it had begun several months earlier. It must be kept in mind that no legal guidelines were available by the beginning of July when the working committees were constituted; the West Berlin Police decided how to proceed with unification. The planning of national unification and the planning of the Berlin Police unification were parallel processes. This is not to deny that the planning of both processes took place in the context of a national debate about unification, nor is it to deny that information was exchanged between those considering the right procedure for unifying Berlin's two police forces and those working in Bonn on the details of the Unification Treaty. Such contacts were far too informal to produce fully compatible results, however.

What seems to be at work here is that common origins existed for the planning of the unification processes of both Germany and the Berlin Police. On the one hand both were made possible by the election results of 18 March, when the GDR electorate endorsed a leadership which opted for quick adjustment of the GDR to the FRG rather than for a leadership which proposed negotiation of a new common state. On the other hand, those origins go all the way back to 1949, when the Parlia-

65. Support for unification as a political goal, at least among West Germans, diminished over time; it was also less popular among younger people. If the same is true for East Germans (for whom there are no data), unification might have vanished as an issue altogether. Perhaps unification would then have come in the form discussed by many West German politicians: the form of an overall European rapprochement.

mentarian Council presumed to speak also for "those who could not partake" in its meetings, thus laying the foundation for a pattern of German-German relations which emphasized the superiority of the West, not only in political decisions or legal battles, but in millions of individual experiences and the stories derived from them. At the moment when unification became available as a historical option, the superior-to-inferior relationship between West and East was a foregone conclusion for almost all West Germans and a majority of East Germans.

What seems to have unified those Westerners working in Bonn and in Berlin to plan, respectively, the unification of Germany and of the Berlin Police is what Wittgenstein (1984, 356, §241, 242) has called "agreement in judgment," which is in his terms constitutive of a "life form." In other, more sociologically common (if also more easily misleading) words, what seems to be at work here is a cultural understanding among many West Germans concerning the proper relationship between the FRG and the GDR—an understanding mirrored by a compatible understanding among a large number of East Germans. I do not refer here to culture as a rule or as a determining factor, but to culture as carried by symbolic forms embedded in countless stories and institutionalized in various ways that are connected by a variety of metaphorical links or, as Wittgenstein (1984, 278, §67) would have said, "family resemblances."

The series of metaphorical links produced by countless mimetic processes does not end here, however. How these metaphorical links extend into the most minute, everyday interactions between westerners and easterners is among the topics of the following chapters.

THREE

Times Ajar

"There the clocks tick differently" *(Dort gehen die Uhren anders)* is an expression frequently used by east and west Germans to summarize their impression of the other half of the country in a simple, yet powerful formula. "There the clocks tick differently" seems to be equally common on both sides of the former Wall, carrying comparable emotional connotations. It is a fairly standard German idiom which is typically used to denote difference in lifestyle, especially in the pace of life. It is, for example, used to capture the difference of life's pace in historical succession. Thus, older people might say, "*Then* the clocks were *still* ticking differently" while remembering their own youth. The expression is also employed in juxtaposing country and city, small town and urban metropolis. In cross-national comparisons, "There the clocks tick differently" is used to point out differences in mentality between various European countries, or between developing countries and a generalized Europe. Frequently, the expression carries some center-periphery connotations, but the emotive and evaluative meanings of its usage are by no means fixed. Depending on the context, it may be suffused with nostalgia, poisoned with contempt, brimming with admiration, or echoing deep anxiety and confusion; it is even employed to ironize times and places, own and other.

I want to investigate in this chapter how east and west Germans use notions of time to identify each other. The widespread use of the expression "There the clocks tick differently" by easterners and westerners in reference to the other part of the country implies the experience of a contemporaneity of different times in unified Germany. After a brief introduction to the theory of temporal modes of identification, I show in the first substantive part of this chapter how identifications lead to a temporal division of the country into an advanced west and a backward east. The second part discusses how ideas about the progression of lives and careers and the influence of unification on these ideas figure in identifications of self and other among easterners and westerners. The third and final part describes how easterners use their experience of continuity and discontinuity during the time spanning the demise of the GDR and subsequent unification as a means to identify themselves.

Temporal Identifications

Identifications frequently connect selves to a past which is owned or disowned, or to a future which can be desired or abhorred. However, the framework of tropes and emplotments I have used until now to analyze identifications does not take proper account of the ways in which selves exist in time. Tropes and emplotments become temporal only on the basis of a narrative. It is the concept of narrative then, which needs to be introduced here as the primary vehicle of temporal identifications. The second concept used to analyze the ways in which selves are linked to time is Fabian's (1983) notion of allochronism which I will discuss in contrast to narrative.

Selves in Time: Narrative

Ricoeur (1984) argues that the temporal form of human experience is narrative: as far as phenomenological time is concerned, narrative constitutes time, and time narrative. In other words, the experiencing person *is* temporal *in* narrative,[1] and the form in which selves are temporal in narratives is character. Through the notion of character, selves can be identified with their own pasts and futures, and thus the notion of character allows selves to be conceived as self-identical in time. However, it also allows self to remain identical while changing.[2] To shed light on this

---

1. In this sense, the theory of narrative is an important extension of Heidegger's work. Heidegger (1986) has argued that the meaning of being is temporality, and he has suggested that this meaning is constituted by comprehending both the temporality of understanding and by assessing life in light of possible alternative life paths from the vantage point of one's own death. Yet Heidegger has remained silent about exactly how this movement proceeds. The theory of narrative can fill this gap.

2. This developmental conception of character is epitomized in the literary genre of *Entwicklungsroman*.

seemingly paradoxical aspect of character, Ricoeur (1992, 2–3) introduces the distinction between what he calls "idem-identity," a recognition
of self as the same across time and "ipse-identity," the qualification of
self through predication. In the language of identifications this means that
Ricoeur distinguishes between identifications of self with itself in time
and identifications of self and the world at large.

The intriguing aspect of Ricoeur's theory of self-constitution is his idea
to conceive the constitution of character as a dialectic between "ipse-
identity" and "idem-identity" through narrative plot. The problem of
bridging difference poses itself in the same way in narrative as it does,
according to Burke, in rhetoric. For Ricoeur (1992, 140) narrative plot
is characterized by synthesis:

> I propose to define discordant concordance, characteristic of all narra-
> tive composition, by the notion of the synthesis of the heterogeneous.
> By this I am attempting to account for the diverse mediations per-
> formed by the plot: between the manifold of events and the temporal
> unity of the story recounted; between the disparate components of the
> action—intentions, causes, and chance occurrences—and the sequence
> of the story; and finally, between pure succession and the unity of
> the temporal form, which in extreme cases, can disrupt chronology to
> the point of abolishing it.

Characters get identified in narrative first and foremost with their own
selves at other points in time, but then they also get identified with the
actions they perform, with the actions of others they have to endure, and
with their own experiences; they get connected to other characters,
places, times, ideas, and objects. Through these identifications with the
world, their permanence and their change, self can recognize itself as self-
identical (cf. Arendt 1958), and it is only through this self-recognition
that identifications with the world make sense. Thus self-recognition
across time, self-sameness, and the meaning of self, that is, identity as
contextualization of self in the world, mutually constitute each other. For
Ricoeur, it is narrative plot which creates this most intricate, multifaceted
play of identifications of the self with itself and with the world. The power
of narrative thus consists, on the one hand, in its enormous ability to
connect many diverse elements such as ideas, relationships, and emotions
to selves, so that it organizes a multitude of identifications into a structured whole. On the other hand, the power of narrative plot consists in
the creation of self-transcendence in time. Narrative plot, according to
Ricoeur, serves as a temporal tracking system through which selves can

recognize themselves as the same while changing all along. In other words, selves at two points in time are connected by a story of being and changing. Easterners and westerners make extensive use of narrative, as I will show, to identify each other as inhabitants of discordant times, to discuss the progression of their lives and careers, and to manage continuities and discontinuities in the face of sweeping changes.

Temporal Displacements of Selves: Allochronism

In an influential critique of ethnographic writing, Fabian (1983) has described techniques of ethnographic object construction. He criticizes ethnography for "denying coevalness" to its object, the people whose life ethnography purports to portray and to analyze. Fabian defines coevalness as "synchronous contemporaneity,"[3] which is the basis for all meaningful dialogue (30–32). Following the hermeneutic tradition (e.g., Gadamer 1993, 207–15; Buber 1995), Fabian insists that dialogue must be based on an open encounter, potentially leading to a self-transformatory experience (cf. Bakhtin 1984a).[4] This is only possible, however, if the other is not merely *encountered* at the same time (i.e., is synchronous), but is also *treated* as an inhabitant of the same time (i.e., is contemporaneous).[5] Fabian uses the term *allochronism* to describe the denial of coevalness, that is, the transposition of the other into another time. In the terminology of this study, allochronism is then a form of oppositional temporal identification which connects at least two sets of human beings and their worlds with disjunct periods of time. Fabian's anthropologists allochronize by rooting themselves and their profession in "modernity," while simultaneously relegating their "natives" and the worlds in which

3. Why this expression is not redundant should become apparent in the next few lines.

4. One might argue that Fabian was among those who prepared the emerging critical discourse on ethnographic writing to give a warm reception of Bakhtin's "dialogism" (Holquist 1990), which holds at least a promise for overcoming some of the apparent shortcomings of ethnographic writing styles, which are in turn taken to be indicative of a problematic epistemology. Many interesting correspondences exist between Fabian and Bakhtin; Bakhtin often seems to provide the answer to problems unearthed by Fabian. Consider, for example, Fabian's forceful rejection of relativism as a technique "circumventing coevalness" (Fabian 1983, 38ff.) and Bakhtin's development of the notion of "polyphony" (1984a, chap. 1).

5. It could be argued that the former is the necessary condition for dialogue; the latter is the sufficient condition.

they live to that vast expanse of time deemed "traditional." By thus producing a radical rift between ethnographers and the people they study, allochronism has, according to Fabian, made anthropology a collaborator of oppression, because it potentially allows for a dehumanization of the other, who, displaced in time, no longer needs to be regarded as an equal, a partner to be engaged in dialogue. Allochronism favors a view of the other as an object which can be instrumentalized within one's own schemes.[6]

A more detailed view of what allochronism is and how it works can be generated by contrasting it with narrative. In its juxtaposition of disjunct times, allochronism is static and mostly concerned with states of being and their hierarchical ordering; it thrives on the creation of distance. Narrative, however, is eminently dynamic and chiefly interested in the process of becoming; thus narrative can be a means to bridge distance by connecting points in time. Where narrative focuses on character, the self-same change of selves relying on metaphorical transformations, allochronism concentrates on the metonymic relationship between selves and human categories. Where narrative emphasizes continuity, allochronism stresses discontinuity. Although both narrative and allochronism can be used as techniques to divide human beings into distinct groups, the ways in which they project the relationships between these groups are very different.

Answering to misgivings like Fabian's that social scientists postulate too much of a disjuncture between their own practices as scientists and the practices of everyday life, *practical* discourses have been used to gain insights for *theoretical* discourses by a process of parallelization (Bourdieu 1977; Herzfeld 1987). The attempt to mirror theory and practice in each other should also be open to the reverse possibility: The strategies of social scientists enacted in their theoretical discourses can find a counterpart in the everyday practices of their subjects. In other words, the metatheory of social sciences (the genre in which Fabian writes) should be gainfully employable as a theory of everyday practice. In what follows I use Fabian's metatheoretical concept of allochronism to make sense of how easterners and westerners relate to each other or, better perhaps, keep each other at arm's length.

6. Fabian's concept of allochronism is in many ways a generalized form of Said's (1978) notion of orientalism, a mode of radical othering employed by Europeans and North Americans in relation to the people they have conquered and colonized around the world.

The Temporal Divisions of United Germany

East and west Germans make extensive use of both allochronism and narrative to identify each other temporally. Frequently, narrative identifications are grafted on top of allochronic ones. This mix of modes of temporal identifications makes, as I will argue, for a very peculiar technique of othering which is, unlike Said's orientalism (1978), not radical, but rather developmental. The following subsections address the questions of how westerners temporally identify easterners, how easterners react to these identifications, and why they react as they do.

Western Allochronizations of the East

Westerners behave much as do Fabian's anthropologists in their temporalizations of the east: they displace easterners into the past. One typical western way to describe visits to the east is in terms of a time journey. The east is presented as a west pushed back several decades in time. Westerners say, for example, "There the time stood still," or "It is like the west but thirty years ago." This is sometimes also followed by a projection of the east into the future. These projections take the form of a discovery of potential that could be developed. Chancellor Kohl and the CDU in the GDR went into the general elections of 18 March 1990 by promising the people in the highly polluted industrial heartland of the GDR "blooming meadows and industrial landscapes within three years." Police officers see the villa neighborhoods of Köpenick, for example, as potential competitors for those of Zehlendorf (the wealthiest borough in the west). These future projections are often initiated by exclamations like "This can be made into something," and "Just wait and see how this will look in ten, fifteen years," followed by a detailed narrative of what precisely would have to be done to turn the homes in Köpenick into spitting images of those in Zehlendorf.

The east is thus considered as thoroughly backward, but also as placed on a trajectory that must ultimately lead to where west Germans stand today. This way, historical development is conceived as a single road that everyone must travel, while people do in fact stand on discernibly different segments of that very road. "There the clocks tick differently" admits in this sense to a simultaneous existence of different times which are all connected by a linear developmental path. The signs employed by western officers to discern backwardness range from the state of buildings ("unkept," "unrestored," "still marked by the war!") and infrastructure ("crumbling!"), to personal and governmental attitudes towards the environment ("predatory"), authority ("submissive"), and foreigners ("hostile"), and to dressing styles ("provincial"). They are the inverse of what many west Germans take as an achievement in their own development of the last thirty years: reconstruction, modern infrastructure, a changed, more protective attitude towards the environment, and a more cosmopolitan outlook on life in general marked by a more critical attitude to authority, tolerance toward things foreign, and a more aesthetic lifestyle.[7]

Western officers frequently sensualize their diagnosis of eastern backwardness in a totalizing olfactory image by summarizing these "anachronisms" as "fug" *(Mief)*, invoking the sensation of bad, used-up air which should long ago have been exchanged for a breeze of innovation. *Mief* is, I should note here, also a temporal marker in West German history.[8] It was used widely by the student movement at the end of the 1960s to denote the old Germany that the protesting students wanted to have exchanged for a fresher, more cosmopolitan, more liberal version of itself. Thus, identifying something as *Mief* (noun) or *miefig* (adjective) has the power to move back in time to a point definitely predating 1968.[9] What is used in identifications between easterners and westerners is by and large what Fabian calls "typological time," the compartmentalization of linear, historical time into various stages that can then be juxtaposed to each other in a totalizing fashion. Easterners are thus identified by westerners as inhabitants of another time, further behind on the road.

Underpinning westerners' allochronization of the east is a narrative of

7. With the help of these allochronizations, easterners and westerners are not only linked with different periods of time, but two entire networks of opposing metonymic relations are established which can then function as a code facilitating easy placement. Thus, temporal identifications can be converted into spatial ones and vice versa.

8. *Mief* is just the kind of linguistic indicator about which Fabian (1983, 75) observes, "In fact, expressions that have a clear temporal referent (a date, a time span, an indication of past, present, or future) are probably less important, quantitatively as well as qualitatively, than those whose temporalizing function derives from the context in which they are used." Fabian's examples in the anthropological literature are *savagery, kinship* (1983, 75), and *neolithic, archaic, mythical, ritual,* and *tribal* (1983, 30).

9. 1968 is considered to be the apex of student unrest. The whole generation which demanded changes then is called the "sixtyeighters" *(Achtundsechziger)*. In 1969 a coalition government under the charismatic leadership of chancellor Willy Brandt was elected, gradually absorbing the student movement into the Social Democratic party and its followers, leaving a radicalized group which turned to terrorism in the 1970s. The year 1968 certainly stands for a cultural revolution in Germany.

development. In principle, this is an understanding of their own historical development which is then projected onto the east. The western past is thus metonymically identified with the eastern present, and the eastern future with the western present. Since most westerners understand their own development as one of improvement, the look backward at their own past/easterner's present is a glance at an inferior state, which is accordingly characterized most suitably in satirical identifications. Satire is thus used again as a bond among westerners in celebration of their common achievement, and it is used to put easterners in an inferior place. Conversely, looking forward from the western past/eastern present, the narrative of transformation is emplotted in terms of a romance. Through this romance, westerners reconfirm with each other their positive commitment to the present while inviting easterners to identify with them over a shared espousal of a common value: the desirability of (western) Germany as it is and thus the proclamation of western Germany as the model for Germany as a whole.

The effect of westerners' allochronizing identifications of easterners can also be expressed in terms of tropes. The negative identification of easterners as nonwesterners ("They are not like us") is not simply the negation of a metonymic identification and thus the denial of membership in the same category (as the same identification uttered by easterners about westerners in all likelihood would be); rather it is the negation of a metaphorical identification which inverts westerners' positive self-identification into its opposite (advanced/backward, rebuilt/still war-damaged, cosmopolitan/provincial, etc.). However, since this opposite is the westerners' own past, the negative metaphorical identification "They are not like us" implies a positive metaphorical identification by calling upon easterners to assimilate themselves to westerners. One could almost say that it is the negative metaphorical identification which produces a prescriptive narrative of change. Negative metonymic or synecdochical identifications could never generate a narrative in the same way. What this example of the functioning of negative identifications shows again is how important it is to differentiate between different modes of identifications: their meanings are markedly different.

Eastern Reactions to Western Allochronizations

The easterner's version of "There the clocks tick differently" is, in contrast to the satiric identifications of the westerners, mostly tragic, thus inviting solidarity in their own misfortune. Typical eastern reactions to

western identifications of eastern backwardness point out that the reparation burdens easterners had to face were much higher than those of
westerners. They explain that the GDR was cut off from the world market
and could not afford costly raw materials. They point out that the GDR
had to sell all its best products abroad to earn hard currency. Thus easterners narrate the backward appearance of the GDR as a product of scarcity tragically impeding infrastructure development. By and large, therefore, the reaction of easterners to western allochronizations is defensive:
they usually acknowledge the gap westerners diagnose by explaining how
this gap has come about in historical development. In other words, easterners almost become something like co-conspirators in their own allochronization.

This reaction of easterners directs attention to the incompleteness of
Fabian's investigations. While he considers the fact that the locutionary
act of ethnographic writing (the writing itself) has an illocutionary corre-
late (the intention of the writing) in the objectification (and potential dehumanization) of the other, he does not take into account what effect
allochronic identifications might have on the other who is thus temporally
displaced. To put it differently, he is not offering a perlocutionary perspective.[10] The circle of communication that he himself invokes with the
notion of dialogue remains therefore strangely incomplete. The fact, however, that on the level of ethnographic writing there is precious little left
of a dialogue in Bakhtin's (1984a), Gadamer's (1993), or Buber's (1995)
sense does not mean that there is no exchange of information.[11] Writing
on Greece in allusion to Fabian's concept of allochronization, Herzfeld
(1991, 273 n. 6) writes, "The hegemony of 'Western'[12] discourse is nowhere more successful than in those places and cultural topoi, such as
Greece, in which its bearers persuade the local population to internal-
ize it to their own disadvantage." This is a pretty accurate statement

---

10. The terminology I use here is that of Austin's (1962) speech-act theory. The
locutionary act pertains to the enunciation of a verbal utterance; the illocutionary
act alludes to the intention connected with the utterance; and the perlocutionary act
finally takes into account the fact that intention and actual effect are not identical.
All three acts share in the production of meaning through the verbal utterance.

11. A possible starting point for presenting a perlocutionary perspective would
be Frantz Fanon's *The Wretched of the Earth,* or perhaps any work dealing with
Third World terrorism in industrialized countries. Terrorism might be read as an
attempt of the allochronized other to bomb his or her way back into the allochron-
izer's time in order to make himself or herself felt.

12. Note the attempt to withdraw possible allochronization through single quotation marks, for "Western" does indeed carry strong temporal connotations.

about the perlocutionary effects of western allochronic identifications, if "western"[13] is substituted for " 'Western,' " and "east Germany" for "Greece."

The question which thus occurs is, How it is possible that the allochronized partake in their own temporal displacement? Why do east German police officers get co-opted into the western schemes of distemporalization and ultimately denial of equality? To answer this question, it is helpful to look at the manner in which easterners temporally identify themselves in relation to the west. The reciprocal use of the idiom "There the clocks tick differently" suggests that eastern officers also allochronize.[14] Thus I explain first how acceptance has come about to show, then, how and why easterners reverse western allochronizations. The answer to the puzzle of acceptance lies, in a nutshell, in the use of the same *formal* set of allochronization criteria by westerners and easterners, a practice which has put easterners at a severe disadvantage.

The narratives of east Berliners' first visits to west Berlin after the fall of the Wall are full of pointers to an acute perception of a different pace of life. Almost invariably they describe west Berlin as fast, as hectic and restless, and *therefore* also as chaotic, disorderly, and ultimately aggressive. One of them said, "I thought that the Wessis had all unlearned walking normally; they were all running." In these narratives the sigh after the return to the east is quite audible (literally so on many of the interview tapes), a sigh that is the watershed between this other Berlin and their own, which is perceived relative to the west as calm and orderly. Through the classical attributes of speed and chaos, which resonate with typical country-city juxtapositions, the west is identified as the more modern part and therefore transposed into the future. Likewise, the east is sentimentally and tragically identified as a shelter, but one which will in all likelihood not withstand the encroachments of modernity: Easterners express the clear expectation that the days of the calm east are numbered. While this picture of the west works mostly with negative evaluations, it does also invoke positive elements. The more modern west is also perceived

13. The word "western" is not yet temporalized to the same extent that "Western" is, so the single quotation marks are not necessary here.

14. While westerners typically identify the east as an inferior past, however, most easterners have originally identified the west as a desirable future, thus basically mirroring westerners' allochronization strategy. Nevertheless, although westerners' allochronizations of the east have only gradually relaxed since unification, easterners have begun to undermine them.

as the place where things happen, the locale of higher liveliness, nicer cafés, better movie theaters—the place of opportunity. Of course, in Berlin the scales are slowly balancing out if not tipping in some respect towards the east.

This post-Wall eastern perception of west Berlin is heightened by a shift of perspective from pedestrian to driver. Easterners told me many stories of how they found themselves lost in much heavier traffic, inundated by the much bigger and faster cars of the Wessis. The driver's perspective, however, also reveals like no other the desirable aspects of the more progressive, more modern west. While western traffic was experienced as anxiety-arousing, western cars were admired; they were the objects of intense eastern desires. Accordingly, most eastern officers went to purchase a new, faster, bigger car as soon as possible.

Technology and Wealth as Measures of Progress

Many easterners describe their lives in newly united Germany as paced by a sequence of car ownership: from a Trabbi (the standard GDR car) to a Wartburg (the GDR higher-end car), a western used car, and finally to a new western car. This narrative is in effect a romantic tale of progress espousing two connected sets of values. The outlined series of cars connotes progress along the lines of technology (the latest model is always assumed to be technically superior to its predecessor) as well as along the lines of economic wealth (the latest model being always the most expensive one ever purchased). Police officers are, perhaps to nobody's surprise, especially fond of technology. Eastern police officers in their tales about the aftermath of unification describe at great length how much fun they had using western equipment, which they quickly acknowledged as more advanced, as technologically superior to their old People's Police equipment. The first opportunity to drive a western patrol car or to use a western computer is for many of them a memorable event. Likewise, westerners remember with a mixture of vexation and amusement how they encountered Eastern technology. They remember countless incidents in which Eastern patrol cars, telephones, and radios proved their hopeless backwardness, their utter insufficiency. Many western officers simply could not get themselves to put up with the Russian-made Lada patrol cars of the former People's Police and deliberately set out to destroy them through what they called "challenging usage."

The westerners' denigration of Eastern technology was not easy for

Figure 15. Changes in car ownership: East Germany's standard car, the "Trabbi" (in front) and a West German standard car (back) in a Potsdam side street. Author's photo.

easterners to take, since the same objects that were now satirized as backward were until recently often the pride of the members of the People's Police (figs. 15, 16). Their Lada patrol cars were not just any Ladas, but souped-up versions especially adapted to the needs of the police (e.g., they could take curves much faster than ordinary models could). These Ladas too, reflected the latest developments, and they were better than the patrol cars used before. In short, they too were a sign of progress.

In countless stories about their own careers, both eastern and western police officers fondly recall the technology they were using at different points in time. These memories are the officers' testimony to the glory of technological progress. They are filled with pride about the chance to use the most current technology, often long before any of their friends could get their hands on it. However, they also satirize the equipment of earlier times by explaining at length what tricks they had to use to make it work reasonably, how cumbersome it was to use, or how unreliable it was in

Figure 16. Former People's Police standard patrol car in new Berlin Police coat (1995). Author's photo.

practice. All this is told from a present perspective in which technology is smoother, more handy, more reliable, simply better.[15]

For both eastern and western police officers, the arrival of new technology is a long-awaited event that is greeted with much excitement. Since new arrivals are never available at the same time for everyone, turn-taking becomes an important issue. Few things seem to have bothered western police officers working in the east more than having to put up with eastern technology at first, and then with western equipment "that was not exactly brand-new either," as some of them said in venting their frustration. Many western officers who serve in the east expressed the opinion that they, who for so long had to deal with inferior technology, should have been first in line for the newest, the latest the Berlin Police could

15. The description of old technology remains satirical and does not slip into nostalgia because of its clear, unequivocal endorsement of modern technology as superior. This does not mean that in the discussion of older technology nostalgia cannot have a part. What typically is nostalgic is their memory of their own skill, their mastery of the more-difficult-to-use technology. Nostalgia also tends to emerge through the identification of a technology with other aspects of a particular time (e.g., a car or a motorbike of a particular type becomes a symbol of the time in which they were young, healthy, full of ambition, and in love).

offer. Many of them stated that they would have considered preferred access to the latest technology as a reward for what they see as their sacrifice for the reconstruction efforts in the east.

A quick look at the coffee table books in which both police organizations present themselves and their history tells a similar story. Besides documenting changes in uniform fashions, they are filled with plates displaying a continuing series of the newest patrol cars, the latest radio equipment, and more advanced weaponry. The emphasis is decidedly not on a depiction of police practices or typical situations but on technology and technology in use.[16] Technology does in this sense become a marker of time, or more precisely of what Fabian (1983, 23) has called "typological time." A particular type of patrol car brackets a whole mini-epoch of police history. Within such a mini-epoch, time seems not to move at all; instead, time seems to leap in discrete steps from one such mini-epoch to another.

Historical accounts too, especially those of the People's Police (MdI 1987),[17] read like progress reports. In these official historical accounts the movement of time is also steplike, but the markers are not generations of technology, but major political campaigns highlighted or proclaimed by the party conferences of the Sozialistische Einheitspartei Deutschlands (SED).[18] These party conferences themselves were embedded in the Marxist philosophy of historical progress on the way from capitalism through socialism to communism. In the *History of the People's Police* (MdI 1987) the fifth party congress is summarized thus:

> The fifth Party Congress of the SED, in session between July 10 and July 16, 1958, in Berlin, could declare that the laborer and farmer power of the GDR[19] has attained significant progress in the institution-

16. Of course, practices are also a lot more difficult to capture in a picture, and often enough they center around a new technical device. But frequently technology does not change practices, yet it is depicted all the same.

17. Every East German officer owned a copy of the *History of the People's Police (Geschichte der Deutschen Volkspolizei)*. That does not mean that they had read it, but it shows the effort made by the People's Police to create a historical consciousness that followed a more official understanding of time.

18. Party conferences were originally scheduled every four years; after 1971 they took place every five years. All eleven party conferences between 1949 and 1985 figure in chapter headings in *History of the People's Police* (MdI 1987).

19. "Laborer and farmer power" is a title that is frequently used to denote the party/state of the GDR. The People's Police accordingly is described as involved in the "struggle for the reliable protection of the first laborer and farmer power on German soil" (MdI 1987, 1: 5).

alization of socialism thanks to the forceful cooperation of the socialist states. It confirmed the policy of institutionalizing socialism. . . . and decided to complete the transitional period on the way from capitalism to socialism during the next few years. (1: 289)

The party congresses not only located the position of the GDR on an objective axis of historical development, but they were also concerned with a much more tangible form of progress: economic growth, as well as the supply of the population with consumer goods. On these accounts, party congresses not only celebrated achievements to date, but they also spun a romantic, future-oriented narrative. Following the example of the Soviet Union (Hough and Fainsod 1979, chaps. 6 and 7; Gregory and Stuart 1981, chap. 10), the party congresses of the 1950s and 1960s expressed tremendous optimism about catching up with the West and surpassing it. The Soviet Union set out to surmount the United States, the GDR ventured to overtake the FRG (Weber 1991). Thus time was measured in economic progress, not only in the capitalist West, but also in socialist Eastern Europe, and perhaps nowhere more so than in the GDR, where economic achievements could easily be compared with those of the other Germany.

The idea of measuring time by economic progress is reflected in the police officers' life histories, which in some ways quite literally take the form of accounting. Many of them, easterners and westerners alike, can recall their precise salaries at various stages of their careers. They also remember the prices of staple items they used to purchase at different times. The price of a roll might just as easily be retrieved from memory as the rent for their apartments or rooms, and the sum paid for their first motorcycle or car. Taken together, prices and income paint a picture of their purchasing power at several points in their lives. While price increases are naturally deplored (and inflation is therefore yet another measure of time),[20] the officers point out that their incomes have usually risen faster than prices. Their biographical narratives are thus also timed by progress in economic well-being, and their life paths have accordingly been planned on the assumption that gradually they could afford ever more.

Easterners were quite aware of the fact that along both measures of progress, technology and economic well-being, the GDR had fallen behind the FRG. While the West had become in the imagination of many

---

20. Time periods may also be marked by prices: in "the good old times," a roll only cost this much and a tram ticket that much.

easterners something of an Eldorado, many police officers say that the
visible difference between wealth in the GDR and the FRG still came as
something of a shock to them. Much of what they had seen on Western
TV was discarded as propaganda, just as most of what they heard and
saw on Eastern TV was identified as make-believe. One eastern officer
told me that after the fall of the Wall he traveled to the shooting location
of his favorite Western TV show, a series of detective stories set in the
industrial heartlands of the Rhein-Ruhr area.[21] He said that he was surprised that things looked there just as he had seen them on TV: the streets
were in good condition, the houses were quite nice, and even the old villas
actually looked just as pretty as they had appeared on TV. Another officer, summarizing his first visit to West Berlin just after the Wall had come
down, explained that the relative wealth of the West did indeed generate
a sense of betrayal in him.

Mostly, easterners came back from their excursions to the west with
an even more acute feeling of relative backwardness; by and large, they
admired the technology and the wealth of the FRG. Westerners, in contrast, came back from their excursions to the GDR or, later, the five new
states with the feeling that "they were much farther behind us than I
actually thought," as one officer put it. The GDR was reputed to be the
most economically advanced of eastern European countries. East Germans were nicknamed "the red Prussians," and the GDR was frequently
said to be perhaps the only country where iron discipline was used to
make central planning work in an exemplary fashion. Many western
officers had formed an image of the People's Police as a perfectly running, perfectly equipped, well-trained organization because they assumed that, just as the U.S.S.R. had put most of its economic and technological prowess into defense, the GDR had put its very best, most
advanced technology in the service of state security. The actual encounter with eastern Germany for the most part destroyed these
images of the relative advancement of the GDR and its police force.[22]
In sum, then, the relative perception of technological development and
economic wealth did exacerbate allochronic identifications of east and

21. For those familiar with German TV, the series referred to is *Tatort,* with its
hero, detective Horst Schimanski of the Duisburg police, broadcast on ARD (one of
the two government-sponsored TV networks in Germany).

22. Actually, a fierce public debate did erupt about who was to blame for that
(in hindsight) unrealistic image of the relative advancement of the GDR. Left-wing
intellectuals in particular were blamed for having produced a completely misleading
picture of the GDR.

west which existed on both sides even before the Wall had come down. The notion of technological and economic progress underlying the political metanarratives of both states, and the importance of technological and economic progress in the individual life narratives and life projections of both easterners and westerners are the foundation on which these allochronic identifications rest. Thus the notion of progress itself has made easterners willy-nilly collaborators in their own temporal displacement. Right after the opening of the Wall, the evidence of western superiority in wealth and technology seemed so overwhelming that easterners had little with which to confront westerners' satiric identifications of their own present, while intensely sharing in the westerner's romantic narrative of the east's transformation to western standards of wealth and technology.

Progress is, however, not only measurable in terms of technology and economic wealth. On both sides of the former Iron Curtain, the discourse of progress has extended into the sphere of social issues. In the West, the "social market economy" (soziale Marktwirtschaft), capitalism tamed by a comprehensive system of social welfare, and corporatist institutions such as collective wage bargaining and industrial codetermination have been heralded as considerable leaps forward. The idea of a social market economy is an essential part of the self-understanding of the FRG, supported by a consensus among the established parties in Bonn.[23] Still, there is poverty in (West) Germany, and unemployment has been a persistent problem ever since the second oil-price crisis in the late 1970s. It is precisely the eastern perception of the failure of the western system to address these social issues satisfactorily which has started to relativize the effectiveness of western allochronizations, smuggling a sense of satire into the romantic discourse of progress.

Reversing Allochronization

With the disintegration of the east German economy after unification and its painfully slow replacement by new companies offering new employment opportunities, unemployment has soared in the east. Virtually nobody has remained unaffected by this transition. Many police employees

23. This consensus seems endangered by the current crisis of the welfare state in Germany. The debate about welfare reform is therefore not only a conflict of interests but also a debate about the identity of the German state. Trade unionists have criticized the CDU government under Helmut Kohl for its welfare cuts by saying that the conservatives obviously wanted "another republic."

have spouses who are unemployed or children whom they cannot properly place in an apprenticeship.[24] Therefore, east German officers claim that as far as social issues are concerned, the GDR with its full employment (even if there might have been what economists call hidden unemployment) was socially much more advanced than the FRG. Here, the allochronization tactics are reversed. The certainty that one could never be effectively out of work is an aspect of the GDR system that almost all eastern officers would want to have reinstituted if they could create a systems mix. Western officers rarely concur in this reverse allochronization, although they share in important respects the easterners' understanding of what social progress means. Still, the fact that the GDR broke down in the end is proof enough for them that the eastern system of creating full employment was ultimately untenable.

Finally, as unification wore on, a third trend developed: easterners started to put their western counterparts firmly back into the here and now. A powerful strategy to achieve this was found in irony and satire. Whenever claims to superiority (which are, on the plane of progress, identical with claims to temporal advancement) are debunked as pompous and unwarranted, the future loses its romantic aura in a forceful *re*presentation. Many western goods have been detected to be much less durable and much less effective than promised. Western clothes have been discovered to come apart at their seams much faster than their eastern counterparts, car parts have been found to be basically unrepairable once they have broken, just fit to be thrown away. Some goods that have been advertised as ultimate everything on glossy paper have proven to be junk. What is true for the world of goods has been ascertained as well for the realm of humans. Postures of professionalism and knowledge have turned out to be unwarranted by actual performance. Eastern officers learned that not all of their western colleagues knew how to handle difficult problems on the street, even if they pretended to be virtual police sages.

For westerners, easterners' satirical identifications of western goods or services are frequently a source of bemusement: they give rise to yet another allochronization. Easterners who reveal their disappointment with the promises of advertisements are thought to be naive. Yet occasionally westerners drop their pedagogical posture and follow the invitations of

---

24. Germany's state governments in conjunction with private companies maintain a system of vocational education, which through a mixture of schooling and on-the-job training (called apprenticeships) recruits and prepares most of the skilled labor force of the country. Thus, not obtaining placement in an apprenticeship frequently precludes persons from later finding higher paid employment.

easterners to bond over ironic or satiric identifications, especially if supe-riors are the butts. After all, some eastern and western patrol officers do find themselves on the same level of the hierarchy.

While satire is clearly the most important, most often used strategy of contemporalization, extreme forms of tragic emplotments are also used to put the GDR and the FRG on the same temporal plane. In several conversations about the technological differences between the FRG and the GDR, eastern officers explained that it was the Cold War confronta-tion, the difficulty of obtaining important raw materials in the world mar-kets, and the importance of earning convertible Western currency to pur-chase these materials which prevented GDR engineers from excelling on a larger scale. Thus the GDR was depicted as being unable to implement its technological prowess by producing, for example, technologically ad-vanced consumer goods. To illustrate this point, one eastern officer ex-plained to me that he *knew* that the Volkswagen Golf, the standard West German car, was actually designed and engineered in East Germany by the enterprise that had also designed and produced the "Trabbi," the standard East German car, which was so often unfavorably compared to the Golf as technologically inferior. He pointed out that the GDR had to sell the blueprints for the Golf to Volkswagen because the GDR could not afford to buy the raw materials to produce it and because it also urgently needed foreign currency. Therefore, he concluded, the GDR was really, au fond, just as technologically advanced as the FRG, but tragic circumstances kept it from developing its potential.[25]

Some officers in Potsdam have pointed out that the western leadership of the police needed to destroy everything that had been in use in the People's Police, including its organizational structure, "because nothing was good enough any more." And they often continued, with a satisfied smile, by pointing out that after just a few years, westerners had to realize that these structures were not so bad after all and reinstituted old People's Police institutions under new names. The examples most frequently men-tioned are the reinstitution of the neighborhood beat patrols in Branden-burg, which were reequipped with a special kind of briefcase (the trade-mark of People's Police neighborhood beat patrols), and the reinstitution of a system of police volunteers who cooperate with the neighborhood beat patrol officers. In this case, the direction of the allochronization does

25. This officer had several more examples of GDR engineering that had to be sold to the FRG. As the source of his information he quoted a tabloid paper, *Super Illu,* which is western-owned, yet deliberately appeals to an exclusively eastern audi-ence, attempting to foster "eastern pride."

get virtually reversed. The westerners' noisy claim to be more advanced is revealed as untenable. The westerners themselves have to admit their own backwardness, at least implicitly, by apparently reversing prior decisions to scrap former People's Police institutions. What eastern officers developed in the course of time was a sense of western inauthenticity and how to discover it, a sense of western make-believe and how to see through it. Having learned about the eastern rhetoric of progress, they have come to learn about its western counterpart.

The use of allochronizations is by no means limited to identifications of police officers among each other. During my presence in Köpenick, several officers (easterners and westerners) actually set out to purchase their first private PCs (note the simultaneity of this move!). This new-found passion for computers gave rise to many complaints about the backwardness of the Berlin Police in relation to other state police forces as far as the use of electronic media is concerned.[26] Thus Berlin was identified as backward vis-à-vis other states, a fact that made the officers quite envious of their better equipped colleagues in Bavaria or in Hamburg. The technological allochronization did, however, also have a societal dimension. The entire public sector in Germany was again and again identified as backward in relation to private companies. One officer pointed, for example, to the word processor in use by one of the secretaries, explaining that this was what the Berlin police would consider high tech. To him, however, the machine was hopelessly outmoded. "Better than nothing," he remarked, "but private companies would at least have a powerful computer instead, in all likelihood even tied to a network."

In sum then, eastern and western police officers identify a host of different clocks, ticking at various speeds. They acknowledge the simultaneity of a multitude of different times. These times are not unrelated, however; they are connected to each other by a narrative of progress which is forward-looking when emplotted romantically and usually backward-looking when satirical. The notion of progress and therefore the possibility to allochronize in particular ways have historically been as much a part of the national metanarrative in the East as in the West. The very idea of progress in the form of a temporal superhighway, along with the notion of a simultaneity of different times, makes all sorts of time travel possible. Officers move themselves on this highway, and they move others—persons, institutions, and even states. In a sense, everything seems

26. My own frequent use of a notebook computer to type some of my fieldnotes on site also gave rise to conversations about technology and the relative advancement or backwardness of certain institutions or even whole countries.

to have a personal temporal identity, its own time. However, this is not a humanist vision of each and every person according to his or her own measure. Instead, time founded on the notion of progress places everything in a rigorous hierarchy in relation to everything else.

The Progression of Lives and Careers

The idea of economic progress within a country is reflected in the expectation of individuals that personal wealth will increase gradually on a quasi-automatic basis. Even if a person hopes no more than to maintain status and position within the hierarchical grid of a given society, the promise of progress is to get carried along with the upward sloping development of wealth and comfort of that society as a whole. Generally, however, people are more ambitious: they expect to improve their relative position within society with the natural progression of age. Police officers do not expect to retire from the same job they held upon graduating from the police academy; instead they count on leaving the police with a much higher rank and significantly increased income. In other words, officers expect to have a career. In sum, then, everyone expects improvement in economic wealth from two different, independent sources: overall economic progress (growth) and one's own career progression. Careers tend to be of two types. There is an ordinary track which reflects, within a certain range of variation, what an officer can expect to achieve on average; and there is an extraordinary, accelerated career track which improves one's standing relative to other members of the same age cohort. This is what police officers mean when they refer to an officer as having "made quite a career for himself." In this sense, careers can accelerate one's movement on the superhighway of progress.

Police forces are hierarchically structured organizations which offer their members relatively clear-cut career trajectories. In imitation of traditional military hierarchies, the People's Police and the Berlin Police have been structured into three distinct, hierarchical layers, each of them reflecting a particular career path: the layer of noncommissioned officers, the layer of commissioned officers, and the layer of staff officers.[27] While

27. For the place of these career trajectories in the (West) German public service, see chapter 2. The German terms for all three hierarchical levels are, for the People's Police, *unterer Dienst* (low service), *mittlerer Dienst* (medium service), and *höherer Dienst* (upper service). The Berlin Police terminology is only slightly different, following the usage of the Civil Service Law (Beamtengesetz); in the FRG they are called

most organizations are more or less hierarchically structured, hierarchy is particularly visible in the police, for all ranks and also the hierarchical layers are prominently reflected in the uniform. Traditionally, in both organizations, everybody had to start from scratch.[28] The entry-gate to each layer is a particular school.[29] Upon entry, it is possible to distinguish an ordinary career, which usually takes place entirely within the stretches of a particular hierarchical layer, and an extraordinary career, which includes a jump into the next higher echelon. While both organizations have always stressed that biological age, tenure within the police, and performance are criteria for promotions, ordinary careers can at best be slightly accelerated through performance, because there is something like a natural age/tenure progression with automatic promotions, provided that officers do not distinguish themselves negatively. Thus ordinary careers are all bound to end at the same rank at retirement. Extraordinary career leaps into the next higher hierarchical level may again lead into ordinary or extraordinary progression on that level.[30]

Many eastern police officers and many older western police officers joined the police explicitly for career reasons. They found themselves potentially stuck in another career, and saw more potential for personal advancement in the police.[31] One eastern officer explained, for example, that he saw little hope for advancement in the factory in which he had been working. All positions for master craftsmen were filled with relatively young incumbents, so that in his lifetime there was almost no chance to get a promotion. A western officer who worked as a carpenter

---

mittlerer Dienst (medium service), *gehobener Dienst* (elevated service), and *höherer Dienst* (higher service). All three levels are also connected to a level-specific career path called in German *Laufbahn* (course).

28. This is true only for the uniformed parts of the police. Criminal investigators had somewhat different career trajectories. All of my informants in both organizations did in fact start as ordinary police officers in riot units and in precincts. In the meantime, the uniformed police have adopted the career system of criminal investigators.

29. They are what I will call police school (People's Police/Berlin Police: *Polizeischule*) for the noncommissioned officers; the police college (People's Police: *Polizeifachschule*; Berlin Police: *Fachhochschule*) for commissioned officers; police academy (People's Police: *Hochschule*; Berlin Police: *Akademie*).

30. The necessary condition for a career-level leap is appropriate secondary schooling. Thus, although all officers entered the police school with secondary-school degrees, their chances of pursuing an extraordinary career were unevenly distributed, depending on the kind of secondary degree they had obtained.

31. The age differentiation is necessary here because most younger western officers joined the police right out of school. Older officers used to complete at least an apprenticeship in another trade.

in a fast-paced construction gang witnessed once how an older colleague's application to join the gang was refused because the gang leader, still young himself, thought the older man would not be able to keep up with their speed. This event made him rethink his future prospects in his craft, and led ultimately to his applying for training as a police officer. Like all public-sector jobs, a career in the police would furnish him with secure lifetime employment.

As I have pointed out, ordinary police careers are not only highly predictable in terms of their final rank, but they also pace the time between entry and retirement. Promotions are comparatively foreseeable and regular. The next promotion is something to be awaited, perhaps to be accelerated somewhat by good performance. Since ranks are indicated in the (West) German police by the color (green for noncommissioned, silver for commissioned, and gold for staff officers) and number of stars on shoulder pieces (one through four), deciding to climb the ladder is aptly called "to reach for the stars"[32] or "to reach for the next star," and if a hierarchy-level switch is intended, officers call it "to go for silver" or "to become silver" or "to get gilded." Regulations prescribe minimum waiting time from one promotion to the next, so that time seems to accelerate around reasonable promotion expectations, and it seems to decelerate after promotions, because the officer is then once again at the beginning of a waiting loop. Once the last rung of the career ladder is climbed, officers tend to wait for their retirement. One of the officers I got to know carried a tailor's standard, two-meter tape measure, clipping off a little portion of its length each day as he was approaching his date of retirement (universally sixty for all uniformed officers). Whenever he was upset for some reason, he would look at his tape and relax: "Just so and so many days left," he would declare.[33]

The People's Police had some other devices to pace life. Officers could pledge upon entering to serve three, six, ten, or twenty-five years. Getting out beforehand was usually quite difficult, because the People's Police thought of itself as notoriously short of personnel. Even leaving at the end of any particular contract period was highly discouraged. Officers

32. The Berlin Police has made this its recruiting slogan, displayed on stickers on most Berlin patrol cars.
33. The idea of a tape measure as a time meter is taken from the *Bundeswehr*, the federal armed forces. There it has become something of a ritual that conscripted soldiers carry a two-meter tape during the last two hundred days of their service, clipping off one centimeter every day. Those who have fewer days to go are considered superior.

who declared their intention to leave were ordered to have conversations with their superiors, political officers, party secretaries, and so forth, usually until they would cave in or it was sufficiently clear that they would not change their minds. On the other hand, at the end of a contract period, officers had the opportunity to press for some help (e.g., in finding an appropriate apartment). In between, officers were awarded loyalty medals in a five-year rhythm. These medals also carried money premiums as part of the award. Although careers in the People's Police could be sped up quite considerably (as two of my interviews have shown), they had a highly predictable pace in the People's Police too.

What emerges, therefore, is a relatively stable association between particular ranks and functions on the one hand, and people's age on the other. I call the habitual association between a position or function in social life and the standard expected age of its incumbent or bearer *social time*. Social time can thus be understood as a cultural form, more precisely a metonymic schema which identifies selves through subsumption under an age category. Officers of a particular age can therefore be identified reasonably well with a particular rank once it is determined at which of the three hierarchy levels they are located (which is usually quickly told from demeanor: level of voice, vocabulary, types of narratives, expectation of deference, etc.). Conversely, the record of rank on paper conjures up an image of an officer of a particular age and demeanor. Due to the demotions of People's Police officers by several ranks, unification has created considerable topsy-turvyness within the well-established schemata of social time used by eastern and western officers. Usually, staff officers became commissioned officers, and most commissioned officers became noncommissioned officers. Thus, in terms of their life experience, they seemed to be pushed back several years, even decades. Through demotion, notions of social time seemed no longer to work properly, because the habitual association between rank/function and age was destroyed.

Demotion after unification was accomplished in several steps. First, as the officers continued to wear their People's Police uniforms, they kept their old shoulder pieces, indicating their People's Police rank. Then they were given western uniforms with blank shoulder pieces, and finally they were awarded their new rank, adding new color and a new number of stars to their shoulder pieces. A former major has narrated this experience as quite ghastly. First, he said, most westerners came to look at him as the "bad major," because staff officers were considered to be "the pillars of the People's Police and as such also of the GDR regime." Then he felt stripped of all rank, and finally western officers came to look at him as the first lieutenant who was a demoted major. In fact, he would have much preferred to enter the Berlin Police with no rank whatsoever rather than to enter it publicly as major, only to be later demoted, a procedure which makes allochronization painfully public. He says that through all these years he felt and was made to feel like an anomaly. From a position of directing operational affairs in the People's Police, he had to step back into the rank and file who carried out orders. The leaders of the shift of which he became a part were younger than he was, and even lower in rank. They had a good deal of difficulty in relating to him, as he had difficulty in relating to them. He felt out of place because he was out of time, not only for himself, but for those around him too.

In her famous analysis of ritual and taboo, Mary Douglas (1966) has defined dirt as matter out of place. What she meant by this is that everything that is perceived outside of routine frameworks of interpretation of experience is perceived at least as an oddity and is also seen as endangering the existing order. The demotion of eastern police officers upset social time, and it has thus also confused traditional notions of authority, in the sense that they have become much more ambiguous. Formal authority in the Berlin Police is generally a function of biological age, tenure, and rank. Within a particular career path, no conflict exists among these three principles, as they are mapped onto each other rather stringently. Across different career paths, the disconnection between rank and age is attenuated by a whole series of cultural forms such as the notions of ordinary and extraordinary careers, as well as a certain cultural segmentation between the three levels of hierarchy. The demotion of eastern officers, in contrast, has created an unattenuated conflict between age and rank. It has also brought the dividing lines between the three hierarchy levels into question. Thus eastern officers find themselves frequently outside of established frameworks, and it is in this sense that demoted eastern officers are perceived and often perceive themselves as not so much out of place as out of time.

As eastern officers faced demotion, many westerners got a chance to pursue extraordinary careers. Since the total number of leadership positions in the Berlin Police increased significantly,[34] while former People's

34. Certain positions increased in number by roughly 40–50 percent. The number of police districts was increased from five to seven, and the number of precincts increased from thirty-one to forty-nine, always at least nominally creating a full range

Police officers were, at least at first, not accepted into any leadership positions, unification afforded initially excellent career opportunities for
medium- to high-ranking western officers. Many westerners were lured
eastward with the explicit but vague promise of their superiors "that their
voluntary commitment to the reconstruction efforts in the east would
certainly pay off in consideration for promotions." Some western officers
told me also that they hoped to escape the dreaded "career jam" *(Beförd-
erungsstau)* by going east.[35] Thus the prospects of career acceleration—
and the adventure of doing something completely different—were allur-
ing to many westerners. Their career hopes were further fired up by the
self-serving myth that the officers who had gone east were indeed the elite
of the (West) Berlin Police. This self-identification of westerners going east
had been stipulated by superiors who, spreading this slogan, wanted to recruit a reliable and successful team of officers to come along with them.[36]

In the end, however, what many westerners found by "going east"
was not the career-Eldorado they had hoped to find. This was especially
true for low- and middle-ranking officers. Beginning with unification, the
State of Berlin slid into a severe budgetary crisis which worsened over
the years as subsidies were phased out.[37] Thus the number of some career
positions was cut again (such as the cherished position of the precinct
administrator) in an effort to save money. The budgetary crisis also led
to delays in routinely expected promotions. This new situation left may
western officers with the feeling that what they considered their sacrifices
for the reconstruction of the east and for their own advancement (e.g.,
longer commutes, the need to work originally without the amenities of

---

of leadership functions from shift leaders to district chiefs. These new functions and
responsibilities did not always, however, translate into the pay level traditionally
associated with these functions.

35. "Career jam" describes a situation in which officers supported by their superiors feel that they should soon be promoted but do not actually obtain promotions
because, as they are told, no positions are available to accommodate an officer with
a higher rank. This problem is exacerbated if these officers, for whatever reasons,
want to remain with their present outfits.

36. The self-declared elitism, in combination with a lack of support from
"above," which translated into a feeling of being abandoned, left to one's own devices, may have helped to generate the "commando" atmosphere sensed by many
westerners who went east.

37. This budgetary crisis occurred because Berlin suddenly lost many of the subsidies it had received from the other West German states and the federal government
because of its "special island status" *(besondere Insellage)*. Not only was the public
sector in Berlin bloated compared to other parts of West Germany because the public
sector created jobs to make up for the severe job losses in the private sector, but the
Berlin administration was not used to working within tight budgetary constraints.

western precincts) were indeed for naught. In addition, many westerners working in the east were annoyed to find that unification increased career prospects in both parts of the city equally, so that officers who had remained in the west, sacrificing nothing, had as much or as little chance of promotion as they did.

Once the eastern officers had finished their retraining programs, getting more and more versed in the western ways of policing, they began to expect that some of their initial demotion would be reversed, that they would be given a chance to move up the career ladder again. Their emerging feeling of deserving promotion coincided with the feeling among many westerners serving in the east that they deserved promotion because they had not yet reaped the benefits of going east. Easterners and westerners have suddenly found themselves pitted against each other in a race on the career highway. Needless to say, the emergence of this situation in full force five years after unification has not contributed to a more conciliatory atmosphere among easterners and westerners.

Experiencing Discontinuity, Spinning Continuity

The Cycles of the Year and of a Life

For east Germans, unification was in many ways a radical break. Not only was drastic change visible in a revolution of material culture and in the physical environment in which they lived, but the pace of life, its very rhythm, was fundamentally disrupted and subsequently altered for good. At the most basic level unification affected calendrical time itself, not in the sense that the number of hours in a day or the number of weeks in a year changed (in this sense the imposition of socialism in eastern Europe had been much less radical than, for example, the French Revolution), but the rhythm of holidays, commemoration days, and workdays was altered significantly.[38] The most important socialist holidays during the year either changed their meaning or were abolished altogether. May Day (the international labor day) changed from a day of massive parades in which it was advisable to participate, a day of speeches (listened to or ignored) about the place of the GDR in the socialist world and the place

38. The changes were probably less consequential in the overall governance of time, because the GDR maintained such major church holidays as Christmas and Easter, wisely attempting to secularize them (following a trend that was visible even in the Weimar republic) rather than to abolish them. Still, socialist countries tried to produce their own rhythm by introducing new holidays (cf. Verdery 1996, 54f.).

of socialism in the scheme of history, to a general family day on which only active trade unionists or union supporters gather for demonstrations and rallies. The Day of the Republic (7 October), the GDR national holiday, as well as the anniversary of Rosa Luxemburg's death (observed on the second Sunday in January) were both abandoned as public holidays.[39] In their place, the religious holidays have resumed greater significance, not in a ritual sense, for most east Germans have not flocked back to the churches, but as focal points for family outings, short trips, and so on. Other commemorating events, like the international women's day, when female members of the People's Police used to receive flowers, or the day of the People's Police, when representatives of other institutions visited the People's Police to congratulate it on it's "birthday," were abandoned without substitute. What made these commemoration days important for People's Police officers was not so much their imputed societal significance, but that they were an occasion for major social get-togethers with colleagues, which most officers seem to have eagerly anticipated.

And not only the rhythm of the year has changed; the socialist rites of passage which had started to mark the life cycle in the GDR on a fairly regular basis were threatened by unification.[40] Entrance into elementary school at age six was usually accompanied by membership in the Junge Pioniere (Young Pioneers),[41] the socialist children's organization; in eighth grade, at age fourteen, young men and women regularly entered the socialist youth organization Freie Deutsche Jugend (FDJ; Free German Youth). Membership in these organizations was fairly comprehensive, because they organized virtually all extracurricular activities in GDR schools.[42] Both organizations were effectively dismantled in 1990.

39. To this day, members and supporters of the reformed communist party, the PDS, assemble at Luxemburg's grave at the cemetery in Berlin-Friedrichshain to commemorate her as a martyr for a better society.
40. The stability of the structured system of life-cycle organization was enhanced when the first generation of parents who had experienced this process in the 1950s or 1960s sent their children in the 1970s and 1980s to institutions that they remembered. This is true, for example, for most of the eastern police officers I got to know during my fieldwork.
41. The full official name of the organization was "Pionierorganisation 'Ernst Thälmann' "; it was named after Ernst Thälmann, communist leader and presidential candidate in the Weimar republic. Grades one through three were spent as Jungpionier (Junior Pioneer), and grades four through eight as Thälmannpionier (Thälmann-Pioneer).
42. Several police officers also reported active repression against nonmembers, describing how nonmembers were actively isolated or otherwise harassed and thus persuaded to join in. Membership in the Young Pioneers stabilized in the 1980s at

In order to replace church-sponsored coming-of-age rituals, such as the First Holy Communion in the Catholic Church and Confirmation in the Protestant Churches, state and party sponsored the so-called Jugend-weihe (youth consecration) as an alternative. More than 80 percent of the youths in the GDR participated in the Jugendweihe. Interestingly, the institution of the Jugendweihe survived the downfall of the GDR, a trend that was evident in the high participation rate in the spring of 1990, while membership in Young Pioneers and FDJ was dwindling rapidly.[43] The Jugendweihe is one of the few institutions of the GDR that have shown surprising resilience. The continuing support it has enjoyed is probably due to its function as a rite of passage in the life cycle, as well as to the lack of acceptable alternatives.

Probably the most traumatic experience of unification for most east Germans was and in many cases still is their sense of an uncertain future. In the preceding section, I described how career projections into the future give human beings a sense of mastery of time. The future thereby loses its threatening openness in relatively predictable closure. Unification rendered virtually all of the career and life projections of east Germans uncertain. For many, these projections were invalidated literally overnight. In Berlin, high-ranking officers (i.e., from lieutenant-colonel upward) were all dismissed (with only one exception); if they have not found employment in other police organizations in any of the five new states (which was quite difficult), they are now working in completely different careers, ranging from insurance brokerage and other financial services to work in private security firms. But even those officers who have remained with the police did not know at first whether their jobs were secure: many officers felt intense anxiety that they might either not pass the final exams in their various retraining programs or that for some reason they might get dismissed for alleged secret police contacts. Life-term employment status was offered to eastern officers only after an extended trial period.[44] Finally, even when eastern officers in general became a little more relaxed

---

around 85 percent (Herbst, Ranke, and Winkler 1994, 1: 293) and that of the FDJ at around 75 percent of a given cohort (Mählert 1994, 93).

43. According to Herbst, Ranke, and Winkler (1994), the participation rate in the spring of 1990, that is, immediately after the fall of the Wall, was still 80 percent; in 1992 roughly 50 percent of all high school students in the former GDR participated in Jugendweihe.

44. Civil service tenure *(Verbeamtung)* started to be awarded only in the course of 1993; most of it was completed by the end of 1994. The exact timing depended on the exact time of graduation from the retraining courses, after which the officers would have to prove themselves for two years in everyday work.

about their own future in the police, at least former commissioned officers and staff officers had to adjust their career aspirations to the demotions they had to suffer.

Narratives and Waiting

In the face of significant changes in the surrounding material world, in the rhythm of the year, and in projections for life in the future, one may wonder if and how eastern officers tried to endow their lives with a sense of continuity. Narrative approaches to identity have explicitly thematized the question of continuity. Ricoeur (1992, 1991) has characterized narrative as a "synthesis of the heterogeneous" (1992, 141). What he means by this is the power of the narrative to weave together events/experiences removed from each other in space and time, encounters with different people, in different circumstances, thus creating a unity by associating these disparate elements into a single plot. Seen this way, continuity is created by the cohesion of a narrative plot. In practice, however life is rarely ever narrated as a whole in a quasi-autobiographic fashion. Thus, the narrative construction of continuity is not to be expected from an overarching narrative of someone's life, but rather from the thematic cohesion of a multiplicity of stories about single projects (cf. Linde 1993). The continuity in the thread of a life is not given by a single fiber, but by a multitude of fibers spun together, some longer some shorter, none of them beginning or ending at the same time, except of course, for birth and death. This image suggests that continuity and discontinuity may be thought of as coexisting in a great variety of ways.

Ricoeur (1992, 1991) argues that the sense of continuity derived from narrative is created by the multiple synthesis of plot. It remains unclear in his analysis, however, how plot creates unity above and beyond the sheer contiguity of actions, places, events, objects, and characters. Peter Brooks (1984) provides an alternative way of conceptualizing the production of continuity in narrative by concentrating on the creation of desire or what he calls "the play of desire in time" (xiii). One simple archetypal example for the creation of desire is the ambition of the hero: "Ambition provides not only a typical novelistic theme, but also a dominant dynamic of plot: a force that drives the protagonist forward, assuring that no incident or action is final or closed in itself until such a moment as the ends of ambition have been clarified, through success or else renunciation" (1984, 39).

Career projections typically take the form of a narrative. At the beginning of a career the desire driving this narrative is advancement in rank, ambition in the above sense. Toward the end of most police career narratives I have heard, it is the desire for the quasi-paradisiacal state of complete self-determination in retirement, the prospect of unlimited time for all the other projects the officers have been working on that drives the narrative. As I have pointed out, after unification these career narratives were stalled. The present was no longer systematically connected with a past and with a future. All attention was focused on the present, the day-to-day worries of staying afloat in a fast-changing world and, as its centerpiece, the overriding concern of maintaining employment. The certainty of work was frequently acknowledged by officers summarizing their troubled sense of an uncertain career by exclaiming, "Thank God, I still have work!" comparing their luck with the pains of unemployment felt by their own relatives or friends. Thus many eastern officers felt that they had to sacrifice their careers for work, but that this sacrifice was well worthwhile, given the general uncertainties of the situation. Nevertheless, the suspension of career narratives, the powerful, overriding concern with the present without a clear picture of what the future held in store for them, was experienced as a severe discontinuity.

As Brooks (1984, 3) writes, however, emphasizing the coexistence of a multitude of narratives: "We live immersed in narrative, recounting and reassessing the meaning of our past actions, anticipating the outcome of our future projects, situating ourselves at the intersection of several stories not yet completed."[45] Career narratives are not the only ones that create a sense of continuity. Other important families of narrative projections include the acquisition of durable consumer goods (furniture, cars, television sets, and video recorders), the renovation of homes, and of course, traveling. The desires underpinning such narratives predate German unification, and just like career narratives, they did indeed have a projective character, connecting a narrative present with a past and a future. The important way in which unification affected these narratives is that the desires that drove them could be satisfied more quickly than ever before. The fact that these narratives originated in the GDR, but frequently came to happy conclusions only in the FRG did indeed create a sense of continuity between the lives of eastern officers then and now.

45. In the same way, the projected life narratives that former People's Police officers had for their children were disrupted and needed reorientation, especially if these children were just about to leave school and needed jobs or apprenticeships. The life narratives people hold for close loved ones are just as important as their own in providing a sense of continuity.

The unexpectedly quick satisfaction of these desires seemed to speed up the progression of time and gave life an apparently faster pace. One officer summarized the shopping spree of the last half a decade since unification as follows: "I have purchased more in the last five years than I would ever have been able to afford in my entire life in the GDR." In stories of the acquisition of durable consumer goods, unification has become something of an unexpected helper for the hero—and the heroes do in fact show their gratitude. Therefore, the narratives of a single project of acquiring some durable consumer good before unification and after were not the same anymore, because neither was a particular good procured in the same way, nor were the goods offered to fulfill particular desires identical (more on this below). Thus, as the life circumstances changed, the narratives changed too. What gives these stories a sense of continuity despite the changes, however, is that the desire itself (much like characters in a narrative) has remained recognizably self-identical in spite of its likely substantive transformations.[46]

While it took GDR citizens between ten and fifteen years just to get a car (regardless of the availability of money), they could buy one immediately in the west (granted savings or credit-worthiness). Perhaps not surprisingly, narrations cover only periods of active pursuit, phases in which the officers could actually do something to get closer to acquiring what they desired. Waiting periods, a common feature of a consumer's life in the GDR, seem to be non-narratable. Still, waiting shortens the time to fulfillment and is therefore just as important in producing a sense of continuity as narrative.[47] The whole time span from the instigation of desire to the moment just before its fulfillment is unified by a common telos. This is as true for waiting as it is for the narrations of active pursuits. The consummation of desire, however, the end of waiting or the end of the story, creates a disjunction. What continuity is about, then, is

46. As the quality of the goods provided to fulfill long-held desires changed, the desires substantively adjusted to the new goods.

47. Schütz and Luckmann (1979, 75–76) are certainly right when they point out that waiting is a neglected phenomenon in the social sciences. Following Bergson, they analyze waiting as "incongruence of different time dimensions," that is, the divergence between individual time consciousness and other temporalities. Their examples involve mostly natural phenomena, such as the dissolution of sugar in water and the healing processes of wounds. But their approach can also be used in the context of diverging time horizons: having to wait to buy a car in spite of available funds can be analyzed as a divergence between the rhythm of five-year plans and individual consumption plans. The gap between desire and fulfillment may be analyzed as disjunction between desire's consummate demands and the means of fulfillment. In this sense waiting is therefore an indicator of limited agency.

a parallelization of a host of waitings/stories, beginning at different times, ending at different times, while partially overlapping. The ending of a story or the ending of a waiting period—at any rate the consummation of a particular desire—is like the tick of a clock: it moves time, simultaneously measuring the progress of other stories or waitings. What seems to structure the experience of time is, therefore, more fundamental than narrative itself. It is the lag between the instigation of a desire and its fulfillment, regardless of whether that lag is bridged by non-narratable waiting or by narratable action. Thus one of the central propositions of Ricoeur (1984), the thesis that there is a mutual constitution of narrative and time experience, is in a very important sense incomplete.

There is, however, still a fundamental difference between waiting and narrative. While the experience of time in action and narrative is self-constitutive, or autopoietic, the time experience in waiting seems to require external clocking, which is provided either by natural devices such as the passage of days, seasons, and years, by calendars and clocks, or by sequences of action/narrations or various periods of waiting. Ricoeur's proposition is therefore still valid as a special case with a limited domain. Narrative is autopoietically clocked because it is composed of heterogeneous elements. Narratives have differentiable ministructures (Barthes 1977, 251–92) that compose the plot, such as differentiable action units or even whole episodes. The beginnings and ends of these elements in narrative clock each other. Thus narrative is not in need of any external timing device; it is self-constitutive, autopoietic. Waiting, however is in its pure form unstructured between the instigation of desire and its satisfaction.

Waiting, like narrative, can be stalled: what one is waiting for may completely disappear from the horizon of time. Many eastern officers were waiting for their next promotion or for the beginning a new phase of schooling when first the fall of the Wall and later unification interrupted the waiting process. Often, waiting periods have become meaningless overnight, either because that what one has been waiting for is no longer available, or it is now *readily* available. Therefore, stalled waiting can be experienced as a disjunction in time. Some eastern officers expressed a strong sense of anger about the fact that many of their waitings were invalidated abruptly.

Unification has not only sped up eventual fulfillment but has changed the very qualities of active pursuit/narration and of waiting. This became strikingly obvious to me when an eastern police officer told me about a conversation with one of her friends. It was early in December, and

Christmas preparations were in full swing. She cautioned me that I would probably find the story somewhat strange, but yesterday her friend had complained to her that, since unification, Christmas had totally lost its charm. The officer said that she was quite baffled at this statement and responded that she found it much nicer now, because the stores had such a wide variety of goods to offer. Her friend replied that *this* was exactly the problem and that she *missed* the typical GDR troubles of getting a nice gift for someone.

This little conversation nicely captures the differences in pursuit and hence the differences in narrative between life in the GDR and life in the FRG. Gone is the old, complex system of barter exchange in which one pursued a variety of paths, arriving at the goal by trial and error. No longer is cunning required to create and mobilize networks of relations to get desired consumer goods (the craft Katherine Verdery [1996, 22] has so aptly called "acquisitionmanship"). In the GDR, the limiting factor in purchasing desired goods was typically not money but the availability of goods.[48] Since scarcity was not managed on the basis of price (i.e., prices were not increased until the number of available goods matched the number of customers willing to buy at this price), scarce goods had to be distributed on the basis of time rationing. One literally had to queue up in front of a shop, or be entered on a list of aspiring buyers. Time rationing thus gives waiting in some sense the character of savings. Accumulated waiting time, partially visible in the form of fewer and fewer people ahead in the queue or, more abstractly, of steadily decreasing rank numbers on various waiting lists, was therefore a resource. These resources were all destroyed by unification.[49]

Today, money is what matters, not availability, since everything seems available at a price. Financial aspects have moved much more to the foreground, as eastern officers point out. Credit has a different meaning, in that failure to pay principal and interest on time are heavily sanctioned now.[50] The role of saving has also changed, for it has become much more of a goal-directed activity. In some ways saving has replaced waiting; a

48. This is why easterners entered unification with substantial savings: they usually had more money than they could spend. The transformation of these savings into convertible currency made the shopping sprees of easterners after unification possible.

49. In this sense, the conversion of eastern savings into western savings at the time of the currency union did not take into account the differences in meaning.

50. Eastern officers have explained again and again that the failure to pay back a debt in the GDR was usually not much of a problem. Not only were debts easily renegotiated, but sometimes employers were willing to pick up the tab.

nonactivity has been transformed into an activity.[51] Today, prices, different suppliers, and competing products all need to be compared, activities that were never much of an issue in the GDR: "You took whatever you could get, if only for later exchange," as one officer put it. In the narratives of eastern officers selective bargain hunting in united Germany has replaced what might be called "omnivorous" hunting in the GDR.[52] But a hunt it has remained, narratable therefore, and productive of continuity.

I want to address one more element in the pursuit of consumer goods and the narratives that are derived from it. The previous quotation, "I have purchased more in the last five years than I would ever have been able to afford in my entire life in the GDR" has a continuation: "And I have bought goods that I never even dreamed of buying in the GDR, such as a video camera or a computer." Not only has the character of the pursuit changed, but goals have emerged and desires stimulated that were not even thinkable before. This too is an experience of discontinuity. In sum, narratives and waiting for consumer goods produce a host of both continuities and discontinuities in the life experiences of east German police officers. There is continuity in the pursuit of home improvement, major durable consumer items such as furniture or cars, and frequently also in dreams of traveling to particular locations. There is discontinuity in the new context of possibilities and most notably in the fundamentally different ways in which desired goods can be attained. Moreover, as John Borneman (1998, 97ff.) points out, the GDR typical consumption restraint must appear as a temporal slowdown. An acceleration of consumption is accordingly experienced as a quickening of time's pulse.

Frameworks of Interpretation

Narrative and waiting are not the only ways in which continuities are spun and discontinuities made apparent. As phenomenologists have

51. Unlike proper waiting, saving is, as an activity, properly narratable, because people can explain how they do it and how savings are accumulating. Saving is therefore, like narrative, autopoietically clocked.

52. Many officers tell stories about how they learned to compare prices from their first encounter with the west. The 100 DM of "welcome money" had to be invested wisely, because nobody foresaw currency union and enventual unification. Thus many officers were afraid that the welcome money might be the only foreign currency they would have for a long while. In painstaking efforts not to squander any of it, some of them undertook extensive price comparisons, which frequently led only to minimal savings after long hours of bargain hunting, as they remark today ironically.

pointed out (Heidegger 1986; Gadamer 1990; Schütz and Luckmann 1979), understanding itself is based on a notion of continuity. This is true in two discernibly different but interconnected ways. First, managing the everyday on the assumption that in very important respects today is like yesterday, and tomorrow will be like today, actions are based on an implicit "and-so-on" and, by extension, "I-can-do-it-again-and-again" (Schütz and Luckmann 1979, 29). This means, for example, that the unfinished work of today can be finished tomorrow, on the assumption that all the major institutions needed to complete the task will still be in place then. It is along the lines of this "and-so-on" of the lifeworld that expectations are implicitly built. These expectations can be frustrated, thus rendering experience problematic. It is on the basis of the "and-so-on" that discontinuities become apparent, and these experiences identify the assumptions underpinning everyday lives. Such identifications can be positive in the sense that the persons thus identified get to know what is important to them, what they really like, and what they stand for. Clearly, the lifeworld assumption that was most severely frustrated in the context of unification was the idea that "no matter what, I will always have work." Frustrations of lifeworld assumptions can also be negative, in the sense that they reveal more clearly than ever what it is that was always experienced as a nuisance: "It took me a while to understand that I did not have to queue up just because there was a line: I can get all the goods I want, always."

Second, understanding itself is what Heidegger (1986, part 2, chap. 5) calls "historical." Present interpretations are based on past experiences and interpretative frameworks learned in the past. If the present is to be understood at all, it is on the basis of the past.[53] These interpretative continuities are revealed perhaps most clearly in the equivalencies that east German officers construct, often in the face of westerners' protests. Arguably the most controversial of these equivalencies is what might be called the generalization of police professionalism, simply expressed in the words of one Potsdam officer: "Police work simply is police work, be it in the East or in the West; we have chased gangsters there, and we chase gangsters here, so what's the difference. Every state needs security." Life in the People's Police and in the Brandenburg or Berlin Police is also made equivalent in more detail. The training in constitutional law is equated with political education in the People's Police; the roles of neigh-

53. Subjectivity is therefore not an impediment to understanding but the precondition for its possibility (Gadamer 1993, 57–65).

borhood beat patrols then and now are seen as one and the same. For western officers, this generalization of police professionalism is an unacceptable depoliticization of the People's Police, implying an illicit identification of East and West. Eastern officers counter their objection by admitting that of course the political rhetoric was different but that, in effect, the bread-and-butter business of police work was the same in the People's Police as it is now in the Berlin Police.

To westerners this equalization becomes particularly visible in easterners' occasional usage of People's Police terminology to denote Berlin (or Brandenburg) Police institutions.[54] Usually, the use of GDR terminology is immediately censored by western officers. They often blame their eastern colleagues for being "caught up in old thinking habits," expressing their surprise that this would still be the case after several years in the new police. Easterners challenged thus might claim then that they use the old terminology inadvertently, that these are slips of the tongue (which certainly they frequently are), just to acknowledge then with exaggerated gestures, such as putting a hand to their mouths in a childlike fashion, that they are also enjoying the provocation their "slip of the tongue" has produced. With the help of this professionalization of police work, equating East and West, eastern officers not only preserve a sense of continuity, but also emphasize the relevance of their prior training and their prior experiences. Generalization of police professionalism is a strategy that positively integrates the GDR past into the FRG present.[55]

Other important identifications of past and present occur in statements about the political systems in both countries. Sometimes eastern officers exclaim exasperatedly that "no matter what, small people always get screwed," emphasizing that in this respect there is no real difference between east and west. One officer declared, for example, that as far as the freedom of speech is concerned, the role of the whip so successfully played in the east by the secret police is played in the west just as successfully by employers who can simply dismiss people. And he added that "in this sense the lines of confrontation have remained the same."

54. Many eastern officers recollect one incident or another in which they have used People's Police terminology in answering the phone (Germans answer the phone by stating their names in private calls and by stating institution and name in official calls) by saying, for example, "Volkspolizeiinspektion Köpenick" (People's Police district Köpenick) instead of saying, "Polizeiabschnitt 66, Köpenick" (police precinct 66, Köpenick).

55. For the apparent political dimension of this strategy, see chapter 2, "The Politics of Identification," where I discuss the issue of the recognition of prior training in greater detail. See also chapter 6.

Continuities in interpretation also become visible in the use of snippets of Marxist theorizing to explain phenomena in unified Germany. For example, the massive closing down of production facilities in the east is interpreted as a means of keeping up profit rates in established western firms. The high unemployment in east Germany is thus explained as completely predictable. Some officers claim that they had expected just that, seeing Marxist theory borne out by the actual path of German unification. Political parties in the FRG are interpreted by some officers either as extensions of monopoly capitalism, or they are deemed completely powerless. On this basis, some officers proclaim that they have been voting for the Christian Democrats because, through their contacts with all-powerful industry, they are the only ones that might actually do something to raise employment levels in the east. It is highly ironic that a belief in the validity of leftist theory may in this way lead to a rightist vote.[56]

Another example of the use of elements of socialist theory and practice to make sense of the new circumstances is the following episode, in which an eastern officer transfers his identification with key socialist values to the Basic Law, which, to his surprise, he found incorporated these very values: "The first thing I did after unification was to get myself a Basic Law, so that I could see whether it was possible for me to identify with it. I fully support the Basic Law with its goals of solidarity and peace." It is highly unlikely that western officers would pick out solidarity and peace as the core elements of the Basic Law. Instead, they would probably stress freedom and democracy as the central values of the (West) German constitution. Given the self-identifying discourses of the FRG and those of the GDR, the difference is not surprising. Of course, the Basic Law includes the values of peace and solidarity, and reading it from the perspective of solidarity could create refreshing perspectives indeed.

In the state of Brandenburg, the practices of the People's Police in structuring and solving problems are seamlessly applied to postunification situations. This is of course unthinkable in Berlin, where nearly all positions of authority have been staffed with westerners. People's Police stations had a formal position for someone who took care of the equipment. The new Brandenburg Police does not provide for a comparable function, completely relegating maintenance and repair to a central office.

56. This is also a good example of why one should be cautious about accepting the simple attitude-behavior link which underlies much of survey analysis (Inglehart 1990). The grammar that links modes of interpretation with behavior only becomes visible in open-ended interviewing or field research, which reveal the process of reasoning rather than merely producing a static inventory of attitudes.

This new way of handling things was found to be rather dissatisfying by the officers in one Brandenburg station, so they created that position informally, "staffing" it with the most qualified officer at hand and redistributing his formally assigned work among his colleagues. Needless to say, the success of this procedure depends on the silent acceptance of everyone involved, including the officers who have to pick up some additional work.[57]

I have already mentioned that westerners tend to suggest a radical discontinuity between the GDR and the FRG, a notion that eastern officers do not accept, as is evident in the examples given of stated continuities. Beyond the question of continuities and discontinuities across the 1989 chasm, east Germans and west Germans attribute continuities and discontinuities in a larger historical way to each other. In particular, each accuses the other of perpetuating the Nazi dictatorship: west Germans stress a continuity of institutions in the East, while east Germans point to a continuity through persons in the West. Stated differently, officers on both sides claim that their respective Germany has broken more radically with the Nazi past. East Germans point to the antifascist activists who were instrumental in founding the GDR, while at the same time they identify leading west German bureaucrats in the postwar period as former Nazis. West Germans in turn insist on the fundamental difference between their institutions and those of the Nazis, discovering a striking similarity between communist and Nazi rule in terms of single-party dictatorship, secret police terror, and political mass organizations which are completely dependent on the ruling party. Thus westerners frequently identify the parties SED and NSDAP, the youth organizations FDJ and Hitlerjugend, and the secret police forces Stasi and Gestapo.

Understanding is used in yet another way by some eastern officers to create a sense of unity between the GDR past and the FRG present. What is at stake is more precisely a self-understanding, which allows for something of a seamless continuity of life in the GDR and in unified Germany. One officer summarized this strategy in a handsome metaphor. He de-

---

57. This situation developed into much more than the mere transfer of tried problem-solving schemes. Once high-ranking officers found out what precisely was going on (the officer taking care of maintenance started to walk around with a gray smock over his green uniform), they tried to enforce the formal procedures. Since then the situation has evolved into a contest of wills with two clearly discernible dimensions: a contest over "western vs. eastern ways of doing things," a dimension which is especially invoked to elicit support for the scheme from other former People's Police officers; and a "center vs. periphery" struggle, in which the remote station tries to escape centralized control.

scribed his life in the GDR as a life in two skins. One skin was his official self that he would show especially to his superiors and to less-trusted colleagues. He disliked this skin, because it was made of lies about some of his private activities, his personal preferences. It was a skin made to protect the other one—his own skin, which contained his true self, his real likes and dislikes. Unification, he explained, was therefore quite easy for him: he just retired the public, protective hide.

What has been shown to be true for narratives and waiting—that they help to weave continuities while at the same time revealing discontinuities—is also true for processes of interpretation. Understandings are by no means all continuous. They have also changed in the course of time, as many incidents readily show. Asked for their interpretations of the secret police, the Wall, or the human rights situation in the former GDR, several officers play elaborately with a "now and then" duality, suggesting a significant change in their perspective. Yet this is exactly what the hermeneutic circle in its modern interpretation by Heidegger (1986) and Gadamer (1990, 1993) is about: "Frequently, the distance of time can solve the critical task of hermeneutics, the differentiation between true prejudices and false ones. The hermeneutically trained consciousness therefore has to contain a historical consciousness" (Gadamer 1993, 64; my translation).

Finally, taped interviews with many eastern officers reveal a very interesting phenomenon. The temporal reference of the shifter *today* is not restricted to the day of the interview itself, but moves within certain boundaries. Roughly, it seems to denote at least three different times, or time intervals. First, it may pertain to the still-intact GDR at the end of the 1980s, thus narrating occurrences from this particular perspective. This happens frequently in stories about life in the People's Police, where the (actually past) "now" is contrasted with another past, for example in describing the changes of life in the People's Police between the late 1970s and the late 1980s. Second, it may pertain to the relatively turbulent time interval between the fall of the Wall and the consolidation of the eastern officers' position in the Berlin Police, a time which has, with its many ups and downs, worries and hopes, left a particularly vivid memory. Finally, *today* may indeed pertain to calendrical time, a time which is characterized as relatively relaxed.[58] Thus, continuities and disjunctures

58. That is the time of the interviews itself, between October 1994 and August 1996, after the first screening for Stasi collaborations had been successfully passed and shortly before most officers were offered tenure as state employees.

are also produced by shifting the meanings of *today* and *now,* allowing for something like a life in memory, creating a perceptible break with the calendrical here and now.[59]

Summary and Conclusions

In this chapter I have explored ways in which time is used to identify self and other. At the beginning, I introduced the concepts of narrative and allochronization as means to create temporal identifications. While narrative links selves to time by identifying characters with actions, places, objects, and events in the form of a contiguous chain, driven by desires, allochronization identifies self and other oppositionally by assigning them to disjunct periods of time. Together, the notions of narrative and allochronization illuminate the peculiar technique of othering used by westerners to deny easterners the status of equal partners. For westerners' othering of easterners is not radical in the sense that Said's (1978) "orientalism" is, or any form of racism or sexism. Westerners do not identify themselves and easterners as members of different, ontologically distinct categories without any bridges that facilitate the transfer from one category to the other. Rather, west Germans consistently displace east Germans into the past, more precisely into their own past. They thereby project a developmental path, a narrative of transformation which east Germans need to follow if they are to arrive eventually in the westerners' present.

Arguably, this allochronization of East Germany started with the promulgation of the Basic Law. That conspicuous sentence in the preamble stating "to have also acted for those Germans, for whom it was made impossible to participate" placed Easterners outside of German history proper. The policies of sole representation and, subsequently, unification by accession upheld the notion that authentic historical development was impossible in the East. Hence, at the point of unification, Easterners were in part thought of as having spent forty years frozen deep in the cave of the Russian Bear. Freed and thawed by the hot Fall of 1989, they were considered ready to catch up and relive the Western *Bildungsroman.* This story of transformation, the history of West Germany and its inhabitants, depicts a character transformation towards a more cos-

59. Altering the referent of "now" in narratives seems to be an interesting instantiation of what Schütz and Luckmann (1979, chap. 2) have called "shifting the accent of reality."

mopolitan, liberal, and less authoritarian self. But even more important, it is a story about the extraordinary accumulation of wealth with the help of discipline and high technology. And it is precisely at this point that easterners got drawn into the westerners' plot, not only by force of their own desires but also by virtue of the fact that they, encouraged by their state, had learned to uphold the values of economic progress and technological development. Thus, easterners have become unwitting co-conspirators in their own allochronization.

Nevertheless, eastern officers try to counteract this temporal displacement in two ways. They insist that the sphere of the social is marked by progress too and that the FRG falls behind the GDR by this measure. More recently, they have also begun to question whether the western achievements are really as advanced as they seemed at first. Thus east Germans begin to make themselves contemporaries of west Germans again, increasingly demanding the status of partners in dialogue. In retrospect, this recontemporalization also throws a much more critical light onto the organization of German unification under the provisions of Article 23 of the Basic Law. Asked whether in hindsight they think unification should have been handled differently, most officers state that today they wish that unification had been more equal, that there had been much more of a give and take on all levels rather than a wholesale takeover.

The second part of this chapter demonstrates that there is a connection between the idea of progress at large and the idea of a career for every individual. Career trajectories take the form of a romantic narrative, connecting past, present, and future through a continuous amelioration of income, rank, and social status. They lend coherence to lives by suggesting a set of common, underlying goals readily packaged with action plans to pursue them. Consequently, lives are turned into rational, continuous pursuits. By providing a contingency map linking possible achievements to actions, career narratives also make the future more predictable. Unification has intercepted the career trajectories of eastern officers, by throwing the possibility of continuing to work as police officers into question, as well as by substantially demoting the officers, thus allochronizing them relative to their own career expectations. In this way unification has unsettled social time, the habitually assumed relationship between social function or position on the one hand and biological age on the other. The ensuing discrepancy between post-unification rank/position and age has led to identifications of easterners, by themselves and others, as misplaced, as out of time in relation to received social standards.

Finally, I have analyzed ways in which east Germans experience and construct a sense of continuity and discontinuity. I have begun my analysis again by investigating narration. But this time, the narratives I found especially interesting dealt with the procurement of durable consumer goods. Continuities and discontinuities in narratives can be found not only in the telos of the narrative but also in the intricacies of plot structure. These plot structures mirror systematic differences in human pursuit which are based on fundamental systemic differences between the two societies. In other words, life in the FRG and in the GDR produced different kinds of narratives regarding the purchase of consumer goods.

A closer look at the experiences of east Germans also reveals that narrative by no means exhausts the possibilities for constructing continuities and discontinuities. Processes of waiting are also of considerable significance. On the basis of waiting processes, I have suggested that the disjunction between the instigation of desire and its fulfillment is the basic clocking device underlying both narrative and waiting. Last but not least I have pointed out that processes of interpretation produce continuities and ruptures too. Narratives, processes of waiting, and interpretation seem to form a bundle of many asynchronous beginnings and endings which together clock experience. For east Germans, unification has been both a fundamental break and a new beginning, as well as a continuation of their lives in the GDR. And it is this latter aspect that westerners need to acknowledge if they want to free themselves from their allochronizations of the east and finally accept easterners as partners in dialogue.

FOUR

Performing Work

Work is a particularly interesting subject for the study of identity, because most people spend a good deal of their adult lives at work. But the significance of work for a person's identity is by no means only quantitative. While the question "Who are you?" is usually answered in Germany primarily by giving one's name, the question "What are you?" mostly aims at the profession or occupation of the person in question.[1] Children are frequently asked what they would like to be later in their lives, and the expected answer is also a profession or occupation. The desire for a particular occupation is taken at least as much for granted as is the desire for a lover or a family. Work, therefore plays an important role in the life narratives that people spin (Young and Collin 1992b), both in the sense of a genealogy of the present and as directive for the future. Historically, and across many European cultures, work has also been a centerpiece of religious thinking, from the Benedictine's famous *ora et labora* to the by now almost idiomatic "Protestant work ethic," and it has also taken center stage in secular thinking, in many worldviews and ideologies, from liberalism to communism and fascism (Bendix 1974; Bell 1988).[2]

There are five different levels on which work can bestow meaning on the self: (1) by the intricacies of the process of working itself (e.g., the thrill of a superbly choreographed police operation); (2) by the results of

1. The question "Who are you?" if the name cannot be expected to ring a bell, will no doubt be answered by mentioning relations with persons who are expected to be known ("I am the son, friend, husband of . . . ") or by naming a position in an organization (e.g., police sergeant at the Babelsberg station) that will be recognized.
2. For a comprehensive, almost encyclopedic overview, see Applebaum 1992.

work, its products (e.g., a gangster caught) and by-products (pay and amenities); (3) by the prestige of a particular kind of work in the recognized universe of occupations (e.g., being a police officer rather than a carpenter); (4) by the prestige of the social context, in modern times especially the type and reputation of the organization in which one works (e.g., a riot unit or a special force rather than a precinct; the Berlin Police rather than Siemens); (5) by the position work takes within the context of other pastimes or activities in a worldview, ideology, or religion (e.g., work rather than contemplation or leisure).

In what follows, I intend to show how east Germans and west Germans identify each other by their respective attitudes to work, that is, their work ethics. The very fact that an ethics of work is at the core of the dispute over identity bespeaks a high valuation of work in relation to other activities (the fifth level just outlined). The appreciation of work ethics must be common to easterners and westerners, or else it would not be one of the principle arenas to fight out their identity conflicts. In the first part of the chapter I analyze in some detail the concrete differences in the concept of work ethics between easterners and westerners, paying particular attention to the codes by which they distinguish positive and negative attitudes to work. Having thus introduced the notion that work is communicative action, which can therefore be analyzed in terms of performance, I proceed to investigate how easterners and westerners differentiate good work from bad work. And although the question underlying the first part, "How can one tell that somebody is ethically good as a worker?" can be differentiated from the question posed in the second part, "How can one tell good work from bad work?" I show how both are related to each other.

The Ethics of Work: Extensive and Intensive Time

Few things are as constitutive of westerners' understanding of themselves as (West) German as the *Wirtschaftswunder,* the economic miracle after the devastations of World War II. Economics is thought to have put West Germany back on the map of the world, if not as a beloved country (and they seem to know that they are not loved) then as an economic power to be reckoned with and as a reliable partner. If westerners are asked what explains the economic success of their country, the almost stereotypical answer focuses on two points: the generous aid provided by the United States through the Marshall Plan, and plenty of hard work. Immediately after the Wall fell, as it became clear how relatively poor the GDR was compared to the FRG, people wondered how to account for this difference in wealth.

The difference was explained at first by the fact that East Germany did not benefit from the Marshall Plan Aid and, even worse, was burdened by extraordinarily high reparation payments to the Soviet Union. Images of railroad tracks and factories dismantled by the Soviets were readily revived from the early years of the Cold War when they were used to highlight the difference between life under the occupational regime of the Western Allies or the Soviet Union.[3] However, the perceived gap between the economic achievement of the GDR and the FRG widened in the course of 1990 as western economists and businessmen gained more firsthand experience of GDR companies and more realistic statistics became available. This prompted a thorough downward revision of the assessed strengths of the GDR economy, gradually changing the picture of East Germans as the "Red Prussians," being perhaps the only ones who might have worked a centrally planned economy reasonably well. At the same time, the image of the East German economy suffered further in Western eyes because of the severe problems caused by the rapid disintegration of its traditional domestic and export markets after the currency union with the FRG. Finally, as it became apparent that east Germans freed from the constraints of a planned economy and supported by a strong currency seemed not to produce an economic miracle mirroring that of West Germany after the currency reform in 1948, westerners started to search for reasons beyond the lack of reconstruction funds and high reparation burdens to make sense of the differential economic achievements between East and West. Thus the suspicion was born that East Germans were after all not as hard working as West Germans. Socialism, it was argued then, took away all incentives to excel. After forty years of communist rule, many westerners (including many Köpenick officers) began to believe easterners had become if not downright lazy, then certainly quite inert, without much initiative. It was pointed out that East Germany was not a *Leistungsgesellschaft*, an "achievement-oriented society"; ideological nepotism was thought to have won over meritoc-

3. Even before it became clear that unification was soon to occur, newspaper articles popped up in which economic historians calculated how much in present Deutsche marks (DM, or simply marks) the FRG owed the GDR due to asymmetric reparation burdens after the war, given the equal responsibility of Germans in both countries for the Nazi dictatorship, the Holocaust, and the devastations of World War II.

racy.[4] The widely published and debated figures on differences in the productivity of labor in East and West Germany, taxing the east at around 30 percent of western levels (Siebert 1992, 121) probably did their share to support the notion of the not-so-diligent easterner.[5] East Germans were then believed not to possess what made West Germans what they were: hard-working, endowed with a sturdy work ethic. After unification many westerners argued accordingly that what easterners needed most was to be taught how to work hard. Almost all eastern officers I got to know told me that in one context or another they had heard from westerners directly that this is indeed what was lacking in them.

All this must have sounded at least strange, if not utterly presumptuous, from the perspective of someone who had grown up in a social system that placed work prominently in the center of society. The GDR called itself a workers' and farmers' state (Arbeiter- und Bauernstaat); everyone with a stake in the GDR therefore self-identified or, if inclusiveness was desired, was identified by the authorities as a laborer. In this vein intellectuals referred to themselves as "mind-laborers" *(Geistesarbeiter).*[6] Thus in the GDR, too, work was one of the most fundamental

4. West German government officials drafting the unification treaties with the GDR were apparently already uncertain about the achievement-orientation of East Germans that the very term *achievement* had to be explicitly used in interesting combinations in the treaty on currency union, as a prescription for how things would have to become in the GDR and how, according to the text of the law, they already were in the FRG. The treaty states in Article I (3) that there was to be *Leistungswettbewerb* (competition for achievement) in the then still-existing GDR (Treaty on the Creation of Currency, Economic, and Social Union between the Federal Republic of Germany and the German Democratic Republic). The social union was not simply to insure "justice" but *Leistungsgerechtigkeit* (achievement-justice). This pronounced position of the word *Leistung* (achievement) is not part of the vocabulary of the (West) German constitution, the Basic Law.

5. Of course, productivity as measured by national income statistics (or even by a factory-to-factory comparison) may have little to do with "working hard," since differences in the production per capita and time unit are also functions of differences in capital endowment and technology. Still, the productivity differences (along with lower costs of living) were taken as the prime reason for fixing eastern wages and salaries immediately after unification at 60 percent of the western level. Economists and government officials pointed out that this was an essential move in order to attract western investment to the former GDR. For a sophisticated discussion of productivity and labor costs, see Sinn and Sinn 1992, especially chapter 5; for a very conservative discussion along productivity-wage lines, see Siebert 1992, especially chapter 8.

6. These labels were ideologically highly significant. The Socialist Unity Party (Sozialistische Einheitspartei Deutschlands, SED) understood itself as the vanguard party of the class of workers and farmers. Thus the number of workers in the party

themes of self-identification. As noted in the investigation of chronotopes of eastern and western life (chapter 1), the workplace was also the center for all sorts of social and political activities, and it was the distribution channel for some of the most desirable goods, notably vacations and apartments.[7] One eastern police officer explained, moreover, that work or, perhaps more precisely, near universal employment was the reason why he believed that the GDR was superior to the FRG:

> Many people in the East believed that imperialism or capitalism must fail, because there are so many people who do not work and who therefore will have to be fed by the state, this mass of unemployed people. It was evident that it must be uneconomical if people get paid for doing nothing.

During a small social event on my second day in Köpenick, some eastern officers explained to me that one of the reasons they did not like to shop in the western part of the city was the presence of homeless people begging for money. All participants in the conversation agreed that "this is something that certainly could not have happened in the GDR," where they claimed all sorts of efforts were made to resocialize former prisoners or alcoholics through work.

Thus work is what makes somebody a valuable member of society in both parts of Germany, but the orientation towards work as the central aspect of life is more pronounced among the eastern officers I got to know than among westerners, a difference that can probably be explained in part by the threat of unemployment, which is perceived much more acutely by easterners than by westerners.[8] Not only do most easterners still feel somewhat insecure in their positions as police officers,[9] but their

---

should have been high, and the SED was trying hard to win more workers into its ranks and to place their children in higher administrative positions. This has raised constant questions about who really was a laborer and why (Hübner 1994, 172) and thus to an interesting politics of identification. The police officers were highly aware of the power of the "laborer" label in explaining, for example, the mandatory waiting time for final admission to the party, the "candidacy," along with the proportions of various professions within the party.

7. Some authors do speak in this context about the GDR as a "work-society" (Kohli 1994).

8. Unemployment rates in east Germany are, depending on the region, at least twice and sometimes three or four times as high as in the west. Berlin, most notably east Berlin, is an exception to this rule due to the enormous construction boom.

9. The main source of this insecurity is the fear of (unwarranted) dismissal for cooperation with the former secret police, the Stasi. For detailed information on this issue, see the section on the Stasi in chapter 6.

own family members are often jobless. Unemployment comes as more of a shock to east Germans, since they had grown up with the idea that luckily—and in marked contrast to West Germans—they would never have to face that problem.[10] Many eastern officers also had to face a spell of time in which they were relieved of their duties, because the (West) Berlin police organization had not made up its mind about what exactly to do with them, whether to continue to employ them at all, in which function to use them, or how to retrain them. While they received a reduced salary during this time, they were effectively sitting at home, partially paralyzed by a very uncertain future. One eastern officer expressed his experience of worklessness and fear of potential future unemployment thus:

> The smaller income wasn't really the problem then. The decisive factor was not knowing what would happen in the future. This sitting at home together with my wife [who was then unemployed] all day, this brooding, this was the worst of times. You need to have experienced that once, to understand what it means to have real work, if you sit at home and you don't know, and you ponder how you would feed your children next year. This was a quite formative experience. I still haven't forgotten that. My wife too says that nobody who has not experienced what it means to stay put at home can possibly assess the significance of work.

In sum then, the very real threat of losing one's job, the experience of unemployment in the family or in the circle of friends, as well as extended periods of time without any real work after unification have probably increased the already relatively high valuation of work by east Germans. All this has to be taken into account if the full force of western allegations that east Germans do not know how to work are to be understood.

The new, more realistic picture of the state of economic affairs in the

10. Recall that full employment has always been heralded as one of the greatest achievements of socialism. One of the most widely distributed textbooks on Marxism-Leninism in the socialist countries of eastern Europe was *Fundamentals of Marxism-Leninism*, written by a "collective" of authors under the leadership of O. W. Kuusinen (1960). In chapter 23, section 5, entitled "Work in Socialism," the right to work and the eradication of unemployment are highlighted: "In Socialism, the right of all citizens to work will be realized. This right is guaranteed by the whole organization of the economy, by the eradication of crisis and unemployment. In Socialism, the partition of society into a working majority and an idle minority living on the exploitation of others will become impossible, because work will be the only source of income" (my translation from the German edition).

GDR that emerged during the interim period between the fall of the Wall and accession to the FRG, and the overwhelming impression of the riches of the west made some easterners begin to wonder if there might be a kernel of truth in westerners' claims about their own work ethic, if not in the allegations about eastern attitudes to work. An eastern officer told me how she expected the Berlin police finally to show her eastern colleagues how to work hard; she expected things to change fundamentally with the arrival of the western officers. She was totally disappointed, however, when she saw westerners unloading camping chairs and beds to make themselves at home! Many eastern officers were surprised by the work mentality of their western counterparts. Frequently they felt that westerners were "lacking in the right attitude." Westerners in turn saw most of their prejudices confirmed: they found the work of their eastern colleagues wanting in many ways. Easterners therefore began to respond to the reproach of a poor work ethic with a counterreproach to the same effect, and so before long the ethics of work were hotly contested between easterners and westerners.[11]

Eastern Visions of Work: Commitment/Extensive Time

This seeming paradox can only be resolved on the basis of a different understanding of what constitutes or, more precisely, what *signifies* a positive attitude to work. Several themes of easterners' perception of what is lacking in their western colleagues emerge in the following statement by an eastern officer:

> As I have said before, now [i.e., in the Berlin Police] every bit of extra time is reimbursed; if you come on Sunday, you get even a certain percentage [of income] more for the time. With us [in the GDR] it was all consciousness; you did your overtime for nothing, and nobody said anything about it, because you knew you had to do it, and still you tried to do your work in a meticulous and orderly way. I wouldn't even want to know what they would say today about that. And if you got a certificate of merit once in a while from the leader of the precinct, or even the chief of police, or ultimately the minister of the interior,

11. Here is a major difference between eastern officers in Potsdam and in Berlin. Since the Berlin police force is mixed, easterners can actually observe westerners at work and assess the validity of western self-identifications. Potsdamers, who work basically with each other, lack such an opportunity. In this sense, east Berlin officers have developed more self-confidence than their colleagues in Brandenburg.

you looked at it as quite a feather in your cap, but you didn't have any material benefits from it; it was just the moral effect. The westerners are laughing, but we used to say, jokingly, in the military, "Thanks during the roll call in free view of the sun." That's because we were thanked during roll calls. The military commanders didn't have any funds either. That is missing here, in spite of all the ideology, the pride in being a police officer, the need [of the individual] to do something for this police force, to do more than what is required by the books. Here [i.e., in the Berlin Police] this all [i.e., the commitment to work] stops at closing the door [of the precinct] behind you; it ceases upon entering one's private car. You pick up these things very quickly. And I am no exception here.

The statement of this officer illustrates what many eastern police officers find wanting in their western counterparts: most of all a lack of *commitment* to their work as police officers. Commitment is indicated in the example above by the acceptance of overtime as a necessary part of police work. In many interviews and conversations at work, eastern officers have claimed that they used to see overtime as a part of their duty. Some of those with administrative responsibilities have told me that in the GDR they regularly took work home to continue with it after dinner. In many examples eastern officers make clear that there was not as strict a division between work time and leisure or private time in the GDR as they experience now in the Berlin Police.[12]

In general, the stricter division between work and leisure is seen by eastern officers as a sign of weakening, a softening. They make the same observations when commenting on other western practices, such as the much wider use of the colloquial form of address (especially among members of different hierarchy layers) and the relatively greater discretion regarding what constitutes a legitimate uniform. Although (West) Berlin police officers wear uniforms, preferences for different legitimate combinations within the repertoire can make them look different. Eastern officers also notice a much greater tolerance in the Berlin police toward violations of this already more liberal dress code, such as not wearing a cap upon leaving the patrol car or not closing one's jacket, to mention the two most common dress-code irregularities.[13] To many easterners,

12. Compare also the sections entitled "Chronotopes of Eastern and Western Life" in chapter 1, and chapter 7.

13. In the East the uniform was ordered, which means on any given day, officers cooperating would wear exactly the same uniform. In the west, however, at any one point, one officer might, for example, wear a leather jacket with a long-sleeved shirt

such behavior indicates a dearth of order and a lack of proper respect, with regard both to the regulations and, by synecdochical extension, to the organization and the state, as well as to superiors. Westerners are thus identified as essentially missing what is seen as quite important for security agencies: *discipline*. Perhaps even more important, however, these western "slips" are also seen as signs of a lack of pride in being a police officer, a want of self-respect, and ultimately a defective work ethic.

The eastern officers' complaints about the deficit of discipline among their western colleagues point to different ideas about authority relationships at work. In order to appreciate fully how eastern officers relate discipline to work ethic, it is important to understand the reasoning behind the specific sense of authority in the People's Police, the "managerial ideology" governing the relationship between different hierarchical levels (Bendix 1974).[14] The rationale that was given for the tight military regimen in the People's Police was that the maintenance of public security in particular required strict discipline.[15] Security as the product of police work was linked up with security within the police organization itself, which was translated into a hierarchical order of secrecy. Knowledge about the police and especially about police actions and action plans was sparsely distributed and carefully guarded. Therefore, police officers always had good reason to assume that their superiors actually knew more than they did and that orders that seemed opaque at their level of knowledge must have made sense at a level where more of the secrets were known.[16] The whole issue of security was further embedded in an ideol-

---

and tie, a second might wear a regular jacket with shirt and tie, and a third might wear an anorak with a turtleneck pullover.

14. Bendix is indisputably a pioneer in studies of managerial ideologies. He raises the fundamental question of why workers submit to the orders of others. Bendix's concern is not so much with why in actuality factory workers did more or less what their foremen and employers wanted them to do, but with the ideologies employers have used to justify their authority. He has little information about what workers or lower level employees actually thought about their superiors or employer's claims.

15. Besides clear work affinities between the military and the police (such as mutual dependence in situations of acute danger), Bittner (1990, 92ff.) traces the military organization of American police departments to attempts at professionalizing the police by ridding it of political patron-client influences. In Germany the linkage is much more direct (cf. Liang 1970; Selowski 1998), as the police has grown out of the military (the Carabinieri in Italy and the Gendarmerie in France are organizationally still attached to the Department of Defense). During the police reforms of the 1970s in West Germany (see Steinborn and Krüger 1993), a deliberate attempt was made to deemphasize the military tradition in the police.

16. This pattern of argument is repeated at the national level. Many east German officers displayed in their stories of the breakdown of the old regime in the GDR a

ogy of internal and external enemies (the class enemy within and without).[17]

Although certain excesses were surely criticized and even ridiculed by eastern officers, the overall complex of security, secrecy, hierarchy, and military discipline made sense to them and gave their own daily work a little more luster too. Since all officers knew some secrets, the system afforded importance to everyone. Some officers have pointed out that these security concerns also kept them from talking about their work with their own wives, husbands, or friends. The connection between providing security for the country, the need to maintain strict internal security and thus hierarchical levels of secrecy, and military discipline was created not only through verbal communication; many practices and objectifications reenacted this notion constantly, serving as constant reminders of its importance. Most documents were safely locked away, many offices were actually sealed upon leaving them in the evening, the precinct itself was secured with barbed wire, and so on.[18] In sum, then, most eastern officers believed that discipline enhanced their work, that it was a necessary, indispensable ingredient of police work. The precise execution of orders given from a position of higher insight is thus virtuous and characteristic of a good police officer. The relative absence of internal security measures and discipline were therefore quite conspicuous to them.[19]

East German officers' complaints about a lack of work ethics among their western colleagues does not center around the issue of discipline

---

trust that the party would know after all what to do, because of its superior insight into the overall nature of the situation. Severe disappointment arose once no action plans based on such presumably higher insight were forthcoming. These narratives have something of the character of the Grimm brothers' fairy tale of the emperor and his new clothes.

17. The figure of the class enemy, creating the constant feeling of living under siege, also comes across clearly in the official history of the People's Police (MdI 1987). Mary Fulbrook (1995, 22ff.) has described the entire "mentality of power" in the GDR as paranoid, linking it to what she calls a "massive, existential insecurity" (26) with roots in Marxist ideology, but also in the personal life experiences of the GDR's ruling elite, and the particular circumstances of the foundation of the GDR as superimposed by Soviet power.

18. For an analysis of how westerners use these security features of the People's Police to identify their eastern colleagues, see chapter 1, especially the section entitled "Reading Space/Identifying Self and Other."

19. Following Bendix (1974), this reliance on hierarchy and secrecy as a managerial ideology can probably be traced back historically from the GDR through the Soviet Union (which was constantly used as a model for the GDR with the slogan "To learn from the Soviet Union means to learn how to be victorious") and back to the factory regimes of imperial Russia. On China, see also Walder 1986.

alone. The officer quoted above also juxtaposes consciousness and money as motivating forces characterizing easterners and westerners respectively. This distinction taps into the stereotypical view of the materialist westerner and the idealistic easterner. The ultimate goal of work for westerners is thereby identified as the material benefit to be derived from it— thus the eagerness to have every hour of work properly rewarded. Easterners are assumed to work ultimately for the inherent benefits of work itself, the achievement of the goal of policing, the provision of security for the population at large. Accordingly they are identified as being content with the occasional recognition of their efforts. My concern here is not to analyze in detail whether these claims are justified or not.[20] What matters is that easterners again identify westerners as lacking in commitment to their work.

After this description of the various deficiencies noted by easterners in the new organization and among their new colleagues, it may be surprising to learn that, on the whole, easterners are happy with the new arrangements. For the most part, they have learned to appreciate undisturbed and more predictable leisure time. They are also content, of course, that overtime is paid now. Easterners' identifications of westerners as lacking a work ethic are mostly defensive; they are meant to reject the presumptions of westerners that they have the right and the duty to show easterners how to work properly. Yet sometimes they miss what might be called the "spirit" of the People's Police, the feeling that they are working together on an important project, that what they do fits indeed into a larger whole. In part it was the medals and the certificates and the speeches which came along with them that provided that larger context.[21] Little acknowledgments for birthdays, women's days, and other occasions gave them the feeling that they mattered personally. Today, in the unified Berlin Police, they no longer experience anything of that sort.

20. The motivation to work for the police is, among all the officers I got to know, a complex mixture: the myth of the profession intersects with particular life-course circumstances, career considerations, and the recommendations of friends or relatives who already work for the police. Career considerations seem to be dominant for easterners and westerners alike. Regarding the monetary issue, it must be borne in mind that salaries at the People's Police were about a third higher than in comparable positions in industry. This is not true for the west, where public-sector salaries tend to be somewhat below those for jobs in the private sector. Public employees benefit from other factors, however, such as absolute job security and rather generous pension programs, health coverage, and so on.

21. Although the same events were often also derided as nonsensical polit-babble, the emotional importance of the individual recognition remains significant.

Compared to the People's Police, the Berlin police organization is a cere-monial minimalist. Thus police work today appears to many easterners as more or less reduced to the status of a job like any other. What binds an officer to the organization is no longer a state of mind, consciousness, duty, an oath, but a contract that specifies the terms of exchange. It is work for money, or so it seems to many eastern officers; that is why extra hours need to be compensated. It is tit-for-tat: the organization gives to the officer what is the officer's due, and the officer gives to the organiza-tion what is the organization's due.

To many eastern officers, westerners appear to act on the basis of con-tractual bundles of rights and duties. For precisely that reason, they tend to perceive that westerners *act as* police officers, while "officers of the People's Police just didn't haggle; they did what they had to do" because they *were* police officers. Thus these identifications juxtapose western *role-playing* with eastern *being*. This distinction receives special emphasis when easterners talk about moments of hardship in their service in the People's Police. These stories regularly end with comments like, "Then nobody complained," or "You just did it because you were a police officer after all," or "Either you are a police officer or you are not." What east-erners are missing in the Berlin police force is a spirit sustaining a feeling of integration into a larger whole. Thus, one of them said, "This is no longer my old police force!"

It is interesting to note that older western officers talk about younger western colleagues in ways that resemble how easterners talk about west-erners. Older westerners describe the work ethic of the following gen-eration in a deprecatory manner as "job-mentality" *(Job-Mentalität)*.[22] Asked to specify what exactly they mean by this word, they point to the same catalogue of indicators as their eastern colleagues: wanting dis-cipline, disorderliness, stricter divisions between work and leisure, a general "softening" *(Verweichlichung)*, in sum a deficiency of "attitude" *(Haltung)* or "spirit" *(Geist)*. Asked further to identify what had brought this change to the Berlin Police, they single out the police reform of 1974 as a kind of watershed (see Steinborn and Krüger 1993). Like their eastern colleagues, they also say that they too had fallen into the same way of

22. In German, the English word *job* is gaining ever-wider currency. It is fre-quently contrasted with the German word *Beruf*, a word that has connotations of *calling* (see Weber 1988, 63–68). To Germans, the word *job* is something quite ephemeral: today it is this, tomorrow it might be something else. *Beruf*, in contrast, suggests permanence, at least some form of continuity. In this sense, *job* also implies role-playing, while *Beruf* is life.

life, simply because it was easier, more comfortable; yet like the east Germans, they are still nostalgic for that other police force, which simply seemed to have more pluck.[23]

In sum, then, for easterners, the idea of commitment is central to their work ethics. Commitment in turn is inferred from behavior relevant to several of the dimensions along which work can become meaningful: it is signaled on the level of results by arguing that true satisfaction is derived from work only insofar as the comprehensive goals of the organization (security in a hostile environment) are set above the narrow aims of the individual (pay); in the dimensions of both the prestige of the kind of work as well as the prestige of organization to work for, the integration of police work into the larger whole of society is emphasized; most important, however, commitment is demonstrated on the level of work process by obedience, pluck, and by pledging, at least in theory, unlimited amounts of time to work. Thus, the easterners' work ethics of commitment is based on a notion of extensive time. This is, I think, very well captured by the line with which one eastern officer ended her musings on the differences between work in the People's Police and the Berlin Police. Thinking back about what work in the People's Police had meant to her, she said, "I have always been there for the police—in a way that this would never be true today: then, it was my life." In the next section on the underpinnings of the work ethic advocated by westerners, I contrast this extensive understanding of time with westerners' sense of intensive time.

Western Perspectives on Work: Initiative/Intensive Time

Westerners have a set of complaints about their eastern colleagues' work ethic which is remarkably different from the rhetoric of the easterners about the work ethic of westerners. What westerners typically find most wanting is independent initiative, as the following statement of a western superior may demonstrate:

> The whole question of delegation is a big problem for me. What should I say? Delegation is a great thing. But I can only do it under circumstances in which the person to whom I delegate a task is actually capa-

23. The date is interesting; it places these changes in the context of overall cultural changes in Germany in the aftermath of the student unrest of the late sixties. Their comments are thus likely to be more than simple nostalgia for the good old days and tougher men.

ble of executing it independently. But many [eastern officers] can't do just that; they have grown up with the expectation of getting very detailed orders about what to do. . . . I have tried to ease things a little bit by working out checklists for the people, although I am a declared enemy of checklists, since they preempt thinking.

Western superiors tell stories about eastern officers whom they have found lounging around somewhere waiting for the next orders to come in. They complain that easterners don't see what needs to be done next. They are annoyed by the way easterners execute tasks more or less literally, without much attention to the specific circumstances at hand. One officer put it this way: "Sometimes I think they [the easterners] just don't know what police work is about." On another occasion, the same officer pointed out how one can differentiate between good and poor police work:

It is the way in which they [subordinate officers] approach their work, how they execute their operations, whether they know what police work is; whether [an officer] just writes down, "At this place at that time somebody has lit up a garbage can," or whether he writes "Then we ran after him and caught him," or that they have asked the neighbors what they saw and whether they knew the person. You know, this is work, a real police operation. Or if someone annoyed an officer a couple of times by driving without a license and if this officer then decides that this guy is his "personal one" and tries again and again to get him, then he is a real police officer, because he tries to achieve something. . . . But if they just drive around in their snow-white patrol cars, enjoying the lovely landscape, just going where they are sent, . . . well, that isn't police work; they are just not getting anywhere.

It should be noted that patrol cars in Germany are not white, but green and green/white. Thus the description of the color as "snow-white" *(blütenweiß)* functions much more as a metaphor of innocence and innocuousness.[24] That then, is precisely what police work cannot be: harmless. The good police officer as defined in the statement above must have the will to apprehend violators and perpetrators. Western officers define good work as driven by the goal of the operation, which ultimately means "to get the villain," the transgressor of the law, to find facts and evidence that will hold up in court and lead to a conviction. Thus, they juxtapose

24. The German term is literally translated "blossom-white."

a kind of work which is ideally task-oriented, in which officers independently involve themselves,[25] and work conceived of as the precise execution of orders. The former relies heavily on taking the initiative in operation; the latter does not. If eastern officers are confronted with this logic, they point to the irony that, after all, the People's Police was much more successful in clearing up criminal offenses than the western police.

Most western officers do not blame easterners personally for their presumed lack of initiative. Westerners hold decades of socialization in a communist system responsible for what they consider ultimately as a form of incapacitation. For them it is just another effect of the militaristic nature of the People's Police, which was an organization based on strict notions of command and obedience, fundamentally different from their own more democratic police organization. The westerner's identification of the People's Police as militaristic again moves the People's Police into proximity with the prewar German police, thus creating strong antidemocratic connotations.[26] Accordingly, western officers have frequently made it a point to let easterners know that form is treated loosely in the west—that "the heel clicking is over."

Undoubtedly, the People's Police was organized much more than the Berlin Police according to notions of military discipline. People's Police officers held military rank (instead of police ranks); they had to salute superiors militarily; they had to drop their work if a superior entered the room to make a report about what they were doing; the patrolmen did indeed have relatively strict orders about where to patrol, what precisely to look at, where to be at what time, and where and when to eat. Many eastern officers agree that they have to work nowadays much more independently, on their own account and taking responsibility for their own actions. It must be remembered, however, that the People's Police was not a unitary organization either. In contrast to the work of regular foot patrol officers, the work of neighborhood beat patrol officers and of officers in highway accident units demanded much more independent initiative as well.[27] Many officers enjoy the greater liberty they now have in

25. The German terms used in this context, *sich einbringen* (literally, "to bring oneself into it") and *mitdenken* (literally, "to follow up in thinking") seem not to have suitable English equivalents.

26. This notion would be true even for the Berlin Police in the Weimar Republic, which has not been seen as a guardian of the fragile democracy but a stronghold of antidemocratic forces (see Liang 1970).

27. In general I have the impression that officers from such units have found it much easier to adjust to work in western police organizations than did former patrol officers.

managing their own work and the responsibility of independent action; some feel overwhelmed by the new demands.

However, the People's Police system, despite its militaristic character, did allow slack sometimes in areas where slack is not so easily tolerated in the Berlin Police. In evaluating the work ethic of easterners, western superiors tell stories about easterners who took liberties with their work time:

> They all of sudden disappeared during the middle of the day and couldn't be found anywhere in the precinct. Nobody knew where they were. In the end it turned out that they had gone shopping, or that they had gone to the hairdresser. They had just left in the middle of the day without telling anyone—you must imagine that!

While such behavior is indeed interpreted as a lack of the proper attitude to work, once again the sociopolitical system is blamed for it. Eastern officers are excused by pointing to the difficulty of obtaining consumer goods in the GDR. As soon as supplies of scarce commodities were available, one simply had to queue up, whether one was at work or not. Waiting until after work meant that the goods would be gone, bought up by those who dropped everything to get themselves in line.[28] Thus shopping excursions of this kind were tolerated in the GDR. Scolding an eastern officer for a shopping spree ("After all, he needs to be told that this sort of thing will no longer fly"), and then excusing him or her by pointing to the system neatly identifies the easterner, the GDR, the westerner, and the FRG: it establishes personal superiority and systems superiority. What upset western superiors about these trips is first the *kind* of private pursuit undertaken during work hours: going to the hairdresser is simply out of the question. Some shopping or running an errand, however, could be tolerated under certain circumstances, but such circumstances, in the eyes of the complaining western officers, were not present. The point is that these activities were carried out by officers whose performance was considered to be substandard. Deviations from the norm tend to be tolerated as long as the performance of the officer in question is deemed satisfac-

28. The common, only half-jokingly suggested shopping maxim in the GDR was that wherever there was a line, it was worthwhile to get in it, since no matter what one got, it could be used subsequently in barter. Both easterners and westerners tell stories dating back to the time after the fall of the Wall about easterners queuing up in the *West* in front of one store or bank while the store next door or the bank around the corner had no customers. Habit, they said, drove people to think that only where there was a line was there a desirable good.

tory, and there are no outside complaints (e.g., by citizens or superiors).[29] The eastern officers who violated these tacit norms were therefore criticized for taking the same liberties as some western officers, but these liberties were not considered to be their right, at least *not yet.*

Taken together, initiative and goal orientation, as well as the stricter separation between work time and leisure induce a sense of time which emphasizes achievement per time unit. In other words, the western work ethic is informed by a notion of time efficiency. Officers who work effectively with limited time receive praise. In sharp contrast to the notion of extensive time embedded in the eastern rhetoric on the work ethic, the comparable western rhetoric implies an understanding of time which can be called "intensive."[30]

The Double-Edged Sword of Missionary Activity

Talking about the work ethic of easterners, western officers frequently make a distinction between "willingness" and "ability." When asked how they can tell someone who is willing or able from someone who is not, their response shows that "willingness" is signified by a set of actions that resemble the elements I have described as signs of commitment in the section on the easterners' criteria for a positive attitude to work: punctuality, courtesy, prompt execution of orders, and playing by the rules. "Ability" indicates the quality of work performance, a combination of initiative and success. Immediately after unification, westerners seemed to fear most that eastern officers might be unwilling;[31] today their concern is much more with ability. Four years after unification most eastern offi-

29. The same measure applies to the judgment of western officers by their own superiors. Thus good performers create liberty for themselves. Differences in performance create difference in the application of regulations.

30. This distinction between intensive and extensive time based on a rhetoric of the work ethic is at least consistent with the prevalent economic policies in both countries to increase output. The GDR tried to increase the participation rate of the potential labor force, accordingly attempting to recruit more and more women into the labor force (see Borneman 1992). The output increase thus produced is therefore extensive. This has certainly not simply happened as a matter of choice; it is due in part to considerable and chronic capital shortages in centrally planned economies (see Gregory and Stuart 1981). Thus, the notion of extensive time is closely linked to what Katherine Verdery (1996, 39ff.) has aptly called the "etatization of time." Western companies usually aim primarily to increase productivity, (i.e., production per capita), which amounts to an intensification of the work process. John Borneman (1998, 97ff.) arrives at a similar result by comparing consumption patterns.

31. West Berlin officers have pointed out that after four years of a united Berlin police force, those who were unwilling to participate have left the police voluntarily,

cers are identified as willing, but only some are also identified as able.[32] Those who are seen as both willing and able are declared to "have mastered unification" *(die Wende geschafft haben)*, while those who are perceived as either unwilling or unable are identified as "not having mastered the turnaround yet" *(die Wende noch nicht geschafft haben)* or sometimes also as "turnaround-damaged" *(wendegeschädigt)*. Thus unification, the turnaround, is understood by these western officers as a challenge to easterners to learn western ways of working and to turn around personally, too—to become for all practical purposes just like a westerner. Thus the highest praise a western officer can give an easterner is that he or she is virtually indistinguishable from a westerner. It is a sign that turnaround has been achieved.

With pride, western superiors have pointed out that for the most part they no longer need to insist on mixed east-west patrols, which were seen as the primary means to achieve western standards on duty in Berlin. One day, as I was leaving the precinct with a western officer who was giving me a lift to the commuter rail station (S-Bahn), a patrol car was just leaving the courtyard. The western officer brought my attention immediately to the car, remarking that it was staffed exclusively by easterners: "This would not have been possible only two years ago," he pointed out. Other western officers with whom I have left the precinct on other occasions have directed my attention to the same fact, with an almost identical undertone of achievement. Western officers like to think of themselves as pioneers who have gone out into the wilderness of the east, which is alluded to as "the wild east" *(der wilde Osten)*, a play on the U.S. term for its frontier, "the wild west" (with a different set of connotations, it is also called "the Congo" or "the bush"),[33] to make unification happen, which is tantamount to teaching easterners western ways in order to remake the east in the image of the west. One mission was to teach

---

or were dismissed, or at least have been transferred to another precinct or office. Police units try to get rid of personnel they judge as unable. Since most of them are tenured state employees, they cannot be fired, which is why units try to "rid themselves" *(los werden)* of unwanted officers. Good occasions for doing so are centrally ordered personnel curtailments requiring individual units to part with a number of officers. Thus individual units often seem to have unofficial "red lists."

32. This is especially so in Brandenburg, where one high-ranking officer from the state of Northrhine-Westphalia in western Germany said, in assessing his eastern subordinates, "They are all willing, but most of them still don't get it." Another western officer in Brandenburg made a statement to the same effect: "Sometimes I wish myself back into police civilization."

33. This is yet another telling allochronism on the basis of a notion of development.

easterners how to work; thus, westerners are proud once their "civilizing task" has been accomplished. But by no means are westerners sure that they have succeeded yet, that what has been achieved is in fact self-sustaining. One day I was standing with a western officer by a window overlooking the courtyard of the precinct in Köpenick. A couple of eastern workers were unloading a truck containing office furniture destined to embellish the quarters of the deputy chief. They did not handle their cargo carefully, making the western officer (and myself, I must admit) flinch at every bump. They also worked at a pace which elicited sarcastic comments from the western officer. Watching the scene for a little while longer in silence, he turned away from it with the comment, "You will see, in the end the easterners will finish us all off."

Policing as Performance

Both eastern and western understandings of a positive attitude towards work are supported by a *sense* of performance, even if eastern and western officers may have different understandings of what constitutes good performance.[34] Theatrical metaphors such as "performance" or "stage" as scientific, heuristic *concepts* for an understanding of social activity have been fine-tuned most notably by Goffman (1959). While the language of the theater has proven to be quite useful as an interpretative device for social scientists, later works, for example by Turner (1974) or Herzfeld (1985), have focused on a *sense* of performance that informs the intricacies, especially the sequencing, of action for the actors themselves. Putting it in terms of Geertz's famous dictum (1973, 93) the emphasis has thus shifted from using theatrical metaphors as "models *of*" to understanding their working as "models *for*" action. What characterizes action as performance is the fact that it is addressed, that it is done to be seen or to be known by others for reasons which may be quite different from its purported intention. In performance, the action does not consume it-

---

34. It is important to keep different uses of the word *performance* in mind. Performance could be defined as the production of results, but the common emphasis on results disregards the production process itself, as when an institution or a machine is thought of as showing good performance (which is usually backed up by a set of indicators such as, to give police-related examples, the clear-up rate of a police precinct or the maximum acceleration of a patrol car). The emphasis here, however, is on the production *process* and less on the result; what is of interest is the *how* of the doing.

self upon completion, it does not rest in itself or exist for itself. Performance aims to convey a relationship between actors, their action, and an audience, and is therefore in many ways the nonverbal equivalent of rhetoric (cf. Burke 1969a).[35]

Performance, then, is just as apt a means to create identifications—links between self and something else—as verbal utterances. An officer who enters a room in which other officers are chatting in little groups can make a statement by associating himself with one group rather than with another. An omitted handshake or a pat on the shoulder at the right time can mean a lot. Licking one's lips over a steaming platter of boiled pig's feet with sauerkraut can be a more powerful identification than the simple verbal statement, "I like boiled pig's feet with sauerkraut."

Since these actions are communications, the analysis of verbal utterances can serve as a metaphor for the analysis of actions as communication. Some actions function like tropes (Turner 1991). The selective association by one officer with a particular group rather than with another can be read, for example, in terms of either a synecdoche (as "I am a part of this group, I stand for the group, the group stands for me") or a metonymy (as "I am like any of them, not like any of the others"). Longer sequences of action can be understood in terms of narratives, as narratives are interpretative representations of action.

As communications, these actions must have recourse to conventions, to codes, for otherwise they would remain unintelligible. Every human enactment of codes is an act of mimesis. Being acts of interpretation in execution, and thus bearing the signature of the actor, all actions as communications are performances (as are a fortiori all verbal utterances). Performances therefore identify not only by the message they convey, but also by the way in which they are executed. This manner of execution in performance has its own poetics (Jakobson 1960). The poetics of performance creates identifications through the choices that have been made, through style, and by the greater or lesser degree of mastery with which a performance is carried out. Police officers who execute a police action in a particular way therefore identify themselves, just as much as the subordinate who tries to convince his superior to nominate him for a promotion identifies himself not only by presenting himself as worthy, but also by the sophistication or the clumsiness of his maneuvers.

35. In this sense one can speak about a rhetoric of action as one speaks about verbal performance.

Narrating Performance

That work is understood as performance by the police officers themselves
becomes immediately clear in such activities as commenting on police
work by saying, "This was a great operation" (Das war ein toller Einsatz),
thus usually introducing a narrative representing what had happened
"outside" *(draußen)*.[36] The primary audience to which police performance is directed is other police officers, mainly for two reasons: first,
only other police officers are fully able to assess the quality of police
work; and second, such quality assessment is the basis on which police
officers get promoted. Since police officers work mostly in pairs, most of
their colleagues and superiors usually do not see any particular work
sequence. While colleagues may observe each other once in a while, because of shifting teams, superiors have few chances to see their subordinates in action.[37] Thus, the chief way in which work performance is made
visible, that is, the principal means by which an audience is constituted
in the police, is through the act of renarrating work sequences to colleagues and superiors both informally in oral presentations as well as
formally in writing.

A good deal of police action is narrated in written reports, which are
read not only by the shift leader, who uses them to stay on top of what
is going on, and who must sign each written report to approve it, but by
the leadership of the precinct (chief and chief of operations), who skim
these reports every morning for general information. Case administrators
read them for further processing (and to turn them into the hottest gossip
about "what is going on in the precinct"). Finally, even peers in the shift
will read them if a police action was particularly interesting. In addition
to these formal written reports, police action is continuously turned into
stories which are narrated and renarrated by their originators as well as
by colleagues who tell them to others. The most colorful ones not only
take their place among the professional yarns of a particular police officer, the personal story repertoire told again and again (e.g., at parties),
but may come to belong to the folklore of a shift or even a precinct.

Narrations of most of the police work in patrol car shifts, in traditional
Aristotelian fashion, consist of relatively closed sequences of action: they
have a beginning, a middle, and an end (1990, 50b24–34). The beginning
is constituted by an event, such as an accident, a suicide threat, a person

36. See chapter 1 for the significance of inside-outside distinctions.
37. Observation by superiors is usually restricted to larger operations such as
major accidents, large-scale traffic control, or other forms of concerted action.

in danger, or a break-in; generally the beginning is some crisis in which police officers are called to intervene. The middle comprises the actions taken by the police, such as securing the location of an accident, assisting the rescue team, interviewing witnesses, and collecting evidence. The end is the result achieved through this action: accident cleared up, endangered person in safety, burglar caught (or escaped) and locale secured, and so on. Thus work narratives of police officers in police action follow a relatively stable, (ideally romantic) plot structure: crisis, intervention, and (ideally desired) result.

Clearly, some police activities are preferred to others, and the preferred tasks are the ones that make for good narrative and, perhaps even more important, are worth narrating. These preferred activities are often referred to as "real" *(richtig)*,[38] whereas other tasks are bemoaned (for example, after being assigned over the radio) as "again nothing real." The first precondition for narratability is that some kind of police action de facto happens. The police officers with whom I rode during patrol car shifts in Köpenick and Potsdam were usually very unhappy about being assigned certain jobs. Typically, family problems, disputes between neighbors, and complaints by possibly psychotic persons (mostly well known to the officers after a while) fell in this category of unwanted, "unreal" tasks.[39] The assignment of such tasks drew remarks like, "I don't really know why we should go there, we can't do anything about it anyway" or, upon leaving a situation in which they couldn't do much, "What in hell are we supposed to write now about that?" The second precondition, which concerns mostly formal, written narrative, is that the action performed be relevant to what are considered true police functions. A reportable incident must minimally involve some form of danger to a person or to public safety and order which the police officers have eliminated through their action (this can be as trivial as removing an obstacle from the road or as spectacular as saving the life of a drowning person, or talking somebody out of committing suicide); otherwise, their action must address itself to the transgression of an ordinance or criminal

38. The word *richtig* has several meanings which reverberate in such statements. On the one hand it means "real" in the sense of something police officers should do, something which is really a police officer's work and thus conforms to ideas about what constitutes police work, the purpose of policing, and so on. The second meaning of *richtig* is "right" as opposed to "wrong," that is, desirable rather than undesirable. On another level, the word can have a moral meaning.

39. See also chapter 7 regarding the problem of embarrassment at the revelation of information usually considered to be private, which creates aversion to certain kinds of police tasks.

law.[40] Of course, for all informal presentations to colleagues, strange occurrences (e.g., involving psychotic persons), even if the police officers could not take any kind of action, make for splendid story material. Unfortunately, strange occurrences are quite unpredictable, and situations which do not promise the possibility of intervention are therefore disliked. Situations in which police officers felt that they should have been able to act (e.g., for moral reasons) but saw no legal ground for intervention are also narratable, but are disliked for the feeling of powerlessness that comes with them.[41]

The question of when exactly an incident is worth narrating does of course reach beyond what a police officer has to do to comply with police regulations. Aspects of personal gratification are very important constituents of narratability. Incidents worth narrating either pose a particular challenge to the police officer's abilities or include events leading to a particularly desirable ending, such as catching a thief red-handed (which is rare enough). The events most worth narrating are those in which the prowess of the police officers actually leads to the ideal outcome, and also those in which the officers did everything in their power, yet circumstances were such that the desirable outcome could not be secured (see Austin 1956; Burke 1969a). Sheer good luck is also worth reporting—the more unbelievable the better. But the best luck is the opportunity seized; therefore, the combination of competence and luck is most desirable. Thus what makes for good narration is what Machiavelli (1978) has identified as the characteristics of a commendable prince: *virtù* and *fortuna*. The best story and thus the most desirable kind of police work is one in which the officer has a chance to deploy her *virtù,* the best of her abilities, her skill and imagination, and is ideally challenged by *fortuna,* so that a great opportunity can thus be seized.

What is needed to turn luck into success is, according to the police officers themselves, "presence of mind" *(Geistesgegewart).* Presence of mind is therefore one of the gifts a good police officer must have; it is part of his *virtù.* In a mundane way, for example, in the everyday practice of police officers in Berlin and Potsdam, presence of mind is revealed in

40. This could also be expressed somewhat differently. In order to be narratable at all, the incident must fall more or less into an established genre. As far as police work is concerned, the genres are represented to some extent by the variety of reporting forms available to police officers (e.g., special forms for accidents without major personal injuries, forms for accidents with major personal injuries, simple reports, charges for damage to property, etc.).

41. Equally undesirable, of course, are situations in which police officers know that they would have to act but don't know what to do.

recognizing a stolen car on the street (car theft being one of the most prevalent crimes since unification). Encountering a stolen car is good luck, but officers must also prepare for this event by memorizing the plate numbers, makes, and colors of stolen cars. "Virtuous" police officers might keep a little notebook for such purposes, collecting information that allows them to recognize an opportunity once they meet it. Another aspect of virtù consists in just that sort of preparation, getting to know what is worth looking for. Recognition of opportunity can be further helped by little "tricks," such as knowing that a license plate with two sets of drill-holes to fasten it to the bumper of a car (indicating that the plate has been transferred from one type of vehicle to another) should at least give rise to suspicion, as one eastern officer in Potsdam pointed out to me. What presence of mind in policing ultimately requires is the piecing together of information acquired in different contexts. The police officer must be able to weave these disparate pieces of information together into a new whole, which at the beginning is often no more than a hunch about an association ("I am sure that this has something to do with that"), but grows in the course of time into a whole story ("This is how it must have been") in the reconstruction of the course of events.

The Social Poetics of Patrol Car Duty

Recently, phenomena of creativity in action, with particular attention to the sequencing of action, have been discussed under the title of a "poetics" (Herzfeld 1985, 1991, 1997; Hallyn 1990; Miller 1986).[42] This metaphorical transposition of a concept used predominantly in literary analysis (e.g., Todorov 1981; Culler 1975) into the social sciences has lent new vigor to social constructivism (e.g., Berger and Luckmann 1967) by contributing to the understanding of process and by emphasizing human creativity. While post-Wittgensteinian (1984) linguistic analysis has benefited from looking at linguistic utterances as forms of action (Austin 1956 and 1962; Searle 1969), the social sciences discovered in a reflection of such thinking which also has its roots in Wittgenstein's late philosophy the power of linguistic metaphors in understanding action. The idea of a poetics of action or a poetics of social life is on the one hand a part of

---

42. Without using the term *poetics*, de Certeau (1984) has discussed the same phenomenon in the context of his version of practice theory, more specifically his *strategy–tactics* distinction (see note 31 in chapter 1), as *making do* (especially chapter 3), as the *enunciation* of action (33, 82–89) tracing this phenomenon of an art of practice back not to the Greek concept of poetics but to *metis*.

this general movement, and on the other it coincides with and draws from the revival of interest in the work of Giambattista Vico (1982) and the reconsideration of rhetoric as a lost tradition of the social sciences (Burke 1969b; Herzfeld 1987).

The main representative of the linguistic structuralism of the Prague School, Roman Jakobson (1960), considers poetics to be not only a feature of poetry but a function more or less implicit in all linguistic utterances. What makes an utterance poetic, according to Jakobson, is the *selection* of words in such a way that their *combination* makes them resonant with each other to create meaning (e.g., by alliteration, rhyme, rhythm, etc.).[43] Taken together, selection and combination constitute an act of creativity within the constraints of available forms: existing words with their known meanings and admissible patterns of stringing them together (i.e., semantics and syntax on one level but also, on a higher level, narrative conventions and genres).

What the police officers call "presence of mind" is not reducible to intentionality. Presence of mind needs careful preparation, prior action. Presence of mind is produced and thus poetic in its selection of elements of information gathered and committed to memory in different contexts so as to be ready for the fortuitous piece of information which will render all of them into a meaningful ensemble, thus giving rise to the recognition that there is an opportunity for police action. Presence of mind in police work is an act of creativity. However, while Jakobson in typical structuralist fashion emphasizes the *equivalence* of the elements poetically related to each other, the elements joined by the police officers are not equivalent in Jakobson's sense; they are disparate and unequal. What holds them together is narrative, the dynamics of plot (Brooks 1984; Ricoeur 1984, 1992).

Presence of mind is not the only part of a police action which can be described in terms of a poetics. The entire action sequence to the degree that it involves skill and creativity and would thus be handled with perceptible variation by different officers within a set of given forms (such as rules and regulations) is conducive to analysis in terms of a poetics. What follows the initial presence of mind in which a situation is recognized as appropriate for police intervention is what is called in police handbook language an "assessment of the situation" *(Lagebeurteilung),*

43. The juxtaposition of selection/combination is inspired by the Saussurian distinction between paradigmatic and syntagmatic relationships. Jakobson (1960) defines the poetic function thus: "The poetic function projects the principle of equivalence from the axis of selection into the axis of combination" (358).

in which the police officers must decide upon and execute a course of action in response to their realization of opportunity.[44] Here, too, police officers have to consider and select among alternatives, and thus there unfolds a secondary poetics—that of the measures taken by the police. The reaction to a car identified as stolen, for example, will depend on whether it is just sitting somewhere or whether it is being driven; whether it looks abandoned, with little chance of finding the thieves in the immediate vicinity of the car; or whether there might be a chance of finding the drivers because the motor is still warm, passers-by saw the driver leaving the car just minutes ago, and so on. Few police actions (or probably any actions for that matter) follow the initial plan devised in the assessment of the situation. In the course of the action, officers need to respond flexibly and creatively to constantly changing circumstances, and they have to reassess the situation as more information becomes available and others act in unforeseen ways. It is precisely this ability to succeed in such unpredictable environments, to improvise in adverse circumstances, which demonstrates ingenuity and is thus conducive to poetic analysis (see Herzfeld 1995, 136ff.). This poetics of measures taken is not one of equivalencies either, and it is not absorbed in itself but is transcended by the final goal: eventual success, whatever that might be under the circumstances given. Thus action has again a narrative structure that retraces sequences of action to their beginning and projects them to their potential end.

Finally, the presentation of action in the police precinct has its own poetics, for certain aspects of what has happened "outside" will be chosen for renarration, tweaked and embellished, and others will be left out. Also the events will not necessarily be presented in the chronological order in which they occurred; that is, they will be emplotted in particular ways. The precise manner of their presentation depends in part on the formal requirements of the reports. The forms that must be filled out and the narrative conventions for reporting police action to superiors and peers direct the interest of the police officers to particular kinds of information at the expense of others. But the presentation also depends on what fellow officers think makes for a good story. Presentation "inside"

---

44. Theoretically one could consider decision making and enactment as two different series of action with their respective poetics. Analytically this would make most sense in cases of large-scale operations in which there is a division of labor between decision makers and enactors. In every kind of practice, however, decision making and acting are intricately interwoven with each other, and since the operations I am talking about here are typically undertaken by patrol officers themselves, a separation between enactment and decision would be misleading.

Figure 17. Potsdam officer taking notes on an accident
in the patrol car for a report to be written later back
in the police station (1995). Author's photo.

requires a skill of its own which is quite distinct from the skills needed
in the identification of opportunity and in the choice and execution of
measures to be taken "outside."[45]

The three levels of poetic action that I have identified here—presence
of mind, measures taken, and renarration—are by no means independent
of each other. Police officers very clearly gear their actions towards the
written report they have to write (figs. 17, 18). In other words, they act

45. Often the formal presentation (e.g., of accidents) requires two parts: a narrative as well as a drawing. Some officers are known in the precinct to make good
sketches of the locale, while they might be considered poor report writers. For others,
it is the reverse. Thus the officer's recognition of skill and style involved in either
acknowledges a distinct poetics for both activities.

Figure 18. Köpenick officer drafting an accident sketch for a report (1995). Author's photo.

with the future presentation of their action in view.[46] This connection becomes visible in formulations which reveal the classification of a situation in terms of the form which is used to write it up. The subsumption of a real-world situation under a form automatically raises a series of questions for which the officers need to find answers at the "locale of action" *(vor Ort)* in order to fill out the forms properly.[47] To use another

46. The relation between action and future narration might have been somewhat exaggerated in my own observations because many of the conversations, especially between eastern and western officers, might have had a pedagogical intention. But even if that is the case, it shows perhaps even more clearly how thinking through an event from the perspective of its relevant end-product, the report, gets habitualized in the process of patrol-duty socialization.

47. The same applies to sketches of accidents, which, professionally done, require certain information, such as the positions of the cars involved in an accident relative

metaphor, the forms function as genres. In this way action and anticipated narration become a unity: action and narration are intertwined in
a two-way mimetic relationship. Narration is as much *mimesis praxeos*,
as action is *mimesis* of narrative.[48]

Performing for the Outside World

Police work has many tangible aspects: accidents are reported, traffic is
rerouted, people are arrested, licenses are revoked, cars are inspected,
hazards removed. But just as important as this tangible feature of police
work is its highly symbolic character. Since police officers (perhaps together with tax officials) are considered to be the representatives of the
state par excellence, police interaction with people is an indicator of how
the state deals with its citizens. For many people, the police are tantamount to trouble: police officers at one's door are rarely considered to
be harbingers of good luck, for even if one's conscience is pure, and one
does not remember any speeding or worse offenses,[49] police officers are
known to bring bad news about relatives in accidents, and so on (Bittner
1990, 94ff.). Needless to say, neighbors also take a lively interest in the
relationship between a particular person and the state. Police interest in
a person identifies this person in some way. Police officers also talk about

---

to the geography of the locale in which it occurred (distance from curb, distance from
intersection, position of traffic signs, etc.).

48. Aristotle has defined drama as the representation of action, as "mimesis praxeos" (1990, 48a28). However, as the shaping of action by awareness of its future
representation illustrates, action can in turn be viewed as enactment of the representation of action. Thus the circular relation between action and representation, between
structure and culture becomes visible (see Giddens 1984). In contrast to Bourdieu's
(1977) theory of "habitus," a framework of "poetics" is much more open to the
creativity of actors. Therefore, in contrast to practice theory with either *habitus*
(Bourdieu 1977) or *structuration* (Giddens 1984) as core concepts, which are both
aiming principally at explaining the reproduction of patterned action in the course
of time, the framework of a poetics of action proposes a dialectical relationship between structure and culture, action and its symbolization, thus giving full credibility
to creative agents. Consequently, the poetics framework recognizing the importance
of consciousness offers completely different possibilities to conceptualize social
change.

49. German radar traps work by taking a picture of every single car passing
through at excess speed. Ideally, the photographs are good enough to clearly identify
both the vehicle and the driver. In cases of conflict, however, the speeder has to be
identified properly, especially if the owner of the car, who will be ticketed, claims
that he was not driving. For these purposes police officers are asked to make house
calls.

their work as "producing security," knowing full well that security is a highly subjective feeling which may be influenced considerably by the presence of police. Thus the sheer presence of a seemingly idle patrol car or a seemingly idle officer still communicates something.

There is an important aspect of performance in police work which I have not touched upon yet at all. I have said before that the primary audience of police performance consists of peers and superiors not only because they are the ones who can actually appreciate the qualities of police work but because the narration of police action taking place "outside" to superiors "inside" is essential for purposes of career development. However, as the symbolic effect of policing makes clear, there is also an audience "outside": victims and witnesses of accidents, bystanders of any kind, the transgressors of laws or ordinances, in short everyone with whom police officers come into contact in the course of their work other than their own colleagues. Police officers even have a particular word for this audience which is conceived as a generalized other: they call it "the citizen" *(der Bürger).*[50] Police officers are asked to act with the citizen in mind. The ideal propagated by the leadership is that of a close relationship between citizens and the police.[51]

There is also a secondary audience "outside," an audience that has an interest in police-citizen relationships as well as in matters internal to the police, composed of the mass media, politicians, citizen's action committees, human rights organizations, and so forth.[52] Police officers are highly aware of the media attention their behavior may attract. Certain actions of the police are especially prone to draw political and media attention, such as the operations in the context of the by-now traditional May Day

50. Lawbreakers have an interesting and ambiguous status within this group of "citizens." On the one hand, they are citizens, too, and thus have rights that deserve respect, but on the other hand they are endangering the generalized "citizen," whom it is the police officer's task to protect.

51. The technical term in use, literally translated, is "citizen-friendly police," *(bürgerfreundliche Polizei).*

52. And of course sociologists are interested in and write about the police. Ethnographers must develop a keen sense for the effects of their presence. I frequently wondered which performances were specifically addressed to me as an outside observer. As I realized during my fieldwork, some performances seemingly aimed at me were similar to performances carried out with neophytes in view: they were meant to teach local ways. I was lucky enough to witness the arrival of newcomers who in some ways received treatment similar to mine. Other aspects transcend the pedagogical intent of certain performances: they are clearly directed toward somebody who will remain an outsider and carry the information gathered somewhere else.

demonstrations of the "left-autonomous scene" *(links-autonome Szene)* in Berlin,[53] which have been regularly accompanied by a great deal of violence in the form of looting, arson, and battle-like confrontation with the police. These operations have an almost emblematic character for the assessment of the police in politics and in the mass media. As countless newspaper articles in the aftermath of these operations show, the quality of police leadership is especially under scrutiny during this one day, which therefore becomes a day of high theatrical significance. Frequently, police officers see themselves also as the whipping boys of pubic opinion. Many officers have explicitly expressed the feeling that no matter what they do the press always seems dissatisfied: either the police are scolded for not being tough enough or branded as a gang of ruffians.[54]

Not only does the leadership of the police try to direct the performances of police officers in ways that it believes will enhance its own relations with the outside world (e.g., the president of police performs through his police officers for the minister), but the police officers have their own agenda, which may or may not be compatible with that of the leadership (see Bittner 1990, 147ff.). Neighborhood beat patrol officers, for example, find it helpful to establish a good understanding with people in their turf, especially with representatives of local organizations such as schools or hospitals, and with the local business community. Police officers also have their "special friends," usually people who have come into conflict with the police on an almost regular basis: they are notorious drunk drivers, or they have been repeatedly caught speeding; they may violate city ordinances again and again, commit petty crimes, and so on. When police officers talk about these "special clients" (another term for "special friends"), they often speak in ways that reveal a high degree of personalized conflict, such as "I will teach him who will finally be at the longer end of the stick," or "I will show him who is the master around here."

---

53. It is called autonomous because it is not affiliated with a political party. It consists of a hodgepodge of small, sometimes quite ephemeral groups, which show a high degree of fluidity in overall organization; therefore, it is more a scene than a fixed structure. If it does have a common thrust at all, it might best be described as anarchic. In most places in Germany its strongholds are in the squatter scene.

54. This is a feature of police work which is, given the highly political character of policing itself, probably unavoidable in a democratic society, in which different parts of society lay claim to the resources of the police. Things were different in the GDR, where the police force clearly understood itself as an instrument of the ruling vanguard party (see MdI 1987). Eastern police officers therefore felt much more appreciated in the GDR, where their work was constantly praised for its contribution to the socialist cause.

Police actions directed at these various kinds of audiences "outside" can have a poetics of their own in that police officers pick a particular tone, select a particular vocabulary, assume a variety of body postures depending on whom they talk to and what effect they try to achieve. One chilly October night at Unter den Linden I approached an employee of the Berlin guard police watching over the premises of the British Consulate General asking him for the closest bus stop. It was late, and he was bored and drew me into a chat. As he tried to forget his duties for a minute, I started to be on duty as soon as he communicated to me that he was a former People's Police officer. Having sensed my interest about life in the People's Police, he began to rave about the pluck it had compared to the Berlin guard police and offered to perform for me as he would have in this same situation (a passer-by approaching an officer guarding a Western Consulate General) if he still wore the garb of the People's Police. He thrust his hips forward, lowered his chin toward his chest, narrowed his eyes behind his eyebrows, which had effectively assumed the role of a visor, and stared at me as if as impermeable as the Wall itself. No doubt, it never would have occurred to me to approach him with anything had he taken this position, which he called the "People's Police guard posture" or "fuck-off position."

Presentations in front of "outside" audiences are recognized by police officers as involving a particular skill. An officer who is good at this kind of performance may be known to his colleagues as somebody "who can talk to people," or as "affable," or he might have a reputation as a mediator in conflicts. The presentations for their "outside" audiences of course have important repercussions for what they present "inside," because police officers depend in many ways on the cooperation of "outside" audiences. Most important, they need information to realize an opportunity, to assess the situation, and to pick the right measures, so as to have a convincing story for renarration back in the precinct.

In sum, then, police work may be seen as suspended between performances oriented toward two different kinds of audiences, the "inside" of peers and superiors and the "outside" of perpetrators, "clients," witnesses, bystanders, and the media. The self-presentation of police officers in front of these audiences, as well as the composition of police action involves various layers of recognizably distinct poetics. Ultimately, there is no poetics without an audience; that is, every poetics must be embedded in performance. The critical boundary case is a performance for one's own self or performances before an imagined audience. In principle, there are as many different poetics as there are culturally *recognized* skills. This point is very important. Only to the degree that skills are discussed and performances evaluated are individual choices of police officers recognizable as such. A poetics thus presumes symbolic distinctions, which are as foundational for the actors and the potential poetic nature of their actions as they are for the appreciation of action. It is the insight into the existence of different possibilities and the resulting awareness that choices actually have to be made which make police officers the primary audience of performance.[55] I have, therefore, followed the police officers' own distinctions of different skills ("presence of mind," "situational assessment," "choice of means," "presentation") in analyzing performance, for these are the ones that are socially effective. Of course, as I have tried to point out, they can only be separated analytically from each other; they all intersect in actual performance. Still, there is no such thing as a totally understood performance: every view of police action is partial, recognizing and reacting only to a part of the poetic activity that composes the whole.

Performance as Rhetoric:
The Blessings of Ambiguity

I have pointed out above that there is a close connection between rhetoric and performance. As rhetoric at times conceals its elements of persuasion to allow the addressee to feel convinced by factual information alone (Burke 1969b), performance at times conceals that it transcends the action itself, that it is actually addressed to and meant to be seen by an audience (Herzfeld 1985). It is interesting therefore to note where police officers explicitly talk about their action as performance and therefore also as addressed, and where the rhetorical character of action is painstakingly concealed. Concealing the rhetorical aspects of performance seems to be acceptable vis-à-vis superiors and citizens, but colleagues do not appreciate it unless it creates explicitly humorous or otherwise entertaining overtones. Concealing the rhetoric of performance from friends constitutes a breach of trust.[56] This is probably the reason why work narrated to colleagues is so often suffused with hyperbole and theatrical gestures.

Rather than pursue the intricacies of concealment, I want to attend

55. Audience and performer have to share a culture; for the interaction between artists and their audience, see Becker 1982.
56. Compare also the section entitled "Valuing Sincerity" in chapter 5.

to the much more curious fact of the openness of performance, the performance of performance as performance, if you like. Superiors sometimes counsel their subordinates on how to improve the "appearance" *(Erscheinung, Erscheinungsbild)* of a written report, which thus gets "brightened" *(geschönt)*. Western superiors frequently express surprise that easterners do not try to present their work in the best possible light ("without violating regulations or a sense of propriety, of course"), while easterners are amazed at the skills westerners use to present their work in the best possible light in front of their superiors. Superiors, in turn, present themselves as being able to see through the performances of their colleagues, "to see the naked truth"; one superior said about the report of a patrol officer, for example, "He can't fool me. I was once a patrol officer myself; I know how that works."

The first clue to why the performance of performance as performance seems to be quite acceptable is the fact that superiors can get quite disturbed if the improvement of appearance, the brightening of a report, does not take place. Superiors sometimes say that they do not even *want* to know every detail as it actually took place. A plausible interpretation emerges from examining a few cases in which officers actually did write (from the perspective of superiors, quite naively) precisely what happened in "graphic detail" *(bis ins kleinste Bischen)*. The problem created for superiors is the conceivable revelation of an explicit violation of a dense set of rules and regulations, a fact that creates intense extra work, as officers who have been faced with the "naïveté" of easterners have pointed out to me on several occasions. In some cases they have even been forced to initiate disciplinary measures, although they felt that the case at hand did not merit such drastic responses, which were better reserved for "real" violations. When asked what "embellishments" they would have suggested, they mention things like "cutting unnecessary detail," "leaving things out that don't have to be said," or "saying everything positive that can be said." What the acceptance of performance as performance seems to create, therefore, is an extra margin of ambiguity;[57] it widens the horizon of defensible interpretations of the reports. The margins of possibility for future renarrations are thereby also widened. In effect, the management of work becomes more flexible on the one hand, and on the other the lines of responsibility are blurred and potential hedges against accusation of neglect of responsibility are created.

57. There is a fine line between tolerable or even desirable ambiguity on the one hand and undesirable insincerity or cheating on the other.

What is confusing about this creation of ambiguity for eastern officers is that westerners point to the lies within the GDR system (e.g., the falsification or "embellishment" of production statistics) as a cause for the breakdown of the GDR, while at the same time tolerating what might look like cheating from some moralistic perspective within the supposedly superior western system.

Performance and Agency

Any poetics assumes agency, the possibility of doing something one way or another. Put differently, a poetics presupposes choice and thus the possibility of making a *difference*. As I have indicated already regarding the narratability of work, various kinds of operations involve different degrees of discretion (Bittner 1990; Manning 1977). What is true within the patrol car service is even more pronounced in other areas of police work. While the patrol car service still involves considerable agency, most of the work of administrating reports affords very little individual agency.[58] Thus subjects of conversation are markedly different among officers involved in these two kinds of work. While patrol car officers talk relatively frequently about their own work, administrators of reports talk more about the work of others; rarely do they talk about their own. I have encountered officers who had second thoughts about climbing the career ladder because it would mean leaving patrol car service to do some kind of leadership work. They were reluctant to experience the potential loss of agency which would come with working "inside," fearing that the very proximity to superiors would deprive them of the independence they enjoyed "outside," where they were "on their own."

Eastern officers who have done patrol duty in both the People's Police and either the new Brandenburg or Berlin Police point out that they had considerably less agency in the People's Police than in the Berlin Police after unification. Particularly bad patrol stretches were called "idiot-patrols" *(Idioten-Streifen)* in the People's Police. Interestingly, their stories about patrol duty in the GDR are much less about policing than about their escapades while on duty. They tell how they secured forbidden supplies of alcohol on duty, or how they managed to sleep, or how

---

58. This reduced discretion in administering cases is reflected in their delegation to civil employees *(Angestellte)* rather than to tenured officers *(Beamte)*.

they outwitted their superiors in other ways. A Potsdam officer tells this story:

> One such idiot-patrol was the Soviet War Memorial. You really went nuts there, you really got a black-out, full twelve hours, always around the Memorial. Then they really came at night to check whether you were still there. What we did then, once in a while, we climbed onto the Monument [the very act they were supposed to prevent] and into the trees. With your uniform, you were so well camouflaged that nobody saw you. Even the controllers went past you, and then you whistled at them to make them wonder where this was coming from.

By contrast, most neighborhood beat patrol officers of the former People's Police have a whole arsenal of stories to tell about their performances at work. That these marked differences in the themes of stories told are not simply a matter of different temperament of different officers is clear from the career biographies of officers who moved from patrol service to neighborhood beat patrol service in the People's Police. The same phenomenon is observable among western police officers who have been employed in different kinds of police practices during their careers. Stories about service in riot police units quartered in barracks are mostly about escapades, about superiors and their idiosyncrasies, or about suffering; they are rarely about the work of policing.[59]

Comparing the western and eastern experience of performing different kinds of police work in Brandenburg or Berlin on the one hand and in the People's Police on the other, and comparing the stories told by officers on different kinds of duties within the same organization yields an interesting result which is quite consistent across organizations and political systems: The less agency there is in any type of work, and therefore the less potential to make a difference in performance through a display of skill, the more likely it is that practitioners of such work will reassert their agency in non-work-related activities.[60] What happens in the wake of deprivation of agency therefore is a reassertion of agency (see Willis 1981).

59. The same is true for stories easterners tell about their military service. Memories of hazing are particularly intense. Westerners working today in the police typically have no experience of the military. West Berliners were not drafted for the *Bundeswehr*, and other westerners joining the police right after school were exempt from military service.

60. This could be read in de Certeau's (1984) terms as the assertion of tactics in cases where strategies are completely defined by others.

With such diverse distributions of agency, within the patrol service of the Berlin Police on the one hand and the People's Police on the other, it is not surprising that the exoneration strategies of officers involved in actions gone awry are also quite different (cf. Austin 1956). In the People's Police the focus was on orders: from below, exculpation asserted that orders came from above, that they were ambiguous or even contradictory; from above, it was insisted that orders were misunderstood or poorly executed. In the Berlin Police hedges against possible complaints have to be built into the written work: whatever ought to have been done should be in the report already; important information transmitted should be noted and kept in the records. This is yet another example of how even potential narrations (imaginary responses to imaginary complaints) influence the course of action. The Berlin officers call these strategies of hedging "getting one's ass to the wall" *(den Arsch an die Wand kriegen)*, thus creating an image of a fighter protected from the back by the wall (i.e., being sheltered from surprise attacks).

These considerations of agency lead back to the question of authority and work ethics. Rosabeth Moss Kanter (1977, 63ff.) has pointed out that in situations in which the performance of individuals is difficult to measure, organizations tend to watch for signs of commitment in the absence of an adequate performance measure. She has also argued (47ff.) that difficulties in judging the performance of individuals may lead to greater conformity pressures because superiors assume that individuals who are more or less like themselves would make decisions and work as they would. The performance of individual Berlin patrolmen, who submit signed written reports, can be evaluated more accurately than the performance of People's Police patrol officers, who had few means to demonstrate that they were good police officers other than their commitment to the organization. Thus there is at least a logical elective affinity between work ethics, performance measures, and the distribution of agency in the two different police organizations.[61]

Conclusions: Work Performance and Identity

The fact that it is possible to identify a poetics of various police practices (however, by no means of all police practices, as I have tried to show

61. This of course does not invalidate any argument about the historical genesis of the structure of the People's Police.

above), allows the officers who perform them to develop their own characteristic style of work, their own signature, as it were. Ideally, performance identifies the performer, who may thus become differentiated as a personality within a field of possible actions which form a conventional repertoire. Police officers do become known in this way as specialists; they are recognized and identified by others as consistently good performers of particular tasks. These known specialties may become the basis for distributing work within a shift. Officers who assign specific tasks to certain patrol car teams have told me that if they can choose among different teams, they pick the one that they believe will be particularly good at completing the task. They say for example, "This is really something for Maier." Sometimes officers come back from a certain task and approach a particular colleague, saying, "This would have been something for you" or "We should have had you with us; it would have been much easier." Thus, on the basis of a poetics, police officers can identify themselves and become identified by others.[62]

Thus the process of working, in the sense of working well by being able to make a difference in the how of the doing, is at least as much a source of identity as the product of work (see Arendt 1958; Kondo 1990).[63] The process/performance orientation in police work is perhaps emphasized because police work often does not really result in a product which could serve as a source of pride, since it frequently aims at the reinstitution of something like an imperceptible state (such as traffic flow after an accident, the removal of a danger, etc.). In most criminal cases, the uniformed police only register a criminal offense, beginning a process which is then taken over by criminal investigators. If the condemnation and punishment of a criminal offender are the final products of criminal

62. I should add that if the notion of skills that are important in the process of policing is recognized, police officers cannot avoid being identified as good or bad performers.

63. For Arendt (chapter 4; also Kondo, chapter 7), the work identity of artisans is primarily derived from the quality of the product of work. Arendt differentiates active human pursuits into three different types: "work," "production," and "action." What she calls "work" is predominantly physical, energy-oriented, without the requirement of skill. The fruit of work, according to Arendt, is ephemeral; it is consumed. Identity can be derived from "work" only in terms of sheer physical strength or by its rhythmical nature. "Production" is linear (in contrast to work, which is cyclical): it aims at a durable product, with which both the producer and the user can identify. "Action" pertains to the human capacity to begin something new; it involves human innovation. Reading Arendt's types of human pursuits as ideal types in the Weberian sense would allow an analysis of police work as a combination of all three forms.

police work, then the uniformed officer sees very little of it. In most cases, uniformed officers never even know whether their reports were helpful for the ensuing legal process. Thus uniformed police officers are frequently left with a sequence of action that has little more than a tentative end, imposed more by the procedural logic of the division of work among several police and state organizations than by the offense that is prosecuted. Thus, all police officers are left with is an orientation towards the process, the poetics of their particular segment of police action, to identify themselves through their work.[64]

After this excursion into the poetics and performance of policing, I return now to the confrontation between easterners and westerners. The problem for many eastern officers was that practices in some important areas (e.g., patrol duty) are very differently organized in the Berlin Police than they were in the People's Police. Suddenly, easterners were forced to perform on a very different stage, before a very different audience, not really being sure anymore what would pass for a good performance. Mastery of performance is typically acquired in long years of practice, within the context of established genres of work which are in turn institutionalized within an organization or across a type of organization. Mastery of performance is in this sense cultural capital (Bourdieu 1984). With the demise of the GDR and the People's Police, much of the cultural capital that easterners had acquired, often in decades of police practice, became more or less worthless, or it was in need of considerable adjustment to new types of tasks and different forms of interaction with colleagues and superiors.

To westerners, who had the advantage of setting the terms of the game, and had little interest in learning more about life in the People's Police, former People's Police officers frequently did not look like police officers at all: they just did not live up to western performance criteria. In retrospect, one western officer said, "They [the easterners] simply did not know what police work was." And right after unification, many westerners missed few opportunities to show them that they did not. Easterners were shocked and outraged at these presumptions, looking back with

---

64. Police officers are quite happy if they learn that their action ultimately led to the condemnation and punishment of a criminal. More often they see indirectly that their work had no effect, because the same individual is arrested for the same offense only a little while later (e.g., a juvenile car thief may be released and arrested yet again just weeks later). Such cases give police officers the feeling that their work has no lasting consequence, and they despair about other state institutions which apparently "do not do their bit."

pride on their police work in the GDR. They were often quite defenseless against the attack, for they had few other means to evaluate the police work of their western counterparts except by using the criteria of the People's Police for what constituted good or poor performance. However, these criteria were no longer backed up by any authority; westerners simply did not care whether they would have made good police officers according to People's Police standards.

It took easterners a while to learn what constitutes good performance in western terms. They had to make the life world of western policing their own. Only then could they begin to see fundamental differences between various western police officers. In Köpenick westerners had created the myth that only the best of the western police officers had come to the east, an interesting self-identification that enriched the significance of "going east" for western officers. This self-serving myth was apparently used by western superiors with quite some success to lure western officers to come along with them to the east.[65] Once easterners had learned to differentiate between the quality of performance of various western officers, this initial tool of creating awe as a means of domination turned into its opposite: every poorly performing westerner shed doubt on the quality of the rest of the western officers. Still, the criteria are set by western officers, and the majority of easterners (with a few notable exceptions) are still judged as underperformers by western superiors. This has decisive consequences in the competition of officers for promotions and further training. As one western superior summarized, "It is very hard for me to suggest an easterner for promotion; if there are many better-qualified westerners, I just can't do that."

The ways in which western and eastern officers think about and habitually go about deriving a sense of self from their work (along the five dimensions outlined at the beginning of this chapter) are markedly different. This difference and the conflicts which it informs have to be understood on the basis of a high valuation of work as a source for positive self-identification, which they both share. On the one hand, the discrepancies between east and west have something to do with how police activities are or were organized, especially with how much agency they are or were

65. It would be interesting to find out why officers bought into that rather obvious ploy. A sensible hypothesis seems to be that the call of the east was particularly appealing to officers who considered themselves gifted and deserving of a promotion but were caught in a career stalemate. The myth seems to have its source in one particular police district which had the duty to "extend" eastward and therefore was particularly concerned to make personnel move.

afforded within the structure of the Berlin Police and the People's Police. On the other hand these differences are linked to the distinct ways in which both organizations have identified themselves and by synecdochical extension their officers; in other words they have something to do with the narratives of identity both police organizations have propagated about themselves. Ultimately, however, they depend on how the officers tend or tended to identify themselves and each other within the context of organizational structures and organizational narratives. In this chapter I have emphasized the different understandings of work process, the prevalent notion of intensive time among westerners and extensive time among easterners. Also, westerners typically do not stress the direct result of their work as a primary source of self-identification because these results are often enough rather elusive; the indirect results of their work, such as pay and benefits, are important to them, however. By contrast, easterners miss the feeling that their work is contributing to the achievement of a long-term goal beyond the ephemeral results of the day and the paycheck at the end of the month, a feeling which was nourished in GDR times through all sorts of rituals, for example, the award of certificates of merit and a People's Police commemoration day. While westerners, especially the younger ones, seem relatively unconcerned with the relative standing of the police as an organization among others, many easterners seem to have cherished the sense that the People's Police, and thus its employees, had a particular place in a larger universe. Of course, not all People's Police officers have shared to the same degree this concern for the embeddedness of their work in their organization within a larger social and historical whole. Yet, despite the cynicism they harbor today about this larger whole, and even though some of them might have had their doubts even during GDR times, the rhetoric of that larger whole seemed to have appealed to what some of them have called "that which is good in me," and they regret the fact that this appeal seems no longer there.[66]

66. This meaning of the larger whole, the humanitarian appeal of socialism, was important even to those who were apparently suffering from other aspects of their work in the People's Police; cf. Fulbrook 1995, 29, n. 7.

FIVE

Challenging Sincerity

The Cold War was not only a conflict of power; it was also a conflict of morals, couched in the rhetoric of right and wrong. Berlin, as the symbol of the Cold War par excellence, as perhaps the place in the world where its effects were most visible, cast in concrete and steel, dividing the once unified city into two antagonistic parts, was also the focal point of Cold War rhetoric and at the same time the place from which this rhetoric could be most effectively disseminated.[1] The police on both sides of the Wall were especially steeped in this Cold War rhetoric, not only because policing is one of the more conservative professions, but because many police officers on both sides had firsthand experience with the border, both as private citizens and in their public function as police officers. A few Western police officers had come of age in the Eastern part of the city and fled with their parents to the West. Some Easterners were actually involved in securing or (while still serving in the Border Troops or in a pioneer regiment of the National People's Army) even directly in building the Wall. Other Westerners serving then in the Berlin Police were detailed to the border, observing events from the Western side. Some easterners I got to know had done years of duty along the Wall; and one westerner I got acquainted with had served decades at the Glienicker Bridge, famous as a location for spy swaps, where he had personally witnessed both successful and thwarted attempts to flee the GDR. Finally, all western Berlin police officers had repeated, unpleasant experiences passing the border stations in Berlin on their way to West Germany.

1. With international visibility, such rhetoric was launched one last time by Ronald Reagan, speaking in front of the Brandenburg Gate while visiting Berlin on 12 June 1987, demanding that Mikhail Gorbachev tear the Wall down.

For almost half a century, police officers in east and west Berlin had learned to see each other as enemies, for, in each other's eyes, they were the ones who upheld the disliked state on the respective other side. The images that the two police organizations produced about each other were similar in their formal properties: Policing on the other side was perceived as a crude, necessarily brutal means of domination, and the officers were depicted as the lackeys either of a dominant capitalist ruling class or of an authoritarian, illegitimate communist regime. Each believed the other's policing was directed against the interest of the average person; it was seen as profoundly undemocratic and therefore immoral.

Accordingly, the unification of the Berlin Police on 1 October 1990 took place in an atmosphere that was highly charged both morally and emotionally. The morality of the People's Police in its role as a stabilizing factor for the East German regime had been under scrutiny within the GDR itself at least since the mass arrests on 7 October 1989,[2] the day of the fortieth anniversary celebrations. The actions of the police on this day and more generally their participation in the suppressive measures of the old GDR regime had become subjects of the various round-table discussions between the government of the GDR and various citizen groups. The more serious beginning of a reflexive evaluation of the People's Police was heralded by the dismissal of the president of police in East Berlin and his replacement by a more reform-minded person early in January 1990. These attempts at inner reform did not, however, assume a directly moral character manifested by rigorous evaluation of the actions of individual officers. Yet they were indirectly aimed at developing a more moral, publicly accountable police organization through depoliticization and professionalization.[3]

While the private encounters between east and west German police officers during the interim period between the fall of the Wall and actual unification were described as rather friendly, the actual unification of the two police forces following 1 October 1990, was described by most east Germans as quite hostile, governed by deep-seated distrust. The westerners were frequently described as conquerors, as bossy and uninterested. Many westerners did indeed describe themselves as liberators, some even as conquerors, and most, at any rate, as just victors of a war—and some

2. The seventh of October, known as "the Day of the Republic" (Tag der Republik) was the national holiday in the GDR, which was usually marked by a carefully orchestrated mass demonstration with parades and flags.

3. For a discussion of these reform attempts, see the section "The People's Police After the Fall of the Wall" in chapter 2.

would admit to being bossy. While easterners thought this behavior un-
justifiable, many westerners thought it quite all right for, as they put it
in allusion to their historical understanding of the Nazi dictatorship, "Did
I know who this other guy was? Did I know what he did in the GDR?"
or on a more personal note, "Perhaps he was one of those guys, who
gave me such a hard time at the border." In order to understand better
how easterners and westerners moralize each other, the organizations for
which they work and have worked, and the states in which they live or
lived, it is useful to consider how in principle selves can be identified
morally, and why moral identifications are important.

* * *

From the perspective of moral theory, the meaning of a person is defined
in relation to and by identification with moral goods. Charles Taylor
(1989, pt. 1) provides a useful analytical framework for tracing the ways
in which selves become moral. He describes the identification between
selves and the moral good as a quest in a moral space. This space can be
thought of as defined by three ideal-typical pillars or dimensions signifying what Taylor believes to be universal types of moral goods. The first
(social) dimension deals with the relation between selves and others—
with the respect they owe each other and the obligations they have to
others. The second dimension addresses what Taylor calls "hypergoods,"
ideas about what constitutes a good life or what renders a life meaningful.
The third (personal) dimension pertains to the relationship individuals
have with themselves, what it is that constitutes their personal dignity.
Taylor suggests that these dimensions should not be seen in isolation from
each other; that is, none is completely independent of the other two. For
Taylor, all moral theories occupy a characteristic corner of this moral
space; that is, they can be distinguished through the relative importance
they afford these three dimensions as well as through the ways in which
they suppose a moral quest can be realized along and across these dimensions.[4] What is true for specialized theoretical discourse in ethics is true

4. A good example of a moral theory that gives primacy to relationships with
others is Kant's ethics of duty. Respect for self flows out of respect for the moral
law that Kant calls the categorical imperative, which he conceives as immanent in
universal human reason. The classical countermodel is Aristotle's, whose ethics give
precedence to the notion of the good life. For him, obligations to others and personal
dignity flow out of a notion of the good life defined in terms of a hierarchy of virtues.
Finally, as Taylor points out, perhaps most removed from contemporary views is the
ancient Greek warrior-ethic as it is known from Homer's epics. There the focus lies
on personal dignity as the guiding principle for moral behavior.

for everyday moral discourses, and Taylor's fra... .work can thus be used to describe more precisely the ways in which eastern and western police officers moralize each other.

Taylor (1989, chap. 2) stresses that orientation within the moral space is absolutely essential for human beings if they are to get guidance for action. It is this orientation that identifies human beings, gives human beings a sense of self, endows the self with meaning. Successful moral orientation is in turn contingent on what Taylor calls "articulation," the ability of human beings to express their moral quest symbolically and thus to reflect on it, to communicate it, to argue about it. Following Wittgenstein (1984) Taylor argues that the ability to articulate moral orientation is ultimately dependent on the speech communities in which human beings live and the symbolic forms they offer for orientation in the moral space.[5]

For Taylor, as for McIntyre (1984) and Ricoeur (1992), the primary vehicle for the articulation of moral orientation is narrative. Yet before somebody can spin a moral tale, a situation must pose itself as morally relevant to a person, and as narratable. Typically, this happens on the basis of a challenge to identifications in the moral space: somebody feels deprived of the respect owed by somebody else; a promise remains unfulfilled; the sacrifices necessary to attain freedom appear to discredit freedom as an ulterior value; the virtues of a person are drawn into doubt.

---

5. Apart from this metatheory of morality, which is more or less a descriptive scheme to tease out the similarities and differences between different moral philosophies (or practical moral discourses), Taylor of course presents his own moral philosophy, which formally emphasizes the necessity of espousing hypergoods, or of committing to what Taylor calls "strong valuations." Lemert (1994) severely criticizes Taylor (and with him Giddens, Calhoun, and Wiley) for their universalist positions (which Lemert calls "the strong-we position"). It is important to note, however, that Taylor's universalism is formal; that is, it is compatible with the most diverse material definitions of what in particular strong valuation is about. Lemert confuses (or rejects the validity of the *analytic* distinction between) the formal and material levels of analysis when he writes, "One may admit, as Taylor does, a multiplicity of goods but only as historical circumstances (ultimately threats) to personhood or Self" (126, n. 22). For Taylor the *concrete* historically or culturally contingent material definition of strong valuation is *necessary* and by no means a threat to personhood, but its precondition. For Taylor they are therefore not "only" in the sense of an inferior copy of an eternal idea, in the sense of a *parole* to a *langue,* but they are, to use a Heideggerian term, "always already" material, in the same sense that the Husserlian consciousness is formal but always already consciousness of something (Husserl 1987, e.g., 38). I do not think it helpful to try to avoid all universalisms, for there clearly are human universals such as the capacity to use language, even though no particular language is universal.

East Germans and west Germans challenge each other morally all the time. Both the challenges and the responses to them, narrative or performative, reveal their moral identifications, their orientations in moral space. My focus here is on the moral conflicts and types of moral reasoning of easterners and westerners. During my fieldwork, I found two distinct symbolic forms of moral reasoning which are unevenly distributed among easterners and westerners. First, there are discourses centering on the truthful presentation of self (sincerity), in which easterners and westerners share, although they are more prevalent among easterners; these discourses are the subject of this chapter. Second, there is a discourse of individual rights, which as a style of moral reasoning is much more frequently employed by westerners. In debates between easterners and westerners, the rights issues, which are the subject of chapter 6, are intricately tied to a discussion of the GDR border regime, as well as to the function of and the collaboration with the Stasi, the secret police of the GDR.

Valuing Sincerity

Describing the ups and downs in her life in the People's Police, one eastern officer has narrated several stories to me in which she identified a former superior as a "false dog" *(falscher Hund)*. What qualified him for this moralization was his duplicity; he said to her, for example, that he would support her in a particular request, only to undermine it "from behind" *(hinten herum)*.[6] In fact, in Köpenick and Potsdam alike, the quickest, most effective way to disavow a person morally is to identify him or her with the adjective "false," to which most frequently the nouns "dog" *(Hund)* or "fifty" [fifty-mark bill] *(Fünfziger)* are added. Somebody who really is being put down may also be called a "left rat" *(linke Ratte)*. Especially the image of the false bill makes clear what the reproach is about: pretending to be something one is not, feigning friendship while acting as an adversary, inviting intimacy and abusing it for egotistical purposes. At the same time, one of the first identifications mentioned in giving praise is to call a colleague "open and honest" *(offen und ehrlich)* or "straight out" *(gerade heraus)*. One Köpenick officer, for example,

6. The expression to "be" or to "come from behind" is somewhat ambiguous. It invokes the idea of an enemy unfairly attacking without warning from an unguarded side, but it also has homosexual overtones, as in "Der ist hinten herum" (he is from behind), meaning homosexual.

filled me in on the character of the various shift leaders, praising one of them as "open and honest; with him, you always know where you stand. If he likes you, he will help you; if he doesn't like you, he will let you know why. But he is never coming from behind." The superior thus praised described his own leadership style with positive self-identification as follows: "I have my principles and I stick to them, so everybody always knows where they stand with me."

What characterizes all of these instances is that they express appreciation for an honest presentation of self, while moralizing anyone who dissembles or deceives others for personal gain. Lionel Trilling (1972, 3) has found one of the earliest literary expressions of this type of moral concern in the words Shakespeare puts into the mouth of Polonius in *Hamlet:* "This above all: to thine own self be true / And it doth follow, as the night the day / Thou canst not then be false to any man." The direction of Polonius's precept is clear: truth in relations with others is a consequence of being true to oneself. Speaking in terms of Taylor's dimensions of the moral space, the type of moral reasoning the officers and Polonius use addresses in a unique way the interdependence between personal dignity, here seen as being true to one's own self, and obligation to others, here seen as truthful self-representation in dealings with fellow human beings. Since the officers themselves do not use any particular term to denote what they value, I will follow Trilling and call the value espoused in the examples above "sincerity."[7] What distinguishes discourses on sincerity from discourses about honesty is that the lies presented in insincerity are lies about self, immediately endangering the moral status of self, while this cannot be said with the same force about dishonesty, which erodes self much more gradually than insincerity.

The issue of sincerity surfaces not only in the evaluation of persons; it also appears in moral evaluations of much wider social contexts, as the following three examples illustrate. In chapter 3, I have introduced a police officer who tried to make sense of his life in the GDR and what had happened to this life in the context of unification by using a dual-skin metaphor. Particularly in relation to his outlawed preference for

7. Michèle Lamont (1992), describing styles of moral reasoning among American and French upper middle class men, has also encountered sincerity as a strongly endorsed value. Although the moral language of her French and American subjects is different from the mostly lower middle class eastern and western police officers in Berlin and Potsdam, they all seem to share a set of core values centering around a forceful disavowal of misrepresentations of the self. Both Lamont's and my findings are a challenge to the frequently postulated postmodern character (e.g., Jameson 1991; Gergen 1991) who is utterly unconcerned with notions of sincerity.

western TV and his secret efforts to maintain forbidden contacts with his relatives in the West, he stated that in the GDR he was forced, especially in his role as an officer of the People's Police, to live with two skins: one was used for public presentation, especially at work vis-à-vis his superiors, while the other, the one he felt to be his own true skin, was reserved for private, intimate use in relationships in which he felt safe enough, that is, with his family, his close friends, and a few selected "reliable" colleagues at work. Unification allowed him, he said, to shed the false skin; it was no longer necessary to lie about whom he saw or what he did on the past weekend.

Another police officer describes his experience of the dissolution of the old regime in the GDR with a considerable degree of relief and retrospective anger:

> At last the pressure was gone to ponder every single word—Whom do you tell what? It was a constant telling of lies: What do you come up with? When one of the superiors asked, "Did you see this or that show yesterday on TV?" and I hadn't because I had watched a Western program, I had to be deceptive; I had to come up with something fast. You had to tell lies constantly, and you had to watch out not to lose track of your own lies. This pressure is gone.

Yet another officer captures a similar situation, but the insincerity is even more heartfelt because it threatens to drive a wedge into his own family. His embarrassment is stressed by a sudden shift from a first-person account to an impersonal ("one") narrator, which seems to allow him some degree of dissociation from his own feelings.

> So, once in a while one watched Western TV. But one had to be careful, one had two children who were not supposed to watch Western TV. If they had told in school that they had watched Western TV, while their father is a staff-officer and their mother a nursery-school teacher, that would have been something. Thus one could only watch the West if the children were not around. And that's why one didn't do it most of the time. Even if nobody believes this today, to be a model for the children, just not to be forced to be insincere with the children, one didn't do it.

All three eastern police officers are describing a particular kind of psychic stress which is the consequence of insincerity. In all three cases they had to identify themselves publicly in ways which are incongruent with self-identifications they felt to be true descriptions of themselves. Especially in the first two cases, the officers cast themselves as victims of an organization or a state which forced them into duplicity. The production of a false facade was the only possible route to travel if they wanted to protect what they felt to be their own, legitimate, morally unreprehensible interest. Only behind this facade could they watch western TV channels or meet their own kinfolk living on the other side of the Wall. If they did not want to produce the false facade, they had to curtail their desire, the solution the third officer seems to have opted for most of the time. The dissembling and feigning they were forced into was not taken lightly by either. All three recount this particular aspect of their past with visible and audible disgust. Neither these accounts nor any stories of similar situations ever expressed the joy one might expect of a trickster who has successfully fooled others. Dissembling was not frivolous play, but a dreaded necessity to protect one's social position while enjoying illicit fruits.

The police officers thus thematize sincerity in three different contexts, and all three of them are present or at least implied in the preceding accounts of insincerity. These contexts are (1) the character of a person, (2) the organization in which they work, and (3) the state.[8]

Personal Sincerity

The identifications of persons as "false" presented at the beginning of this section show that sincerity is first and foremost used by the officers, east and west alike, to qualify the character of a person. Moral evaluations of a person usually begin with the assertion or denial of sincerity. As a property of character, sincerity is not only socially expected and valued, but personally aspired to. Sincerity is also seen as an attribute of

8. Common parlance in Germany recognizes yet another level at which the concept of sincerity is used to make moral sense. The term has also been applied to characterize not a person but, in a Herderian sense, a people. German folklore claims that Germans are a sincere people (which implies that they are also plain, direct, and at times naive and vulnerable). This idea is paradigmatically portrayed in the infamous "great" aria of Hans Sachs at the very end of the final act of Richard Wagner's *Die Meistersinger von Nürnberg,* where German truthfulness and sincerity are contrasted with the falsehood of the Romance people. German romantic nationalism has made excessive use of the adjective "German" as a synonym for "sincerity." What remains of this is the use of the term "German" in the expression *auf Deutsch sagen* (to say it in German) as a synonym for "to say something straight out," not to beat around the bush. The larger ideological implications as set forth by romantic nationalism are gone, however.

individual actions. In this sense, a person's action can be characterized, for example, as "deceiving somebody" *(jemandem etwas vormachen)*. What can unfold then is a dialectic between character and action which is the hallmark of narrative constructions of identity (Ricoeur 1992). The insincerity of any particular action can only be judged in light of the knowledge of character, while the establishment of insincerity of character must rely on the observation of action which somehow reveals insincerity. Insincerity in action is therefore bound to diminish the sincerity of character; conversely, the assumption of an insincere character puts every single action into doubt. Polonius himself is an excellent example for this dialectic. His avowal of sincerity stands in stark contrast to his inability to live up to it in action, which ultimately reveals the insincerity of his character.

Insincerity can be revealed in two different ways. Duplicitous behavior may first be observed in a particular person: for example, a commitment may be entered and vouched for by reference to character but not honored in the end. In a way this is a reversal of Polonius's movement of thought, in that it approaches sincerity from the perspective of social interaction. Since it is open to external observers, I call it the *external* perspective. Officers' questioning the morality of their colleagues usually proceed from this vantage point. The second method of questioning sincerity—I will call it the *internal* perspective—follows the movement of Polonius's proposition; it starts from the awareness of a gap between a presented self and another, true image of self.

The internal perspective presupposes a notion of who one really is, that is, a sense of identity. People without an understanding of their own identity have nothing to be true or false to. The three eastern officers struggling with the fact that they had to lie about their preferences for western TV or their meetings with western relatives to protect their social position discover insincerity in the disgust and anxiety they felt about their self-misrepresentation. However, this internal perspective is not to be confused with a concern for authenticity. Trilling (1972) argues that the ideal of sincerity was gradually replaced during the nineteenth century by the ideal of authenticity. Taylor (1989, 1994) follows the lead of Trilling, describing modern European moral history as a relocation of moral authority from without (God, Reason) to a moral feeling within human beings. This feeling, according to Taylor, becomes in the course of time highly individualized, specific to each human being. It is the concurrence with this inner moral voice which, according to Taylor (1994), lies at the heart of the concept of authenticity: "Being true to myself means being true to my own originality, which is something only I can articulate and discover" (31). The quest for authenticity is primarily concerned with finding one's true identity. In terms of Taylor's moral space, authenticity is almost exclusively focused on the dimension of personal dignity without direct connection to the social axis of obligations to others.[9]

Yet the police officers in Köpenick do not speak about sincerity in this way; they do not make the concern for an authentic internal voice central to their moral deliberations. One reason why authenticity seems to be less of a concern among them is what might be called the recursive foundation of sincerity as an absolute human value. For them, sincerity is part of a universalistic concept of what they call "human decency" (menschlicher Anstand). Every human being with a claim to morality must be endowed with this human decency and by necessity must be sincere in character. Sincerity of character, in turn, is thought to manifest itself in action. It is discovered by taking the external perspective, by observing a particular person acting in different circumstances, at different points in time, and in relationship with different people. The officers themselves are acutely aware of the dialectical relationship between sincerity of character and sincerity in action; they are thought of as mutually constituting each other. This is why the easterner's and westerner's mutual suspicion of insincerity was hard to break at first. It led east Germans and west Germans to avoid contact as much as possible. But this is also why, since cooperation became increasingly unavoidable, officers explicitly stated that they wanted to get to know each other in different situations: alone, in different groups, with equals, with superiors, during work and in socials, in stressful situations and in relaxed ones. Thus sincerity is thought to manifest itself in a certain degree of constancy, congruence, and predictability within and across different types of social situations.[10]

The constancy which is looked for, however, is not simple sameness, but a sameness in difference. This notion of a sameness in difference comes very close to Ricoeur's (1992) argument about the synthesizing

9. Accordingly, Taylor's (1989) discussion of the "sources of the self" shifts for the modern era to ways in which human beings can find this true self—through the epiphanies of art, for example.
10. In chapter 7 I analyze in detail how the hope of getting to know the other beyond the masks of professional roles at precinct parties and other kinds of socials gets thwarted.

powers of plot in narrative.[11] None of the officers would expect colleagues to speak in exactly the same way to a superior as they would speak to their peers, and yet it would be unacceptable for them to be kind and friendly to superiors while being uncooperative and abrasive with their own kind. Sameness in difference also implies, however, that people who seem to be simply the same in all different circumstances are not trusted either because they are felt to be at least potentially insincere. People who are simply the same are felt to be "slick" *(glatt);* they are felt to be hiding something. It is interesting that both easterners and westerners experienced each other as slick and therefore as not truthfully representing themselves. Easterners felt that westerners always pretended to know everything, to be never at fault, and to present themselves consistently in the best light possible. Easterners typically describe westerner's slickness as "so much better in selling themselves" *(die können sich viel besser verkaufen).* Westerners found easterners to be impenetrable, to be so docile as to "say yes all the time," to "show no resistance." One western officer allegorized this feeling one day in the context of explaining the origin of the military salute. He said that this habit dated back to the knights in the Middle Ages who, in greeting each other, raised the visors of their helmets so that they could see each other's faces and look into each other's eyes. He felt that easterners never removed their visors.

Role Sincerity and Personal Sincerity

Sincerity also has a very strong professional dimension for police officers. In behavioral codices, both the former People's Police and the Berlin Police commit police officers to a sincere execution of their respective roles.[12] Both organizations have issued these codices in small reference booklets which officers are supposed to carry around for quick reference. The People's Police version reads as follows:

> My service as a police officer is an honorable duty of class and constitution. I will therefore place all my powers and capabilities in the service

11. Compare chapter 3, especially the section "Modes of Identification."
12. The behavioral codices issued by both police organizations are especially insistent on that point (for [West] Berlin, the Polizeidienstverschrift 350, *Verhalten der Polizeibeamten* [Senator für Inneres 1986]; for the People's Police, *Merkbuch für die Schutzpolizei* [MdI 1973]).

of the Socialist Fatherland, and I will commit any time selflessly to the maintenance of public order and security.

Here is the (West) Berlin version:

Through their entire official and extra-official behavior, police officers have to demonstrate commitment to the liberal democratic order which they pledge to preserve without reservation. They have to be ready to commit their entire person. . . .

In addition to issuing behavioral guidelines and regardless of the very different formulations of the role of a police officer (which I discuss below in the section entitled "Sincerity and the State"), both the former People's Police and the Berlin Police ask their officers to pledge sincere execution of their roles in an official oath. The function of the oath in each case is to link the sincerity of role execution to the sincerity of the person. Negligence of duty by police officers is thus meant to reflect badly on the character of the officers as persons.[13]

Sincere role execution pledged in an oath is, therefore, more than just a contract between an employer and an employee. This is not to say that a breach of contract could not also have a moral dimension, but a contract consciously shelters self; in a way a contract disregards the self. A contract asks only for fulfillment of obligation, regardless of what the person thinks or feels. Role sincerity tied through an oath to personal sincerity, however, puts self at risk, draws self into the role.[14] Sincerity then, is not only a property of character but also, and this is the second level on which it is important, a matter of role-execution.

This moral dimension of police work is quite different from the performative aspects discussed in chapter 4. As far as the police officers are concerned, a bad performer can still be a very sincere role executor. What counts in sincerity is the good intention, not the success. Each aspect of the work has different moral qualities. While sincerity, as I pointed out above, is a conceptual movement from the axis of personal dignity to the

13. Conversely, both organizations emphasize in their personnel selection guidelines that a police officer needs to have a reliable character as a person to function well as an officer.

14. This aspect of the official oath is taken to extremes in some versions of the oath of the People's Police which included a self-condemnatory formula: "Should I breach this solemn vow, the laws of our Republic should chastise me" (MdI 1987, 2: 36).

axis of obligations to others (in Taylor's view), the excellence of performance conceptualizes primarily a relationship between personal dignity and the meaning of life.[15]

While personal and role sincerity involve moral demands in their own right, the conjunction of these two demands poses the greatest challenge. And it is precisely at their intersection that the hostile, Cold War police images of the respective other side have been built up. The catch in these images is that one cannot possibly be a good (i.e., sincere) police officer and a good (i.e., sincere) human being at the same time. Publicly, the GDR spread an image of the western police as henchmen of the capitalist ruling class, as "ruffian police" always ready to beat up any demonstrators in pursuit of their legitimate right.

These images were somewhat abstract at first, but after the student unrest in 1968 they were fed by the TV pictures of the violent clashes between riot units, especially of the Berlin Police, with mostly left-wing demonstrators. Not only did these clashes become a regular feature of police work in Berlin during the 1970s, but by the end of the 1980s they had become almost ritualized in the May Day encounters between police and the anarchist and squatter scenes in Kreuzberg. These images showing hundreds of police officers in riot gear (boots, helmets with visors, huge see-through plastic shields, and bats), sometimes facing stone-throwing demonstrators in black hoods, sometimes beating up demonstrators struggling to protect themselves with their bare hands, were not only widely televised in the West and thus accessible to the East; they were also shown in the east with running commentary by Karl-Eduard von Schnitzler, the anchorman of the so-called Black Channel, as living proof of the fascist character of the FRG.[16] These images were indeed disquieting to some eastern officers, especially since violent clashes were decidedly not a feature of their everyday experience. Some of them were led to question seriously whether they could serve in the unified (Western) police after unification. One police officer told me that he was thinking

15. For an elucidating analysis of the moral qualities of performative excellence of practices as an "internal good," see McIntyre 1984, chapter 14.

16. The "Black Channel" *(Der schwarze Kanal)* was a weekly TV show in the GDR that attempted to subvert the effect of Western TV by unmasking it as propagandistic. Although many officers watched the Black Channel regularly, some with the feeling that "if you see it all, you probably know better what really is going on," it was also generally understood that the Black Channel was one of the crudest propaganda instruments of the GDR regime and was for that reason the butt of many jokes.

about alternative plans. He considered opening his own little business in
a craft to which he was apprenticed as a young man. He put his doubts
thus:

> My commander said to me, "Everybody has to scrutinize his own con-
> science to decide now for himself whether he can really continue to
> be a police officer there [in the (West) Berlin Police]." . . . Seen from
> a moral perspective, I thought it would be best just to wait and see
> what kind of a police [force] that really is; what are they doing? Is
> that really such a gang of ruffians as we got to know from TV? And
> if this is the case, I wouldn't stand it for long anyway.

Undoubtedly, the economic situation and the general insecurity after unification made such moral concerns somewhat "luxurious." Still, many
police officers voluntarily left the police after unification. Whatever else
their motives might have been, this moral dimension seems to have been,
at least for some of them, part of the decision.

Immediately after unification, the majority of western officers considered the People's Police as the club of "one hundred and fifty percent
believers" *(Hundertfünzigprozentige)*, loyal adherents of the GDR regime
who would do almost anything to protect it. The neighborhood beat
patrol of the People's Police and high-ranking officers were especially
scorned by westerners. Two western officers, born and raised in the East,
explicitly stated that they could not imagine having become police officers
in the GDR, because they were afraid police work there would have violated their conscience. In particular, they thought it unethical to write
"travel-reports" *(Reiseberichte)* assessing the "reliability" (i.e., the likelihood of return) of people who had applied for permission to travel to
the West. What they found particularly appalling about writing travel
reports is that they would have had to gather information they considered
private, such as the kind and degree of political convictions, the stability
of marriages, quality of relationships with children and friends, and so
on. Another western officer pointed to certain aspects of the People's Police oath that he found personally reprehensible (he actually handed me
a copy of the oath on which he had highlighted the passages in question
with a yellow marker). The wording he found especially repulsive was,
"As officers we are ready to teach our young comrades . . . a deep, class-
based hatred of imperialism and its armed agencies." Nobody, he insisted, should be taught hatred of anyone, and he took publicly prescribed
hatred to be the marker of a dictatorial regime, likening the prescribed

hatred of Jews in the Nazi dictatorship to the prescribed hatred of the class enemy in the GDR.[17]

The moral basis for the rejection of police work in the other Germany has a rather similar structure on both sides of the Wall. The self-images of police officers define police work as a profession in the service of the honest, sincere, common human being. "Helping people" was mentioned by eastern and western police officers alike as one motive for joining the police and certainly one factor that made police work a satisfying occupation. Police officers in east and west thus not only acknowledge a personal obligation, but also a role obligation to the common citizen, while allegiance to the state is derived primarily from their role as police officers. According to the images the two police forces developed about each other before the fall of the Wall, police work in the respective other part of Germany betrayed the interest of the common human being, whose interest police work was meant to protect in the first place. Thus both images state an internal contradiction in the moral role of the police officer; each image assumed that, given the nature of the other state, it was impossible to meet obligations to both the citizens and the state. In addition, each image presumed a conflict between personal sincerity and role sincerity. Thus officers on each side felt that being a police officer in the other Germany implied either being insincere with respect to role execution, or being insincere as a person; in any case, being a police officer in the other Germany was construed as something of a moral paradox.

Sincerity and the State

The tensions among the role obligations of a police officer and the possible incompatibilities between personal and role sincerity raise the question of why these problems came up in the first place. The answer is given by the police officers themselves in describing the characteristics of states and political systems, the third level on which the concept of sincerity is applied. The state is thought of as being connected to sincerity in two different ways. First, the state is held at least partially responsible for creating an environment in which human beings can actually dare to be sincere. Second, the state itself as an actor can be sincere or insincere. I

17. Pointing out this passage, of course, has still another catch: the armed agencies of the imperialists are clearly identified to include the police forces in the West. Thus, he pointed out, the new colleagues he was working with who have sworn the oath were once taught to hate him.

have pointed out already, that the police officers see it as part of their own role to create an environment in which sincerity can be lived. Also, since police officers execute state action, insincere role behavior on the side of the police is coextensive with insincere action of the state. Now west Germans claim, and east Germans agree, that the GDR forced both its citizens and its police officers too to be insincere, as the examples given at the beginning of this chapter illustrate. The stories of eastern officers are full of references to occasions which they see today as imposing false-hood on the people, in spite of the all-pervasive socialist party rhetoric exhorting people to be open, honest, and critical. East Germans tell stories about how they were forced to be personally insincere, to lie about watching Western television, or about their contacts with Western relatives, and to keep back their own feelings, their own criticisms in all sorts of discussions. In what appeared to many officers as a mind-boggling twist of doublespeak, they were also *ordered* by superiors, who otherwise admonished them to uphold the ideals of the People's Police, to be professionally insincere. Thus some of them told me stories of how they were forced to disregard breaches of the law (having caught local party officials speeding or driving drunk), or how they were encouraged to falsify statistics in order to feign attainment of some planned target.

Many eastern police officers say they learned to accept personal and role insincerity as a way of adjusting to the system. They vividly recall the measures they took to avoid being caught red-handed watching Western TV or meeting Western relatives. Family routines were established about never answering the door before tuning TV and radio back to an eastern station, and precautions were taken to prevent children from betraying their parents, either by never watching Western TV in the children's presence (especially as long as they were younger) or by rehearsing answers to questions likely to pop up in school. Easterners never received Western relatives in their own homes but always in the homes of other relatives or friends, preferably outside of areas in which the police officers were known, that is, areas in which they never worked and in which no superiors or colleagues lived. Even then, they would park their cars around the corner and check the terrain before going in to meet their Western relatives.[18]

18. The consequences of being caught meeting Western relatives clandestinely could be very grave. I have heard stories of colleagues who were dishonorably discharged. The consequences of being caught watching Western TV were not as grave, but they could still be quite disagreeable, such as being ineligible for premiums and promotions for a certain period of time.

The feelings attached to these clandestine activities were never of the victorious, cunning, "let's beat the system" variety; they were usually accompanied by fear. Interestingly, these experiences did not, in GDR times, lead to intense anger at the state which forced them to behave in this way; rather, they led to a form of resignation to fate: the circumstances were acknowledged as unchangeable reality. "That's just how it was," is the usual answer to questions about how it felt to have to cover up.

East German police officers also tell stories about how they tried to fight some forms of forced role insincerity, sometimes successfully. Curiously, the plot structure of these success stories is highly standardized: a report of unlawful behavior was ignored by superiors, leading the reporting officer to pursue the issue further, asking questions about measures to be taken, and so on. Typically, this is followed by some intimidation from the superiors, which the officer answers by addressing higher authorities, usually the next higher administrative unit, which in turn resolves the dispute, vindicating the insistence of the officer on lawful conduct. As officers tell these stories, they reveal a fundamental ambiguity about the GDR, especially about being a person living in the GDR.

Several conclusions are usually drawn from these episodes: They assert the existence of political patronage in the GDR, which led to the People's Police to cover up a breach of law. At the same time, however, officers attribute these problems not to the political system as such, but to personal failures—failures of the holders of offices rather than systemic failures of the institutions. Frequently, there is a self-critical note as well: the officers point out that a little more courage on the part of everybody involved would have made the GDR a better country.[19] Thus sincerity is again upheld as a moral value. Stories of unsuccessful resistance to forced role insincerity reveal traces of bitterness much more profound and disturbing than do the stories involving personal insincerity. On the basis of a self-identification with the moral good, all of these stories, whether of success or failure, are sources of considerable personal pride, and they show beautifully what Taylor means by connecting a moral quest with identity.

Blaming the system for inducing insincerity can be an effective tool of

19. It is probably no accident that the personalization of failure found in these accounts of many policemen follow the scripts of exercises in "self-critique" (see Leonhard 1981, e.g., 270ff.), which are a systematic feature of socialist rule in Eastern Europe. The system is sanctified by the objective laws of history: thus failure must necessarily originate in the personal failures of human beings.

moral exoneration. A Brandenburg officer who explained to me what kind of superiors he could respect showed, for example, that people may quite successfully shift negative moral identifications from self to system by presenting a conflict between role sincerity and personal sincerity as system-induced:

> I know some people, commissioned officers and party-members, . . . who would give people a dressing-down, right in front of the whole outfit, because they didn't do this right or that, because they were polit- ically wrong, and once everybody was gone, they would come up to the poor guys and tell them not to let themselves be put down by that, because they just had to do it as their superiors. Then I knew he was a commissioned officer and he was in the party, but I knew that he thought and felt internally just like me, and that he just had to do that because of his function. I still respect such people.

What the commissioned officer in this story seems to do is to balance role sincerity and personal sincerity, giving public precedence to the former and honoring the latter off-line, so to speak, by indicating that personally he would not have acted in this way. He thereby rejects responsibility for what he has just done, blaming his behavior on the role he is pledged to play and thus ultimately placing the blame on the system. He tries to cancel the personal insincerity that the role forced him into by falling out of his role later. Thus he communicates a distance between self and role and thereby takes back some personal responsibility while at the same time communicating the constraints of the role. For the police officer who told me this story, this maneuver demonstrated, after all, that the commis- sioned officer personally knew right from wrong, that he shared in his own understanding of human decency. By his acceptance, the officer who told me this story also shows that he accepts the boundaries of agency outlined by the commissioned officer. By making use of a satirical emplot- ment (i.e., by identifying himself as powerless in the face of the system), the commissioned officer has ultimately succeeded in creating an identifi- cation and thus a community with the victim of his own behavior.[20]

---

20. In an interesting essay on the sources and functions of fantasy, Žižek (1997: 18–27) identifies this peculiar movement of social interaction as characteristic of total institutions such as the military (cf. Goffman 1962, chapter 1). He argues further that ideologies governing interaction within such institutions depend on reference points outside of themselves to remain effective (their internal functioning is so rigid that permanent literal obeisance would ultimately destroy them). The off-duty (out- of-role) humane behavior of the archetypal drill sergeant, or the underhanded apol- ogy of the commissioned officer in the example above are cases in point. Žižek is

The very fact that eastern police officers are willing to work for the unified Berlin police force makes it difficult for them to maintain a negatively charged image of an immoral western police force. Put differently, maintaining such an image while taking the oath of a civil employee of the State of Berlin would cast them as insincere human beings. However, the negative western image of the moral status of the People's Police has remained in full force. Instead of losing persuasive power, it seems to have become more scathing with every new scandal about human rights violations in the GDR, with every new insight into the workings of the former regime in the GDR. Many eastern police officers started to feel cheated and in part also abused by the political system, feelings which in turn seemed to validate the western image. Eastern police officers were faced simultaneously with the attacks of their western colleagues and their own doubts, and they had to hide their doubts, because many westerners would have mercilessly exploited them.

Western officers point out that the GDR was missing one fundamental precondition for a sincere life: freedom of speech. For both eastern and western officers, sincerity is intimately connected to the possibility of voicing one's opinion. This is highlighted by the close connection they make between sincerity of character and "speaking one's mind" *(sagen was man denkt)* or "saying one's opinion straight out" *(seine Meinung gerade heraus sagen)*. While most eastern officers share the western opinion of the GDR, some of them are not so sure that freedom of speech is in fact a feature of the sociopolitical system of the FRG. They point out that where freedom of speech matters most, at work, the Western system is at least as restrictive as the Eastern one, because everyone who ventures an opinion is potentially subject to disadvantages or even to dismissal by the employer.

That the GDR forced its citizens into a life of insincerity, that the GDR could not even have continued to exist if it had allowed its citizens to express themselves sincerely, has been the claim of the FRG government since the founding of both states. In fact, this claim was the basis of the principle of sole representation which characterized the policy of the FRG toward the GDR at least between 1949 and 1969.[21] The state-sponsored

---

right, of course, that this out-of-role behavior, paradoxically, has the potential to increase role compliance. Žižek is too narrowly focused on issues of systems homeostasis, however; he presents this out-of-role behavior merely as a function of the system itself, thus depriving the actors of any real agency.

21. See chapter 2, especially the section entitled "Historical Identifications of the Other Germany."

discouragement of sincere expression pertained not only to freedom of speech, but also to the secrecy of elections. In 1950 the prominent Social Democrat Herbert Wehner said before the Bundestag (Diemer and Kuhrt 1994, 201),

> The preparations for October 15 [election day] make clear that the people, driven to the election booths with all possible means, will this time be forced to cast their so-called ballots openly. The people will be deprived of the possibility to say no or even to invalidate their ballot. Thus human beings are forced to deny their own convictions and to elect candidates whom they hate and scorn.

Thus the GDR has always been seen in the West as a state of lies in a double sense. Not only did it lie to its own population by manipulating election results, for example, but it forced its citizens to lie too.

In conclusion, the importance of sincerity as a moral good guiding action and serving as a criterion of moral judgment needs to be placed in perspective. The reason is that the depth of moral discourse of most westerners (and increasingly of easterners) is not wholly exhausted by sincerity as an absolute value; many important moral arguments are cast in the language of rights.[22] The two types of discourse are not neatly separable; they do not just complement each other, but intermingle and ultimately compete in leading to divergent prescriptions. This is immediately clear, for example, in the notion of the right to withhold information; that is, people are not, in terms of rights, obliged to be sincere but are instead granted and—as the following example will show—even expected to exercise the right to distinguish between what they think is true about themselves and the presentation of self. There is one context in which this has become especially visible to me in my fieldwork. Western superiors reproach their eastern subordinates for being *too* sincere in reporting incidents in which they have made a mistake or done something wrong (for example, parking the patrol car where they are explicitly not allowed to park and thus causing an accident). Sometimes these reports about their own mistakes are written in such a candid way that the superiors would be obliged to undertake disciplinary measures against their

22. One problem involved in any rights discourse should be borne in mind: the language of rights is ambiguous insofar as it might be either moral, or legal, or both at the same time. Law might even be invoked to silence moral doubt, in an attempt to state that whatever is legal should be at least not considered as immoral. For reasons which are perhaps apparent, this is an argumentative approach which is especially significant for police officers. I discuss these problems further in chapter 6.

subordinates (e.g., for neglect), while they themselves might see simple ways of framing the incident in less self-incriminating ways. What is involved here is the concept of a presentation of self that does not take full advantage of the rights of the officers in question "to present themselves in the best possible light." Sincerity in these cases is seen as the result of an almost childlike naïveté.

Turncoats: Commitment, Time, and Sincerity

The significance of sincerity as a virtue of character and action is further underlined by the prominence of a stark figure in the public discourse on the moral dimensions of unification: the "turncoat." It is he who has become the antihero of unification. The turncoat has a somewhat indeterminate existence, for although everybody seems to know instances of turncoat-like behavior, few people are identified as complete turncoats. Thus he is a little bit everywhere and nowhere at the same time. He is perhaps best thought of as a symbol, ringing true with a variety of personal experiences, mingled with rich layers of historical connotations. The turncoat is the allegory of insincerity in German unification.

So far, I have discussed two different ways of identifying insincerity: the failure to stay within the acceptable limits of variation in self-presentation between different social situations (the external perspective) and a perceived tension between a "true self" and a presented self, the internal perspective. A third way of identifying insincerity is particularly important in the context of German unification because it is much argued about: the *timing* of certain actions.

Many east German officers tell stories about so-called "turncoats,"[23] fellow easterners who have supposedly changed their ideological allegiances "overnight." Typically they are described as former "one-hundred-and-fifty-percenters," often as especially self-righteous and constantly ready to reprimand their fellow officers for their "false consciousness" or "lax attitudes" vis-à-vis the class enemy. The same people are then said to have shifted abruptly from preaching socialism to preaching or at least openly supporting capitalism. This "stupefying change of mind"

---

23. The German term is *Wendehälse* (wryneck: a woodpecker that can turn its head easily in all directions). The reason why the image of the *Wendehälse* is particularly apt to capture this phenomenon is that the political changes in East Germany since the fall of 1989 and the subsequent unification with West Germany are in their totality called *Wende* (turnaround). Thus the Wendehälse are the wrynecks produced by the Wende, they are the suddenly and therefore awkwardly turned people.

as one eastern officer put it, is according to its critics, expressed by unexpectedly dismissive, even derogatory statements about the GDR, or by certain actions such as suddenly entertaining especially lively contacts with the West (after having vigorously condemned such contacts during GDR times) or visiting the West before everyone else (while reminding others that it was still illegal to do so for police officers).[24] Turncoats are also said to have been "the first in line to return their party membership cards," after priding themselves on their "communist attitude" before. Sometimes turncoats are discerned as telling boastful stories about their suffering under the former regime and their intense dislike for it, purportedly "stylizing themselves as victims." Worse, they are reported to describe minor forms of noncooperation or internal difference of opinion as "resistance."

In Germany the very term *turncoat* has strong historical connotations which must be considered to understand the full force of the reproach. Since the overall German resistance to Nazi rule was small and most of the population cooperated with the Nazis, both postwar regimes had to make wide use of members of the former Nazi party to create a functioning government and civil service. The folklore of both Germanies has it that especially the ruling elites of the respective other Germany were heavily staffed with turncoats, former Nazis who had successfully reinvented themselves, if not as "victims" or even as "resistance fighters," then at least as truthful adherents of "democracy" or "socialism." Moreover, the GDR leadership worked from the beginning on a metanarrative legitimizing the "first laborer and peasant state on German soil" as antifascist and grounding it in a tradition of resistance to the Nazi dictatorship (cf. Meuschel 1992). The victimization of some members of the GDR leadership during the Nazi dictatorship, and their struggle as resistance fighters has been widely publicized in the GDR, and many police officers remember these stories.[25] In light of the outward similarities between institutions in Nazi Germany and the GDR, this antifascist rhetoric has always been mocked as insincere in the West. Aided by a string of scandals about the Nazi past of leading western officials and politicians, the

24. Immediately after the opening of the Wall, members of the "armed agencies" *(die bewaffneten Organe)* were still not allowed to visit the West, which aggravated them. Within two weeks, noncommissioned officers were allowed to go, and after about a month all travel restrictions were removed.

25. Especially vividly when their own grandparents or parents had suffered from intimidation and incarceration during the Nazi period.

East missed no opportunity to unmask the so-called democracy of Western leaders as fascism in disguise. Thus the identification of turncoats as self-styled resistance fighters or victims conjures up images of postwar conflicts over morality and the legitimacy of regimes.

In talking about turncoats both east and west Germans pick up on these historical resonances, though often with different aims in view. The gamut of possibilities in invoking this complex of historical connotations is quite far-ranging. At one extreme, the identification of present-day turncoats with Nazis who have tried to pose as good democrats (with overtones of metonymic identifications between the GDR and the Nazi dictatorship) is used as a means to discredit the resistance-fighter/victim narrative of many former GDR leaders. At the other extreme, the posing of turncoats as resistance fighters/victims is contrasted with the sincerity of real resistance fighters/victims during the Nazi dictatorship, whose example is seen as besmirched by the presumption of the turncoats. In between lie all the subtle shadings of ironizations which, for example, already use the terms *victim* and *resistance fighter* as mockery (much to the chagrin of the few people who really resisted). Easterners and westerners meet in ironization, but tend to cluster around the two opposing ends of the outlined spectrum.

What makes these turncoats morally despicable in the eyes of those who talk about them is their *sudden* shift of allegiance, which is read as utter insincerity with respect to the life they had lived before, thereby raising suspicions about their present commitments. Therefore, turncoats are discredited as lacking the very capacity to be sincere, which (as I have outlined above) is a precondition for being moral in the first place. It is sincerity as a constitutive part of "human decency," sincerity of character, which is doubted because individual acts betray abrupt shifts in commitment. Sincerity, therefore, implies a certain degree of constancy. Just how constant is, of course, contingent on the type of commitment. What is at stake here is the commitment to persons and ideologies, and neither can be changed "as often as shirts," as a popular expression goes.

The irony for turncoats is that westerners are as suspicious, if not disgusted, about them as fellow easterners. In principle, western officers are especially suspicious of eastern police officers who disown their former lives in the GDR too vocally, because they assume that as a police officer, one is supposed to have a special commitment to one's state. In the eyes of many westerners every eastern police officer who has tried to continue to work for the unified Berlin Police, the former class enemy, is a potential

turncoat and therefore cannot be trusted easily because he or she might
have shifted allegiances too quickly. Many westerners say that they prefer
"honest communists," standing up for their former beliefs, freely admitting their membership in the party, and defending the GDR at least to
some degree, to somebody who embraces western ways of thinking too
rapidly. Not that they would particularly like such an "honest communist," but, as some have put it, pointing to the value of predictability in
a person, "at least you know what you have." The lack of constancy and
predictability ascribed to turncoats is further emphasized by associating
them with soft, malleable material like rubber.

The image of the turncoat offers a convenient way for westerners to
metonymically identify all easterners as unprincipled opportunists who
trim their sails to the wind. At least at the beginning, critical statements by
eastern officers about the former GDR were in danger of being misunderstood as attempts to ingratiate. Easterners thus have reason to signify
clearly that they are not turncoats. Often enough, my first talk with easterners about their past in the GDR started with statements like, "I was not a
resistance fighter," or "I must admit I have not been a victim of the regime;
to the contrary, I fared rather well," thus beginning to explain their sincere
belief in the value of their party membership and in socialist ideology.

At the same time, westerners, especially in Berlin, tend to get upset
about any praise of the former GDR by their eastern colleagues. Even
too spirited a defense on the part of easterners in response to a western
provocation might lead westerners to identify them as "incorrigible," as
"having not learned anything from history"; westerners claim to be baffled that despite all that easterners now know about the GDR, "they *still*
cling to it." In the face of the Nazi dictatorship and the Holocaust, "learning from history" has become a very strong moral imperative in both
parts of Germany. Both countries have developed narratives in which
"learning from history" is the raison d'être for the particular form both
parts of Germany have taken (Grosser 1974; more specifically for the
police, MdI 1987; and Steinborn and Krüger 1993). After the moral abyss
of the Third Reich, learning from history has been a way for both parts
of Germany to reacquire a sense of moral integrity through change for
the better. Therefore, an east German identified as not willing or able
"to learn from history" is moved again into the proximity of a Nazi by
creating a metonymic relationship between the GDR and Nazi Germany.

Westerners feel especially provoked by easterners who defend the reformed socialist party (PDS), successor to the former Socialist Unity Party

(Sozialistische Einheitspartei Duetschlands, SED).[26] Voting for the PDS is to them completely incomprehensible and can only be understood as a clear sign of "backwardness." The German expression most frequently used in this context is *zurückgeblieben sein* (to have remained behind). The same word is employed in German to denote mental retardation, and its use in the context of westerners identifying easterners clearly carries this connotation, "for how could a reasonable adult do something like that [vote for the PDS]?" as one of them put it. Another term used frequently in reference to PDS supporters is *Ewiggestrige* (literally, "eternally yesterday's"). This term has again strong historical resonances which do not escape most German speakers, since die-hard Nazis were called just that after 1945. Thus, the term *Ewiggestrige* also produces a metonymic identification between the GDR and Nazi Germany, respectively between a supposed adherent of actual socialism and a Nazi. The irony in all of these formulations based on metaphors of moral development in time is that they were used in the GDR to denounce political opponents, who were identified as "back-stepping forces" *(rückschrittliche Kräfte)* who were "thwarting progress." Thus, in identifying easterners as backward, westerners, for moral reasons, demanded change of their eastern colleagues, visible change, as well as a renunciation of their own past.[27]

By and large, easterners reject all attempts of westerners to associate the GDR with the Nazi dictatorship. And they are certainly not ready to renounce their past wholeheartedly. Still, they are concerned with the failure of the GDR, and they pose the problem of learning from history. Thus change is something that they thought was bound to happen in the GDR anyway, because the structures apparently could not survive as they were. What is doubtful, however, is whether change has gone in the right direction. Put differently, they have second thoughts about whether the FRG is really the answer to all of the questions—moral and otherwise—posed by the demise of the GDR and a new understanding of its internal workings.

26. The general elections in October 1994 gave me ample opportunity to observe exchanges between easterners and westerners about the better than expected results of the PDS, which managed to send four directly elected candidates to the Bundestag, the lower house of parliament. Three of them were elected in east Berlin electoral districts of Marzahn, Prenzlauer Berg, and Lichtenberg. The PDS candidate in Köpenick narrowly lost to his Social Democratic competitor.

27. For more on the topic of temporal identifications, see chapter 3.

The simultaneous demands of sincerity and change put easterners into a serious dilemma. On the one hand, sincerity, if it is to be credible, requires substantial constancy of opinion and behavior over time. Fast change gets identified by easterners and westerners alike as frivolous, at best, and as an indicator of an complete lack of morality at worst. On the other hand, western police officers do want to see a profound change of allegiance as proof that their eastern colleagues are learning their lesson from history. Both demands are almost impossible to fulfill at the same time. Therefore, as one eastern officer put it, east Germans must be "careful now of how they talk to whom [so as] not to be misunderstood." In other words east Germans need to think carefully about how to present themselves and must once again choose between keeping quiet and misrepresenting themselves within certain boundaries. They need to be insincere to protect the appearance of their sincerity, at least in confronting many westerners, and since most superiors in Berlin are westerners, they once more cannot talk openly to their superiors about how they feel and what they think. Psychologically, this has effects comparable to the insincerity they were forced into when watching Western TV and meeting Western relatives in the GDR. The dance they have to perform between the constancy of commitment and the morality of historical lessons is difficult, if not impossible. Their little insincerities threaten the moral integrity of their character, which is felt as depression. Thus east Germans face a dilemma that amounts to a veritable paradox.[28]

The question, then, is this: If western demands force easterners into a paradoxical situation, what do westerners think that easterners could do to get out of it, to reinstate their moral integrity in their eyes? To undo the paradox, there must be an accepted path of action that allows for sincere change.[29] The answer to this question is quite simple. Many westerners entertain the idea that what would befit the "pillars of the GDR regime," including former People's Police officers, is some form of atonement, some sign of humility and recognition of error. One suggested form of atonement would be to accept the demotion all east German officers had to cope with if they wanted to continue to work for the Berlin Police *without complaint*. Atonement is by no means a device suggested

28. In the next chapter I discuss how this experience is the starting point for easterners to criticize the political, social, and economic institutions of the FRG.

29. Sincere change is, for example, possible in the context of rites of passage: forms of behavior and commitments are allowed to change virtually overnight if the person in question has undergone a legitimate ritual keeping the moral status intact, because the moral demands change with the rite of passage.

only by westerners, however. I have encountered several low-ranking east German officers who thought it not only acceptable, but a matter of justice that at least some of their former superiors be demoted. This pertains especially to those officers who were thought to be particularly closely aligned with the politics of the East German regime.

> There were those [commissioned officers] who were totally enmeshed in politics, condescendingly dealing others a dressing down, insisting on their political point of view in all circumstances, emphasizing their partiality, and I just can't accept that somebody like that stages a full turn to reappear as my superior again. I am very much in favor of their demotion; they shouldn't be dismissed, but if they used to have the rank of lieutenant colonel they should now have the rank of sergeant, just like me. That's quite all right, I think.

In sum, sincerity has a very important temporal dimension, in that it is based on the fulfillment of temporally stable commitments which cannot be undone at will without endangering one's moral status. While sincerity as a moral value seems to favor unflinching stability, the notion that especially Germans need to learn from history, a notion developed in response to the horrors of the Third Reich but now applied by west Germans to the "moral processing of GDR history," seems to mandate decisive change. Both demands taken together pose a serious dilemma. Changes in commitment may need to occur, but they must be orchestrated extremely carefully. In the eyes of many west Germans, but also some east Germans, the potential insincerity of change may by healed by atonement.

Conclusions

The recursive foundation of sincerity in itself was an important reason why easterners and westerners did not trust each other at first. They did not even talk to each other much. Each had a hunch that the other might have a stake in being insincere, misrepresenting themselves in conversation. Westerners believed that nothing easterners would tell them about the former GDR was to be trusted since their stories would be created to exonerate themselves from any responsibility in suppressing people in the GDR. Many easterners believed in turn that most westerners, suspicious enough to consider every easterner a potential Stasi mole, would want to spy on them. Easterners also felt that nothing they could tell westerners about life in the GDR would be understood correctly, because they sensed (accurately) that westerners not only knew little about the former GDR, but they were unwilling to learn from them what life in the GDR was like. Trust is built on the belief that the other is sincere. In a situation of distrust—a situation in which one believes the other to be insincere, as in the unification of both police organizations in Berlin—the belief in the sincerity of the other can only be established slowly through countless personal interactions. This task has taken years to accomplish and in its finer aspects, it is still under way.

The GDR deprived its citizens of the freedom to travel and the freedom to utter their opinions, and it strove to restrict access to uncensored information. The People's Police made it an offence for its officers to watch Western TV and to maintain any contact with people living in Western countries, even if these people were parents, children, brothers, and sisters. What strikes many westerners as odd in the context of this suppression is that, explicitly asked, almost all eastern officers uniformly said that none of these restrictions ever made them angry. In my own conversations too, none of these measures was ever used as a basis to develop a reproach against the state or the People's Police, a reproach by which officers would have identified themselves as being against their state. This is so despite the fact that most easterners would have wanted to travel to the West, that they wanted to watch Western TV and to receive their relatives openly in their own apartments. Thus the eastern officers I have talked to did not identify themselves as being against the state which they had served. Contrary to Foucault's (1969) hypothesis, power, although certainly felt and at least partially circumvented, did not lead to identity formation in resistance.

Most People's Police officers identified with their work, and with the organization and the state which employed them. Yet their state and their police force asked them to comply fully with any rules established by the state or police if they really wanted to count as "true officers" and "true communists." Some of these rules, however, conflicted with their desires to watch the TV channels they liked best and to meet the people they loved. Moreover, the transgression of these rules was heavily sanctioned. Anyone caught watching Western TV or meeting Western relatives stood to lose his or her job. Thus, eastern officers either had to betray the police force or their desires. Worse, wanting both a life in the police and a life according to their desires, they had to be insincere, in spite of the fact that sincerity was to them a highly cherished moral value. Whatever they decided to do, they were bound up in what Bateson (1972) has aptly termed in his research on schizophrenia a "double bind" (cf. Laing

1969, pt. 2). Double binds are, as Bateson has shown, dilemmas, paradoxical demands which cannot be escaped because a further identification or prohibition holds them firmly in place. The double bind situation in this case is due to incompatible identifications with the People's Police and its norms as well as with personal desires, and it is rendered inescapable by the valuation placed on sincerity, which emphasizes the validity of both identifications. Each officer caught between these conflicting identifications had to find his or her own balance between desires, duty, and sincerity. In the end most officers compromised on all three, living a fearful life as officers while never quite fully enjoying the fulfillment of their desires because they felt morally at fault and because they feared discovery. Although not all officers were equally affected by this double bind, those who valued highly their relationships with people in the West suffered most severely.[30]

One eastern officer who moved suddenly from having no problems to being deeply steeped in the double bind just described because his nephew tried to flee the GDR, was caught, imprisoned, and later "bought free" *(freigekauft)*[31] by the FRG recalls this situation thus:

> Because the big one [an endearing term used here for his nephew] was bought free, I, as a People's Police officer, was forced to break off all contact with my sister-in-law. I said to my wife, "What are we going to do about it?" [He had explained before that they had a very lively, good relationship with his wife's sister.] But I had my work, my wife had her work, and we both liked it, and so we never thought of fleeing. So my wife said, "Look, we have to live in this state and we are not the only ones whose families get divided; we have to take it as it is. Let's leave it at that." So we broke off the contact but always with the feeling, I as brother-in-law, my wife as sister, Why? Why is this so?

30. Other paradoxical demand constellations intersect with the double bind I have just outlined: An identification with the GDR—the state, or the place, or both—on the one hand, and on the other a desire for things that seem simply unavailable in the GDR; or, even more pragmatically, a desire for the privileges that come with service in the police, such as an income which was about 30 percent higher than that in comparable positions in industry, and the special restrictions such as the strict prohibition to meet Western relatives that came with employment in the People's Police.

31. The FRG regularly "bought" the freedom of political prisoners from the GDR, who were therefore allowed to leave GDR prisons for the FRG. Between 1963, when this practice began, and 1989, the FRG bought the freedom of a total of 31,391 prisoners (Garton Ash 1993, 658–59).

I do not want to go as far as to suggest that this double bind necessarily leads to schizophrenia. The individual responses to this situation were just too different. But I do want to suggest that it did indeed lead to a form of emotional paralysis, which in most cases prevented effective moral criticism of the GDR.

Not only their lives in the GDR, however, put eastern officers into a double bind; their incorporation into the Berlin Police, an organization which, for most of their own history had been interpreted as an antagonist, also posed substantial challenges to their personal sincerity. Westerners have not made this incorporation any easier, because they demand on the one hand full allegiance to the new organization with a corresponding repudiation of the old one, and on the other hand they ask that the embrace of the new organization be not too strong and the disavowal of the old one not too fast, because such a quick and complete change of allegiance would have to be frivolous and insincere. What prevents unification from developing into a full-blown double bind is that there is a path out. It is a narrow path, however, with moral abysses on both sides. And since traveling on it is more like a delicate dance, it takes time too. For nobody, neither westerner nor easterner, thinks that one cannot have a change of mind, that de-identification and re-identification cannot be credible. However, as the shared eastern and western abnegation of turncoats proves, a change of mind cannot be too sudden if it is to convince others of its integrity. It requires a carefully paced narrative of transformation, a story of commitment, disillusionment, atonement, and new commitment.

What this chapter may also show is that even where easterners and westerners agree, as in their high esteem for sincerity, this agreement works out very differently in their lives. There are two reasons for this difference. Unification has put easterners and westerners in very different positions of power with regard to each other, because westerners have appeared as rule-setters and easterners as rule-followers. Moreover, life in the two Germanies was very different, creating very different biographies with very different claims on the present.

SIX

Individual Rights and the Morality of States

Political scientists and sociologists have debated the degree to which it makes sense to speak of the state as an autonomous actor. While the liberal theory and orthodox Marxism of the postwar decades have both, if for different reasons, denied the state any agency above and beyond the projection of societal forces, the pendulum has swung back since the beginning of the 1980s to assert the character of the state as a semiautonomous actor (Skocpol 1979, 1985; Nordlinger, 1981). The everyday discourses of police officers, too, wrestle with the question of whether or not the state can be treated as a proper actor. This becomes especially visible in their conversations about the morality of states, because some notion of the state as independent actor is the precondition for its effective moral identification, that is, moralization (Moore 1993). In fact, the officers' discourses oscillate widely between wholehearted moralization of states, thus considering states as proper actors, often experienced as adversarial to self, and the flat refusal to moralize states, attributing real agency and thus moral competence instead (much in the fashion of liberal or Marxist theory) to societal formations.

The question is, then, When and under what circumstances are states considered proper moral subjects? At this point a fundamental distinction must be made between the totalizing moralization of states as wholes (e.g., westerners' frequent "the GDR was a state of injustice") and a moralization of certain aspects of states, of particular policies, institutions, and incumbents of offices. Totalizing moral identifications of states are most common among easterners and westerners, if the state in question is experienced as other. This is clearly the case for foreign states, which are freely moralized from without. States as wholes are also moralized

257

from within by people who do not positively identify with the state in any way. In the latter case, the moralization of the state is often a simultaneous moralization of the self, in that the powerful agency of the state is paired with the overpowered agency of the self. State and self are understood in terms of a victim-victimizer dichotomy.

Westerners systematically moralize the former GDR from a particular vantage point: they moralize the GDR on the basis of a juxtaposition between an authoritarian regime and a suppressed people; that is, they moralize the state from without by identifying with an assumed victim-victimizer dichotomy from within. This is precisely the rhetorical strategy of the principle of sole representation.[1] Westerners create a metonymic identification between themselves and the suppressed people of the GDR. Thus the FRG is cast, if not as the liberator, then at least as the guarantor of the new-found liberty of the formerly suppressed people of the GDR. The shock for westerners comes when easterners reject the notion of liberation, instead insinuating occupation. These conflicting perspectives of easterners and westerners emerge clearly in the debates about the continuing electoral success of the reformed communist party. As one western officer put it to an eastern colleague, "I simply cannot understand how you can still vote for your former suppressors." To this the easterner responded, "Because they are the only ones who speak up for us," thus reversing the suppressor-suppressed insinuations of his western colleague, effectively moralizing the FRG rather than the GDR.

Westerners rarely moralize the FRG as a whole. If they do, it is mostly in comparative perspective, either in contrast to the GDR or in contrast to other historical German states—the Nazi dictatorship or the Weimar Republic. In this context the FRG is often praised as the "best state ever on German soil." Rather than the FRG as a whole, western officers moralize individual policies enacted by a particular government, decisions of certain institutions, or actions of individual representatives of the state, while the state as a whole recedes into the background as a given. Sometimes the state is even placed beyond the sphere of the moral, especially when citizens identify state and police and, by synecdochical extension, state and police officers. In the context of citizen complaints about police action, the officers deny active, independent state agency, which as a rhetorical strategy follows the liberal doctrine. In a discussion about a widely criticized police maneuver on the occasion of the May Day demonstration in Berlin, one western officer said, "Who in the end

---

1. See the discussion in chapter 2.

is the state? It is all of us taken together!" while portraying the police leadership and by synecdochical extension the state as driven by electoral considerations.

Easterners' moralizations of states are much more conflicted. The exact circumstances of their moralizations must be seen from a concrete historical and situational vantage point to get an accurate picture. Thus, in what follows I make a distinction between how eastern officers saw the GDR during GDR times and how they have come to see the GDR and the FRG after unification. Today, some easterners moralize both the FRG and the GDR as a whole, communicating a disenchanted distance from politics and states in general; some heavily moralize the FRG as an "occupying force" *(Besatzungsmacht)* while sparing the GDR as a whole; but only a few follow the western path of only moralizing the GDR as a whole (e.g., as "state of lies") while refraining from totalizing moral identifications of the FRG. By contrast to the use of totalizing moral identifications, easterners extensively moralize specific policies, institutions, and office incumbents of both the FRG and the GDR. Easterners' moralization of the FRG takes place most notably either in the context of political concern about the treatment of easterners in unified Germany (notoriously in the ongoing debate about their own lower pay), or in response to western moral attacks on the former GDR.[2] Their moralization of the GDR as a whole most frequently recedes, just as the FRG does for westerners, into the amoral background of givens, even if they are today highly critical of the GDR leadership.

Easterners' moral identifications of the GDR during GDR times followed a completely different pattern (as far as one can tell from their retrospective narratives). As westerners moralize policies while avoiding the moralization of the state as a whole, easterners, during GDR times, seem to have moralized persons as incumbents of offices, not institutions (perhaps with the sole exception of the Stasi) or policies (cf. Fulbrook 1995, 75). This moral acquittal of the state in favor of a judgment of persons seems to have been common practice in GDR times, as some

2. Sometimes easterners place the FRG beyond the sphere of morality. This is perhaps most apparent when eastern officers try to explain their own wholesale depoliticization or at least their decreasing interest in electoral politics. By using an orthodox Marxist theoretical framework, some of them describe the state as an "executive organ of monopoly capitalism," thus pointing to a ruling class which is credited with agency and is accordingly to be moralized. This placement of the state beyond morality is connected to the perceived powerlessness of the state to do something about what most easterners consider the most pressing problem after unification: unemployment.

eastern officers remember. The blame for the lack of provisions, for example, was put on persons—mostly anonymous bureaucrats negligent of their duties. Thus not even the top of the political hierarchy got blamed, but the faceless layer somewhere in the middle. Eastern officers have in the past frequently contrasted a good (if not perfect) system with imperfect people who cause most of the problems.

One eastern officer recalls, for example, a visit by Honecker to a construction site in Köpenick to celebrate the completion of the millionth apartment. Suddenly everything around was cleaned up, the parks were nicely planted, and there was an abundance of otherwise very scarce fresh paint, while the stores in the neighborhood were well stocked with tropical fruits and other hard-to-come by delicacies. He recalls today that he then said to himself that some officials were constantly fooling the leadership about the true state of the GDR and that this was the reason why so many things went wrong in the GDR. Another officer, commenting on the same kind of window dressing which was regularly staged on the occasion of visits of higher officials, said that during GDR times she truly believed that the leadership did not know what was going on, and that she was shocked to learn after the breakdown of the GDR that Honecker himself ordered these shows for his own visits.[3]

There may be yet another reason why the GDR as a whole was not moralized during its existence and is still not moralized today. One easterner said in the context of an interview about the disintegration of the former GDR and subsequent unification,

> Perhaps I would have done everything for my state. I have always considered it my home. Everywhere something gets messed up, everywhere something is wrong. But this was my home, yes, this was my home, I grew up there.

State and country, a set of political institutions with a particular history, fuse here into a whole with the notion of a place. This is further highlighted by the fact that the same person, in talking about unified Germany, uses the term *home* only in reference to place, not in reference to the state. And again, the new state is still considered as something other, foreign, something of which self is not a part, and this other, the FRG, is indeed extensively moralized by her.

3. The deflection of moral judgment away from the state and away from the political system to persons may even be exacerbated today because the debate about the meaning of the former GDR is first and foremost driven by the lawsuits against officials of the former GDR.

In many encounters between eastern and western officers I could observe that the moralization of parts of a state—a policy, an institution, a person—could lead to a discussion, a peaceful exchange of ideas, attitudes, and feelings. Communication for the sake of understanding would stop, however, with the synecdochical use of parts to denounce the whole. Such a rhetorical move was invariably understood as a provocation which led immediately to strong emotional reactions, usually turning a discussion between easterners and westerners into a highly personalized argument. It seems that for understanding to have a chance in a highly conflicted social field, there must be something like trust in the exclusion from the conversation of what might be called *synecdochical mischief.* Synecdochical mischief is the readiness to use any information attainable about parts to reconfirm preset notions about the whole. Typically, neither easterners nor westerners were willing to accept negative judgment of the whole state/country, no matter how critical they were about any single part.[4] Therefore, even eastern police officers who had refused to enter the party, thus forfeiting possible promotion to the ranks of commissioned officers, would counter wholesale western attacks on the GDR, defending a state which they would otherwise mostly criticize. What seems to underlie this pattern is a basic identification with a state/country, which does not necessarily imply an identification with any single part making up the whole.[5]

Michael Herzfeld (1997) has discussed a complementary phenomenon in terms of "cultural intimacy." Knowledge about the failures of one's own cultural group are only discussed inside this group, while the outside is presented with a homogeneous, positive picture (the officer in the example above says, "everywhere something is wrong"). Moreover, precise knowledge about inside failures is a reason to close ranks, a source of internal cohesion. The symbolic boundary between inside and outside is then also defined by what is discussed with whom. Discussion of failures or unpleasant facts is a sure sign of inside status. East and west Germans were much more ready to discuss the shortcomings of their respective states and politi-

4. At the beginning, I too had strong feelings when east Germans negatively evaluated the morality of West Germany as a whole. It showed me the extent to which I identify with the FRG as *my* country and have investments in its political institutions as a whole, even if I personally do not approve of the way in which unification was handled and could sympathize with easterner's specific complaints.

5. Edward Said (1992) makes a similar point about the exchanges between the first and the third world, where the moralization of whole states (e.g., as between France and Algeria, India and England, the United States and Iran) leads to constant misunderstandings, even involving otherwise rather critical intellectual elites.

cal systems with other easterners or westerners than with colleagues from the other part of the country. And it is precisely this play with inside-outside status which attests to strong east-west identifications.

In sum, then, the moralization of states as wholes, in contrast to the moralization of particular policies or officials, is connected to a political agenda usually based in a perspective that sees itself as outside the state in question. The moralization of states as opposed to the moralization of policies or officials favors a wholesale endorsement or rejection of a state.[6]

Both easterners and westerners share a basic identification with the GDR or the FRG respectively. This identification is typically provoked by synecdochical mischief, and it is protected by cultural intimacy. The degree to which synecdochical mischief is experienced as provocation and the degree to which cultural intimacy is practiced are useful indicators for the strength of the basic identification with a particular state *within a particular arena of contestation.* And it is precisely in this context that easterners' support for the reformed communist party (which is not necessarily electoral support) and their anger at the treatment of the reformed communist party on the national level must be understood. In what follows, I analyze the debates over the moralization of states between east Germans and west Germans in the context of their focal points: the Wall (or more generally the border between the two parts of Germany); the Secret Police, or Stasi; and state-citizen relations.

Viewing Self and Other through the Wall

During my stay in Berlin, all of my visitors who had come to the city for the first time asked me to show them the Wall. Most of them were rather disappointed to learn that most of it was gone. Typically, they also wanted to walk through the Brandenburg Gate. As for the rest of their sightseeing, they usually left it to my imagination to come up with some good ideas of how to spend our common time in Berlin. Since the 1960s the Wall had become West Berlin's most famous tourist attraction, and a visit to Berlin should have at least included a view of the Wall. Since

6. The moralization of states as a whole is a feature of social revolutions. Thus it is no accident that Skocpol's theorizing of the state starts from an analysis of social revolutions. Starting points for the moralizations of states are, accordingly, political concerns, which are not represented within the institutions of these states. It is the perceived otherness of the state (again not of one particular government, or of particular policies) which gives rise to moralizations of the state from within.

its fall, walking through its most famous stretch at the Brandenburg Gate was added to every tourist's short list of "must dos." I myself, upon arriving in Berlin, had taken my bicycle to explore the former boundary between the boroughs of Mitte in the east and Kreuzberg and Tiergarten in the west. I too was somehow thrilled that the course of the Wall was still discernible, and I took great pleasure at transgressing that once most real—in the sense of most tangible—of geographical boundaries, which had become more or less imaginary. The Wall was the foremost symbol of the East-West divide; crossing it without difficulty in turn was the best proof that Europe was no longer a divided continent, or so it seemed.

In western officers' tales, the Wall emerges as the location of political drama; it was the boundary between freedom and authoritarian tutelage, it was the boundary between good luck and bad, a hurdle for many Easterners who would risk their lives to reach the Western side, the lucky side of history. Every attempt to flee across the Wall, successful or thwarted, made news in Berlin. The Wall also signified to west Berliners the special political status of their city, neither independent nor fully part of West Germany, a special place between the worlds under the suzerainty of the three Western Allied Powers who guaranteed West Berlin's freedom. But the Wall also stood for much more mundane things, for some of the hardships of everyday life. Effectively cut off from the surrounding countryside, West Berliners were deprived of their recreational hinterland and thus forced on the road for weekend trips to faraway places in northern Franconia and Lower Saxony. The Wall was also the symbol for the chicanery of GDR border controls on the transit routes to the FRG. Finally, it was blamed for the higher prices of groceries and gasoline. West Berliners liked to talk about themselves as "walled in" *(eingemauert, zugemauert)*, triggering associations of brutal "oriental" methods of torture.[7] This feeling of being walled in would invariably trigger what they called in metaphorical assimilation an "island fit" *(Inselkoller)*, the urgent need to leave, to get away to a place where life was "normal," that is, non-insular. In sum, then, to west Berliners the Wall was a monstrosity, a symbol of abnormality, and constantly remembered as such. As an integral part of west Berliners' identity, the Wall was kept firmly in view.[8] It

7. This being of course the punishment for Aida and her lover Radamès in Verdi's opera.

8. The Wall was also made the locale for many happenings: sprayers and graffiti artists used it as their canvas (the only place where Western authorities could not do anything against their spraying, since the Wall was strictly speaking on GDR territory), and rock concerts were held in front of it.

identified West Berliners as victims of communist violence and at the same
time as the avant-garde of Western freedom. In short, the Wall identified
West Berliners as West Berliners.

East Berlin officers remember that they viewed the Wall in a different
light altogether. It had by no means the deep emotional significance it
held for westerners. Rather than remembering the Wall, making it visible,
East Berliners chose to ignore the Wall—if they could, that is. The overwhelming majority of eastern officers considered the Wall during GDR
times as a simple fact of history; in the words of one of them, "The Wall
was just there, that's it." Often, west Berliners justify moral condemnation
of the GDR by pointing to its agency in erecting the Wall. Thus provoked,
easterners typically defend "the right of the GDR to protect its own, inter-
nationally recognized state boundaries." Asked whether the border between the two Germanies, and especially the border between the two
Berlins was not markedly different from other international boundaries—
for example, those between the GDR and Poland or the GDR and
Czechoslovakia—easterners point to the fact that the border between the
two Germanies was of course at once the frontier between not only different, but antagonistic political systems. Given these circumstances of international politics, most of them argued, the Wall was quite normal. Accordingly, the erection of the Wall in 1961 is almost universally justified
by the eastern police officers as a legitimate act aiming at the economic
protection of the GDR on two accounts: first, to prevent smugglers from
the West from buying up cheap, subsidized consumer goods in the East,
and second to prevent qualified Eastern workers and professionals from
fleeing to the West, since their labor was urgently needed in the GDR.
The second point was defended on the grounds "that the GDR had financed the education of those who were fleeing and could thus not simply
allow them to walk off with it," as one of the eastern officers put it.

Some of the eastern police officers had done service along the Wall.
All of them claimed that they had dreaded the job, not, however, because
the Wall itself posed a particular moral problem for them, but because
the service itself had several severe downsides.[9] The work was exceedingly
boring; usually nothing much happened on patrol, and since there were

9. This is one of the places where my own western emotional investments became
pretty apparent to me. When eastern police officers would talk about dreading the
service at the Wall, their dismay was in my mind quickly connected with the moral
repulsiveness of the Wall itself, and I was disappointed to find I had made a prema-
ture, deeply cultured assumption. I myself could at first not believe that there could
be anyone who would not find the Wall almost "naturally" repulsive.

no people allowed near the Wall, there were also few possibilities to divert oneself with a little chat. Service in police precincts all along the wall was also avoided, if possible, because the security systems on and around the Wall would frequently lead to alarms, which meant also a high risk of pretty regular overtime work until the cause of the alarm was found: perhaps a stray dog or cat, and sometimes really a human trying what was called in GDR official jargon "an illegal break through the border" *(illegaler Grenzdurchbruch)*.

What creates the most severe controversy between east and west German police officers about the Wall is what has been called on the western side the *Schießbefehl* (order to shoot), the sanctioning of the use of deadly weaponry to prevent anyone from crossing the border. Between 1961, when the Wall was built, and 1989, when it came down, more than five hundred people died attempting to cross either the Wall around West Berlin or the heavily fortified boundary between the FRG and the GDR. These "dead of the wall" *(Mauertote)* constitute the prime evidence for western officers, and for western authorities in general, that the GDR was a "state contemptuous of human beings" *(menschenverachtender Staat)*, protected, kept alive with the help of the eastern police officers who suddenly became their colleagues. The (western) authorities have been trying since unification to identify and to persecute the so-called Wall-gunners *(Mauerschützen)* as well as their commanding officers and party officials, who could be held responsible for these approximately five hundred deaths. Several of them have been found guilty of manslaughter or abetting manslaughter. At the beginning it looked as if the legal system could only successfully cope with the lower-ranking officers who actually carried out the orders to shoot refugees. As documents became available, however, proving the active encouragement of the soldiers to prevent refugees at any cost from crossing the border, even members of the politburo could be successfully indicted and sentenced to prison terms.[10]

Again, most east German officers claim that there never was such a thing as an "order to shoot" *(Schießbefehl)*, that the border between the

10. In the trial against Egon Krenz, Honecker's immediate successor, the state prosecutor based his argument on a memo of the National Defense Council of the GDR (Nationaler Verteidigungsrat) from 1974 which says that development along the border has to be such that "there is everywhere a clear line of fire" and that "as before, firearms should be employed ruthlessly," while "those comrades having used their firearms successfully should be commended" ("Anklageerhebung im Todschlagsprozeß gegen ehemalige DDR-Führung," *Süddeutsche Zeitung*, 13 March 1996). Krenz has in the meantime been sentenced to six and a half years in prison (appeal pending).

two antagonistic socioeconomic systems simply was a military high-security zone, which it was forbidden to enter, just as it is forbidden to enter
other military high-security areas, which are all marked in German "Attention! Use of firearms." They maintain that all persons who tried to
approach the border knew about its dangers and therefore willfully endangered their own lives in trying to cross it. Of course east German
officers say they feel sorry for everybody who was killed. However, they
also insist that those who tried to flee took their chances, while there
were other (legal) means to leave the GDR.

Westerners also claim that the Wall in itself constitutes a blatant violation of human rights, that no state has the right to keep its citizens from
leaving its territory if they so choose. I have asked eastern officers again
and again whether the Wall as the epitome of highly restrictive travel
regulations did not upset them as citizens, whether they were not angry
at their own state for keeping them from going where they wanted to
go. They all answered that although they might have had the wish to
travel to West Germany, to France, or to Italy, it never made them angry
that the GDR tried to keep them from doing so. They often add that they
see things differently now, but then they were definitely not upset about
it. They argue that during GDR times, it appeared much more as an un-
questionable fact of life, something that could not be changed anyway.
The same response followed inquiries about their feelings and thoughts
with respect to the interdiction of any sort of contact with Westerners,
including close relatives, to the censorship of the mass media, or to the
tapping of their telephones. There was never a response in which eastern
police officers identified themselves as bearers of individual rights—rights
that could be violated by others, especially the state; rights that could or
at least should also be defended. None of these issues, which every western police officer typically framed in terms of rights, was ever seen within
such a framework by eastern police officers during GDR times. In short,
a moral discourse in terms of rights was absent at least as far as rights
of freedom are concerned. In all likelihood, the assumption of individual
rights would have led, given the numerous GDR state actions curtailing
these rights, to a self-identification of the presumed bearers of rights as
victims, thus creating an internal opposition between state and self. A
sustained self-identification in opposition to the state might eventually
also have led to a positioning of the self outside of the state, destroying
the basic state/country identification, thus creating the potential for a
moralization of the state as a whole. In the absence of a rights framework,
however, such self-identifications did not suggest themselves as easily. To

be precise, they were absent *then*. Easterners explain that *today* they would see individual rights at stake and that they would understand and share some of the feelings of their western colleagues *now*. But then, things were different![11]

I am uncertain to what *extent* the notion of rights was absent from eastern police officers' vocabulary and to what extent this impoverished vocabulary was shared by others in the GDR.[12] It is clear that eastern officers did not make much use of a rights framework for their daily police work either. Also, in all descriptions I have heard of why people tried to leave the GDR, the violation of individual rights seems to have played a minor role. What is given as a motivation (at least by those who stayed and had someone in their family who fled) is the expectation of a better life "over there," not the protection of rights. Altogether, there is little indication that the notion of individual rights played any major part in the moral vocabulary and therefore in the identity of east German police officers. Thus it is rather peculiar that they should emphasize the right of the state to protect itself by erecting the Wall, even shooting at those who tried to flee.

There is one group of east German officers who did have a much more ambiguous attitude to the Wall. While they still use the rhetoric of a system in need of defending itself, they still never could get themselves to accept the Wall as normal, because in some ways the Wall inflicted pain on them, making it next to impossible to ignore it. This is the group of officers who, disregarding the strict official interdiction, went out to meet their Western relatives and friends clandestinely or who otherwise tried to maintain contact with persons in the West. Some officers became part of this group simply because a dear relative had fled to the West, all of a sudden rendering the Wall significant, whereas before it might have been little more than a gray line on the horizon beyond which they had no urgent desire to explore. Others became good friends of people who suffered because of the Wall, and thus they started to think differently.[13] In general, the way in which the Wall was seen, and this is as

11. Compare the section entitled "Experiencing Discontinuity, Spinning Continuity" in chapter 4.

12. In contrast to the police officers, the GDR opposition did indeed use a language of rights, but then the opposition was indeed a very small minority.

13. Of course, there remains the difference between those who did sever ties with western relatives and subsequently normalized the Wall; those who severed ties, but for whom the Wall was a constant reminder that things were not as they were supposed to be; and those who refused to sever ties, never normalizing the Wall (and all shades in between). I have nothing further to offer to explain differences of this

true for westerners if the difference between West Berliners and West Germans with no important ties into the east is considered, depended strongly on the importance—or in phenomenological terms the relevance—of the Wall for each individual. On average, of course, East Berliners could much more easily choose to ignore the Wall in their everyday life than West Berliners.

Clearly, as the Wall came down on 9 November 1989, to the surprise of almost everyone in Berlin, eastern police officers were as curious and as eager to visit the West, as most of their fellow citizens. That does not mean that they were universally joyful about the fall of the Wall. Some were, but others were a lot more cautious, even anxious about what the event might mean and what it would bring eventually. Still, the fall of the Wall was welcome, if only as an opportunity to get any of the scarce goods so hard to come by in the GDR.

Relating Selves to the Secret Police

Considering the heat of the controversies about the East German secret police (Stasi),[14] and in view of the considerable complexity of the topic, it seems necessary to begin this section with a few clarifying remarks. What is at issue here is by no means an attempt to understand the Stasi, the function and position of the Stasi in GDR society, its contribution to the sustenance or the downfall of the GDR. There is not even an attempt to understand the relation between the Stasi and the People's Police in the GDR in any comprehensive way, although what I have to say might contribute to such an undertaking. I want to focus exclusively on the ways in which east German and west German police officers identified the Stasi and how they identified themselves and each other in relation to the Stasi.

---

kind. Many factors might have played a part in each individual way of dealing with the Wall: the importance of relatives on the other side, personal courage, the question of how important it was to be a policeman, the degree to which people could imagine doing something else, and so on.

14. Two different names for the secret police are in use: it is either denoted by the acronym for the name of the secret police bureaucracy, MfS, for Ministry of State Security (Ministerium für Staatssicherheit), or by the acronym for its purported function, "Stasi," visible in the title of the bureaucracy, namely, State Security (Staatssicherheit).

The Stasi has become in the public discourse of Germans in east and west perhaps the epitome of all that was wrong with the GDR. With nearly a hundred thousand full-time employees[15] and almost a hundred and ten thousand unofficial collaborators in 1988,[16] the Stasi has produced literally tons of observation records about the GDR and its citizens, as well as about foreign countries, especially the FRG. The Stasi prided itself on being the "sword and shield of the party." How devastating a sword it was has only become fully apparent after its dissolution in December 1989; how protective a shield the Stasi was will certainly be open to much debate among social scientists and historians in our generation and the next. Doubtlessly, the Stasi was a most significant element in the power structure of the GDR, whether for its real powers or for its imagined ones.[17] Five years after unification, the opinions about the GDR may still diverge considerably, but nobody seems to doubt the depravity of the Stasi. In the identity contests between east Germans and west Germans, two related issues emerge: the relative proximity between the institutions of the People's Police and the Stasi on the one hand, as well as the extent to which each police officer had something to do with the Stasi on the other. What is debated, therefore, is the question of whether and to what degree the People's Police and each officer must share in the negative moral evaluation of the Stasi.

Differentiation against Metonymic Identification

The confusion starts with the border experience of West Berliners, who habitually identified those who did control them on their way from and to Berlin as members of the People's Police. Thus, many western police officers aired their anger accumulated in years of tense border cross-

15. Including the personnel of the Guard Regiment "Feliks Dzierzynski," Gill and Schröter (1991) calculated 92,000 full-time employees.

16. See Vollnhals (1994) and Gill and Schröter (1991) for structure and staffing of the Stasi. Given the turnover rate of unofficial collaborators, there are estimates that more than two hundred thousand citizens of the former GDR at one point or another in their lives worked for the Stasi. Given a total population of sixteen million people, more than 3 percent of the adult population may have been involved actively in Stasi work.

17. And who would want to differentiate the one from the other, for power seems to be in its effect on its supposed subordinates a little bit like the spell the Devil holds over his believers, about whom Thomas Mann has fittingly remarked "He who believes in the Devil, already belongs to him" (Doctor Faustus).

ings in their initial encounters with members of the former People's Police. One of them expressed this sentiment thus:

> For us it was clear that they were part of the security apparatus which had harassed us at the border. . . . Now you had the opportunity to dress them down for it all . . . at the first encounter I really let go.

While it is indeed true that the officers at the border were wearing the uniforms of the People's Police, "It must be clear by now to everyone that it was not us who did these border controls but the Stasi guys," as one eastern officer put it somewhat exasperatedly.[18] For east Germans that confusion indicates clearly where part of the problem really lies. In their opinion, west Germans know far too little about the institutional makeup of the GDR, especially the organization of and responsibility for security matters, to be able to judge properly who is guilty of what. A proper differentiation between the Stasi and the People's Police is demanded here to divert some of the moral blame of westerners, whose negative image of the People's Police as a grumpy, unfriendly crowd specializing in harassing Westerners was indeed formed by encounters with Stasi border officers. The Stasi is in this way posited as a distant other, easily instrumentalizeable as a convenient scapegoat.

Right after unification identification as "Stasi" was frequently used as a metonymy for all other security organs of the former GDR, which were thought to form a whole. After the fall of the Wall, People's Police officers were frequently attacked in public as "Stasi pigs." Most officers remember this as a time in which their authority had reached an absolute low. Especially the People's Police seems to have been perceived as little more than the most visible, most present part of a massive, homogeneous security machine which was rejected as a whole. In part this echoes the official political rhetoric in the GDR, which presented a unitary view of all security agencies by referring to them summarily as "the armed organs of the GDR" *(die bewaffneten Organe der DDR)*.[19] In the course of time, this security machine was then in public awareness differentiated more and more into its component parts. This differentiation was also in the interest of western authorities, who needed the continuing services especially of

18. To be precise, it was Department 6, responsible for passport control, tourism, and the state hotel chain, Interhotel (Gill and Schröter 1991).

19. The phrase *bewaffnete Organe der DDR* included the National People's Army (Nationale Volksarmee), the Border Patrol (Grenztruppen), the People's Police, the Stasi, and Customs (which played a relatively minor role in the GDR).

the People's Police (to a much lesser extent those of Customs and National People's Army).[20] Thus, there was a certain congruence of interest between eastern police officers and western authorities to single out the Stasi as that part of the security machine which was illegitimate. What remained to be done was to "purify" the People's Police of Stasi influence. Therefore, the authorities of the five new states, Berlin, and the federal government started to check every single eastern public servant for Stasi connections.

Eastern officers are highly aware of the fact that many westerners think of Stasi contact as morally contaminating, a fact expressed in western exclamations like, "I don't want to have any business with someone who had dealings with the Stasi," which were especially frequent directly after unification. This general attitude of western officers toward the Stasi found reconfirmation in at least three different types of experience. First, the Berlin Police was until recently quite rigorous in dismissing officers with Stasi contacts.[21] Officers whose unofficial connections to the Stasi have been uncovered were dismissed immediately or, if the case was not clear enough, were immediately relieved of their duties and sent home to await further notification. Within the precinct, the visibility of such dismissals was regularly amplified by intensive exchanges of rumors about the exact nature of the Stasi contacts. Second, as I have just pointed out, eastern citizens frequently demonstrated a hostile attitude to former People's Police officers. Sometimes they explicitly expressed their relief to western officers that the police force was now different. In daily encounters, eastern citizens often ignored former People's Police officers, making it a point to converse only with the westerner.[22] The distinction was still easy at this time because eastern officers were still wearing People's Police uniforms. Finally, the media played a large role in producing an image of the morally contaminating Stasi contact in taking a huge interest in possible Stasi connections of leading public figures, politicians,

20. There is an interesting difference here also between the state of Berlin (which could much more easily do without the former People's Police officers because the former West Berlin Police was very well staffed compared to other large city police forces in Germany) and any of the new states which effectively depend for police services on the former People's Police officers. Accordingly, the Berlin Police seems much more rigorous in pursuing Stasi connections than, for example, the police in Brandenburg.

21. For an extensive discussion of this policy see chapter 2.

22. Occasionally, the reverse happened also, but this was much less frequent.

artists, lawyers.[23] The tenor of the media reports on these public figures has generally been that someone with a Stasi past is unfit for public office.

Naturally, eastern officers perceive the investigations into Stasi contacts as a real threat to their economic and social existence. Despite the fact that the Federal Court of Labor has established relatively stringent criteria for justifiable dismissals, in that "conscious and goal-oriented work for Stasi"[24] must be proven, a rule which chiefly affects the diverse categories of "unofficial informants" (inoffizielle Mitarbeiter, usually abbreviated IM), eastern officers fear that their names might come up somewhere in the files, putting their position with the police at risk. One put it thus:

> I don't know whether there is something in the files. I can only say, possibly. Oh dear, how often did you sign something, or [how often did] he [the contact officer of the Stasi] say, "Could you write this down for me?" How often did you do this in all these years? You really can't tell.

Western officers dismiss these fears as unfounded. They argue that people who have worked for the Stasi must know themselves best. For westerners it is a rather clear-cut matter: Whoever has signed an agreement with the Stasi to transmit information to them, perhaps in exchange for a "second income," *is* Stasi. In contrast, easterners think of involvement in the Stasi rather as a matter of fine shades and gradations, and the line of dismissal seems to be for that reason somewhat unclear, perhaps even arbitrary.

Experiencing and Mythologizing the Stasi

This raises the question of how easterners did in fact experience their contacts with the Stasi during GDR times.[25] On the one hand, eastern

23. This process began right after the final dissolution of the Stasi, barely a month after the fall of the Wall. In the spring of 1990, right before the first free general elections in the GDR, the head of one of the new civil rights parties, Demokratischer Aufbruch, the prominent lawyer Wolfgang Schnur, had to resign for collaboration with the Stasi. Just after the elections the head of the eastern Social Democrats, Ibrahim Böhme, followed suit. This process continues right into the present with accusations of Stasi collaboration against the prime minister of the state of Brandenburg, Manfred Stolpe, as well as against the most prominent figure of the reformed communist party (PDS), Gregor Gysi.

24. Bundesarbeitsgericht (Federal Court of Labor), for example, AZR, 496/1993.

25. Especially in this case, in which the Stasi was made the perennial topic of consideration and reconsideration, it seems particularly difficult to try to reconstruct what the Stasi meant then, during GDR times, to the police officers. Their memory

officers point out, the Stasi was simply another state security agency. They stress that any country maintains a secret service, and they point to the fact that the Stasi and People's Police frequently cooperated on certain routine security issues. In Köpenick the most perceptible form of co-operation involved security on the so-called "protocol-stretch" *(Proto-kollstrecke)*, the route on which guests of state traveled from Schönefeld, East Berlin's international airport, to Niederschönhausen Castle, the official residence of the head of the Council of Ministers of the GDR. The protocol stretch passed for several miles through the city borough of Köpenick. While the Stasi seems to have had the overall leadership in this enterprise, the People's Police provided much of the staffing. Other points of potential professional contact which I have encountered in my field-work were the highway accident units, and the border patrols of the People's Police. People's Police officers were aware of a significant amount of parallel surveillance, suspecting that some People's Police documents, such as the travel reports of the neighborhood beat patrols, were routinely transferred to the Stasi. Of course there were also routine contacts between both organizations in addition to cooperation on certain concrete tasks. The borough heads of the People's Police and the Stasi conferred regularly.[26] the Stasi did also have official contact officers who visited People's Police offices, stations, and precincts at least once every fortnight. Often People's Police officers knew them on a first-name basis because they remained in their positions for years. Their visits were described to me as friendly chats in which these officers would lounge around asking more or less innocent questions.[27] However, the Stasi also infiltrated the People's Police with secret informants on all levels, from

---

is almost bound to be tinted by present perspectives. In order to get as few present-day perspective corrections as possible, I have focused on concrete encounters and experiences with the Stasi as the informational basis for this section, rather than on a general discourse on the Stasi.

26. These were the so-called "directions of operations" *(Einsatzleitungen)* which were established in the main administrative units of the GDR: the county *(Kreis;* the equivalent in Berlin would be the city borough [*Stadtbezirk*]) and the sixteen regions (*Bezirke;* the whole of Berlin would be equivalent to a *Bezirk*). The directions of operations were considered to be an organ of defense organization, thus comprising not only the People's Police and the Stasi, but also the National People's Army (NVA), as well as the administrations. See also Herbst et al. 1994, vol. 1.

27. Some of the police officers humorously likened these Stasi contact officers to me. They were described as just popping in to hear what was going on. They would also take notes (like me) and would once in a while ask for pieces of written information (as I might ask for a sketch of organizational charts, etc.).

simple ordinary patrolmen to high-ranking staff officers.[28] The extent of this penetration (revealed only after unification) came as a surprise to many eastern police officers.

While this routine side of the Stasi-police interaction definitely existed, there was another side that made the Stasi into much more than just another state security agency. Officers who were regularly part of the dreaded (because extremely boring) security operations along the protocol stretch report, for example, a certain animosity towards the Stasi, if only because the Stasi could always appear in the garb of the People's Police, with police identity cards and all, while the reverse was of course not true. Police officers serving in the highway accident units felt as if they were under constant surveillance by Stasi officers whom they knew sat on watchtowers along the transit motorways and whom they suspected of patrolling the forests left and right of it too.[29] Thus the Stasi was perceived also as policing the police. Thereby a certain sense of hierarchy was created, which also stimulated some invidious comparisons between the police and the Stasi.[30] This impression was furthered by the fact that People's Police officers knew quite well that their counterparts of the same rank at the Stasi earned substantially more than they did (about two-thirds more).[31] This sense of hierarchy helped also to further a certain myth of the Stasi as an almost omniscient, nearly omnipotent organization within the power structure of the GDR.

28. The infiltration also encompassed all possible levels of Stasi involvement: part-timers reporting occasionally to the Stasi, part-timers who would, meeting at least weekly, write hundreds of reports over the years, all the way to full-time Stasi officers living as undercover agents in the People's Police.

29. They argue that for this very reason they had to be especially careful in their interactions with Westerners involved in accidents: the acceptance of a cigarette or a bar of chocolate would have, so they feared, been dutifully registered by the Stasi, thus possibly leading to serious problems because they allowed themselves to be corrupted by Western materialism.

30. One officer even went so far as to describe the Stasi as the superior agency to which the police reported, which is bureaucratically speaking not true. The Stasi and the police were independent bureaucratic hierarchies with their own respective ministries. It is worth noting, however, that the head of the Stasi, Erich Mielke, was one of the longest-serving ministers (since 1957) and most influential members of the Politburo, while the minister in charge of the police, Friedrich Dickel, also long-serving by any western standards (since 1963), never made it into the Politburo and thus into the core group of power-holders in the GDR (Lang 1991; Präsidium der Volkspolizei Berlin 1988).

31. Some officers knew about the income differential between the Stasi and the police from recruiting attempts of the Stasi; others heard it firsthand from Stasi officers whom they encountered in training, and so on.

Many officers tell stories about unexpected (or even imaginary) encounters with the Stasi. Directing a detachment of police officers to secure a state visit of Sanssouci castle in Potsdam, a People's Police staff officer all of a sudden saw an iron eagle adorning the castle move. Immediately he suspected Stasi with a periscope behind or underneath it. After the dissolution of the Stasi, he tried to find out whether there actually was such a device installed. To his disappointment there never seems to have been one. Another officer was posted somewhere along a highway over which the former chancellor Helmut Schmidt of West Germany was supposed to travel on the way to a state visit in East Berlin during an icy December in 1981. As he moved a little bit away from the pavement into the bushes, he heard a voice say, "If you budge one step further, you will be standing on my hand." He found "the forest full of Stasi officers," freezing—as he laughingly pointed out—in their low shoes and trench coats, while he was wearing full-scale People's Police winter gear with boots and cotton-padded coat. This last story satirizes the omniscience of the Stasi with a mixture of ridicule and pity. A certain degree of respect and again pity are sensed in the identifying punch-line of another officer's story about an encounter with the Stasi. He rejected their advances to become a full-time Stasi employee repeatedly, because he feared losing a highly cherished private life in a job described to him as involving continuous vigilance, utmost secrecy, and twenty-four-hour availability. In another typical attempt at satirizing the Stasi, eastern police officers also claim that they could "smell" Stasi officers, because they were reputed to resemble the cartoons of undercover investigators: "trench, sunglasses, the party newspaper, Neues Deutschland, tucked under their arms, walking in that ambling Stasi-way." Moreover, the Stasi was ridiculed by police officers in the GDR, much as they were by the rest of the population in countless jokes. Reflecting critically on these jokes, however, one officer dramatically relativized the success of the satiric identifications of Stasi, effectively weaving a tragic tale of self-identification: he claimed to know that almost all of these jokes were invented by the Stasi itself in a highly conscious effort at self-mystification. Thus, in what amounts to a scenario of Orwellian proportions, the Stasi is credited with the ultimate power over the imagination and thus the minds of the people. Still other officers looked to the Stasi as a possible source of positive change in a situation that looked completely hopeless. They told me that they communicated their grievances to the contact officers in the hope that they might set matters straight. The attitude of ordinary police officers in the GDR towards the Stasi during GDR times was therefore highly ambiguous: the

Stasi was normalized as a state security agency, it was admired for its presumed influence, celebrated for its successes ("the best secret service in the world"), but it was also ridiculed for its all-too-apparent secrecy, which of course might well have been staged; the Stasi's employees were envied for the material benefits they enjoyed, and they were pitied for having to sacrifice even more privacy than police officers. Overall, the police are depicted as rather powerless vis-à-vis the Stasi, itself a victim of sorts: admired or pitied, the otherness of the Stasi is emphasized, thus illuminating the self-perception of former GDR police officers.

Moralizing the Stasi/De-moralizing Stasi Involvement

What is it that now makes the Stasi immoral in the eyes of both easterners and westerners? Stasi officers were considered by most eastern police officers as sleuths, concerning themselves with matters that should really have been none of their business. Thus the Stasi was thought to transgress the private-public divide in illegitimate, even immoral ways. I know of one case in which a police officer claims to have rejected the appeals of the Stasi to work for them as an informant on precisely these moral grounds. Another officer, who has worked for the Stasi, became morally increasingly disgruntled with his own role, as his Stasi guidance officer[32] demanded more and more personal information about his colleagues after he had begun to write rather "atmospheric statements," which were essentially useless for Stasi purposes. For many east German officers the moral problem was not so much in working for the Stasi as such; many of them could conceive of a perfectly legitimate relationship with the Stasi, even as secret informants. In retrospect they considered it more or less a stroke of good luck that they had never been asked to become informants.[33] In keeping with the ambiguous image of the Stasi just outlined, however, everyone I have asked draws a line between information which could be forwarded to the Stasi without moral harm, a category

32. Each informant was led by a "guidance officer" *(Führungsoffizier)*, who was the interface between an informant and the Stasi. Guidance officers typically tried to build up a personal relationship with their informants, honoring birthdays and so on. Meetings were usually held "conspiratively" in private apartments or rooms (see also Müller-Enbergs 1995).

33. In describing what they would have done if the Stasi had approached them, eastern officers typically answered, "I don't know, really." Only a few said that they would under no circumstances have worked for the Stasi.

which chiefly contains work-related information, such as problems with equipment, or even failures in task performance, and information which should not have been transmitted to the Stasi, such as stories about the private lives of colleagues, friends, and family members.

After the dissolution of the Stasi, the general public has become increasingly aware of the extent of its involvement in extraordinary human rights violations, such as minutely planned destruction of personalities (Behnke 1995; Fuchs 1995), torture, and even planned killings (ZERV 1993, 1994), which easterners claim they would have never thought possible in their own state. Usually they are also shocked about the sheer magnitude, the actual scale and scope of Stasi operations, which seems to surpass even the myths about the Stasi. Easterners also express surprise about the degree to which the Stasi penetrated the People's Police with a dense network of informants. And the fact that some colleagues might have betrayed private information about them to the Stasi makes many of them quite angry.

Westerners add to this catalog that the entire organization was illegitimate, that the Stasi was the backbone of a societal system of insincerity that created a stifling atmosphere of angst (a claim which east Germans dismiss as exaggerated). West Germans also metonymically identify the Stasi with the secret police of the Nazi dictatorship, the Gestapo, as the whole system of denunciation and political incarceration is seen as a repetition of Nazi methods of authoritarian rule. High-ranking officers in the west are also concerned about the integrity of the police, which they assume would lose trust in the eyes of the citizens if it continued to employ former Stasi informants. The top leadership of the organization also argues that it would be unbearable for all the victims of the GDR regime to see their former tormentors still at work for the new state.[34]

It is not surprising, then, that easterners and westerners propose different standards about the degree of Stasi involvement which should lead to a dismissal. In general, west Germans are far more rigorous than east Germans, and younger west Germans are, as many easterners have pointed out, even more rigorous than older ones.[35] Westerners show some

34. The last two arguments were much less frequently presented at the lower echelons of the organization, by noncommissioned officers and low-ranking commissioned officers.

35. The reason why many older westerners seem to be more cautious is that they have a sense of the arbitrariness of history; they can imagine and they do actually speculate about what their lives would have been like had they ended up on the

forgiveness when informants were recruited into the ranks of the Stasi while they were still very young, working for the Stasi, for example, only during their military service.[36] These are considered pardonable "sins of youth." Westerners, especially those who have informed themselves about Stasi practices, also reject the notion of fortuitous Stasi offers to work for them as informants. They point to the rigorous screening techniques the Stasi typically applied before they would actually approach a potential informant, carefully selecting candidates who were considered ideologically reliable (cf. Gill and Schröter 1991, 414–77). Thus, in the eyes of these westerners, selection by the Stasi suggests a high degree of conformity with the regime, a considerable degree of ideological investment in the GDR.[37] While westerners seem to have become more lenient in their attitude as they have learned more about the details of life in the GDR, they still generally support a policy of dismissals for Stasi collaboration.

The formula that most easterners use first when asked under which circumstances it might be justified to dismiss former Stasi informants is "if they have done harm to somebody." This is a utilitarian principle based on the consequences of action rather than on the value of the particular action itself. What they mean is simply this: if people have lost their job, could not attend university, or were even imprisoned because their political attitudes were denounced to the Stasi by a secret informant, it would be justified to discharge this respective officer from active police duty. Westerners think far more in Kantian terms: what matters most is the intention to do a certain kind of act regardless of its consequences. Thus the very willingness of an officer to spy on others for the Stasi is decisive; the officer is thus thought not to be fit to do service in a democratic police which is founded on respect for the personal rights of indi-

---

other side of the Wall, a thought that understandably does not even occur to younger westerners, for whom living in the West is simply a given. An argument that is also more frequently heard from the young is that one of the biggest mistakes after the Nazi dictatorship was not having been rigorous enough with former Nazis, a mistake that should not be repeated now.

36. One Köpenick officer was dismissed, however, for working as an informant for the Stasi during his military service, when he was still in his late teens.

37. While this is true, this argument overlooks the degree to which the Stasi has also worked not only on the basis of ideological conviction but also by playing on the interests of their candidates and even using blackmail to assure the services of potential informants (Müller-Enbergs 1995, 104). Thus, identified lawbreakers or people with debt problems were systematically targeted by the Stasi.

viduals. Many easterners supplement the utilitarian argument by a notion of decency: a blatant violation of the private-public divide along with the insincerity of covering up this violation, as in the betrayal of trust between friends or within the family, is for them also sufficient ground for reservations. Easterners are keenly aware of the fact that a person to whom they confided their disenchantment about politics in the GDR or their liking of some western TV show might have betrayed this confidence and done their career irreparable harm.

Despite all this, however, most easterners feel some pity for and even solidarity with those who are dismissed for Stasi collaboration. Again a utilitarian principle is invoked to justify their sympathy (or at least their absence of antipathy). Most say that they did not suffer in any way in the GDR, that they did have all in all a good life and that therefore they would have little reason to morally condemn someone who worked for the Stasi. What is also important here is that they see Stasi involvement not so much as a matter of choice but almost as something that happened or did not happen to a particular person. In keeping with the conflicted Stasi image, eastern officers attribute to themselves much less agency than westerners would attribute to them. The lack of choice they have experienced is captured well by a joke: The meaning of the Stasi is rendered as follows: "Either you come to us or we come to you!"[38] Thus what is created by these Stasi-related dismissals is a community of destiny, a destiny that easterners share in contrast to westerners. Conversely, many eastern officers say they would understand that anyone who had suffered in some way from Stasi-related denunciation would want the informant to be removed from public service.

The utilitarian principles invoked to evaluate Stasi involvement constitute an interesting, far-reaching privatization of morality. In the absence of perceptible consequences for third parties, the relation between individuals and the state, even in their function as police officers, is relegated to the realm of the private. And if a third party is concerned, this concern is still viewed as more or less private to all those directly involved. They see no need to concern the community at large, except in extreme cases such as those involving the members of the former Politburo, who are thought to bear real responsibility. In principle, this privatization of morals is tantamount to what might be called the removal of Stasi involve-

---

38. The one officer I got to know who refused to collaborate with the Stasi did indeed have to endure negative career consequences.

ment from the moral sphere, or the "de-moralization"[39] of Stasi involvement, and ultimately to a de-moralization of the GDR itself. Thus, part and whole are separated, allowing for the attribution of moral blame while saving the integrity of the whole. In this operation, the state is sheltered, at least partially, to remain a viable object for positive basic identification, which would be much more difficult to sustain if the state as a whole were considered morally tainted.

This de-moralization of Stasi involvement is in accordance with the fact that most former People's Police officers I have encountered think that it is about time to stop the general Stasi-connection investigations, to close the files at the Stasi document center at least in part.[40] Eastern police officers, especially in the state of Brandenburg, support the prime minister of the state of Brandenburg, Manfred Stolpe, a former leader of the Protestant Church in East Germany, who has been accused of being a secret informant for the Stasi on several occasions. Most officers defend him by pointing out that someone in his position simply could not avoid dealings with the Stasi, arguing again along utilitarian lines that he probably did more good in the end than harm. Stolpe's popularity contrasts sharply with the intense dislike all eastern officers I have talked to feel for members of the civil rights movement in the GDR, who take a quite rigorous moral stance towards Stasi involvement in the sense that they do not favor allowing continued employment in the public service. What is important in this context is that most members of the civil rights movement do, of course, insist on moralizing any Stasi involvement as misguided action, while emphasizing the agency of individual collaborators.

---

39. I use the term *de-moralization* faut de mieux as an antonym to *moralization*. The hyphen distinguishes it from the term *demoralization*, which does not carry the meaning I intend.

40. The office of the Bundesbeauftragter für Stasi-Unterlagen is better known as Gauck-Behörde (Gauck office), from the name of the director of this agency, the former east German Protestant minister Joachim Gauck. While I was doing my fieldwork in Berlin and Potsdam, the public debate about closing the files was in full swing and was fought out with much fervor. What is most interesting about this debate is to note who takes which side. The coalition-building in this debate by no means follows traditional party lines or a simple left-right pattern. The main supporters of keeping the files open indefinitely are the members of the former civil rights movement in the GDR, most visibly supported by the Greens, joined by the old guard of conservative anti-Communists. The other side is not only represented by members of the reformed communists, but most forcefully by moderate and liberal eastern and western members of all the established parties who wanted to put an end to the "Stasi witch-hunt."

The reservation of eastern officers is particularly strong vis-à-vis Bärbel Bohley, one of the most prominent members (along with Jens Reich) of the civil rights movement in the GDR. She is perceived as taking out her own private grievances, which are accepted as quite justified, against GDR society at large, an action which is incomprehensible to most people. Accordingly, she is frequently described as a hysterical personality. Strong moral judgments of Stasi involvement, whether from westerners or eastern dissidents, are thus equally rejected.

Nevertheless, east German officers typically support the trials of "bigshots," former leading party members. The one important and notable exception is Markus Wolf, the legendary former East German spy chief,[41] who symbolizes for many east German officers the normal, presentable, even admirable aspects of the Stasi. Eastern officers argue that putting him on trial doubtlessly smacks of "victor justice." This impression is exacerbated by the fact that foreign espionage is certainly one of the few areas in which the East very clearly outdid the West. It is seen as an attempt to take revenge on a highly successful man who has pursued the perfectly legitimate profession of spying for his own country.

How is the de-moralization of Stasi involvement thinkable in face of the moralization of the Stasi institution itself? The key to the puzzle is knowledge. Eastern officers claim that they did not know about the involvement of the Stasi in the graver kinds of human rights violations such as torture and murder, the use of personal information for blackmail, and systematic personality destruction. They also maintain that they were not aware of the extent and comprehensiveness of Stasi operations. While they knew that the Stasi committed acts of indecency by transgressing the private-public divide and by asking people to be insincere, these moral misdemeanors could be excused by the particular historical

41. Markus Wolf was in charge of the HVA (Hauptverwaltung Aufklärung: the Intelligence Department) until 1987, when he stepped down for reasons that are not yet fully understood. Under his leadership the HVA was very successful in undermining the West German intelligence services. He presented himself during the fall of 1989 as carrier of a reformed communism, peaking in his appearance at the famous demonstration of 4 November 1989 at the Alexanderplatz in East Berlin, where leading members of the GDR opposition like Jens Reich and Bärbel Bohley, but also more moderate members of the SED, spoke in favor of "socialism with a human face," but he was almost silenced by the shouting crowd. The media identify Wolf's demeanor, in notable contrast to that of other leading members of the SED, and especially to that of the Stasi's head, Erich Mielke, as "Western" or "grand bourgeois," which has won him sympathies also in western Germany.

circumstances, the Cold War confrontation, the notion that a besieged GDR had to defend itself, even if with somewhat doubtful means. Thus, given the historical circumstance and the available knowledge about the Stasi, working for the secret police could be justified to a certain degree as positive service to the state.

* * *

In sum, while westerners tend to moral fundamentalism in relation to the Stasi, easterners emphasize the contingency of institutional arrangements and individual acts. Westerners view both the Stasi as an institution as well as personal collaboration of individuals with the Stasi as morally reprehensible. The Stasi is constructed as a radical other which stands for everything a democratic police force in a democratic state is not supposed to be. Especially to higher-ranking officers, looking into the face of the Stasi is not so much like looking into a mirror perverting one's own self, but much more like looking into an image of one's own antonym. The gap that is felt between the Stasi and western security agencies is infinite. This categorical otherness of the Stasi precludes any attempt to use the Stasi experience as a reason for critical self-evaluation. The Stasi's otherness is so fundamental that it does not even give rise to self-congratulation. The Stasi and western security agencies are thought to be incomparable. Since the Stasi has an unambiguously and thoroughly negative moral connotation, almost any identification of westerners insinuating proximity between an eastern officer and the Stasi is a moral devaluation.

Most easterners have a much more differentiated, multifaceted, and conflicted view of the Stasi and their own role in relation to the Stasi. Although most easterners have a generally negative image of the Stasi as an institution, this image is tinged with awe for the foreign espionage section of the Stasi and its partial legitimation as an ordinary security agency of the GDR. Eastern officers take pains to differentiate police and the Stasi from each other, but they also need to salvage part of the Stasi because any attempt at preserving the integrity of the People's Police would have to include those aspects of the Stasi where both organizations did officially cooperate. As far as their own involvement in the Stasi is concerned, easterners are aware of the many shades of cooperation and collaboration. The majority of them suggest that eastern police officers had or would have had (if asked) hardly any choice in the decision to work for the Stasi. The perceived (and, in the one case of refusal to collaborate, very real) threats to their own career progress within the police were experienced as outside constraints, aspects of life they could not do much about. However, they see agency in the kind of information a single officer in his or her collaboration with the Stasi could and should transmit. Many would argue that nobody could have been forced to spy on the personal lives of colleagues, friends, and relatives. The experience of trade union representatives, who by law have to be involved in all personnel issues and who therefore took part in the process of evaluating former officers for unofficial Stasi collaboration, confirms this point. They argue that they have seen very different attitudes shining through in the reports of unofficial informants. As one trade union representative put it, "You can write this way, or you can write that way. Some described the confrontation between two billy goats as class struggle; others were sniffing out their neighbor's life all the way into their breadboxes [i.e., in excruciating, shameless detail]." They have also seen great variation in the intensity of collaboration, the eagerness to relay information to the Stasi. As the union representatives point out, the Stasi did discontinue collaboration from their side if the information were for some reason not satisfactory for them (see also Schmidt 1995). While thus collaboration per se gets indeed de-moralized, the kind and degree of involvement remains moralizeable. East Germans therefore demand Stasi investigations which are a lot less formalistic but do take into account the very specific circumstances of every single case of collaboration.

The concentration of westerners on the mere fact of unofficial Stasi collaboration signals to easterners how little westerners know, and care to know, about the intricacies of GDR life. One aspect of this life is singled out to overshadow all others, developing a dynamic of its own. The Stasi does get demonized, almost in keeping with its own myth of itself, and relations of individuals to the Stasi do get fetishized; that is, the complexities and intricacies of their lives do get reduced to this one aspect. The sheer presence of millions of document pages with their promise to prove wrongdoing and therefore to justify the moralization of the GDR past seems to galvanize most westerner's minds, to the degree that they care at all. The Stasi therefore allows westerners an incredible economy of judgment in a grandiose synecdochical swoop. In part easterners reject demonization of the Stasi and fetishization of Stasi relationship; but in part, they are also willful participants in it because demonization and fetishization of the Stasi and Stasi relationships (as far as one is not immediately concerned) offer tempting ways of discarding the shadows of the past, while preserving some of its sunshine.

The Rule of Law, Politics, and Justice

When in particular higher-ranking western police officers (including teachers at the police college) are asked where they see the differences between the People's Police on the one hand and the Berlin Police or other western police organizations on the other, they regularly point out that the latter is a police force acting in accordance with the principles of a pluralist democracy, in short a democratic police force, while the former was not. If asked further what it is that characterizes a democratic police force, the answer is invariably that a democratic police force is restricted by the rule of law, which means that no police action can take place without legal foundation. What characterizes the People's Police as undemocratic in the eyes of many western officers is that it was guided more by political opportunity than by law. The evidence which is usually presented for the political character of the People's Police is the degree to which any training in the People's Police was oriented toward the so-called political subjects: Marxism/Leninism, the history of the communist parties in the Soviet Union as well as in Germany, and the discussion of the latest party directives, such as the resolutions of party congresses.[42] Moreover, western officers maintain that the police were prone to treat people differently depending on their place in the power structure of the GDR. Thus the People's Police is depicted as a guardian of privileges.

One western neighborhood beat patrol officer exemplifies this by a little story. When he took charge of his new area, the former eastern leader of the station responsible for the neighborhood in which his area is situated told him that he would have plenty of difficulties with the people who were living there. Asked why, the eastern officer responded that it was the area in which many high-ranking officials of the former east German government and party (ministers, army generals, Stasi generals) lived alongside other GDR celebrities. The western officer said that he responded that even if Hannelore Kohl lived there (the wife of the chancellor) and parked her car at the wrong spot, he would give her a ticket. After all, as he said, "Law is law." The easterner, he reported, remained skeptical, warning him that in the long run he would see how difficult an area this really was. In this little story, the western officer identifies himself as the guardian of the rule of law. He explains that he feels comfortable assuming this role, because he is confident that the po-

42. Compare the section entitled "Personnel Selection after Unification" in chapter 2.

lice in particular and the law and justice system of the FRG in general would back him up in case of conflict. The real hero of that story is not the western officer himself, but the principle of rule of law, and by implication the villain is not the eastern officer but the system that he defended, a system which would in the end not have backed up a legally correct decision if it violated elite privileges or political calculus. Needless to say, the purity of the rule of law is certainly idealized in this story, as police officers feel frequently left alone trying to defend a virtually indefensible law.[43]

Eastern officers sometimes answer identifications of this kind by pointing out that the GDR not only had laws, but that the laws of the GDR were even the same, more or less, as the laws in the west. Some officers have actually compared the legal codes line by line, marking the differences, which they found to be minimal. Some claim that they even mixed up the paragraph numbers during the retraining programs because the biggest difference between laws East and West was the sequencing of the articles. Their equation is plain and simple: murder East equals murder West, burglary East equals burglary West, from which they proceed to the conclusion that therefore police work in the East and the West is fully comparable, at least as far as its bread-and-butter aspects are concerned.[44]

Teachers at the police college, confronted with these identifications of law in the FRG and the GDR, continuously tried to convince easterners that these similarities were superficial. In interviews covering their experiences during the retraining programs of former People's Police officers, they said that they tried to argue the different character of legality in both Germanies by pointing out that there was no administrative law in the GDR. Without administrative law, they argued, citizens had no legal means to fight decisions of the police (or of any other administration for that matter). The means of "complaint" *(Eingabe),* which was offered by eastern officers as a GDR alternative to procedural law, did (so said the teachers) not even follow a clear, orderly procedure. Accordingly,

43. In what follows I will not try to assess whether this self-understanding of the police as guardians of the law is accurate in light of what the police actually do. In particular I will not go into the question of what "law enforcement" would actually mean in concrete circumstances, especially the issue of how determinate this really is. For literature on these issues consult Manning 1977 and Bittner 1990.

44. At the same time, however, several eastern officers have pointed out that now they do indeed enjoy the protection of the law, telling stories about legal violations in the GDR which were brushed under the rug, although they tried to be the guardians of the law. Compare the section on role sincerity in chapter 5.

there was also no distinction between public and private law, and consequently there was also no administrative judicature (see Friedrich 1994, 485–86).

In contrasting police practice in East and West, eastern officers do not primarily see a difference in law, but they point out that the police did whatever they could to alleviate problems that might not even have anything to do with police work in a more narrow sense. One officer, for example, described how he was able to secure material for a playground of a kindergarten. Another tells a long and engaging story about how he helped a farmer with his cattle. "Work at and with human beings" (Arbeit an und mit dem Menschen) is a formula that I have heard very often used by eastern officers as a rock-bottom description of what police work ultimately means. Eastern police officers, especially the former People's Police neighborhood beat patrol officers, describe this often as "being there for the people." And they complain that the western police force is not there for the people in this sense. They bemoan the fact that cases are regarded first from the angle of jurisdiction, and not from the angle of justice. In the GDR, they claim, they could always talk to a superior, who might talk to the civil administration, and thus needs could be met and injustices could sometimes be set aright.

The eastern officers are not the only ones who complain about the fact that the police force, according to a common complaint frequently heard by the citizens of Köpenick and Potsdam, "is no longer doing anything." Frequently citizens call the police in order to ascertain the authority of the state to intervene in conflicts they have with others in which they may very well be treated unjustly. These are usually cases such as property conflicts between neighbors that are considered by the (West) German legal system a matter of private law, which is in general outside of the purview of the police. All the police can do in instances like that is to alert the people to the fact that a particular kind of legal situation needs to be produced (such as an eviction notice issued by a court of law against undesirable tenants) in order to make it legal for the police to intervene in any way. While western officers have learned to shrug their shoulders in instances like these, counseling those with grievances to seek legal advice, easterners frequently point out that in the GDR they would have been able to do something for a person who seemed to have been treated unjustly.

What eastern officers seem to claim here is that the People's Police could help to secure particular outcomes which were considered to be desirable for reasons of justice, consideration for the needs of people, and humane interaction. Thus, the logic of action of the western police is identified as following a sense of formal rationality, while the logic claimed for the People's Police is one of substantive rationality (Weber 1980, 447).[45] These claims attributing the cold heart of bureaucratic inhumanity to the western police and an almost parental care to the People's Police undermine the stark moralization of the People's Police launched by western officers. While these arguments partially appeal to western officers because they too feel a discrepancy between their own sense of justice and their permitted or required intervention as police officers, they also counter this argument by pointing out that it is precisely the seemingly cold procedure which prevents patronage.

These descriptions insinuating and juxtaposing formal rational procedure in the west and substantive rational procedure in the east also capture significant differences in the policing practices of both police organizations. High-ranking eastern officers point out that the guiding question they were asked to pose in any new situation in which they would have to make a decision is "Who benefits from it?" These officers explain that the adequacy of police action was not primarily argued on the basis of a norm (a formal criterion) but on the basis of the actual political desirability of the outcome of the police action in terms of progress for socialist society.[46] Thus an action under suspicion of supporting the declared class enemy could not be justified even if it might be called for on the basis of law, as one officer put it.

The point is that any disregard for the political desirability of police action by recourse to a norm would have betrayed a grave misunder-

45. Jurisdiction is a typical formal criterion that is tied to the notion of procedure: every administrative course of action, that is, every administrative procedure, begins ideally with a test of jurisdiction. The affirmation of jurisdiction leads then, again ideally, to a flowchart-like prescription of process.

46. The political aspect of policing is systematically downplayed in the self-understanding of western police officers. Thus the unashamed primacy of politics over law in the regulation of the police in the GDR is especially provocative. In view of what Manning (1977, 6) writes about police work in general, the GDR view seems quite realistic: "They [the police] serve to maintain the relative placement of social groups upon the political-moral ladder. By enforcing the law, they are always enforcing someone's interest against someone else's." Although Manning is right to criticize the view that policing is simply law enforcement for obfuscating the fact that policing is always selective and hence eminently political, his implied view of the law as automatically subservient to ruling-class interests is far too simple, precisely because it overlooks the partial, institutionally grounded autonomy of the police. If he were right, the police in the GDR would not have had to emphasize the primacy of the political goals over laws, since the two would effectively be congruent (see below).

standing of "socialist law" *(sozialistische Gesetzlichkeit)* itself (cf. Dilcher 1994). The political instrumentality of the law is well captured in a summary of the fifth party congress of the SED in 1958 which, among other things, dealt with the notion of socialist law:

> The party congress decided to adjust socialist law to match the objectively working economic laws of socialism ever more perfectly, in order to improve their effectivity in implementation, as well as to contribute ever more comprehensively to the education of the workers so that they can consciously create a socialist future for themselves. (MdI 1987, 290)

Thus law is not above politics (or administration), but it is in fact subservient to it.[47] Seen from that point of view, the political training of GDR police officers (and the expansive space given to it) is not some form of mindless indoctrination, as some western officers try to assert, but it is a highly rational way to try to secure the outcomes of police actions which are actually desired. The political training of People's Police officers was as much a preparation for their job as the legal training is for FRG police officers.

But does this all mean that there is no substantive rationality underlying western administrative action, including police action? Is the rule of law really as universally and blindly applied as western officers in their depiction of western superiority would have it? Can east and west really be understood in such neat juxtaposition? For one thing, easterners have found that the rule of law was not applied to them blindly. They feel that the very way in which they have been incorporated into the Berlin Police was not in keeping with the letter and the spirit of the rules devised in the Unification Treaty. Easterners have some doubt that it was legally correct to dismiss high-ranking officers out of hand; they question whether everybody who was charged with Stasi collaboration was

---

47. This can also be shown beautifully by analyzing the thesis written as partial fulfillment of the degree requirements at the People's Police Academy (Hochschule der deutschen Volkspolizei, HSDVP). Arguments are deduced in the first line from the acknowledged classics: Marx/Engels, Lenin, and (depending on the time) perhaps also Stalin. In the second line the argument is backed up with experiences from the histories of the communist parties in the Soviet Union and in Germany as well as by adequate statements from party congresses, and only in the third line are laws an important source for argument. It may be noted as well that many official texts of the People's Police consequently speak of "socialist law" *(sozialistische Gesetzlichkeit)*. For a characterization of the theory of socialist law, see Dilcher 1994, and for Soviet law, see Butler 1988 and Berman 1963.

dismissed rightly; and they doubt that their demotions or regroupings were done in accordance with the law. They feel that the Berlin police organization took advantage of their own fear of the future, of their own ignorance of the means of legal action. Many easterners suspect that the Berlin Police simply tried to get rid of as many former eastern officers as they possibly could to control exploding personnel costs. Thus here too, they point out, the substantive result was the guiding principle. Eastern officers suspect that those who preach formal rationality practice substantive rationality, that those who preach the rule of law make eminently political decisions too. Of course, what eastern officers have discovered in the meantime is the advantage of an administrative judicature: increasingly, they are resorting to legal procedures, suing the Berlin Police if they do indeed feel mistreated. Increasingly they assert what they have come to understand as their rights, thereby echoing the behavior they have observed on the street, that eastern citizens do indeed become more knowledgeable about their rights vis-à-vis the police.

Moreover, it has also become clear to eastern officers that breaches of law are always policed selectively. Not every violation of the law is investigated by the police; sometimes breaches of the law are simply ignored "because nothing would come of pressing charges anyway." Thus, violations are ignored for practical reasons: the principles underlying such a decision are therefore not just a matter of legality but also a matter of effective and efficient policing. Many eastern officers point out that they did not have to make such decisions in the GDR because there were simply not as many violations to follow up.[48] The sheer size of the problem requires a selectivity which undermines belief in the notion of the rule of law. Selectivity also implies that there is political discretion in policing.[49] Selectivity in this sense also produces particular issues of justice. "Why

48. Of course, the Stasi might have faced similar problems: the "crimes" they were dealing with were just so prolific that they had to focus on uncovering some especially useful violations.

49. While I was in Berlin, the issue of illegal (mostly Vietnamese-controlled) cigarette vending was especially acute. This is a typical example of a violation that might be tolerated for a certain amount of time, which is basically also a political decision. But so is any campaign to crack down on a particular type of crime. That doesn't mean, of course, that a crime not particularly policed does not remain a crime in the strict legal sense. There may also be a core set of crimes which is more persistently prosecuted—murder, for example. But it does mean for all practical purposes that the chances of getting away with some crimes are much higher than the chances of getting away with some others, regardless of the sheer technical problems of policing, simply because political decisions steer police resources in one direction rather than another.

me?" is a question that police officers face incessantly in discussions with citizens who have violated something they would themselves consider a minor law, thus being subject at least to an administrated fine (e.g., a ticket). A typical reaction of someone receiving a parking ticket is to point to major crimes and ask why the police do not focus on them instead of wasting their time with minor issues such as parking tickets.

Some easterners continue to use the interpretive frameworks they have acquired in the GDR to evaluate the western legal system and the role of the police in it. Thus some of them identify the western legal system by invoking the Marxist apparatus critiquing "bourgeois legal systems" as "rich man's justice," pointing out in effect that citizens certainly are not equal before the law in united Germany, contrary to what westerners would want to suggest in pointing to the comrade-nepotism in the GDR and juxtaposing it to the western system of the rule of law. Easterners, after their experiences in both political systems, are much more prone to believe that "no matter what, no matter where, the little guys get screwed," as many of them have summarized their disillusionment.

In sum, the politico-legal bases on which the Berlin Police and the People's Police operated were indeed quite different. For a variety of typical police cases, it would not have made a difference in which of the two systems a particular violation occurred—the outcome would have been similar. This is clearly the case for most of the crimes attracting public attention, such as murder, burglary, or robbery. In general, westerners espouse the rule of law as a defining hallmark of their work as police officers, providing a sense of identity through a stipulated superiority of the rule of law in the FRG vis-à-vis other political systems, especially in comparison to the other two recent German experiences with policing and law, the Nazi dictatorship and the GDR. While easterners have in general also started to identify with the rule of law, seeing its advantages sometimes plainly against the background of their own history in the GDR, their present experiences also point to the inconsistencies and ambiguities of the system. For the tensions in the three-way relationship among the rhetoric of the rule of law, the practice of policing in a much more crime-ridden society than their old one ever was, and a sense of justice seem to be much more apparent to eastern officers who slowly move into and adjust to this new system than to their western colleagues who have learned to live with these tensions in the course of the years. Thus, although the new might look attractive to easterners, they clearly also see its difficulties, which puts into perspective for them the western claim to superiority. For easterners, the difficulties of the western system are the less acceptable, the more westerners tend to moralize the GDR, stressing the superiority of the FRG.

Conclusions

In a cultural context where people with disjunctive synecdochical or metonymic identifications meet, such as people who identify as east Germans and west Germans (or French and Americans, men and women, Catholics and Protestants), synecdochical mischief is an effective means to emphasize and strengthen symbolic boundaries. Put differently, synecdochical mischief is a potent means of other-objectification. The effect is heightened if the synecdochical mischief aims right into the core of cultural intimacy (Herzfeld 1997), the received understanding of a group about its own shortcomings. This is so precisely because groups can be intensely aware of their own vulnerability to synecdochical mischief and because cultural intimacy is an effective means to create in-group solidarity. Thus, cultural intimacy and synecdochical mischief are complementary dynamics of what has aptly been called boundary work (Lamont 1992; Lamont and Fournier 1992). From another vantage point, this insight into the dynamics of boundary closure can be reformulated in terms of preconditions for effective boundary transcendence in what Buber (1995) and Bakhtin (1984a) have called dialogue: knowledge about cultural intimacy, and the absence of synecdochical mischief.

In the conclusion to the last chapter I described the situation of eastern police officers in the former GDR in terms of a double bind leading to an emotional paralysis which effectively prevented a moralization of the GDR. As shown in that chapter a moral discourse organized in terms of sincerity is an essential aspect of this double bind because it serves as a lock-in device. In this context, the absence of an alternative moral language which might have helped to redefine the situation is important. In particular, easterners had no language in which it would have been possible to moralize parts of the state while preserving an overall identification with the state as a whole. One reason for the impossibility of moralizing parts without running the risk of undermining the basic identification with the whole state was that the GDR presented itself not as a fractured composite, but as a unitary whole. State, party, security organs, all were thought to dovetail neatly into one solid block. Mistakes were not supposed to get discovered and corrected through a system of checks and balances, by a multitude of divisions of powers, functional and regional; rather, mistakes were not supposed to occur in the first place due to a system of highly centralized control. Without competing redundancies of power, however, every attack on any part amounts to synecdochical mischief—every attack on a part is an attack on the whole. The unitary appearance of the GDR was intensified for the People's Police officers by a very high degree of internal and external security routines, a multitude of locks and seals, barred windows and security fences, security measures which were taken very seriously. Thus, internal cohesion was strengthened by the constant practical reminder of the existence of an enemy of the state.[50]

Discourses in terms of rights are uniquely suited to moralize parts without simultaneously threatening the whole. Rights are always conceived of as a bundle; together they form a composite which may or may not have an organizing internal structure, but mostly rights are given in the form of a catalogue: it is possible to violate one without violating another; it is possible to have one without having another. Western officers have no problem in moralizing certain parts of the FRG, because the FRG presents itself as a composite of organized redundancies of power, thus opening the possibility of a basic identification of the whole while subscribing only to identifications with some parts but not with others. Western officers, in contrast to their eastern colleagues (again, the situation is changing slowly), are comfortable with invoking a language of rights to moralize individual policies of the state. This view is consistent with the different positions of law in both societies. For westerners, the language of rights has a lively presence in their everyday practice as police officers. It is emphasized in the formal rationality of due process. This use of a language of individual rights was much less a feature of People's Police practice, which was, relatively speaking, more tilted towards the production of politically desirable outcomes.

In sum, then, it was difficult for easterners to moralize parts of their state or their political system without threatening the whole. Seen from

50. How far-reaching the effects of this construction of an outside enemy have been may be gauged from a statement by Vera Wollenberger (1993, 155), a very well known GDR civil rights activist, who explains why they did not attack the Stasi in their critique of the GDR regime (a critique which attempted to be selective while preserving a basic identification with the state). "I don't think it was fear which made us exclude the Stasi from our aggressive critique of the Honecker regime. It was a rest of a mode of thinking which saw the real enemy on the other side of the iron curtain to whom one didn't want to show one's weak spot, at least not more than was absolutely necessary" (my translation).

this perspective, it is perhaps not surprising that as a decision for the organization of unity came up, GDR citizens shed their old state with some ease. And it is for that reason perhaps equally unsurprising that to the same degree that easterners have acquired a notion of the state as a composite as well as a notion of rights, they regret that hasty decision.

So what does all this imply for a theory of moral identities? Taylor (1989) has described moral identity as a pursuit of moral goods in a moral space. He has argued that this pursuit is in need of an articulation in the form of a narrative which has to be cast in a moral language. What the explorations in the previous chapter and this chapter have shown is that not every moral language is equally well suited as a guidance system in the moral space of all social circumstances. They have also shown that not in all social circumstances are all moral languages readily available. Moral identities are therefore deeply interrelated with the particular historical and cultural circumstances under which human beings live. And although Taylor barely says a word about this interconnection, I do not think that he would disagree.

SEVEN

Building, Shifting, and Transgressing
the Public-Private Divide

For several reasons, the public-private divide is an especially interesting aspect of the police officer's east-west identifications. The sociopolitical and economic systems of the Federal Republic of Germany (FRG) and the German Democratic Republic (GDR) are thought to be characterized by diverging, systemic, public-private divides. In the rhetoric of political systems analysis as well as in the rhetoric of Cold War politics, Western individualism is typically played out against Eastern collectivism and vice versa. Thus, the encounter between easterners and westerners affords particularly interesting opportunities to see how officers react to each other's public-private boundary delineation. Moreover, police officers as representatives of the state, that is, as agents of the institution which is seen in some traditions as the center of the public sphere, must frequently cross public-private boundaries to perform their duties. Given these circumstances, I pursue the following three sets of issues in this chapter. First, how different are the uses made of the public-private divide by eastern and western police officers, how are they different today, and how were they different before unification? Second, note that the rhetoric of the modern nation-state is founded on metaphors of kinship and intimacy, projecting a particular kind of public-private divide onto the boundaries of the nation-state (Herzfeld 1987, chapter 4; Borneman 1992; Herzfeld 1997, especially chapters 1 and 5). In the light of nation-state rhetoric, encounters between members of the same nation have therefore a private character of sorts, while encounters between people of different nationalities have more of a public feel. During the Cold War, West German political rhetoric in particular has upheld the notion of one divided German nation, thus implying a heightened intimacy between East Germans and West Germans. I examine this presumed national intimacy/privacy by investigating the attempts of easterners and westerners to socialize in the context of work in order to befriend each other. Third, studying the rhetoric and practices that allude to the public-private divide offers interesting possibilities for studying the way in which human beings understand themselves and each other. The public-private divide is a symbolic form, an aspect of culture which is specifically used by the police officers as a basis on which identifications of self and other proceed. The public-private divide can, therefore, also serve as a heuristic for the sociological study of the hermeneutics of self and other.

Two Models of the Public-Private Divide

Distinguishing public and private is a time-honored practice in the social sciences. There are two different traditions of dividing the private from the public in Western political thought which, for the sake of clarity, I need to distinguish here before analyzing how this symbolic form is used by the police officers in everyday discourses. The older of the two goes all the way back to Aristotle (1957), who introduces a fundamental distinction between *polis* and *poikos*. *Oikos,* the household, is for Aristotle the realm of production and reproduction; women, children, and slaves; the sphere of necessity. *Polis* is, in contrast, the arena of communal/political action; the sphere of freedom; the place where men rise above the animalistic. Within this tradition, the public is essentially the political understood in its widest possible sense as life in and for the community as a whole. While for Aristotle the good life was one lived in the publicity of the polis, contemporary authors might sympathize with Aristotle (e.g., Arendt 1958) but diagnose the modern condition as much more ambiguous about the value of public/political engagement. Arendt sees in modern times an outright reversal of Aristotle's order of value between public and private in that the public has become for the vast majority of people the realm of necessity, whereas the private has become the sphere of freedom.[1] Hirschman (1982), writing after the civil rights

1. What Arendt means by this is simply that a person today would seek fulfillment in the pursuit of a career or even in the pursuit of a hobby, rather than in the pursuit of public office or political involvement.

movement, is much less gloomy than Arendt, but diagnoses "shifting involvements," cycles of interest in public (political) affairs, and a withdrawal into the privacy of home and career. I call this approach the political perspective or the political distinction between the public and the private.

Arendt's and Hirschman's interpretations of modern life point to the second tradition, which has its origins in what Taylor (1989, part 3) calls the "affirmation of ordinary life" in consequence of the European Reformation. The good life is seen by most Reformers, according to Taylor, as a life in pursuit of work and family. In contrast to Aristotle, the political does not enjoy any particular *moral* status in Reformation thought.[2] It is this ordinary life suspended between home, workshop, and field which is seen as private. It is the private as the intimate, accessible only to a select few, the private "as if behind the drawn curtains of home." But this ordinary life also has a public side, that which is done under the eyes of the many, "as if in the lime-light of the village square."[3] In Europe, these distinctions become more and more pronounced during the nineteenth and twentieth centuries with the increasing separation of workspace and homespace (Benjamin 1982; Perrot and Martin-Fugier 1991; Perrot and Guerrand 1991; Prost 1991). This latter distinction between the public and the private (I call it the "intimacy perspective" or "intimacy distinction") is the one foregrounded by the police officers themselves. I examine the private-public distinction in three different sets of relationships: the relationships between the police officers and the police organizations in which they work or have worked, the relationships of police officers among themselves, and finally the relationships of police officers to citizens.

2. Keep in mind here that Reformation thought is not coextensive with Renaissance thought. Of course, political entrepreneurship has strong (Aristotelian) moral connotations for Burckhardt's (1956) Italian condottieri or in the political thought of Machiavelli (1978). Of course their vision of the political is fundamentally different from Aristotle's understanding of polis. Some aspects of Renaissance politics can in part even be understood as a privatization of the political in the sense that politics is not the matter of a community but the sole pursuit of a prince and his entourage (which of course is not true for cities, especially imperial free cities in Germany and also for some of the city-states which were not at the same time principalities in Italy). It is against this background that the de-moralization of politics by Reformation thinkers has to be understood.

3. Of course this notion that the public as the nonintimate is of moral concern to the community at large can extend very far into the various rooms of a house, as the open-window policies in some Protestant communities show.

Private Home and Public Work?

During a conversation about the differences between life in the People's Police and the Berlin police, one officer pointed out that one aspect about the Berlin police he enjoyed very much was that when he went on a vacation now, nobody asked him where he was going, nobody demanded an address or a telephone number at which he could be reached. In the GDR, in contrast, he said he had to register in detail when exactly he would be leaving his private home, at what time he would arrive at the vacation location, the address and telephone number of the location, and so on. Another eastern officer said in the same context that he thought it nice that nobody cared anymore which party he voted for, or whether he would vote at all,[4] or whether he had an extramarital affair or not. Both closed their statements with the remark that all these things would nowadays be considered "private business" *(Privatangelegenheiten)*. Both officers perceived what they considered as characteristic differences in organizing the realms of the public and the private in both police organizations. The narration of these differences not only identifies past and present practices, but also identifies the police officers themselves as preferring something over something else. Each officer used different principles to divide public and private, principles which can shed some additional light on the meaning of such a divide.

Time/Space as Dividing Principle
between Public and Private

The first officer's statement invokes the idea of a segmented time/space continuum. In his case, the division between private and public is one of rules regulating the acceptability of access to an individual or a group in a particular time/space zone. There are general rules, such as "one cannot call a family after 9 P.M. in the evening," or "One should not make an

---

4. Eastern officers recount a high pressure to vote in the GDR. Here, too, the house-communities were instrumental. Whereas the voting stations had separate booths, one was expected not to use them. Using them would in any case have spelled trouble, eastern officers insist. Voting in the GDR was thus experienced as public, whereas voting in the FRG is experienced much more as a private matter. Participation in the public (political) realm is therefore experienced now as a private choice. The privacy of voting for westerners goes so far that they do not directly tell each other for which party or for which candidate they have cast their ballot. If asked, nevertheless, it is legitimate to pass the question. In the context of elections, therefore, officers can engage in extensive speculations about who has voted for which party.

unannounced house-call, especially not on Sunday morning," but these rules are usually embedded in a more complex casuistry. The most important conditions in regulating acceptable access which I could discern during my fieldwork are the type of relationship with the person or group whose privacy is disturbed, the reason why access is sought, and finally the particular demand placed on the person or group whose privacy is violated. It does make a difference whether the person seeking access is a colleague, a close friend, or a close relative; the boundary is drawn differently in cases of an emergency or for purposes of simple diversion; and access is granted more readily if the demand requires a simple, five-minute phone call rather than a longer, face-to-face meeting. While formally the criteria used by eastern and western officers are the same, substantively the rules are very different, leading to divergent practices. In the above example, the Berlin police does not demand any kind of accessibility to holiday time, which is in this sense considered strictly private (for the organization, the holiday time of its employees gets bracketed). In contrast, the People's Police made it a point to ensure accessibility (in fact it did not allow any sort of total bracketing). This, of course, does not necessarily imply that it would have regularly recalled police officers from their vacations.[5] The symbolic value of the request may be at least as important, if not more important, than its practical value (e.g., the ability to multiply the number of officers available on short notice). The access of the People's Police to its officers was ascertained, in addition to space/time tractability, by the fact that many of the apartment buildings in which officers lived were fitted with alarm systems. Former People's Police officers also talked about practice alarms, which were apparently sounded once a year to test the accessibility of the police officers and to see whether the telephone alarm-rings actually did work according to plan.

What, then, is the symbolic value of these accessibility rules which perforate the boundaries between home and work space, leisure and work time—in short, the boundaries between public and private? The answer is given by the eastern officers themselves, in comments (often proud comments) about their readiness to serve, encapsulating the interesting double identification that, in contrast to their western colleagues, they "were police officers 24 hours a day and 365 days a year." In this sense, to be a police officer was not just to *have* a job; the officers emphasized that

5. Some were recalled, however, in the aftermath of the opening of the Wall, where especially the passport and registration services of the police were hopelessly overworked.

life *in* (not *with*) the police was a *way of being*.[6] This does not mean that police officers were happy about times when they were asked to practice their encompassing police-officerhood. But this unhappiness is part of the very meaning of accessibility. What was involved in the idea of un-bounded accessibility was a sense of sacrifice, and it is this sacrifice which (begrudged or not) identified easterners as police officers; it gave them a sense of self. It has to be borne in mind that in order to make the time commitment apparent as a sacrifice, a notion of a usual division between private and public is necessary; there has to be a line of demarcation which makes the demands put on the time/space of People's Police offi-cers unusual, and thus defining.[7] In this sense, the demand on the private space or time gives the person to whom access is sought the feeling of importance, because he or she is needed. Lacking interest in access to the private can just as well be read as a sign that the person whose privacy is always respected is highly fungible and thus unimportant.

A public-private distinction along the lines of rules regarding accessi-bility to time/space segments can also be cast in the language of chrono-topes:[8] A high degree of accessibility implies a very fuzzy boundary be-tween concrete chronotopes in the case discussed here between home and work. By focusing attention on the dynamic and direction of narrative, the analysis of the connection between concrete chronotopes, that which I have called plot chronotope, raises the question of *how* precisely these

6. This notion of life in the People's Police, the notion of *living* a job rather than *having* one, is immediately related to the question of wearing the uniform from and to work, which I discussed in the section "Chronotopes of Eastern and Western Life" in chapter 1. It is also related to what I have called "extensive time" in the section "The Ethics of Work." Cf. Verdery 1996.

7. What becomes apparent here is that the theory of definitions can also be helpful for an understanding of the working of identifications: The classical theory of defini-tion analyzes a definition as a composite double predication *(definiens)* of the *defini-endum* by *differentia specifica* and *genus proximum*. The *differentia specifica* is the identifying aspect of the background of the *genus proximum*. Easterners might define a police officer *(definiendum)* as a citizen *(genus proximum)* who is available 24 hours a day and 365 days a year *(differentia specifica)*. Thus the defining/identifying aspect of a police officer is that, in contrast to the ordinary citizen, he is continuously avail-able.

8. See also the section "Chronotopes of Eastern and Western Life" in chapter 1. To some degree, and as far as this first distinction of the intimacy perspective of the public-private divide is concerned, an analysis in terms of chronotopes is much more precise than one in terms of the much more ambiguous terms *public* and *private*. What a chronotope analysis is missing, however, is the important connection between the intimacy perspective and the political perspective (see the conclusion to this chapter).

boundaries get perforated and from which side the perforation occurs. A fuzzy boundary in the narrative direction from work to home does not imply that the boundary in the narrative direction from home to work is equally fuzzy. Of course it may be fuzzy too: female eastern officers were, for example, allowed one household day per month, and they could also officially go to the hairdresser during their regular work hours.[9]

Concern as Dividing Principle between Public and Private

The second officer's statement in the examples given above—his felicitous "nobody cares anymore"—suggests another principle for dividing public and private, a principle which is not based on access to persons in particular time/space zones, but on a notion of what kinds of actions should or should not *concern* others—persons or institutions. What is at stake here is not interest in the sense of a desire to know, for anybody may be interested in anything at anytime. Interest cannot legitimately be used as a reason for interference, unless the word is used as a synonym for concern, which establishes a ground for intervention. The People's Police was in particular ways actively concerned with the lives of its members above and beyond work. It was concerned with whom its officers befriended, especially that they did not maintain contacts with Westerners, and it was also concerned with its officers' sexual mores: People's Police officers were not supposed to have sexual contacts with anyone other than lawful husbands and wives.[10] Both eastern and western officers tell stories about the affairs their colleagues (or even they themselves) might have entertained, but only eastern officers tell about the negative consequences that the publicity of an affair would have had within the organization: public rebuke by superiors, even public, dishonorable discharge, including expulsion from the police college.

Facing unexpected demands about what to reveal, encountering disinterest in what used to be demanded, or learning about new possibilities of concealment identifies a person as being surprised by otherness. This

9. In their sexual one-sidedness, these may very well have been measures to ease female participation in the GDR workforce (cf. Borneman 1992) while maintaining a traditional division of labor at home.

10. I have never encountered a story about a homosexual officer. However, a social services officer of the Berlin police told me that he was told by homosexual eastern officers that they had to hide their sexual orientation, for it would have been a reason for dismissal.

experience may be liberating, leading to a reorientation, to a realization of other possibilities, but the encounter may also be alarming, and the otherness may be rejected. While the encounter with a different set of public-private distinctions in the examples above was welcomed by the officers, other aspects of newly emerging practices that divide public and private were not welcome. In the chapter on space, I introduced the house-communities. While neighbors used to be nosy, penetrating the enclosure of the family with requests to get involved in the house-community, they also offered opportunities to socialize, as well as assistance when needed. Moreover, the dovetailing of work and home allowed for the exertion of pressure on those who did not do their share of communal work in the house, and it ensured that the work got done in the end. Many east German officers now complain about the breakdown of these house-communities, which they knew not only as members, but also as police officers, especially on the neighborhood beat patrol.[11] These officers report that in the absence of effective means of control, some people have begun to dodge their obligations (for example to sweep the hallways), inviting others to follow suit. Many eastern officers have described this as a regrettable withdrawal into the private sphere; one officer said he felt that it indicated a "nobody-gives-a-damn attitude."[12]

Ambiguous Practices

The line between public and private, though apparently crystal clear in rhetoric when claims are staked or rejected, is rarely ever sharp in prac-

11. The breakdown of house-communites makes the work of the neighborhood beat patrol more difficult. Not only do people know less about their neighbors, but with changing notions about public-private distinctions, they know also that even if they know, they might no longer be supposed to know (revealing undue curiosity), and furthermore, they might develop doubts about whether it is the police's business to know.

12. The reasons for this decline of the house-communities are, however, much deeper than just the absence of control through the workplace. Unification has profoundly shattered social hierarchies in the GDR. While the apartment blocks used to house people who were socially and economically rather similar, unification has led some to be suddenly much better off than before; others may have maintained their status, and still others may, mainly through unemployment, have become impoverished in relation to their fellow housemates. These differences have, on the one hand, created envy, as several neighborhood patrol officers have complained, but they have also created less carefreeness in conversations. They no longer ask how people are and how they are doing at work, for fear that the others might have lost their jobs.

tice. Several institutions within the People's Police reveal interesting ambiguities about the public-private divide. These ambiguities derive from the fact that public-private distinctions are deeply engrained culturally, and cannot be just changed around at will. These examples bespeak how and in what ways socialism had to put up with but also tapped into older petit bourgeois forms of dividing public and private spheres. In the first of the following examples, the ambiguity seems more or less staged: a public mission is clothed in the garb of a private occasion by adopting the petit bourgeois code of a formal private visit.

Eastern superiors were asked to make house calls on their immediate subordinates at least once a year. The leader of a shift would visit his patrolmen, the leader of a station would visit the shift leaders, and so on. The superiors and their subordinates would agree beforehand on a date when the spouses of the subordinates would be able to attend the meeting. Typically the superiors did not come in uniform, but in plain clothes, and they carried a gift of flowers or sweets purchased with the proceeds of an official fund maintained expressly for this purpose. While the staging of the visit followed the rules of formal private visits (clearly inspired by bourgeois codes of politeness), the superiors did indeed have a public mission: to get an idea of the general life circumstances of their subordinates and their families in order to assess hazards to the proper functioning of the subordinates within the organization. Such a visit usually included, for example, an effort to get a sense of the family's financial situation.[13] Apparently, this home call was handled very differently by different superiors. Some checked radio and TV dials and screened the kitchen closets for traces of illicit contacts with the West; some tried to keep a rather low profile; and others emphasized the paternalistic aspects of the endeavor and tried to find out whether they could be of any help to the family. Help was possible, for example, in finding a more adequate apartment, and so on. House calls could also be made for more specific purposes. If an officer was officially asked to attend the police college, and if this officer was hesitant to jump at that opportunity, superiors might try to persuade the wife of the officer in question that the career leap of her husband was desirable.

The party is another institution which east German officers found confusing with respect to a division between public and private spheres. In

13. As one former eastern shift leader told me, this was to discover possible sources of corruptability or susceptibility to potential blackmail. Westerners consider their financial situation as one of the most private areas, to be shared with one's spouse, but usually not even with one's best friends.

general, this reflects the peculiar relation between party and state in the GDR. Here, too, both a conflict with and the instrumentalization of another tradition seems to become apparent. Party membership was in principle voluntary, a matter of private decisions. Yet, if police officers wanted to attend the police college to launch themselves into the career path of commissioned officers, they were obliged to join the party, thus lending party membership a decisive public touch. Although party dues were considered private contributions, they were withheld from salary payments very much like taxes in the West. The People's Police also undertook systematic and sustained efforts to convince/persuade the few non–party members to join. While the police did have a typical, hierarchical, bureaucratic structure, it was penetrated by a semiautonomous hierarchy of so-called political deputies, who were ultimately not answerable to the bureaucratic hierarchy proper. Problems at work could therefore not only be discussed with a superior, but also with the political deputies, who had their own resources for intervention in the bureaucratic process, for example, by jumping a hierarchy level or two. The workplace was also the unit on which the party organization was based. The smallest unit was a party group, which could encompass, for example, all party members in a station (or if the station was large, then also in a shift, etc.). These party groups were chaired by party secretaries. Thus yet another hierarchy was created, which was again formally independent of both the bureaucratic hierarchy proper and the system of political deputies. In keeping with the notion that party membership is voluntary and private, party meetings were supposed to be held after work; however, the issues discussed during these party meetings were mostly work-related. Most eastern officers I spoke to were quite disturbed about this discrepancy.

While superiors and subordinates were supposed to use the polite third-person-plural form of address during official work hours, they were asked to use the colloquial second-person-singular form of address in party meetings. But then, everybody within the police was addressed also, no matter whether in polite or colloquial form, as "comrade" (*Genosse*), the official word for party consociates, irrespective of whether the person in question actually was a comrade or not (thus again expressing the implicit expectation that police officers should be party members). Many officers have remarked that one funny aspect of the party meetings was that they supposedly established a space in which critical thoughts could and indeed should be voiced in the presence of superiors, who sat as comrades with them at the same table, whereas during work, a strict military discipline was enacted, based on order and obedience. Hence, most said they decided to shut up, for who knew whether the superiors would be able to distinguish between a private statement as party member and one made in one's role as a subordinate police officer, lest criticism might smack of disobedience. But the presence of superiors is not the whole story. Many officers who have prepared political training sessions that they hoped would generate some real discussion contrast the lively exchange of opinions during coffee breaks with the blandness of the exchanges during official discussion time. As some officers have indicated, the difference seems to be that the frame of the debate in party or political training sessions was essentially public and official, thus lending some definiteness to words: they could not easily be recalled. A careless word might have triggered institutionalized sequences of action which were better avoided. Coffee-break discussions had a much more tentative character, offering many more opportunities to reinterpret what had been said.

There were thus three different, interpenetrating levels of hierarchy within the workplace: the police hierarchy itself, the political deputy hierarchy, and the party hierarchy of the various group secretaries. Whereas the first two were surrounded with the paraphernalia of the official— uniform, rank, office, box in the organization chart of the police—the latter was not. This reverses the relationship between bureaucracy and party in public political life, where the party organizations usually took precedence over the bureaucratic ones. Honecker was first known as party secretary and chair of the Politburo, and only after that as chair of the Council of Ministers. In the lives of the police officers, the party therefore occupied an intermediate position somewhere between the public sphere of work and the private sphere of home. This view is further supported by the fact that grievances, trouble with superiors, were best channeled through the party, perhaps with the help of the political deputy, but never through the official police bureaucracy. The organizational structure itself, therefore, contains more or less private channels of communication, institutionalizing the semiprivatization of certain information. This form of privatization is meant to serve the public purpose of functionality. It is as if the public could not work without the private. Organizations rely not only on formal and informal structures but also on formal-informal ones. This role is played in the West by personnel representation and unions.

All this, of course, does not mean that the Berlin Police is not concerned with the private lives of its police officers at all. Radical political activities might get a police officer into trouble.[14] Official concern for the physical and mental health of police officers leads to measures such as supporting and even demanding sports during work hours ("Sports is service!" as I was told), as well as offering assistance with problems ranging from substance abuse to gambling and difficulties related to "same-sex lifestyles."[15] Physical fitness is a precondition for continuing in active service as a police officer, making health tests a potential tool of personnel policy.[16] A particular aspect of the German civil servants law which runs especially against the grain of understood private-public distinctions in (West) Germany has gained renewed attention in the context of unification: Civil servants, including police officers, can in theory be posted anywhere within the jurisdiction of their employer. Thus a federal civil servant has to accept in theory a posting anywhere within the republic, and the civil servant of any of the sixteen states must accept being sent anywhere within the state. Much as the People's Police officers' twenty-four-hour readiness served as a justification for higher pay, the civil servants' mobility serves as a justification for all sorts of public service perks, such as full job security, state pensions, and a waiver of the duty to contribute to unemployment insurance and to the general pension fund. Both of these forms of availability have been clad in the rhetoric of sacrifice for the state, a sacrifice of the private which would go beyond ordinary expectations.

In theory, therefore, moving the federal government from Bonn to Berlin should have been not much of a question, as far as moving the civil servants is concerned. Of course, when actually called to duty, civil servants found it difficult to comply, and massive resistance was mobilized on the political level trying to keep as many jobs in Bonn as possible. The entire debate about the reasonableness of the move for civil servants circled around the question, Which degree of infringement into the private sphere is justified, and indeed justifiable, in terms of the public service

14. The so-called radicals-decree *(Radikalenerlaß)* forbids civil srvants to engage in any kind of political activity which would contradict their oath to protect the "liberal-democratic basic order" (freiheitlich-demokratische Grundordnung; ironicized in acronym as FDGO).

15. Literal translation from the German *gleichgeschlechtliche Lebensweise,* the official Berlin police expression for homosexuality. It is interesting, of course, that the police force views homosexuality as a "problem" which gets classified and institutionalized alongside gambling and substance abuse (mainly alcohol).

16. An officer who is found unfit for active service will usually not be dismissed, but will be employed in some other capacity, which might mean a much less desirable job and will, in all likelihood, also mean a significant loss of income.

law?[17] Likewise, some west Berlin police officers who were transferred by decree after unification to a department or a precinct in east Berlin did not like the idea at all. Understandably so, since the distances to and from work frequently doubled or even tripled, leading in extreme cases to nearly two-hour commutes in each direction (which is, incidentally, also true for all easterners transferred to the west, though they are not even thought of as having the right to complain). Transfers of this kind do indeed severely curtail the amount of available private time, and they also increase nonrefundable transportation costs. Western officers regularly point to these foregone resources, either negatively interpreting them as unwarranted forms of taxation or seeing them somewhat more positively as their "sacrifice for German unity." Those who volunteered, however, feel all the better for it. Western officers who did so never fail to identify themselves as volunteers. They did, in their own eyes, live up to the call of duty, and not only to that of the Berlin police, but to that of country and nation as well. Here, the Aristotelian notion of the public as the political assumes importance: demonstratively, the life of the *polis* is put above that of the *oikos*. What differentiates these western police officers from Aristotle's ideal citizen, however, is that the *oikos* is not held in contempt; it is indeed the value of the *oikos* which gives the sacrifice its significance.

Privatizing/Publicizing Self and Other

The very words *public* and *private* are, as the explorations of these examples suggest, extreme positions within a gamut. Every action, every time/space area, is just relatively public or private. Just how private or public is also a matter of circumstances and a matter of frames. Also, cultural understandings of the *appropriate* dividing lines are contested in many areas. What some claim to be a private affair ought to be regarded as of public concern according to others.[18] Several other important points

17. Of course the settlement agreed upon is one of sweetening the transfer, for example, by creating subsidized housing in Berlin. Needless to say, these sweeteners constitute a substantial portion of the costs of moving the government.
18. This is typically the case for what Hunter (1991) describes as "culture wars." Also, debates about multiculturalism are based on a contested public-private divide in several ways. Two of them are pertinent here. In a first step, something that has been considered of public concern (e.g., certain sexual practices) is taken out of the realm of the public and made private (i.e., by decriminalization). What seems to

should be noted. In practice, people who do not agree with the prevalent boundaries try to work around them. For East German officers during the time of transition, a day trip to the west not registered and not remarked remained a private trip; an extramarital adventure kept secret remained private. In practice, then, actions are made public (i.e., they are revealed), or they are made private (i.e., they are concealed) above and beyond normative notions of what is supposed to be public and what is supposed to be private. Thus the public-private divide attains in practice a much higher degree of fluidity. From a cultural point of view, therefore, it makes very little sense to conceive of the public-private divide as a practical equilibrium, as Perrot (1991) and her collaborators do. The fascinating aspect of the public-private distinction is precisely what people do with it to create meaning; thus what is interesting is not in any way an actual balance but the permanent, practical unsettling of a rhetorical balance.

The revealing and concealing are done with respect to one's own life as well as the lives of others. Police officers tell all sorts of stories about their private home lives, while they also retell those of others. People exploit the difference between a cultural ought and actual performance in order to create meaning. Revelations and concealments have meaning against the evoked backdrop of normative understandings of the public-private divide. Revelations and concealments can change the key in which human beings converse; they move people on the scale of intimacy: thus, friendships are made, annulled, or broken.[19]

The Production of Intimacy

The revelation of something private in order to make friends is a very delicate and precarious kind of social action. In Goffman's (1967, 5–45) terms, it requires a considerable degree of "face-work." In revelation (publication of the private), an existing public-private boundary is breached with the expectation that the breach will eventually be healed by a kind of concealment (privatization of the public) due to a general shift of the public-private boundary between the interactors in the direc-

---

follow this in some important instances is a sort of re-publicizing of the once private in what Taylor calls a "demand for recognition" (1992).

19. Compare Herzfeld's (1985) report of the sheep-thieves' intricate dance of concealment and revelation used to create social proximity and distance. Here, too, the boundaries between the public and the private are constantly moved in front of a background of normative understanding of these boundaries to create meaning.

tion of greater intimacy between them. This increase in intimacy trans-
forms the revelation ex post into legitimate private communication. The
maneuver is ultimately only successful, however, if the addressee of the
revelation reciprocates in kind. A mere concealment (for example, assuring the revealing person of confidentiality) is not enough, because it leaves
the revealing person naked, as it were, even if it is a shielded nakedness.
Those who initiate this process put themselves into a precarious position
because their advances, dangling in the air, might not be honored. To
use Goffman's terms again, the revealing person puts his face at risk and
depends for maintenance on the addressee of the revelation. What usually
unfolds, therefore, is a dance of revelations and counterrevelations slowly
establishing a new level of intimacy which is comfortable for both partners. Any choreography which fails to establish a new comfortable level
of intimacy is experienced as embarrassing.

Successful fieldwork itself relies on such a delicate dance of revelations
and counterrevelations. During my fieldwork, I found myself in situations
in which this dance worked beautifully and to the mutual satisfaction of
me and my informants (which is usually felt in the ease of further meetings). At the end of an interview, the interviewee would sometimes turn
the tables and ask me questions. In the medium to long run, these are
the informants I was most comfortable with. I also encountered situations
in which the revelations almost went too far for me to be able to recipro-
cate accordingly, thus immediately creating a tension which would en-
danger the relationship. Getting a good feel for the local understandings
of public and private as well as for the significance of deviations is thus
an absolutely indispensable aspect of ethnographic fieldwork. Slash-and-
burn interviews, in which interviewers ask questions with the aggressive-
ness of an investigative journalist, are useless in fieldwork, because they
preclude the possibility of sustained positive encounters. Also, the value
of interviews advancing too far too fast seems highly dubitable since interviewers would understand little of the emotional investment in certain
aspects of somebody's life, which come to the fore much more clearly if
the dance is danced and the degree of a revelation, the risk involved, is
acutely perceived. The dance itself, the choreography of revelations and
counterrevelations, is identifying; it makes apparent the ties of self to the
world and reveals and constructs identity in showing. Since this is true
for the relationship between ethnographer and informant just as much
as for the relationships between informants, it is a good example of how
an ethnographer not only gets field data from observations of others, but

from self-observation. The generation of field data is thus just as much an emotional process as it is a cognitive one.[20]

Assessing the Strength of Identifications

The dance of revelations and counterrevelations just described shows that identifications are of very different emotional strength, thus pointing to a significant gap in the analytical theory of identifications so far presented. Analyzing identifications in terms of their cognitive and emotional form, that is, on the basis of tropes, emplotment structures, performance, and narrative primarily conveys a sense of their quality but not necessarily of their intensity. One possible way to assess the strength or intensity of identifications is through psychoanalysis. Freud (1960b, 183–88; 1974a, 98–103) distinguishes two ways: "object cathexis" *(Objektbesetzung)* and "identification" *(Identifikation),* in which selves emotionally connect themselves to subjects and objects of the world. Both are constitutive for the dynamics of the oedipal conflict, mass-psychology, and the phenomenon of melancholia. "Object cathexis" aims at the possession of the desired object; its ideal-typical form is sexual desire, consuming itself in orgasm. "Identification" by contrast aims at assimilation to another subject; its ideal-typical form is the emulation of the father by the son, and it is consumed in their acknowledged sameness. Freud's "identification" and "object cathexis" are, in the terminology suggested in this study, both different modes of identification, and both can be gainfully analyzed in terms of the tropical modes of identification introduced in chapter 1. Freud's "object cathexis" has, in its drive for possession, basically the gestalt of a metonymy which ideally tends towards a synecdoche (in the consumption of the possession in sexual intercourse). His "identification" has, as a process of assimilation, the gestalt of a metaphor which tends towards a dissolution in metonymy (once similarity is thought to have given way to sameness).

Although Freud's terminology is much less flexible than the framework of modes of identification presented here, the notions of "object cathexis" and "identification" explicitly raise the question of the strength of the

20. In this sense I fully agree with reflective ethnography (Clifford and Marcus 1986; Clifford 1988; Van Maanen 1988). This doubling of self-observation and other observation is well captured for example in Kondo's (1990, ch. 1) "eye/I," which apparently occurred to her as she was straddling the public-private divide as a Japanese-American in Japan.

connections between self and the world as they are built on the foundation of an economy of drives. Freud's "identification" and "object cathexis" can be of varying intensity, depending on how much libido, drive
energy, is invested in them. While considering identifications, it must be
taken into consideration that there is a fundamental difference between
an officer suggesting first, "I like boiled pig feet with sauerkraut" and
then, "I was proud to be a member of the People's Police." Both are
identifications which differ not only in quality but probably also in *intensity*.

Even more important, Freud emphasizes the fact that all connections
between a self and the world have their own respective history, that they
have their own background of gestation. The context in which they are
generated has, for Freud, considerable ramifications for the *relative importance* of any identification made. In other words, Freud's theory suggests that there are relatively more and relatively less important connections between self and the world. Some are supporting beams and pillars
in an architecture of connections, others hold parts and subgroups together, and still others are little more than trimmings and embellishments.
The way of differentiating the one from the other is of course the business
of psychoanalysis proper.

There are different possible ways of addressing the issues of strength
and relative importance. The avenue Freud travels is to privilege certain
phases in life (early infancy), certain key relations (to father and mother),
and certain interactional patterns ("oedipal conflict") to differentiate between strong and weak, important and unimportant. But he also takes
his cues from typical, conspicuous aspects of the therapeutic interaction
("defenses" and "pathological" types of behavior). In other words,
Freud's understanding of weak and strong, important and unimportant,
is based on an elaborate psychoanalytic theory.

Psychoanalysis, as useful as it may be, is not the only way to assess
the strength of identifications, however. The lifeworld itself is very rich
in cues to the importance and strength of identifications. I have already
mentioned the dance of revelations and counterrevelations as an everyday
practice which provides vital cues for an assessment of the strength of
certain identifications. Also, participants in conversations usually have a
pretty good understanding about which parts of self-identifications are
strong and important and which ones are not. For how else would people
be able to insult one another with a fair amount of precision; how would
they otherwise be able to convince and persuade? The choices of alternative pursuits people make can be important leads regarding the strength

of identifications.[21] Moreover, the choice of words, modes of speech, differentiating gestures, and the invocation of contexts all help to differentiate the strength and importance of identifications made. Certain cultural conventions, for example, certain words, suggest a stronger tie than others: "like" is typically taken to be weaker than "love," unless, of course, these words are used in ironic inversion signaled by the context of the interaction, the theme of the talk, or a literal twinkle in the eye, a tongue in the cheek. Self-identifications voiced to a dear friend in a conversation about one's own problems in a marriage that threatens to break apart have in all likelihood a different ring than those made in a conversation with acquaintances about the last vacation trip. In other words ethnographers, just like the people they observe, can begin to assess the importance of identifications with ordinary fieldwork techniques.

Making Friends at Socials

Typically, east and west Germans complain that for some strange reason it seems to be impossible to get closer to one another. An easterner said, "They [the westerners] never tell anything about themselves." One western officer put it metaphorically in explaining the historical origins of the military salute: "They [the easterners] never open their visor," and another western officer said somewhat exasperatedly, "Even after five years, I still do not know who they are." The others always seem to be not forthcoming enough, or too rash, or they reveal the wrong thing at the wrong moment at the wrong place. The time/space that both designate as the appropriate one "to get to know each other as human beings [as opposed to as police officers]" arises in the different forms of "socials" (east German: *Geselligkeiten*). Socials are, therefore, again interesting intermediaries between the public and the private. They are tolerated and even supported by the organization, because it is assumed that a more intimate knowledge of colleagues will also improve their work relationship. The public and the private are thus seen as interdependent. If the social stretches from the workplace into the private, as it were, then invi-

21. These choices may pertain, for example, to a rank order of rules which are invoked in decision-making processes (see Shweder 1996, and selections in D'Andrade and Strauss 1992), where people identify with a whole set of rules but with each of them to a different degree. Or they may pertain to choices of roles in situations when different roles could have been taken, thus conveying a sense of which role a person identifies with more strongly (see Stryker 1992).

Figure 19. Köpenick officers on a hiking day (summer 1995). Author's photo.

tations from colleagues to grill parties at individual officers' garden plots extend the locus of the private, home, into the public.

The "lowest" form of a social in Köpenick is a "breakfast" of varying degrees of inclusiveness in which one colleague treats others to sandwiches and coffee.[22] In contrast to other treats, breakfasts are typically not ad hoc: people are invited to attend and are asked beforehand whether they will be able to make it (to get the number of sandwiches right). Also, a table is set formally with tablecloth, china, silverware, and (paper) napkins. A breakfast typically has an occasion, some of which are work-related, such as promotions, departures to another office, or arrivals from another office. Others are private: for example, birthdays, returns from vacation, a new house/apartment, marriage, or the birth of a child. Breakfasts are held during work hours, therefore in uniform and within the precinct building. The next higher form is a party, for which several officers usually team up as sponsors. Parties can have the same occasions as breakfasts, but since major sponsorship is needed the occasion is usually important; typically it is a retirement. In addition, there can be Christmas parties, hiking days, shift outings, and so on. Parties

22. *Sandwich* is something of a misnomer: what is served are *belegte Brötchen,* that is, buns and rolls cut in half, spread with butter and different kinds of sausage, cheese, fish, and—especially popular—seasoned, minced meat.

Figure 20. The Köpenick lounge with Christmas decorations (1994). Courtesy A-shift, Precinct 66.

are celebrated after hours (though an hour or two might be slashed from the workday), attended in plain clothes, and held somewhere in a pub or restaurant with separate rooms. The separate room is important, because the officers want to be, as they put it "amongst themselves" *(unter sich)*, thus creating already a new public-private boundary, stipulating an atmosphere of intimacy within.

In light of the many socials in Köpenick, it is quite curious that easterners and westerners reproach each other for being unable to celebrate properly. Asked what in particular they mean when they reproach their colleagues from the respective other part of Germany in this way, officers seem to be unable to pinpoint exactly what they mean, but they insist that the atmosphere at joint parties is typically wanting. Discernible (but meager) indicators which are used are the frequency of such events, especially those organized by the precinct (easterners: too few) and the degree of participation (westerners: easterners often absent, leave too early). What it seems to boil down to, however, is a certain reserve vis-à-vis the other side, the lack of atmosphere is related to the mixing of easterners and westerners.

My observations during the socials at Köpenick suggest that eastern and western officers still have great difficulties in choreographing the dance of revelations and counterrevelations in such a way that at the end they are able to suffuse a public part of their lives into private components, to increase intimacy among each other by rendering co-workers into colleagues, and colleagues into friends. Many revelations lead to embarrassment, and concealment still leads to disappointment over a lack of closeness. One reason is that revelation is often seen by easterners as too risky a business. Not only do they constantly feel under scrutiny by the police organization for possible links with the former secret police, but also by their colleagues for their competence as well as their moral integrity.[23]

A closer look at the actual verbal exchanges at such socials, especially at parties, reveals what seems to go wrong. "To get to know the other as human being," one of the explicitly stated purposes of parties, aims at the revelation of the real person hidden behind the masks of roles. Socials in this sense are cultural forms in which officers can individuate in respect to each other; they provide a framework in which dialogue is thought to take place. Officers express this expectation of individuation in dialogue quite clearly by saying, for example, "I am glad that this party is coming around. There we will finally really have a chance to talk." Thus, socials also offer a chance to round out and complete the picture of the moral character of their colleagues.[24] What is supposed to help in the process of character revelation is sociability over eating plenty of food (boiled pig-feet preferred) in connection with lots of alcohol. Socials are, then, looked at as a sort of oracle of identity: they are thought to reveal the truth about the other. What is hoped for is "that people really move out of themselves to show who they really are," as one officer put it. Alcohol is an important, indispensable ingredient in the process; the Roman idiom "in vino veritas" is invoked and half-believed.[25] Officers pay close attention to how much the others consume, and not consuming enough is tantamount to "not really participating." The officers continuously invite each other to drink more: "Come on, let's get another

23. See the section "Personnel Selection after Unification" in chapter 2 for the danger of Stasi linkages; see also the evaluation of competence in the section "Policing as Performance" in chapter 4, and the section "Valuing Sincerity" in chapter 5 for the connection to the question of moral integrity.

24. Compare the section "Personal Sincerity" in chapter 5.

25. In the northeast of the country, a region inhospitable to wine (climatically and culturally), "vino" means of course mostly beer and schnapps.

round." And as they drink, and eat, and effervesce, they are supposed to "speak their mind" (sprechen wie ihnen der Schnabel gewachsen ist [literally: "talk as their beak has grown"]). And they do! Supposedly freed from conventions, supposedly certain that revelations will be honored, Goffman's faces saved, western officers reveal their dislike for the whole GDR, inviting their eastern counterparts to agree finally; hoping that while they are drinking together, this should not be too difficult anymore, since "How could a reasonable person disagree? . . . ," Eastern officers in turn reveal their attachments to their lives in the GDR and praise the People's Police for its success in catching every thug. Easterners' criticisms of their own old country is gleefully exploited by westerners, who (practicing synecdochical mischief) seem to welcome any critical statement with a great halloo of "finally you admit it," thus using it as yet another confirmation of their idea of what the GDR was really like. In return, partial criticism of westerners is read as a wholesale attack by easterners. Thus ranks begin to close again around issues of cultural intimacy (Herzfeld, 1997), and the atmosphere of the party seems to get increasingly clouded. Thus, the combination of the practices of synecdochical mischief and cultural intimacy spoils their sport, preempting most attempts at understanding.[26] The western moralizations of the GDR raise eyebrows east, the praise for this or that positive aspect of the GDR leads to an exchange of glances west, and thus the Wall is resurrected quickly over picked bones and empty glasses of beer. Embarrassed, some easterners leave the party early (or in anticipation of such embarrassment, they have made arrangements to be picked up early), and westerners take it as a sign that easterners just cannot celebrate. The revelations mostly fail to be honored. Luckily, much can be excused the next day on account of alcohol, which, used excessively, can be conveniently thought to conceal because revelations under the influence of alcohol can be disregarded, thus saving face after all. This two-faced nature of alcohol as an agent of concealment

26. Synecdochical mischief is of course also a permanent danger for the labor in the vineyard of ethnography, in that explanatory frameworks are deployed too fast, too rigidly, preempting sustained efforts at understanding. Coles (1986) maintains that psychotherapeutic efforts benefit greatly from time-suspended closure, in what Anna Freud once termed, adopting Woodrow Wilson's words on the U.S. position in World War I, "watchful waiting." Coles quotes Anna Freud (my apologies for the indirect quotation): "Children have their small wars, and often we have to suspend our judgment about their significance until we know enough; and it takes time, a long time, to know enough." What Freud has said here about therapy seems just as true for ethnography, for understanding in general. "Watchful waiting" as a hermeneutic principle helps to undermine synecdochical mischief.

and revelation, is the ideal safety net for the social tight-rope dancing of shifting public-private boundaries.[27] Yet, at the end of the day, a stale taste always remains, for there is a belief in the truth of the identity oracle.

What was said and done during a social is painstakingly registered and is evaluated in little groups the day after. The result is mostly an exasperated feeling that the gulf between east and west remains, freshly reconfirmed by the experience of the night before, which once again made it clear that it is almost impossible to speak one's mind, to be "open and honest," to be sincere with the other Germans without risking considerable misunderstanding. The public-private boundary maintained by one person vis-à-vis another tells the other what kind of relationship really is at stake here, because relationships are at least partly defined by recourse to the public-private divide.[28] What east and west German officers find out through their socials as identity oracles is that although friendships are desired, they do not happen, or they themselves would probably say that they cannot happen. That does not mean that there are no friendships at all between east Germans and west Germans, but there are precious few. Failed east-west parties are then contrasted with successful west-west or east-east parties, where jolly harmony is seen to reign, where at least no de-energizing hiding of one's own thought—insincerity—has to be practiced.

The confraternization envisioned by the national metanarrative does not take place; Germans "cannot speak German with each other"; that hallmark of what it means to be a German (to speak freely without any beating around the bush) cannot be practiced in unison; the other still fails the ultimate test of nationality.

Policing as Publicizing

Policing itself is about actions that by law have to concern the police. All criminal acts are defined as of concern to the general public. Police officers

27. This dual perception of alcohol may explain why it is rarely missing at German socials, eastern and western. It would be interesting to study what other methods are available for the same purpose in different cultures.

28. Luhmann (1982) shows how the significance of love relationships has changed in this respect during the last 250 years. A love-relationship today implies a very different understanding of intimacy than in previous centuries, which did not share modern notions of an all-encompassing, all-accepting knowledge of the other. While the historical facts Luhmann unfolds are undoubtedly very interesting, I am much less convinced by his highly functionalist explanation for the change. He is arguing that certain social structures imply certain forms of intimacy codes for self-sustenance.

also constantly come into contact with the private worlds of citizens. Police contact is almost always a form of revelation; it makes the private public in a particular way. This is true in a much wider sense than just the uncovering of crime. In reporting the death of accident victims to their relatives, police officers face the expression of feelings which are— in most contemporary, western, industrialized cultures—relegated to the private; being called onto the scene by a quarreling couple confronts police officers with a situation regarded as almost archetypically private; much of police work is not done on the street, but behind the doors of private apartments that the officers would never have seen as private citizens. Thus, policing is about crossing the public-private divide.

In the FRG such crossings are legally highly regulated. For example, police officers can enter an apartment or demand identification only under certain conditions; they can only ask certain questions, store certain data, and their choice of means must be in accordance with the much-touted principle of adequacy.[29] Such legal provisions mostly deal with transgressions that the police officers themselves initiate, where they are actively pursuing information. Eliciting the revelation of information that the police want is a matter of professional cunning. These revelations never cause embarrassment because they simply bring into the public arena what is, given the laws and the legitimate concerns of the state, supposed to be public in the first place. In this sense, what might look like a transgression at first is healed by the fact that the private was not really violated; rather, illegitimate concealment was undone.

Any notion of a right to privacy, a sphere in which police officers may not interfere, or in which they may interfere only under certain conditions, or even only with the permission of another controlling agency, makes the work of police officers more difficult. To police officers, these rules sometimes make their work appear like playing a game with an artificially imposed handicap. Especially the rules of data protection, which prohibit them from keeping any private records about persons, appear far-fetched to them. The privacy rights of individuals at times seem to mock their efforts as police officers. Many officers argue (and there is no difference between easterners and westerners in this respect), that privacy rules protect criminals rather than decent human beings, since decent human beings do not have to hide anything anyway. At the same time, however, these privacy rules are proclaimed to be the hallmark

29. In recent years, one of the major public debates in Germany in this respect concerned the question of whether the police should be allowed to tape conversations in private apartments, which until recently was unlawful.

not only of western democracy but of universal human rights. Thus, there is a tension inherent in police work between the obligation to honor the constraints of democracy and the function of providing security.

Western officers argue that states identify themselves and their citizens in the laws protecting privacy. Even more important, the police force identifies itself, the state, and the citizens in keeping or disregarding these laws in daily practice. The protection of privacy is, however, not only a matter of law but also a matter of "human decency" universally conceived. Westerners reproach the GDR and, by extension, their eastern colleagues for having violated these privacy rules, thus transgressing "the most primitive rules of human decency." The so-called travel reports of the People's Police's neighborhood patrol officers (ABV: Abschnitts-bevollmächtigte) are taken as a case in point. The ABVs tried to assess the likelihood of return of persons who had demanded permission to travel to the so-called non-socialist currency area (Nicht-sozialistisches Währungsgebiet, NSW). The criteria for assessing the likelihood of return were based on a notion of rootedness in the GDR. This encompassed such indicators as the quality of relations to significant others, to children, relatives, and friends; investment in realties, such as houses, garden plots, etc., and so on; job satisfaction and reputation at work; and finally political ties to the GDR, such as membership and activities in socialist mass organizations and parties. Western officers take issue with the state's concern with where its citizens wanted to go, and especially with the issues investigated in order to make an informed guess about the likelihood of return. Western officers see in these issues a clear, unwarranted violation of the private sphere of citizens.

Even in comparing the quality of police dogs, westerners discover the undemocratic nature of the People's Police. Eastern dogs have been found in tests to be generally unfit for service in the unified Berlin police, because, as western dog-handlers explained to me, they bite far too readily, thus violating the most sacred of private rights, the inviolability of the human body. Thus, on grounds of what they see as an unwarranted violation of the private sphere, westerners identify the GDR as well as the police officers who acted on its behalf as immoral, claiming that they themselves would never have "prostituted" (sich hergeben) themselves "to do something like that." Sometimes, however, western officers talk admiringly about the "possibilities" of investigation in the GDR, pointing to the fact that this made success possible. Even if the clear-up rate in the GDR was higher, one high-ranking western officer enviously pointed out, it was achieved by undesirable means.

Most eastern officers who wrote travel reports did not like the task at all, but they did not have the feeling that they were violating a right to privacy, though several said that they were not "happy stirring around in the private matters of others," taking the investigation as lightly as possible.[30] One of them said that nobody told him exactly how to investigate the return-likelihood, so one could do a tough check-up, or one could take it less seriously. Thus, officers saw it as within their own discretion to respect boundaries they found important. However, all of them agree that the problems with travel reports multiplied with the sheer number of applications during the late 1980s. People who did not come back after a positive report could cause serious problems for the reporting officers. One ABV told me of a forty-eight-hour interrogation he went through after eight persons in his area did not return. He was also sure that after that incident the secret police tried to find out whether he took his job seriously. Luckily, he added, a few months later the Wall came down. Thus, easterners did indeed have a sense of privacy, and some of them also felt that they were transgressing a boundary that they were somewhat uneasy about violating. Still, this did not lead them to reproach the political regime in the GDR. Rather, they felt that the work was disagreeable but that somehow it had to be done.

The transgression of the private-public divide is also a matter of tact, at least in those cases where police officers are faced with revelations they have not sought and that are not part of any investigation because they are not considered to be of any concern to the public. There are ways of dealing more or less successfully with the potentially embarrassing fact of such revelations. The problem for police officers is that it is neither desirable nor in any sincere way possible for them to answer revelations with counterrevelations, thus embarking on the dance of exchanges that could lead to a degree of intimacy that would heal the transgression of the private. Professionally, this is also not desirable, since any form of intimacy might undermine the active concerns of the police.[31] Officers do not act only in the interest of the revealing person (though they do so much more often than is generally assumed),[32] but if there is a conflict

30. This is yet another example of the effects of a missing discourse on individual rights.

31. I hesitate to use the more common term *fraternization* here because it has negative overtones.

32. There is a fundamental difference here between the daily work of criminal investigation officers *(Kriminalpolizisten)* and uniformed policemen *(Schutzpolizisten)*.

between the interest of the revealing person and the interest of the state where something is revealed that the state has declared to be of its concern, the police officer has to act, so the officers claim, unflinchingly on behalf of the state's interest.[33]

Unlike a physician or a priest, therefore, a police officer cannot even offer absolute secrecy, but only the assurance (if it is an assurance) that only authorized persons will get to know. Many police officers develop (much as do physicians, therapists, priests, and undertakers) a certain professionalism in dealing with the transgression of the private-public divide. Different officers prefer different techniques, different styles of face-work, which are meant to protect themselves at least as much as they are meant to make it easy for their counterparts. Getting it right most of the time is a high art. Some officers exude the air of a jovial acquaintance; they seem to say "You can tell me anything, it won't shock me."[34] Some prefer the more gentlemanly discretion of nonchalance, saying as it were, "I have not heard anything. I have not seen anything." Many try to cut interaction short, presenting themselves as rough and edgy, saying almost "Do not tell me too much; I am not a buddy." Perhaps the most common response is to take the lead in keeping things on a relatively technical level: "What is the problem here? Is it something for us? [meaning, is the police force responsible or answerable in any way?]. If so, what can the police do to solve it? If not, then for whom is it something?" And some just remain slightly embarrassed, nervously rushing to finish the job.[35] The respective success of all of these techniques is highly dependent on the police officers' momentary interlocutors. Whatever the technique, however, the purpose seems to be to heal the transgression of the public-private divide in ways that allow the officer not to respond in kind, but to listen without having to become intimate. While some police officers do enjoy these more human encounters and pride themselves in

33. Thus citizens are advised of their rights to withhold information.

34. This is the down-to-earth version of Terence's "Nothing human is alien to me."

35. I remember quite well how uneasy I felt during my first patrols when we would be called to a house. At first I chose to remain in the car, since I had the strong feeling that I had no right to intrude into the private sphere of the persons who might have called the police but certainly did not count on a sociologist accompanying them. Some police officers made it easier by introducing me, asking the people whether they would mind having me with them. In the course of time I became less scrupulous. However, a feeling of unease never quite left me, which made me sometimes dread my patrol-car observations. I was always grateful to be on the road with at least one officer in the team who could handle revelations with professional bravura.

being able "to talk to people," others find them rather disturbing, much preferring the emergency task-oriented side of their work.[36]

Some eastern officers claim that their western counterparts often do not find the right tone in relation to eastern citizens. They claim especially that westerners are too downright technical, speaking in a lingo which confuses people in the east. They advocate a much more jovial attitude which aims at cajoling citizens into voluntary cooperation. The attempt is thus to transform a public state-citizen transaction into a more private negotiation between two human beings who understand each other. Eastern officers are also surprised at the ways in which western citizens frequently deal with the police. They are said to know their rights extremely well; therefore, westerners are contrasted with easterners for using a language of rights in dealing with the police. But eastern officers state also that eastern citizens are more and more following western models of behavior. They are said to learn their rights rather fast.

Conclusions

Easterners and westerners both make comprehensive use of private-public boundaries. Both use transgressions of these boundaries to create meaning: the acceptance of a transgression, for example, is interpreted as a sacrifice for a higher purpose; transgressions are also initiated to make friends. Working with the private-public boundary is highly identifying in several ways. A transgression of the boundary is felt, and thus its very existence is realized. The question that arises at transgression is how to react to it. Transgressions can be invitations to change the boundaries by incorporating the formerly public into the private, or by making public what was thought to be private. Any deviation between a boundary maintained in practice and a normative idea of the same boundary is highly signifying. Police officers find out what they mean to others by inspecting behavior regarding the private-public divide in relation to citizens, in relation to the police organization, and in relation to each other. In order to function in this way, privacy itself must be valued. As such, privacy is then something that can be given—it is a gift.

36. The very fact that there is a whole repertoire of possible responses to the typical situation of revelations which are neither professionally wanted nor answerable by counterrevelations, the very fact that officers handle these situations with more or less style and bravura, deriving very different senses of identity from such situations, attests to the existence of a whole poetics of handling such situations.

Normatively public and private were divided in quite similar ways in East Germany and in West Germany. Even the normative reference points, which find a relative anchor in the social boundaries of the family, the spatial boundaries of the apartment, and the temporal boundaries of leisure were almost the same in East and West. All in all, the socialist regime in East Germany seems not to have done away with rather bourgeois notions of the public-private division. The politically opportune transgressions of the authorities were accepted and are still justified in terms of the extraordinary situation of a life at the frontier between the two sociopolitical world-systems. However, for easterners, the boundaries between work and home were much more fluid than for westerners; there were more and different institutions to bridge them. These intermediary institutions have been partly despised, but their merit has also been recognized. Thus there are some remarkable continuities between popular understandings of the public-private divide under socialism and its bourgeois predecessors. Despite the diminished respect of the state for the public-private divide and the introduction of a host of intermediary institutions, the private has ironically been strongly emphasized in the former GDR. The relatively strict routines governing what might be said to whom or what should be done in response to the arrival of an unexpected visitor are indicative of this rather solidified boundary, which testifies again to the adherence to a more bourgeois understanding of the private.[37] Substantively, the formal similarities of eastern and western ways of creating intimacy do contribute, however, to a fundamental confusion, because the procedures do not, in the face of very different life experiences, lead to redeeming extensions of intimacy: the brotherhood of nationality does not find confirmation in east-west socials.

Finally, the history of the GDR has also shown how interdependent are the two models of the public-private divide developed in social philosophy; the political perspective and the intimacy perspective (cf. Maier 1997, 42). The state's disrespect for the desired protection of intimacy can contribute to political atrophy, or upheaval, or both, and a disregard for the political embeddedness of intimacy can lead to its very dissolution.

---

37. Gauss (1983) has talked in this respect about a "nitch-society (Nieschengesellschaft) in the East.

CONCLUSION

Dialogue, Individuation, and the Other

The unification of Germany has effectively divided the country. Until 1989 Germans in East and West could nourish the idea that division was merely political, superimposed on Germany by historical circumstances, by powers outside of Germany's control. Until 1989 Germans could believe, if they had not long ceased to care, that their national unity has survived in a shared culture. The idea of an essential unity of "the German people" was sustained by the political establishment in West Germany, as well as by thousands of visitors who used to cross the Iron Curtain every year. Although in the West the invocation of German unity had acquired for many the character of a ritual devoid of meaning, and although more liberal-minded West Germans found it chic in the 1980s to stress their cultural proximity to Germany's western neighbors, thus deemphasizing German-German similarities, the idea of unity regained enormous momentum in the context of the rapid disintegration of the GDR after 9 November 1989. For a short moment, in the euphoria about the revolutionary changes occurring not only in East Germany but in Eastern Europe as a whole, it looked as if that so-often-stipulated "sisterhood and brotherhood" among the people living in the FRG and the GDR was not a fiction but a living reality. It looked as if the conservatives with their insistence on an essentialist German nationhood, supported by easterners' enthusiasm for quick unification, were somehow right after all. At any rate, it was the old, conservative, essentialist vision of German-German relations embodied in the FRG's old claim to sole representation which won the day. And it is not surprising therefore that Germany's

323

neighbors (along with German liberals) started to get seriously worried about a resurgent nationalist chauvinism.

Political unification was a moment of truth, however. Now Germans on both sides of the former Iron curtain were asked to live their unity. And at this point the idea of cultural unity, which had been questioned by liberals before, finally broke down, as it became clearer that easterners supposedly freed from socialist tutelage, supposedly liberated to be who they had always been, did not produce a *Wirtschaftswunder* (economic miracle) of their own. East Germans did not repeat West German history in fast-forward mode. Ever since, a closer look at the Germans from the respective other side seems to confirm and reconfirm every day that easterners and westerners are quite different, that they are other, even foreign. Overcoming the reality of a political division made the intensive experience of a cultural division possible. It became apparent to Germans from East and West that forty years of separate histories, of increasingly divergent biographic experiences within a set of diverging institutions, and participation in fundamentally different discourses had indeed made a difference.[1] And thus the Berlin Wall, symbol of the political division of the country, gave way to a discourse on the "wall in the heads of people," a symbol for the experiential division of Germany.

In this study I have tried to explore wherein precisely that experience of difference lies. In the light of countless identifications of self and other discussed in the previous chapters, I would like to differentiate two aspects of the experience of difference. Identifications of the other as other have two mutually reinforcing sources. Usually the other-identifications of east and west German officers begin with the encounter of the unexpected: they start with a breach of lifeworld assumptions. This breach may, as I have tried to show, originate with almost anything: with linguistic differences, with the perception of an alien object, with demeanors or attitudes outside of the repertoire of the everyday. At least initially, the effect of such a breach is intensified by the stipulation of shared nationhood and culture. The breach itself is followed by an accounting for the breach, which is in the case of east and west Germans easily found in identifications that suggest, after all, membership in different categories.

1. That this difference is not just the difference among Germany's various regions, in the same way that somebody from Hamburg may strike somebody from Munich as odd, is highlighted by the fact that these differences are felt not only between persons from various parts of the country—between a Saxon and a Swabian, let's say, who have their distinct histories, differences in food and language, and so on—but also by Berliners, who share a common history, a common dialect, and—even after forty years of separation—a taste for certain foods.

These are, in the absence of the typically invoked national distinction, the makeshift categories of Ossi and Wessi. From there on, categorization and the experience of a breach of lifeworld assumptions feed each other: categorization leads to the expectation of breach (sure to be found), and breach leads to categorization.

The identifications invoked by this categorization draw on the stereotypical images of the typical easterner, the Ossi, and typical westerner, the Wessi, as they have emerged in the context of unification and as they have been spread widely by the mass media. These images have a history, however, which is as old as the division of Germany. They are suffused with elements of Cold War rhetoric which in turn makes use of identifications between the respective other German and Germany's common Nazi past. West German political rhetoric, for example, has always constructed a dual, almost gnostic image of itself in relation to East Germany. The borderline between night and day was that between apparatchiks on the one side and the people on the other. The apparatchiks were painted as the villains who kept the people from being basically like any other (West) German. When east Germans, freed from the domination of the apparatchiks, turned out not to look like any other (West) German after all, it was an easy move to utilize the picture of the apparatchik to make sense of the difference. The categorizations also draw on interaction patterns between East and West which have developed in forty years of German-German relations, from sole-representation in the 1950s to "giver of presents" and "receiver of presents" relationships in the 1970s and to the organization of unification by simple accession of the former GDR to the FRG. These interaction patterns are invoked in everyday exchanges by identifications with states created through a web of tropes and narratives.

This "othering" of the other German, despite the fact that it is catgorical indeed, is not a radical othering in the same sense that Said's (1978) "orientalism" is. The other is not assigned an essential and thus timeless difference in the projected eternity of a moral universe, such that bridging the categories would be unthinkable without at the same time resurrecting the categorical boundaries with every incidence of interaction. The othering of east Germans by west Germans is a developmental one; it follows the pattern of a particular type of allochronization. West Germans place easterners into a space which is thought of as different, but only for the time being, while it is under massive reconstruction. Westerners place easterners into a time through which they themselves think they have long since passed, a time which they have left behind to advance to better shores. Thus, westerners spin a story of metamorphosis, a narrative of transformation which connects the two categories easterner and westerner with each other. In effect westerners propose a blueprint for easterners to use in maneuvering themselves from one category to the other so that the categorical distinction may fully disappear, thus eventually restoring the essential unity of all Germans.

This story of transformation as a blueprint for assimilation has a particular, very interesting twist. Often enough, westerners try to overcome in their relations with easterners the negatively evaluated pasts of Germany. What is called "processing the past" *(Vergangenheitsbewältigung),*[2] something west Germans have been asked to do with themselves, they perform now on east Germans. Processing the past is the prescription of liberal-minded Germans for coming to terms with Germany's Nazi past in general and with the Holocaust in particular, by squarely facing the facts and working through the troublesome emotions that are connected with them.[3] For West Germans this is not only a matter of taking responsibility for autocratic rule and the consequences of collaboration in an infinite number of suppressive measures, but much more generally a restaging of their own presumed transformation from bad to good. Yet, while they themselves felt treated as students of the Allied Powers in their own transformation, they feel now that they can play the teacher in the transformation of the easterners. The allochronization of easterners is a necessary first step in this restaging of self in the other.

This operation has many facets, and it pertains to a variety of pasts, but the most salient one is Germany's Nazi past.[4] Many western officers have commented on the militaristic makeup of the People's Police, and they have made it clear that they were glad that the (West) Berlin police

2. I have very deliberately chosen the psychotherapeutic term *processing* because it mirrors perhaps more closely than other possible translations (coming to terms with the past, or mastering the past (cf. Maier, 1988)) the use of the term *Vergangenheitsbewältigung,* which implies a conscious working-through of the past with the intention to free oneself from its negative, potentially destructive influence.

3. It is highly ironic that at a time when west Germans prescribe processing the past for east Germans, remembering the Nazi past remains a troubling experience for many Germans. This has been made sufficiently clear again by the sometimes pained reactions to Daniel Goldhagen's *Hitler's Willing Executioners* (New York: Knopf, 1996) as well as by similarly strong emotional reactions to an exhibition organized by the Hamburg Institute for Social Sciences (Institut für Sozialforschung) about the role of the Wehrmacht, the regular German army in World War II, in the mass murder of Jews.

4. For many liberals, another past to overcome is the Adenauer era, with its intellectual narrow-mindedness.

had more rigorously shed the militaristic origins of the police.[5] How widely spread this impression of a militaristic east amongst westerners actually was can perhaps be illustrated by how Helmut Kohl (1996), then chancellor, remembers his first contact with Egon Krenz, chair of the Council of Ministers of the GDR right after the opening of the Berlin Wall:

> The conversation ended on a bizarre note. The SED-Chief asked me how one should handle the press-communiqué about the phone call. I responded, "Simply say we had an intensive conversation." Krenz repeated militarily, "Intensive conversation conducted." When I added that he could also say that we would continue the conversation, if necessary, by phone, he answered, "Continue by phone."

It does not matter whether Kohl's memory about the phone call is correct. What is significant is that for one, Kohl portrays the most powerful man of the GDR at this time as a person used to thinking in terms of orders and obedience, a man with a quasi-militaristic demeanor. Of course, Kohl also makes Krenz into a recipient of his orders, thus establishing a hierarchy between him and the leader of the GDR, and by synecdochical extension between the FRG and the GDR, in effect living sole representation all over again. Here too, Kohl allochronizes the GDR. He finds militaristic demeanor, the famous Prussian heel-clicking, which has been used in so many caricatures of the ugly German all around the world, still characteristic of the eastern leadership. In recognizing and satirizing it, self is identified as having overcome this, while other is morally held accountable for overcoming it too.

The attempt to defeat the ugly German in the east German is even more explicit in the following account. One western officer diagnosed a readiness, especially of high-ranking eastern officers, to ingratiate themselves as a sure sign of lacking "male pride" (Männerstolz). Then he proceeded to liken this "ingratiation with a victorious power" to what he had seen after World War II, when Germans also tried to endear themselves to the victorious powers. He thus identifies the FRG with the Allied Powers after World War II, the powers which were to become the models for both new Germanies, which were incidentally also the powers that taught Germany how to transform itself into a better version of itself. He went on to say,

5. See "The Unification of the Berlin Police" in chapter 2, where I quote an officer who identifies the east as militaristic.

Wouldn't it have been better from the perspective of People's Police officers, wouldn't it have been so much more respectable—well, not to continue to praise socialism—but not to depreciate themselves so much. But they did. And this made me very reflective. I said to myself, "Allow yourself the question whether that is not an aspect of German mentality." I thought a French officer would not be able to do that. He just wouldn't do that, and neither would a British officer. I was very worried that this could be typically German.

What is present here is an uncertainty whether a negative self-evaluation of Germans, a category in which he as a person shares metonymically, has really been overcome to the extent that he would like to see it overcome. The vehemence with which he rejects the negatively identified easterners, spurred by self-doubt, leads to an intensified effort to overcome the ugly German in easterners.[6] Preaching to easterners the gospel of transformation is thus partly an attempt to come to terms with the specters of Germany's past.[7]

Westerners thus cast the present west, the already transformed part of Germany, as a model for the east, as a metaphor which easterners by their own volition are supposed to turn into a metonymy. Westerners generally assume that one-sided assimilation is wanted, and how could it not be, westerners reason: the path mapped out is one of improvement from dictatorship to democracy, from prison to freedom, from technological backwardness to the newest frontier, from modest wealth to riches. Westerners thus create a hierarchy which easterners must reject for its sheer presumption. Nevertheless, easterners become co-conspirators in

6. In psychodynamic terms one would have to analyze this pattern as a projective defense triggered by anxieties that self is what other is made into. Vaillant (1993, 46) says about projection, "In projection, subject is turned into object, and object into subject. Projection turns self-loathing into prejudice." Vaillant classifies projection as an "immature defense," stressing that the immature defenses are "irritating to others," that they have a particular capacity to poison human relationships.

7. There are many more examples of this effort by westerners to defeat the ugly German in the east German. Liberals find rampant illiberalism among former GDR citizens, finding in them again the illiberal, culturally stifling atmosphere not only of Germany's past in general but of the early years of the FRG in particular. The embarrassing attacks on foreigners everywhere in Germany are frequently discussed as a particular east German problem. East Germans are found to be lacking a cosmopolitan *savoir vivre*, a lack that many Germans think was an aspect of their own past which they hope to have overcome. In connection with the reintegration of many leading Nazi officials into the public service of the FRG, the treatment of the higher echelons of the civil service of the GDR is frequently commented upon by saying, "We shouldn't make the same mistake again."

the western scheme not only for a lack of alternative models which could be the source of effective counteridentifications, and not only because easterners and westerners are steeped in formally similar discursive structures on the merit of progress, but because the scheme of transformation laid out by westerners plays into easterners' own long-held desires.[8]

The way of transformation suggested by westerners is strewn with near paradoxes for easterners. On the one hand change is encouraged and wanted, and a disavowal of the GDR socialist state is expected, while at the same time rapid change and a wholesale avowal of the west by "turncoats" is mistrusted as insincere opportunism. Resistance to change is, on the other hand rejected as inability to learn from the past, which carries added moral weight not only because it is gauged as portraying an inability to differentiate between right and wrong, but also because it moves those unwilling to draw the lessons from history into the neighborhood of die-hard Nazis. The majority of easterners also reject the extremes of sudden change and stubborn resistance. Sudden change is understood as a betrayal of all that is good and worth preserving from the past; no change in contrast undermines the "then" and "now" narrative of many east Germans, which they use to motivate their own gradually shifting identifications by pointing to differences between what they knew in the past and what they know today. In this sense, both easterners and westerners seem to demand a credible narrative of change, a narrative which is *paced right* to preserve the integrity of character.

Until westerners are satisfied that assimilation is achieved, the categorization of the other has the effect that westerners typically do not accept easterners as partners in dialogue. Most westerners have no intention of learning from easterners, of engaging with them in such a way that they themselves might change in the course of the interaction. They are concerned that easterners might use them in some kind of scheme thought to be motivated by easterners' attempts to reestablish themselves, a move which is frequently suspected as a cover-up for a morally reprehensible past. Easterners fear in turn that westerners are only interested in getting rid of them to take leadership positions at easterners' expense. The relationship from the westerners' perspective is something like that between adults and children, where adults do not consult with their children on serious matters until they have grown up to become adults themselves. Thus the language about the respective other as well as the interactions

---

8. Easterners tend to mask their own materialism by projecting it onto westerners, whose own materialism then looks magnified.

with the other German are frequently caught up in highly standardized patterns which do not allow either side to individuate vis-à-vis each
other. The categorical identifications of Ossi and Wessi preempt the
possibility of understanding and appreciating the other as a distinct
personality.[9]

It is important to recall that dialogue and verbal interaction are not the
same. Dialogue (see Bakhtin 1981, 1984a; Gadamer 1993; Buber 1995) is
a very particular, rather difficult kind of human interaction. The main
aspects of dialogue—equality, trust, openness, readiness for the new and
unexplored—are rarely ever present in the interactions between easterners and westerners. What is missing so far is a mutual recognition of
easterners and westerners as different and equal (Todorov 1992). In their
identifications of the other, east and west Germans so far prefer de-indi-
viduating strategies such as allochronization and placement in conjunction with metonymic or synecdochical identifications of persons with
larger organizations, states, and social systems. This is coupled with an
attitude which I have called synecdochical mischief, the readiness to derogate the wholes once certain parts are found to be objectionable, and
amplified in its effect by what Herzfeld (1997) has called cultural intimacy. Through all these means of identification, the other is never fully
allowed to become a person; thus, it is not surprising that there are only
few east-west friendships. The situation is aggravated by the fact that
individuating self-identifications in performance are often not understood
across the former Iron Curtain, because the codes in terms of which they
take place are frequently not known to the observer from the respective
other side: thus jokes fall flat, or individuating differentiations (e.g., in
writing spaces or in work performance) go unrecognized because they
are overwhelmed by the perception of otherness of code (in contrast to
difference within one and the same code). This situation is changing
somewhat, however, as east Germans develop a facility with western
codes and learn to use them. Of course, as westerners will never care to
learn eastern codes, a privilege they have acquired through unification

9. It is not surprising that the preemption of individuation in the interaction between easterners and westerners sometimes bears a striking similarity with the
theoretical discourses on the "modern" and the "traditional" in the sense that easterners depict westerners as antisocial, individualistic, and ruthlessly egotistic, but also
as beyond meaning, as alienated—in short much as the theory of "modernity" sees
the "modern" human being. Westerners sometimes characterize easterners as collec-
tivistic, unable to care properly or speak for themselves, but also as more caring for
each other, thus replicating depictions of "traditional" societies.

by accession, easterners will always remain more foreign to them than westerners are to easterners.

One might have surmised that the rhetoric of a shared nationhood ostensibly subjugating any other categorization under that of nationhood itself by means of stipulating nationwide intimacy might have facilitated dialogue among east and west Germans. Yet, in the context of German unification, this means failed in the face of the everyday experience of difference. The appeal to nationhood has not proved a strong enough moral imperative for Germans in east and west to perceive each other as equals. At the same time, however, only the insinuation of a shared nationhood makes the pains of unification palatable at all, even if that sharing is conceived at times as little more than the company of guilt in the atrocities committed by Germans in the Nazi period and the common responsibility for the consequences of World War II. The appeal to nationhood has also prevented the construction of the other German as radically other. In sum, then, national rhetoric has received a highly ambiguous response. This also has a lucky side, I hasten to add, since the facilitation of dialogue based on the premises of romantic cultural nationalism all too frequently, and most notably in German history, has meant the denial of dialogue and individuation within the boundaries of the German nation as well as across national boundaries, however defined.

It has been pointed out repeatedly, in our time perhaps most forcefully by Habermas, that dialogue is at the very root of democracy. Democracy is not, as Cold War rhetoric might have made us believe, something a state has or has not, a structure achieved once and for all; it must rather be understood as an ongoing process that has to be made and remade, lived and relived. This process can benefit enormously from critical voices pointing to practices which are undemocratic, although frequently veiled by make-believe. It is sad for democracy in Germany that the critical voices, the critical questions of east Germans concerning, for example, the meaning of the freedom of speech in the workplace, are often simply brushed aside in a rather self-righteous fashion. For the most part westerners see easterners' criticisms of the western "liberal democratic order" (*freiheitlich-demokratische Grundordnung*) as the senseless ruminations of the not-yet-properly initiated, especially if easterners raise rather unfashionable concerns about the reconciliation between a capitalist economy and a democratic polity. Here a chance has been missed to help to reinvigorate a debate about the roles of the state, of parties, the media, and the economy in a democratic process (cf. Verdery, 1996, 10ff.).

On the Continuity and Consistency of Selves

Postmodern theorists of the non-self (e.g., Baudrillard 1990; Jameson 1991; Gergen 1991) argue that human beings are always completely absorbed in the social contexts in which they find themselves in any particular instant. Thus, non-self theorists discard the self by denying it *any* transcendence from one social context to the next, from one time period to another.[10] The theory of the non-self therefore moves far beyond a mere fragmentation of the self, which has been described in one way or another in modernist theories from Marx to Freud, from Weber to Sartre, who all analyze various forms of breaks, tensions, and inconsistencies in the self while preserving some form of unity.[11] When modernists talk about fragmentation, it is in recognition of a complete form. Their idea of fragmentation is that of a discernible, if not always beautiful vase that has gone to pieces, while they may (e.g., Freud, Marx, Heidegger) or may not (e.g., Weber) think that they know the glue that can put the pieces together again. When postmodern theorists of the non-self write about fragmentation, they invoke the image of an arbitrary mix of pieces, of a collage, that never had a unity beyond its haphazard contiguity and never will. While modernists recognize an origin, an anchor, or a goal of the self, postmodern non-self theorists ridicule thinking in terms of either.

Like much of social theory, the postmodern theory of non-self is given descriptive and prescriptive readings. On the basis of my field observations, I maintain that as a description of social reality, the postmodern theory of non-self is of little help in making sense of the life circumstances, problems, and joys of eastern and western police officers in the city of Berlin, a city that has been described by some authors as "the ultimate postmodern space" (Borneman 1992, 1). If postmodern non-self theorists were right in their description of present-day selves, east Germans would have few problems in moving from one social system to another, and likewise west Germans would have no second thoughts about accepting

10. I will continue to use the word *transcendence* in this reduced sense, a sense which might be called transcendence with a small *t*. I clearly do not want to speak about the possibility of the Transcendence of the self. Transcendence with a capital *T* may pertain, for example, in a religious sense to an immortal soul, or in the sense of Enlightenment philosophy, it may pertain to a universal and timeless principle of reason. In short, transcendence with a capital *T* pertains to the relation of selves to a metaphysical substance.

11. It is therefore somewhat bewildering to find authors who identify themselves as postmodern, such as Kondo (1990) or Battaglia (1990), writing as if they had to defeat Descartes's *cogito!*

them. As a matter of fact, transition and acceptance would not even be an issue for either west Germans or east Germans, who would both easily and without friction move into new contexts of interaction, of which they would then be simply a function. Nevertheless, postmodern theorizing on the non-self is helpful as a polemic against easy assumptions about self-transcendence. Through the polemic it becomes more urgent to analyze the problem of transcendence empirically.

The drama of unification has indeed produced something like a character without a transcendent self: the turncoat.[12] Yet, while turncoats are talked about a lot, they seem to be hard to come by in reality, which is not surprising since they are the most despised characters on the scene. Turncoats are evaluated negatively because the officers feel that they cannot be trusted, and trusted they cannot be precisely because their selves are cast as non-transcendent. Trust is an impossibility without *some* transcendence of self (Ricoeur 1992, 123 ff.).[13] I found the most salient value that officers employed in their moral judgments to be sincerity. The officers try to assure themselves of the sincerity of a person by checking for transcendence from one social situation to the next and from one period of time to another. Sincerity is meaningless without transcendence; commitment, the anchor of east German thinking on the ethics of work is basically a precept requiring transcendence. The pains experienced by eastern officers at the demise of the GDR were at least in part also caused by the insincerity of this state towards them, by the state's apparent duplicity, that is, the state's non-transcendence between public speeches and secret actions. They were further exacerbated by the question of what sincerity might possibly mean for their own behavior in the wake of the revolutionary changes they had experienced.

After the radical break in their lives in 1989, east Germans did not simply bid farewell to their history. They continued to understand themselves as products of their biographies, and to make sense of their lives in the present, they felt that they needed to salvage something from that past, all the more so because the uncertainties of the future had increased sharply. The debates that go on between east Germans and west Germans about the quality of the GDR, about the preservation or destruction of monuments from GDR times, about the naming and re-naming of streets

12. See the section on turncoats in chapter 6.

13. Any theory denying any transcendence to self must ultimately account for stability by pointing to structures outside of human consciousness. In this sense postmodern theories of the non-self are, in their denial of self-transcendence, the ultimate form of structuralism.

and squares are all in part a fight over legitimate memories, about ways
to integrate life experiences into a whole. East Germans try to spin continuities by pointing to similarities in their present lives and in their past
lives, and by reinterpreting past and present in new lights. All this attests
to the fact that east Germans are looking actively for ways to transcend
their selves in time. The destruction of continuities, on the other hand,
which have been taken for granted, are often experienced as painful, as
in the disruption of career trajectories, or in the effects of the wedge unification has frequently driven into their sense of what I have called social
time.[14] And finally, nothing seems to attest more to the desired unity of
work and leisure as a complementary relationship than the widespread
fear of unemployment; nothing attests more to the interdependence, the
unity of self at work and self at leisure, than the disheartening experience
of protracted idleness some east Germans have had to go through. In sum
then, east Germans do indeed conceive of their selves as wholes, and not
as independent, uncoupled parts, or as happenstance baskets of roles.
And so do west Germans who hold east Germans responsible for what
has happened in the GDR, being obsessed at the same time with the idea
that Germany after unification is little more than the old Federal Republic
with a new appendix, with the idea that their lives have remained on the
same trajectory. It is their insistence on a particular kind of transcendence
that has urged them to resist even mild suggestions of change.[15]

The question that thus arises is what precisely transcendence means
to the police officers and how it is produced. Self-transcendence seems
to have two main dimensions: the first one concerns the relationship of
self within different social situations, in different roles, and with different
partners of interactions; this is what may be called the "consistency of
self." The other dimension concerns the connection of self to itself at
different moments in time; this may be called the "continuity of self."
None of the officers I got to know think that continuity and consistency
imply perfect sameness of self, a sameness understood as the definitional
or analytic equivalence of two sides of a mathematical equation. Quite
to the contrary, consistency and continuity seem to imply difference of
sorts.

The very notion of social time implies a development of a person. In
this sense persons are understood as characters. Social time associates not
only career steps and physical time, but also forms of behavior, demeanor, dress, and so on, etc. with physical time. One day, I witnessed

14. See chapter 4.
15. See especially chapter 2.

an interesting conversation between a commissioned officer and a patrol-
man. The older one went out of his way to convince the younger one
that he should indeed attend the police college (he had just been admitted
to sit for the entrance exams), to launch himself into the career of a commissioned officer. The younger one was not sure he really wanted to become a commissioned officer. He was afraid that assuming a commanding role would also imply more bureaucratic work, which would lead
him away from the excitement of the streets, which he described in vivid
colors, indicating the satisfaction he derived from his work as a patrol-
man. Then the older one said, "You don't want to just receive orders all
your life long. That is fine now, but it doesn't feel good anymore when
you are fifty." What the older officer insinuated in beseeching the younger
one to move ahead with his career was that in order to stay identical with
himself, to continue to like his work as a policeman as he does now, he
would have to change, because by sheer age progression his realtive position in the police organization would change somehow.

The same notion of identity in difference is at play in the consistency
checks that officers undertake to ascertain sincerity. Nobody assumes that
a particular officer speaks quite in the same tone to a superior as she
would speak to a peer; people expect each other to act differently at work
and at a social occasion, over a glass of beer in a pub, and they even
consider it fine that people behave differently depending on who participates in the social. I heard, for example, a debate over whether the presence of spouses was desirable on a common hiking day. The arguments
on both sides were made according to the difference in the way people
could behave or would behave. One officer said that she preferred spouses
to stay home because everything would be "more relaxed." Another preferred the spouses to attend because it would be "more of an occasion."
Here too a sameness in difference is implied.

Yet, the difference from time to time, from situation to situation, is
not fully open. There are limits to what difference is still acceptable. Turncoats have overstepped these limits; they are regarded as neither consistent nor as continuous; at best they are considered consistent in their
inconsistency and discontinuity. So what then constitutes acceptable variance and what does not? How is transcendence in difference conceived?
One can begin to answer this question by looking at the ways in which
these differences in transcendence are talked about in everyday interaction. Any *accounts* of difference, as well as the *moral evaluation* of difference in behavior are instances which shed light on the construction of
transcendence. For the police officers the necessary condition of accept-

able variance seems to be that it can be explained at all, that it can be accounted for. Unaccountable difference is perceived as a case of insanity. The sufficient condition for the assertion of transcendence in difference seems to be a certain regularity in these accounts of difference. It is the very regularity in the accounts of difference, their predictability, which are implied in the notion of character. Moreover, certain of these accounts of difference, including their regularity, find approval in moral evaluation, and others do not.

If eastern officers are asked whether they themselves think that they have changed after unification, they most frequently answer that they have not, that they are still the same. Yet their life-narratives are full of changing identifications, they are shifting back and forth between a "now" and a "then," and in the sense that I have defined identity in chapter 1, their identity has changed indeed. Thus, they are the same and yet different. However, they think that they can explain their changing identifications. "If I had known then what I know today," begins one officer's explanation why he is no longer a socialist. "Today I am more knowledgeable," summarizes another officer in her explanation of why she no longer wants the reinstitution of the GDR, in spite of the fact that she had strongly identified with the state she called home. Thus, differences in knowledge seem to be one of the factors in the relationship between officers and their environment which are accepted to account for change while preserving transcendence.

The various possible accounts of difference in continuity and consistency draw on an immense stock of cultural forms, which I cannot even begin to outline here. Difference in knowledge is just one such form widely used by east Germans in the context of German unification; notions of sincerity, commitment, and social time are others. The degree to which they are convincing is a matter of agreement in judgment (Wittgenstein 1984, §§241–42), a matter of acceptability within an interpretative community (Fish 1980). Selves are, then, as transcedent as they can be made by convincing stories connecting self at different points in time and across different situations (cf. Linde 1993). It is the acceptable account of differences in behavior from situation to situation and the believable narrative of transformation from time to time which makes selves transcendent.

This is precisely the point where the notion of a postmodern non-self as a normative or political concept becomes relevant again. It is possible to use this theory in an attempt to undermine forms that account for the transcendence of selves. It must be kept in mind that transcendence as such is by no means to be equated with the moral good, although many forms of morality are contingent on a notion of transcendence of the self. The assertion of morality and immorality may for this very reason imply transcendence of moral approval or disapproval of a character. And in this way transcendence can be used as a powerful tool of moral stigmatization, as western German officers have shown time and again in their exchanges with easterners. Thus undermining the notion of transcendence from the perspective of a postmodern theory of the non-self may very well reap liberating effects. As a totalizing scheme, however, the theory of the non-self has grave consequences. As a thought experiment, a world of completely non-transcendent selves is imaginable. Yet the world of these postmodern non-selves would be very different from the world of the police officers I got to know. It would be a world without promises, responsibilities, commitments, oaths, sincerity, or narrative biographies in the traditional sense. Of course it would also be a world devoid of anxiety about an uncertain future, of guilt, shame, desire, wishes, and dreams. It would be a world devoid of consciousness, a world devoid of memory, a world devoid of culture. It would be a world no longer recognizable as human. Transcendence is therefore not something that should be assumed or rejected, but it needs to be empirically investigated.

From Identifications to Identity

In the previous chapters I have made extensive use of the concept of identification. I have shown how eastern and western officers attribute meanings to selves by contextualizing them within the world. For the Berlin and Potsdam officers, I have shown especially how they identify themselves and others with buildings and places, with notions of time, their own biographies, and German history; with the states they live in, the organizations they work in; with particular attitudes to work, work practices, and skills; with moral goodness; and finally with different ways of viewing the world. I have demonstrated as well that these identifications are cast in different modes that can be analyzed as following fundamental cognitive schemata in the form of metonymies, synecdoches, metaphors, and other important tropes. I have argued that such an analysis reveals the specific qualities of identifications affecting the dynamics of the interaction in which these identifications are placed. By using the concept of narrative, I have pointed out how identifications can be made temporal, and how selves can change from context to context as well as across time while remaining identical. What I have not discussed yet at all is how a myriad of identifications can add up to something like an identity.

As the exchanges of identifications and counteridentifications between east and west Germans reveal, processes of identity construction are eminently social. Mead (1962) describes the emergence of consciousness and reflexivity, that is the emergence of a self, and also the development of the personality of a self as processes of internalizing the attitude of others toward a self. Unfortunately, Mead offers little concrete help in analyzing the precise path of the dialectic between self and others in identity formation processes.[16] Erikson (1986) emphasizes the role of others, especially of caregivers, in the formation of identity in the more or less successful resolution of a series of ontogenetic crises spanning the life cycle from early infancy to old age. While I have advocated here a much more continuous approach to studying identity-formation processes independent of but compatible with ontogenetic models, Erikson's insistence on the importance of relevant others (who can be peers or colleagues too)[17] in their identification of self, especially in times of identity crisis, is quite pertinent to the encounter between eastern and western officers. To develop an understanding of how the dialectic between self and others might unfold in identity-formation processes characterized by an exchange of identifications, I found Wittgenstein's (1984, §§179–242) deliberations about what it means to follow a rule and his result, the rejection of the possibility of a private language, especially useful.[18] The gist of Wittgenstein's argument is this: Every course of past behavior is compatible with an infinite number of possible rules, and there is no good reason, no criterion by which to choose one of these rules over the other as more likely. Thus he concludes, "Therefore, 'to follow a rule' is a practice. And to *believe* one is following the rule is not the same as following the rule. And

16. Mead (1962) also remains somewhat ambiguous about the kind and degree of the input of the self into this dialectic. While the third part of the book offers a picture of personality as almost completely socially determined, he envisions in the fourth part of his book a larger, more creative part for the self. These tensions may very well be due to the nature of "Mind, Self and Society" as a compilation of lecture notes (cf. Joas 1985).

17. The role of peers, colleagues, and superiors becomes particularly apparent in Erikson's (1962) discussion of the formation of Martin Luther upon entering the Augustinian Order.

18. The importance of this central insight of Wittgenstein's later philosophy for the social sciences cannot be overstated. In fact, I believe that this is the very core of the sociality of human beings. Unfortunately, I cannot develop this argument here in extenso. For a brilliant discussion of the private-language argument from a philosophical perspective, see Kripke (1982).

therefore it is impossible to follow the rule privately, because otherwise to believe one is following a rule would be the same as following the rule" (1984, §202; my translation). Following a rule is therefore embedded in what Wittgenstein calls a "lifeform," which is basically a community of interpretation (cf. Fish 1980). In other words, stability or regularity can only be constituted by asserted agreement of a human community. Any process of meaning making is therefore ultimately dependent on its grounding in sustained forms of human interaction. To hold on to an identification of self or of other is very much like following a rule. Identifications can therefore only be stabilized in collaboration with others who need to confirm the identification.[19] If one officer self-identifies as "having a strong sense of duty," she cannot hold onto this self-identification in the absence of the reconfirmation of others: "Yes, we all know, you have a strong sense of duty." She will be able to stand up against some destabilizing counteridentifications, for example, "At heart you are flighty and negligent," but only if she has others who back her up and tell her so. The stabilization of an identification is, therefore, labor in a communal vineyard.

The identity-formation process can then, perhaps, be pictured as follows. A person gets identified by another person in a particular way: let us say she has been called "able." She finds this identification flattering and thus uses it a little later in a narrative to her best friend, who starts to support the identification by repeating it. A little later this person is confronted with a task which is a little out of the ordinary, and she handles the situation well. As she drives home, she hears the identification "able" again and finds herself reconfirmed. Henceforth, she might be encouraged to volunteer for tasks which require extra skills and also give an opportunity to prove ability and to get reconfirmed by self and by others. If she has not heard the identification in a while, she will have to find out whether it still is true. Identity formation is, therefore, a ping-pong of identifications between self and other. The stability of an identification is produced in human interaction, but so is its destruction.

Maybe, by borrowing another great Wittgensteinian metaphor, I can

---

19. Of course, the awareness of the importance of others in confirming self-identifications as "recognition" or "validation" goes back to Rousseau, Herder, and Hegel (Taylor, 1989) with present-day reverberations into social psychology (Weigert et al. 1986) and the debates about multiculturalism (e.g., Taylor 1994). What Wittgenstein (1984) adds to this discourse with his private-language argument (with Mead [1962] as a less pronounced precursor) is a radical rooting of the social dialectic of identity formation in the very possibility of meaning creation.

illuminate now what I mean by identity. Wittgenstein (1984, §18) likens language/life forms/cultures to a city: "You can look at our language as a city: a maze of alleys and squares, old houses and new, and houses with extensions from different times; and all this is surrounded by many newer suburbs with straight and rectangular streets and uniform houses" (my translation). In a similar fashion, identity as our language of ourselves embedded in the language of a community can be likened to a house. It is the house in which we live (Heidegger 1947). We take part in its construction, but by no means are we the sovereign architects of it. Willy-nilly, identity-house-building is a collaborative effort in which many persons and institutions participate, not all invited, and those who work on it often do so in an uncoordinated fashion. Identifications are the bricks of which this house is built, and the reconfirmations are the mortar, which makes them stick, which holds everything together. It takes many bricks to build a room, and thus many rooms have been begun without ever reaching the state of completion. Some of these rooms have been patched up quickly, others have been built solidly in the course of years. The house may have a plentitude of rooms or just a few. And all these rooms are of a different kind, some are little more than chambers, others serve as grand reception halls; some are at the center of the house, frequently visited, while others linger at the periphery and are used only once in a while. As everything is given to decay by nature, this house always requires maintenance work to keep its rooms livable. Broken bricks need to be replaced with new ones, and mortar needs to be refilled. Some rooms, for want of care, may fall to ruin; others may be added, here and there, and so the house grows and falls apart. And as long as human beings live, the smell of mortar and new bricks will never leave the house. Identity is nothing other than the state of this construction site, this house, at any one point in time.

Culture, Identity, and Understanding

The embeddedness of identity formation in social interaction suggests a close relationship between identity and culture. Selves cannot be identified with everything and in every way. In the most fundamental sense, for the identification of a self with a particular aspect of the world to be even thinkable, a community of interpretation needs to recognize not only the existence of a self, but also the existence of the aspect of the world with which the self is supposed to be identified. Yet, the ontological grid of an interpretative community is only a necessary condition, and by no means sufficient to make an identification possible. The connection itself needs to be deemed meaningful. The eastern officer who suddenly, after the breakdown of the GDR, discovered an interest in the landscape of churches in and around the city in which he lived and who started to identify with these churches as tangible remains of his history is a good case in point. "Church" as a particular kind of building with certain functions was of course a part of the ontology of the interpretative community in which he lived, but apparently nobody in his circle had the idea of either connecting him or themselves with the churches in town. The churches seem not to have been relevant objects for identifications of this group of police officers (at least until they spelled trouble for some of them in the tumultuous late summer of 1989).

Although the officer who found a new pastime in visiting churches insisted that he had "never even dreamt of looking at churches in the GDR," thus denying the very possibility of an interest in church buildings, another interpretation might be possible too. For it is of course by no means surprising to find that in the GDR especially police officers would not want to identify themselves (or find themselves identified by others) with anything reminiscent of churches as institutions. To the degree that the churches as institutions could not be overlooked altogether, they were identified as "antistate" and "antisocialist," and thus they were (at least officially) negatively evaluated identification targets for police officers who had vowed to protect the state and to advance socialism. This negative evaluation of the churches as institutions might, by synecdochical extension, well have pertained to church buildings as well, especially since they were regularly open for religious services only. Therefore, besides the ontology and the set of possibly meaningful connections implied in a particular worldview, publicly accepted or even favored linkages between objects, persons, and institutions on the one hand and moral and aesthetic values on the other hand, provide a background grid against which any particular identification acquires its distinct meaning.

The possible (or meaningful) range of identifications is also highly contingent on the definition of a particular situation. While recording an accident, it is meaningful to identify an officer as tactful or rude, as a skilled observer, or a bad draftsman of sketches, but it would be completely out of place to identify him then as a good ping-pong player. The exception is, of course, if the interpretative community in which both interlocutors maneuver would recognize the possibility of making inferences between seemingly unrelated types of social situations by classifying both of them, for example, as potentially involving physical movements of a particular kind. Thus, a connection between "playing ping-pong" and "recording and accident" might be made in such a way as to consider a particular movement of the officer's hands or a particular posture as a sign which would betray his natural aptitude for or even skill at this sport. Yet, even if this is the case, the officer identified as a possible ping-pong player would in all likelihood demand an explanation for this identification, and his acceptance of the explanation as reasonable would typically depend on the existence of a cultural form in at least one of the communities of interpretation in which he partakes.

In the previous section I began to discuss ways in which selves can be made transcendent, that is, consistent between situations and continuous across time. I have concluded, then, that transcendence is produced by recourse to symbolic forms which are embedded in interpretative communities or cultures. These forms are types or genres of narratives which provide a credible story explaining why a particular officer acts differently from one social context to another, in conversations with his wife, friends, colleagues, and superiors, and how he is still the same even if he preferred "outside" to "inside" work at twenty-five, while the relationship is actually the reverse at age fifty. What passes for an acceptable account of differences in transcendence at one time and place within one particular interpretative community may not pass for such in another. Accordingly, it can be expected that the way in which transcendence is produced changes over time with the kind and availability of transcendence-producing narrative patterns and the types of situations for which they are deemed relevant.

Beyond ontologies, conventional understandings of the range of possible identifications, typefications of situations, and a repertoire of admissible narratives of change in transcendence, there is one particular aspect of cultures which is especially important for identity-formation processes. Cultures seem to designate genres of interaction in which human beings can distinguish themselves from their fellow human beings, in which they can acquire a distinct personality. Any genre of interaction recognized within an interpretative community as allowing for style or skill, thus providing for a poetics of action, is such an area of distinction in which human beings can individuate within this community. Police officers become known for their style of talking with citizens, for their skill at finding stolen cars, for their handling of superiors or subordinates, for the ways in which they wear their uniforms. Their personalities are shaped and acknowledged within these genres of interaction.

If this is the case, then police officers can only recognize the personalities of their colleagues if they are familiar with the interaction genres which are, through their poetics, designated as offering possibilities for personality development. To recognize skill or style, one has to have a sense of the alternative possibilities for action; then one can appreciate the specific selection and combination a particular officer has realized. In other words, another person can only be perceived as a personality on the basis of some familiarity with the interaction genres and their poetics. A person who is unaware of the poetics of an interaction genre is bound to perceive all practitioners of this interaction genre as similar, as unindividuated; in other words they will seem to be an undifferentiated, homogeneous mass. Throughout this book I have pointed to differences in the poetics of the interaction genres in which east and west German officers have individuated. Easterners and westerners had, for example, very different means at their disposal to inscribe themselves in the spaces which they controlled; the ways in which they could demonstrate commitment to work made use of diametrically opposed understandings of time; the very different organization of patrol services involved a significantly different path for developing a patrol-officer personality. It is therefore not surprising at all if the officers perceived each other at the beginning of their initially hesitant collaboration as rather homogeneous blocs of others.

In cultures in which the perception of personality is often perceived as the reason to initiate friendship, and in which friendship is in turn the preferred place of dialogue, an unhappy dynamic may unfold in relation to members of other cultures or interpretative communities. Friendship is not initiated because the other is not seen as a personality; thus dialogue, which would be the only way to understand the personality of the other, is not even begun, and the interlocutors remain strangers. This is a classic vicious circle, which can only be overcome by a strong countervailing force such as a positive valuation of anything other or different as worthwhile exploring, investing difference with "watchful, waiting" curiosity.[20] East and west Germans were at least in part caught up in this vicious circle. If this circle is breaking, then it is not because easterners and westerners are terribly curious about each other, but because easterners are forced to participate in westerners' interaction genres and to learn and adopt the poetics underpinning their way of life. Easterners become personalities to westerners to the degree that they adopt western interaction poetics, and westerners become personalities to easterners as they

20. To use Anna Freud's congenial phrase for the suspension of judgment and classification one more time (see note 26 in chapter 7).

learn western ways of decorating, of communicating work ethics, and of being excellent at patrolling. Once, more, the burden of learning and adjustment is squarely put on the shoulders of easterners.

Divided in Unity: For How Long?

Germans are worried about the "walls in the heads of people" that seem to have replaced the Berlin Wall. This study attests to the depth of the division of Germans in east and west by studying the example of the Berlin Police. Politicians are right to worry about a longer-lasting cleavage of German society along geographical lines.[21] Yet, one must remember that the perception of the depth of the divide is judged from the assumption of an essential unity. The notion of a shared nationhood with its stipulated metonymic sameness in synecdochical integration into a superindividual whole, which was the basis for rapid unification by accession, provided a counterproductive frame of reference. Had east Germans been assumed to be of a different nation, had unification not at the same time thrust east Germans into a competitive situation with west Germans, the perception of similarities might have overshadowed the differences. Yet the fact remains that the perception of difference is strong, the gap seen between the two parts remains wide. So will this gap narrow, or will it remain open for a long period of time? Will there be such a thing as a separate east German identity?

An answer to this question must remain hypothetical. What follows is based on a very simple movement of thought: Given the validity of the theory of identity construction I have outlined in this study, what preconditions must be fulfilled to make a separate, effective, relatively stable east German identity viable? Two sets of issues must be raised: following the building metaphor I have developed here, these two issues may be called the "issue of the bricks" (i.e., there must be a will to identify as well as something to identify with), and there is what might be called the "issue of mortar" (i.e., there must be a social arrangement of some kind to reconfirm the identifications made).

21. Such a cleavage would be especially damaging if this geographical line were coextensive with a considerable gap in wealth and income. In this context it is frequently feared that Germany might develop a problem akin to Italy's division into a wealthy north and a much poorer south. I have no authority to speak on the prospects of the east German economy. What I will consider is exclusively the emergence of an east German identity (which is of course related to the question of lasting, perceptible wealth differentials).

With regard to the first issue, there must be a set of identifications (a set of various types of bricks) which can jointly be labeled "east German." All the bricks in the set must bear family resemblances (Wittgenstein 1984 §67) with each other, so that a connection between all of them remains visible. A sizable number of east Germans must then be willing to draw on this set in order to construct their house of identity. Nobody has to draw on the entire set, but everybody must draw on some subsection of the set. I say that what east Germans build with these bricks should be pillars and beams, because what is interesting in the political debate is not so much some rather unimportant aspect of east German identity, but a central aspect of it, something east Germans would act upon.[22] Thus, these identifications would organize and sustain other less important identifications, which would crumble if the pillars were not in place.

At the moment it is hard to see how such a set of possible identifications should be composed from what might be called "the heritage of the GDR." Among east Germans, most aspects of the former GDR are not only strongly disputed, but many of them are seen also in a very ambiguous light. One aspect of the former GDR that is constantly seen as superior to the situation in the FRG is the higher degree of solidarity in GDR society. Yet, if this solidarity is discussed a little bit more concretely, it erodes quickly as a basis of identification. A good example for this ambiguity is the institution of house-communities. They did indeed provide a forum for mutual help and enjoyable common activities, but they were also an instrument of control; they were fertile ground for Stasi surveillance. In discussions among each other (i.e., not with westerners) easterners very quickly point out these ambiguities.

Identifications with the GDR heritage are further undermined by the fact that most east Germans are better off today in material terms than they used to be in the GDR. Thus, the FRG has made it possible for east Germans to fulfill long-held desires for an improved material life. Needless to say, east Germans enjoy their new-found wealth, which creates in the possibility-space that it opens a host of novel identifications. As one officer put it, it has even significantly changed his outlook on life:

22. In this sense the nostalgia easterners exhibit for former GDR products or their enthusiasm for revived GDR brands may very well initially have been little more than a preference for an acquired taste. The wholesale dismissal of western values that westerners sometimes want to read into it, their incessant complaints about these forms of "Ost-Nostalgie," or "Ostalgie" for short, may very well be instances of synecdochical mischief, which only produce in reaction what they diagnose to begin with: the political significance of consuming eastern brands.

> If one goes on holiday today, one feels that one can achieve something with the D-Mark. I have just been to Malta and Tunisia; all of a sudden the goals one has in life are changing. . . . One didn't even think of these possibilities before, because they were impossibilities then. . . . All the measures have changed: TV, videos, computers, the whole thinking is different about what one can do with the D-Mark in the world. If I go to Poland today, then I can do something with my money. I see that it constitutes value, and that I therefore constitute value as well, a bigger value than I have had before.

Identifications of this kind would be even more prevalent and less ambiguous or less guilt-laden, if unemployment was not such a stifling and persistent problem in east Germany. Unemployment has to a certain extent split the GDR population into beneficiaries of unification, that is, all those who have work and more wealth, even if the social prestige of their work has declined (which many experience as a profound paradox), and those who do not have work and whose income has stagnated. Many eastern officers point out that one reason why the former house-communities have broken apart, why there is no longer a sense of solidarity among many east Germans, is that different people have done differently well in the context of unification. Income differentials have widened significantly, and with these differences envy, the suspicion of envy, and perhaps even some guilt have started to burden the relationships between neighbors. As one officer said about the house in which he lives, "Before, we all chatted a great deal with each other. Today we just greet each other and pass. You never know—does this guy still have work or does he not? It is just not so easy anymore to chat."

As much as the new-found wealth has undermined identifications with the GDR, the relationship between east Germans and west Germans in general, and the treatment of east Germans by the FRG state in particular has created identifications with the former GDR. Not surprisingly, it is the experience of the west as different, as alien or as hostile, which since unification has been by far the greatest source of identifications of east Germans as east Germans. The experience of the west is, therefore, also the most significant basis of east German identifications with each other. Ironically, it may be said that unification by accession gives east Germans, in their blatant disenfranchisement, a sense of togetherness. Ironically, unification by accession with its wholesale rejection of everything GDR has created a rationale for an east German politics of identity. In this sense, the radical elimination of the GDR has resurrected it to a certain extent. All policies which represent further attempts of westerners to overcome the GDR, to defeat it once more, such as the totally misguided attempts of conservative Christian Democrats to outlaw the PDS, to treat the reformed communists as the lepers of the political parties, and to trick them out of the seats they have in the Bundestag, are prone to lead east Germans to identify explicitly as east Germans.

With regard to the second issue, in order to assume the role of pillars, there must also be a source of continuous reconfirmation for these identifications whatever their source; something must provide the mortar to keep these special east German bricks together. This brings the issue of the political organization of identification to the fore again. The question arises of who or what could provide that mortar on a regular basis. In principle this can only be done by some form of institutionalization, for which there are basically two alternatives. On the one hand, the reconfirmation of a basic east German identification may be provided by the state FRG. The entire political organization of German unification and the differential treatment of east Germans in terms of pay have done much to create institutionalized reconfirmation of a GDR-identification among east Germans. On the other hand, reconfirmation could also be provided by some form of east German political organization, a party, let's say, that does what some fear the reformed socialist party, PDS, may do—become a protest movement for the concerns of east Germans. Even more effective would be a conjunction of both, a reconfirmation of an east German identification by the state and a successful political protest movement. The PDS has become a viable force in the political scene of east Germany. It is represented in all state parliaments; in the state of Saxony-Anhalt, a minority government of Social Democrats is dependent on the toleration of the PDS, and in the state of Mecklenburg-Vorpommern the PDS is junior partner in a coalition government with the Social Democrats. Yet, the PDS itself is bedeviled by strong internal factionalism. The party is torn between the neo-Stalinism of the communist platform and the social democratic outlook of its current leadership. In part due to these internal inconsistencies, the PDS is much more effective as a force in local politics, and it has not been able to formulate a vision for east Germany as a whole, which would have found wider support.

In sum, then, the historical heritage of the GDR is far too conflicted a source of identification for east Germans to build a basis for the formation of an eastern German identity. The crucial factor will be the political attitude of the FRG state toward the east, its willingness to continue with reconstruction efforts in the east, and its treatment of east Germans. In this respect, the established political parties have to play an integrative role, which they have not been able to do as thoroughly as they should have. This is mostly due to strong western reservations about the former GDR, and their difficulty in accepting east Germans as equal partners. One small first step toward such an acceptance could be to elect an east German to the office of Federal President.[23] For the elections in 1994 and in the preparation for the elections of 1999, both large parties, but especially the Social Democrats, have failed to pursue the option of an eastern candidate seriously enough. The unwillingness to listen to people from the former GDR has so far prevented a positive public discourse on how the history of the GDR can be integrated into the history of the FRG above and beyond outright rejection. A plethora of narratives of integration must be found, ranging from personal to local and national histories, which grant a visible place to the GDR without smoothing over the violence of forty years of authoritarian rule but also without degenerating into unqualified praise for the western part of the country. However, such narratives, difficult as they are to weave against the temptations of synecdochical mischief and the instincts of cultural intimacy, are rarely even attempted. What remains much more typical, especially in official tales, is an attempt to delete the GDR from any narrative about the past, present, and future of the country and its institutions. Again, the Berlin Police may serve as an example. In 1998 the Berlin Police issued a commemorative volume on one hundred and fifty years of uniformed police in the city (Der Polizeipräsident in Berlin 1998). While the volume covers

23. While in 1993 Chancellor Kohl sensed the symbolic desirability of an east German Federal President, his candidate of choice, Saxony's Minister of Justice Steffen Heitmann, who would have been assured a majority in the Federal Electoral Assembly, had to be dropped after he had issued long series of highly controversial, ultraconservative statements. Instead of producing a more conciliatory easterner, the Christian Democrats went into the 1994 elections with the western president of the Federal Constitutional Court, Roman Herzog, as their candidate. The Social Democrats, driven by old, western-style party jockeying about positions, failed to produce an eastern candidate and missed out on a chance to support Jens Reich, a leading member of the GDR civil rights movement, even though their own candidate stood no chance then to win, and together with the Greens, who backed Reich, might have stood a slight chance. For the 1999 elections, the Social Democrats, this time in a strong position to assure a majority for their candidate, renominated their 1994 candidate, the former North-Rhine-Westfalian prime minister Johannes Rau. The Christian Democrats, knowing that their candidate stands no chance to win in 1999, have nominated the completely unknown Thuringian physicist Dagmar Schipanski in an effort to snatch stray votes from disgruntled easterners and women among Social Democrats and Greens.

the West Berlin developments, tracing them back through Nazi, Weimar, Imperial, and Royal Berlin, it failed to include a chapter on the People's Police, thus effacing 40 years of the most recent East Berlin police history. And it is precisely in this context of integrating the GDR symbolically into the history of Germany as a whole that debates such as the one about the preservation or destruction of the former parliament building of the GDR, the *Palast der Republik,* must be seen. The closure of the political unification process and the confrontations it has created have to be overcome now by an openness of interaction which should be easier for the western side to initiate. The relative ease of political unification through accession has to be counterbalanced now by a sophisticated politics of east-west integration which is acutely aware of the effects of symbolic choices.

Of course, one could also wait for the generations to come, those not entangled in four decades of German-German politics, to heal the divisions created by unification. Asked whether an east-west confrontation would be important in the freshmen classes of the Berlin police school, one seventeen-year-old eastern policewoman in training said, "No, not at all. I think we are even more easterners than westerners, but I am not even sure. If they [the westerners] would say something stupid, we'd just tell them to get lost." As forty years of life in different institutional arrangements, of participation in different discourses have created markedly different east and west German styles of thinking and acting, participating in the same discourse and the same institutional arrangements can slowly erode these differences. This presupposes, of course, that the situation of easterners and westerners within these institutional arrangements and discourses is equal, characterized by partnership. This also means that east Germans must feel that they shape these institutions and discourses at least as much as westerners do. This is especially true if the hope for overcoming the German east-west division is placed on the younger generation. Starkly different rates of youth unemployment in east and west, visibly different chances to find an apprenticeship in the two parts of Germany, and vastly different opportunities to pursue particular interests or hobbies with like-minded people are bad preconditions for the integration of eastern and western Germans as equal partners in a joint enterprise, even in the next generation.

The unification of Germany was a stunning success in modernizing the infrastructure in the former GDR and in equalizing the consumption opportunities in east and west. It has also established the same formal political rights across Germany. With the help of truly dedicated eastern and western public servants, such as the police officers of precinct 66 in Berlin and the Potsdam police station in Brandenburg, a functioning public administration could be built up everywhere on the territory of the former GDR. While there are remarkable stories of economic entrepreneurship and investment in eastern Germany, the former GDR has also been ruthlessly exploited by slash-and-burn capitalists. However, the unification of Germany has not yet created equality of participation in wealth and power, and it has not yet created the same sense of belonging in both parts of Germany. Thus Germany remains divided in unity. This does not mean that this division could not be overcome by decisive political commitment to equalize life-chances while acknowledging, ironically, that easterners and westerners are different.

ACRONYMS OR ABBREVIATIONS

ABV	Abschnittsbevollmächtigter (People's Police beat patrol officer)
CDU	Christlich Demokratische Union (Christian Democratic Party)
DVP	Deutsche Volkspolizei (People's Police)
FDJ	Freie Deutsche Jugend (Free German Youth)
FDP	Freie Demokratische Partei (Liberal Democratic Party)
FRG	Federal Republic of Germany
GDR	German Democratic Republic
Gestapo	Geheime Staatspolizei (secret police of the Nazi period)
KOBB	Kontaktbereichsbeamter (Berlin Police beat patrol officer)
KPD	Kommunistische Partei Deutschlands (Communist Party)
MdI	Ministerium des Innern (of the GDR) (Ministry of the Interior)
NATO	North Atlantic Treaty Organization
NSDAP	Nationalsozialistische deutsche Arbeiterpartei (National Socialist Workers' Party)
PDS	Party of Democratic Socialism (reformed communist party)
SED	Sozialistische Einheitspartei Deutschlands (Socialist Unity Party)
SPD	Sozialdemokratische Partei Deutschlands (Social Democratic Party)
Stasi	Staatssicherheitsdienst (secret police of the GDR)
ZERV	Zentrale Ermittlungsstelle Regierungs und Vereinigungskriminalität (Central Investigative Unit for Government and Unification Crime)

REFERENCES

Appiah, Kwame Anthony, and Henry Louis Gates, Jr., eds. 1995. *Identities*. Chicago: University of Chicago Press.

Applebaum, Herbert. 1992. *The Concept of Work: Ancient, Medieval, and Modern*. Albany, NY: State University of New York Press.

Arendt, Hannah. 1958. *The Human Condition*. Chicago: University of Chicago Press.

Aristotle. 1957. *Politics*. Edited by W. D. Ross. Oxford: Oxford University Press.

———. 1990. *Poetics*. Translated by Leon Golden, with comments by O. B. Hardinson Jr. Tallahassee, FL: Florida State University Press.

Ariès, Philippe, and Georges Duby, eds. 1991 [1987]. *A History of Private Life*. 5 vols. Cambridge: Harvard University Press.

Auerbach, Erich. 1946. *Mimesis: Dargestellte Wirklichkeit in der abendlänischen Literatur*. Tübingen: Francke.

Austin, John L. 1956. "A Plea for Excuses." In *Proceedings of the Aristotelian Society 59*: 1–30.

———. 1962. *How to Do Things with Words*. Cambridge: Harvard University Press.

Bachelard, Gaston. 1969 [1958]. *The Poetics of Space*. Translated by Maria Jolas. Boston: Beacon Press.

Bakhtin, Mikhail M. 1981 [1975]. *The Dialogic Imagination: Four Essays*. Edited by Michael Holquist, translated by Caryl Emerson and Michael Holquist. Austin: University of Texas Press.

———. 1984a [1963]. *Problems of Dostoevsky's Poetics*. Edited and translated by Caryl Emerson. Minneapolis: University of Minnesota Press.

———. 1984b [1965]. *Rabelais and His World*. Translated by Helene Iswolsky. Bloomington: Indiana University Press.

Barthes, Roland. 1977. "Introduction to the Structural Analysis of Narratives." In *A Barthes Reader*, edited by Susan Sontag. New York: Noonday Press.

Bateson, Gregory. 1972. *Steps to an Ecology of Mind: Collected Essays in Anthropology, Psychiatry, Evolution, and Epistemology*. San Francisco: Chandler.

353

Battaglia, Deborah. 1990. *On the Bones of the Serpent: Person, Memory, and Mortality in Sabarl Island Society.* Chicago: University of Chicago Press.

Battaglia, Deborah. 1995a. "Problematizing the Self: A Thematic Introduction." In Battaglia, ed. 1995b.

———, ed. 1995b. *The Rhetorics of Self-Making.* Berkeley: University of California Press.

Baudrillard, Jean. 1990 [1979]. *Seduction.* Translated by Brian Singer. New York: St. Martin's Press.

Becker, Howard. 1977 [1970]. *Sociological Work.* New Brunswick, NJ: Transaction Books.

———. 1982. *Art Worlds.* Berkeley: University of California Press.

Behnke, Klaus. 1995. "Lernziel Zersetzung: Die Operative Psychologie in Ausbildung, Forschung, und Anwendung." In Behnke and Fuchs 1995.

Behnke, Klaus, and Jürgen Fuchs, eds. 1995. *Zersetzung der Seele: Psychologie und Psychatrie im Dienste der STASI.* Hamburg: Rotbuch.

Bell, Daniel. 1988 [1960]. *The End of Ideology.* Cambridge: Harvard University Press.

Bellah, Robert N.; Richard Madsen; William M. Sullivan; Ann Swidler; and Steven M. Tipton. 1986. *Habits of the Heart: Individualism and Commitment in American Life.* New York: Harper and Row.

Benda, Ernst; Werner Maihofer; and Hans-Jochen Vogel, eds. 1983. *Handbuch des Verfassungsrechts der Bundesrepublik Deutschland.* Berlin: de Gruyter.

Bendix, Reinhard. 1974 [1956]. *Work and Authority in Industry: Ideologies of Management in the Course of Industrialization.* Berkeley: University of California Press.

Benjamin, Walter. 1983. *Das Passagen-Werk.* Frankfurt/M: Suhrkamp.

Benveniste, Emile. 1971 [1966]. *Problems in General Linguistics.* Coral Gables, FL: University of Miami Press.

Berger, Peter L., and Thomas Luckmann. 1967 [1966]. *The Social Construction of Reality: A Treatise in the Sociology of Knowledge.* New York: Anchor Books.

Berman, Harold J. 1963. *Justice in the U.S.S.R.* Cambridge: Harvard University Press.

Bittner, Egon. 1990. *Aspects of Police Work.* Boston: Northeastern University Press.

Blumer, Herbert. 1969. *Symbolic Interactionism: Perspective and Method.* Englewood Cliffs, NJ: Prentice-Hall.

Borneman, John. 1992. *Belonging in the Two Berlins: Kin, State, Nation.* Cambridge: Cambridge University Press.

———. 1998. *Subversions of International Order: Studies in the Political Anthropology of Culture.* Albany, NY: State University of New York Press.

Bourdieu, Pierre. 1977 [1972]. *Outline of a Theory of Practice* [Esquisse d'une theorie de la pratique]. Cambridge: Cambridge University Press.

———. 1984. *Distinction: A Social Critique of the Judgment of Taste.* Cambridge: Harvard University Press.

Brooks, Peter. 1984. *Reading for the Plot: Design and Intention in Narrative.* Cambridge: Harvard University Press.

Brubaker, Rogers. 1992. *Citizenship and Nationhood in France and Germany.* Cambridge: Harvard University Press.

Bruner, Jerome. 1990. *Acts of Meaning.* Cambridge: Harvard University Press.

Buber, Martin. 1995. *Ich und Du* [I and thou]. Stuttgart: Philip Reclam jun.

Burawoy, Michael. 1979. *Manufacturing Consent: Changes in the Labor Process under Monopoly Capitalism.* Chicago: University of Chicago Press.

———. 1992. *The Radiant Past: Ideology and Reality in Hungary's Road to Capitalism.* Chicago: University of Chicago Press.

———. 1998. "The Extended Case Method." *Sociological Theory* 16:1.

Burckhardt, Jacob. 1956 [1860]. *The Civilization of the Renaissance in Italy.* Translated by S. G. C. Middlemore. Vienna: Phaidon Press.

———. 1988 [1860]. *Die Kultur der Renaissance in Italien: Ein Versuch.* 11th ed. Stuttgart: Körner.

Burke, Kenneth. 1969a [1945]. *A Grammar of Motives.* Berkeley: University of California Press.

———. 1969b [1950]. *A Rhetoric of Motives.* Berkeley: University of California Press.

Butler, Judith. 1990. *Gender Trouble.* London: Routledge.

Butler, William Elliot. 1988. *Soviet Law.* Stoneham, MA: Butterworths Legal Publishers.

Calhoun, Craig. 1991. "Morality, Identity, and Historical Explanation: Charles Taylor on the Sources of the Self." *Sociologial Theory* 10: 2.

———. 1995. *Critical Social Theory: Culture, History, and the Challenge of Difference.* Oxford: Blackwell.

———, ed. 1994. *Social Theory and the Politics of Identity.* Oxford: Blackwell.

Carrithers, Michael; Steven Collins; and Steven Lukes, eds. 1985. *The Category of the Person: Essays on Marcel Mauss.* Cambridge: Cambridge University Press.

Certeau, Michel de. 1984. *The Practice of Everyday Life.* Translated by Steven Randall. Berkeley: University of California Press.

Clifford, James. 1988. *The Predicament of Culture: Twentieth-Century Ethnography, Literature, and Art.* Cambridge: Harvard University Press.

Clifford, James, and George Marcus, eds. 1986. *Writing Culture: The Poetics and Politics of Ethnography.* Berkeley: University of California Press.

Coles, Robert. 1986. *The Moral Life of Children.* Boston: Houghton Mifflin.

Crapanzano, Vincent. 1992. *Hermes' Dilemma and Hamlet's Desire: On the Epistemology of Interpretation.* Cambridge: Harvard University Press.

Culler, Jonathan. 1975. *Structuralist Poetics: Structuralism, Linguistics, and the Study of Literature.* Ithaca, NY: Cornell University Press.

———. 1982. *On Deconstruction: Theory and Criticism after Structuralism.* Ithaca, NY: Cornell University Press.

Czarniawska, Barbara. 1997. *Narrating the Organization: Dramas of Institutional Identity.* Chicago: University of Chicago Press.

D'Andrade, Roy, and Claudia Strauss, eds. 1992. *Human Motives and Cultural Models.* Cambridge: Cambridge University Press.

Danto, Arthur. 1985. *Narration and Knowledge.* New York: Columbia University Press.

Der Polizeipräsident in Berlin. 1994. "Zentrale Ermittlungsstelle Regierungs- und Vereinigungskriminalität." Berlin: Landespolizeiverwaltungsamt II C 33–Polizeiliche Veröffentlichungen 147.

———. 1998. *Festschrift: 150 Jahre Schutzmannschaft 1848-1998.* Berlin: Der Polizeipräsident in Berlin, Referat für Öffentlichkeitsarbeit.

Derrida, Jacques. 1976. *On Grammatology.* Baltimore, MA: Johns Hopkins University Press.

Diemer, Gebhard, and Eberhard Kuhrt. 1994. *Kurze Chronik der Deutschen Frage.* München: Olzog.

Dilcher, Gerhard. 1994. *Politische Ideologie und Rechtstheorie, Rechtspolitik, Rechtswissenschaft.* In Kaelble, Kocka, and Zwahr 1994.

DiMaggio, Paul. 1991. "The Micro-Macro Dilemma in Organizational Research: Implications of Role-System Theory." In Huber 1991.

Douglas, Mary. 1966. *Purity and Danger: An Analysis of the Concepts of Pollution and Taboo.* London: Routledge.

Dumont, Louis. 1986. *Essays on Individualism: Modern Ideology in Anthropological Perspective.* Chicago: University of Chicago Press.

Eco, Umberto 1979 [1976]. *A Theory of Semiotics.* Bloomington, IN: Indiana University Press.

———. 1984 [1979]. *The Role of the Reader: Explorations in the Semiotics of Texts.* Bloomington, IN: Indiana University Press.

Elias, Norbert. 1983 [1969]. *Die höfische Gesellschaft.* Frankfurt/M: Suhrkamp.

Elmer, Karin. 1995. *Ein Vertrauensverhältnis ist zu schaffen.* In Behnke and Fuchs 1995.

Erikson, Erik H. 1962 [1958]. *Young Man Luther: A Study in Psychoanalysis and History.* New York: Norton.

———. 1986 [1950]. *Childhood and Society.* New York: Norton.

Evans, Peter B.; Dietrich Rueschemeyer; and Theda Skocpol, eds. 1985. *Bringing the State Back In.* Cambridge: Cambridge University Press.

Fabian, Johannes. 1983. *Time and the Other: How Anthropology Makes Its Object.* New York: Columbia University Press.

Fernandez, James. 1986. *Persuasions and Performances: The Play of Tropes in Culture.* Bloomington, IN: Indiana University Press.

———. 1991a. "Introduction: Confluents of Inquiry," In Fernandez 1991b.

———, ed. 1991b. *Beyond Metaphor: The Theory of Tropes in Anthropology.* Stanford, CA: Stanford University Press.

Fish, Stanley. 1980. *Is There a Text in This Class? The Authority of Interpretive Communities.* Cambridge: Harvard University Press.

Foucault, Michel. 1969. *Surveillir et Punir.* Paris: Editions Gallimard.

———. 1976. *Histoire de la sexualité, tome I: La volonté de savoir.* Paris: Editions Gallimard.

———. 1984a. *Histoire de la sexualité, tome II: L'usage des plaisirs.* Paris: Editions Gallimard.

———. 1984b. *Histoire de la sexualité, tome III: Le souci de soi.* Paris: Editions Gallimard.

Freud, Sigmund 1960a [1920]. "Jenseits des Lustprinzips." In *Das Ich und das Es und andere metapsychologische Schriften.* Frankfurt/M: S. Fischer.

———. 1960b [1923]. "Das Ich und das Es." In *Das Ich und das Es und andere metapsychologische Schriften*. Frankfurt/M: S. Fischer.

———. 1972 [1938]. *Abriß der Psychoanalyse*. Frankfurt/M: S. Fischer.

———. 1974a [1921]. "Massenpsychologie und Ich-Analyse." In *Kulturtheoretische Schriften*. Frankfurt/M: S. Fischer.

———. 1974b [1929–30]. "Das Unbehagen in der Kultur." In *Kulturtheoretische Schriften*. Frankfurt/M: S. Fischer.

Friedrich, Paul. 1991. "Polytropy." In Fernandez 1991b.

Friedrich, Thomas. 1994. "Aspekte der Verfassungsentwicklung und der individuellen (Grund-) Rechtspositionen in der DDR." In Kaelble, Kocka, and Zwahr 1994.

Frowein, Jochen A. 1983. "Die Rechtslage Deutschlands und der Status Berlins." In Benda, Maihofer, and Vogel 1983.

Frye, Northrop. 1957. *The Anatomy of Criticism: Four Essays*. Princeton, NJ: Princeton University Press.

Fuchs, Jürgen. 1995. "Bearbeiten, dirigieren, zuspitzen: Die "leisen" Methoden des MfS." In Behnke and Fuchs 1995.

Fulbrook, Mary. 1995. *Anatomy of a Dictatorship: Inside the GDR, 1949–1989*. Oxford: Oxford University Press.

Gadamer, Hans-Georg. 1990 [1960]. *Wahrheit und Methode: Grundzüge einer philosophischen Hermeneutik*. 6th ed. Tübingen: J. C. B. Mohr (Paul Siebeck).

———. 1993 [1986]. *Wahrheit und Methode: Ergänzungen*. 2d ed. Tübingen: J. C. B. Mohr (Paul Siebeck).

Garton Ash, Timothy. 1993. *In Europe's Name: Germany and the Divided Continent*. New York: Vintage.

Gauss, Günter. 1983. *Wo Deutschland liegt: Eine Ortsbestimmung*. Hamburg: Hoffmann und Campe.

Gebauer, Gunter, and Christoph Wulf. 1992. *Mimesis: Kultur-Kunst-Gesellschaft*. Reinbek: Rowohlt.

Gebhard, Winfried, and Georg Kamphausen. 1994. *Zwei Dörfer in Deutschland: Mentalitätsunterschiede nach der Wiedervereinigung*. Opladen: Leske+ Budrich.

Geertz, Clifford. 1973. *The Interpretation of Cultures*. New York: Basic Books.

———. 1983. *Local Knowlege: Further Essays in Interpretive Anthropology*. New York: Basic Books.

———. 1988. *Works and Lives: The Anthropologist as Author*. Stanford, CA: Stanford University Press.

Gergen, Kenneth J. 1991. *The Saturated Self: Dilemmas of Identity in Contemporary Life*. New York: Basic Books.

Giddens, Anthony. 1984. *The Constitution of Society: Outline of a Theory of Structuration*. Berkeley: University of California Press.

———. 1991. *Modernity and Self-Identity: Self and Society in the Late Modern Age*. Stanford, CA: Stanford University Press.

Gill, David, and Ulrich Schröter. 1991. *Das Ministerium für Staatssicherheit: Anatomie des Mielke-Imperiums*. Berlin: Rowohlt Berlin.

Goffman, Erving. 1955. "On Face-Work: An Analysis of Ritual Elements in Social Interaction." *Psychiatry* 18: 3.

358 References

——. 1959. *The Presentation of Self in Everyday Life*. New York: Anchor Books.

——. 1961. *Asylums: Essays on the Social Situation of Mental Patients and Other Inmates*. New York: Anchor Books.

——. 1967. *Interaction Ritual: Essays on Face-to-Face Behavior*. New York: Pantheon.

——. 1986 [1974]. *Frame Analysis: An Essay on the Organization of Experience*. Boston: Northeastern University Press.

Grasemann, Hans-Jürgen. 1994. "'Wenn die Partei Weisung gibt, folgen die Richter': Politische Strafjustiz als Instrument von SED und Staatssicherheit." In Weber 1994.

Greenberg, Jay R., and Stephen A. Mitchell. 1983. *Object Relations in Psychoanalytic Theory*. Cambridge: Harvard University Press.

Greenfeld, Liah. 1992. *Nationalism: Five Roads to Modernity*. Cambridge: Harvard University Press.

Gregory, Paul R., and Robert C. Stuart. 1981. *Soviet Economic Structure and Performance*. 2d. ed. New York: Harper & Row.

Grosser, Alfred. 1974. *Geschichte Deutschlands seit 1945*. München: Deutscher Taschenbuch Verlag, 2. Auflage.

Gutman, Amy, ed. 1994. *Multiculturalism: Examining the Politics of Recognition*. Princeton, NJ: Princeton University Press.

Habermas, Jürgen. 1981. *Theorie des Kommunikativen Handelns*. 2 vols. Frankfurt/M: Suhrkamp.

——. 1983. *Moralbewußtsein und kommunikatives Handeln*. Frankfurt/M: Suhrkamp.

——. 1990. "Der DM-Nationalismus: Warum es richtig ist die deutsche Einheit nach Artikel 146 zu vollziehen, also einen Volksentscheid über eine neue Verfassung anzustreben." *Die Zeit*, 30 March 1990.

Hägerstrand, T. 1975. *Space, Time, and Human Conditions*. In Karlqvist 1975.

Hallyn, Fernand. 1990. *The Poetic Structure of the World: Copernicus and Kepler*. New York: Zone.

Hannerz, Ulf. 1992. *Cultural Complexity: Studies in the Social Organization of Meaning*. New York: Columbia University Press.

Harvey, David. 1989. *The Condition of Postmodernity: An Inquiry into the Origins of Cultural Change*. Oxford: Blackwell.

Heidegger, Martin. 1947. "Über den Humanismus: Brief an Jean Beaufret, Paris." In *Platons Lehre von der Wahrheit: Mit einem Brief über den Humanismus*. Bern: Francke.

——. 1986 [1927]. *Sein und Zeit* [Being and time]. 16th ed. Tübingen: Max Niemeyer.

Herbst, Andreas; Winfried Ranke; and Jürgen Winkler, eds. 1994. *So funktionierte die DDR*. 2 vols. Reinbek: Rowohlt.

Herdt, Gilbert. 1994. "Introduction: Third Sexes and Third Genders." In *Third Sex, Third Gender: Beyond Sexual Dimorphism in Culture and History*, edited by Gilbert Herdt. New York: Zone.

Herzfeld, Michael. 1985. *The Poetics of Manhood: Contest and Identity in a Cretan Mountain Village*. Princeton, NJ: Princeton University Press.

————. 1987. *Anthropology Through the Looking-Glass: Critical Ethnography in the Margins of Europe.* Cambridge: Cambridge University Press.

————. 1991. *A Place in History: Social and Monumental Time in a Cretan Town.* Princeton, NJ: Princeton University Press.

————. 1997. *Cultural Intimacy: Social Poetics and the Nation-State.* London: Routledge.

Hesse, Konrad. 1991. *Grundzüge des Verfassungsrechts der Bundesrepublik Deutschland.* 18th ed., enlarged. Heidelberg: C. F. Müller.

Hirschman, Albert O. 1982. *Shifting Involvements: Private Interest and Public Action.* Princeton, NJ: Princeton University Press.

Holquist, Michael. 1990. *Dialogism: Bakhtin and His World.* London: Routledge.

Hosking, Geoffrey. 1990. *The Awakening of the Soviet Union.* Cambridge: Harvard University Press.

Hough, Jerry F., and Merle Fainsod. 1979. *How the Soviet Union Is Governed.* Cambridge: Harvard University Press.

Huber, Joan, ed. 1991. *Macro-Micro Linkages in Sociology.* Newbury Park, CA: Sage.

Hübner, Peter. 1994. "Die Zukunft war gestern: Soziale und mentale Trends in der DDR-Industriearbeiterschaft." In Kaelble, Kocka, and Zwahr 1994.

Hunter, James Davison. 1991. *Culture Wars: The Struggle to Define America.* New York: Basic Books.

Husserl, Edmund. 1987 [1931]. *Cartesianische Meditationen: Eine Einleitung in die Phänomenologie.* Hamburg: Felix Meiner.

Iser, Wolfgang. 1976. *Der Akt des Lesens.* München: Fink.

Jameson, Frederic. 1991. *Postmodernism, or the Cultural Logic of Late Capitalism.* Durham, NC: Duke University Press.

Inglehart, Ronald. 1990. *Culture Shift in Advanced Industrial Society.* Princeton, NJ: Princeton University Press.

Jakobson, Roman. 1960. "Closing Statement: Linguistics and Poetics." In *Style in Language,* edited by Thomas Sebeok. Cambridge: MIT Press.

Joas, Hans. 1985. *G. H. Mead: A Contemporary Re-Examination of his Thought.* Translated by Raymond Meyer. Cambridge: Polity Press.

Johnson, Chalmers, ed. 1970. *Change in Communist Systems.* Stanford, CA: Stanford University Press.

Kaelble, Hartmut; Jürgen Kocka; and Hartmut Zwahr, eds. 1994. *Sozialgeschichte der DDR.* Stuttgart: Klett-Cotta.

Kanter, Rosabeth Moss. 1977. *Men and Women of the Corporation.* New York: Basic Books.

Karlqvist, A. 1975. *Dynamic Allocation of Urban Space.* Farnborough: Saxon House.

Kohl, Helmut. 1996. *Erinnerungen.* Partially reprinted in *Der Spiegel* 40.

Kohli, Martin. 1994. "Die DDR als Arbeitsgesellschaft? Arbeit, Lebenslauf, und soziale Differenzierung." In Kaelble, Kocka, and Zwahr 1994.

Kondo, Dorinne. 1990. *Crafting Selves: Power, Gender, and Discourses of Identity in a Japanese Workplace.* Chicago: University of Chicago Press.

Kripke, Saul A. 1982. *Wittgenstein on Rules and Private Language.* Cambridge: Harvard University Press.

Kuusinen, Otto Wille, ed. 1960. *Grundlagen des Marxismus-Leninismus: Lehrbuch*. Berlin: Dietz.

Ladd, Brian. 1997. *The Ghosts of Berlin*. Chicago: University of Chicago Press.

Laing, R. D. 1969. *Self and Others*. London: Penguin.

Lakoff, George, and Mark Johnson. 1980. *Metaphors We Live By*. Chicago: University of Chicago Press.

Lamont, Michèle. 1992. *Money, Morals, and Manners: The Culture of the French and the American Upper Middle Class*. Chicago: University of Chicago Press.

Lamont, Michèle, and Marcel Fournier, eds. 1992. *Cultivating Differences: Symbolic Boundaries and the Making of Inequality*. Chicago: University of Chicago Press.

Lang, Jochen von. 1991. *Erich Mielke: Eine deutsche Karriere*. Reinbek: Rowohlt.

Lasch, Christopher. 1984. *The Minimal Self: Psychic Survival in Troubled Times*. New York: Norton.

Lash, Scott, and Jonathan Friedman, eds. 1992. *Modernity and Identity*. Oxford: Blackwell.

Lemert, Charles. 1994. *Dark Thoughts about Self*. In Calhoun 1994.

Leonhard, Wolfgang. 1981. *Die Revolution entläßt ihre Kinder*. Cologne: Kiepenheuer & Witsch.

Lewin, Moshe. 1991. *The Gorbachev Phenomenon: A Historical Interpretation*. Expanded ed. Berkeley: University of California Press.

Liang, Hsi-Huey. 1970. *The Berlin Police Force in the Weimar Republic*. Berkeley: University of California Press.

Lienhardt, Godfrey. 1985. *Self, Public and Private: Some African Representations*. In Carrithers, Collins, and Lukes 1985.

Linde, Charlotte. 1993. *Life Stories: The Creation of Coherence*. Oxford: Oxford University Press.

Lüdtke, Alf. 1994. "'Helden der Arbeit'—Mühen beim Arbeiten: Zur Mißmutigen Loyalität von Industriearbeitern in der DDR." In Kaelble, Kocka, and Zwahr 1994.

Luhmann, Niklas. 1982. *Liebe als Passion: Zur Codierung von Intimität*. Frankfurt/M: Suhrkamp.

Machiavelli, Niccolò. 1978 [1532]. *Der Fürst* [The prince]. Stuttgart: Kröner.

Mählert, Ulrich. 1994. "'Die gesamte junge Generation für den Sozialismus begeistern': Zur Geschichte der Freien Deutschen Jugend." In Weber 1994.

Maier, Charles. 1988. *The Unmasterable Past: History, Holocaust, and German National Identity*. Cambridge: Harvard University Press.

———. 1997. *Dissolution: The Crisis of Communism and the End of East Germany*. Princeton: Princeton University Press.

Manning, Peter K. 1977. *Police Work: The Social Organization of Policing*. Cambridge: MIT Press.

Marcus, George E. 1995. "On Eccentricity." In Battaglia 1995b.

Marquart, Bernhard. 1995. "Menschenrechtsverletzungen durch die Deutsche Volkspolizei." In *Equete-Kommission "Aufarbeitung von Geschichte und Folgen der SED-Diktatur in Deutschland."* Vol. 4. *Recht, Justiz, Polizei*. Baden-Baden: Nomos.

Marx, Karl. 1973 [1846]. *Die Deutsche Ideologie.* Vol. 3 of *Werke,* by Karl Marx and Friedrich Engels. Berlin: Dietz.

———. 1974. *Manifest der Kommunistischen Partei.* In Karl Marx, Friedrich Engels: *Werke,* by Karl Marx and Friedrich Engels, vol. 4: 459–93. Berlin: Dietz.

Maunz, Theodor, and Günter Dürig et al., eds. 1963–. *Grundgesetzkommentar.* München: C. H. Beck.

Mauss, Marcel. 1985 [1938]. "A category of the human mind: The notion of person; the notion of self" [Une catégorie de l'esprit humain: La notion de personne, celle de 'moi']. In Carrithers, Collins, and Lukes 1985.

McIntyre, Alasdair. 1984. *After Virtue: A Study in Moral Theory.* 2d. ed. Notre Dame, IN: University of Notre Dame Press.

MdI (Ministerium des Innern der DDR), ed. 1973. *Merkbuch für die Schutzpolizei.* Berlin: Ministerium des Innern der DDR.

———. 1987. *Geschichte der Deutschen Volkspolizei.* 2 vols. Berlin: Deutscher Verlag der Wissenschaften, zweite Auflage.

Mead, George Herbert. 1929. "The Nature of the Past." In *Essays in Honor of John Dewey.* New York: Henry Holt.

———. 1962 [1934]. *Mind, Self, and Society: From the Standpoint of a Social Behaviorist.* Chicago: University of Chicago Press.

Meuschel, Sigrid. 1992. *Legitimation und Parteiherrschaft in der DDR.* Frankfurt/M: Suhrkamp.

Miller, Nancy K., ed. 1986. *The Poetics of Gender.* New York: Columbia University Press.

Moore, Barrington. 1966. *Social Origins of Dictatorship and Democracy: Lord and Peasant in the Making of the Modern World.* Boston: Beacon.

Moore, Sally F. 1978. *Law as Process: An Anthropological Approach.* London: Routlege & Kegan Paul.

———. 1986. *Social Facts and Fabrications: "Customary" Law on Kilimanjaro, 1880–1980.* Cambridge: Cambridge University Press.

———. 1991. "Inflicting Harm Righteously: Turning a Relative into a Stranger: An African Case." In *Fremde der Gesellschaft: Historische und sozialwissenschaftliche Untersuchugen zur Differenzierung von Normalität und Fremdheit,* edited by Marie Theres Fögen. Frankfurt/M: Vittorio Klostermann, 1991.

———. 1993a. "Introduction: Moralizing States and the Ethnography of the Present." In Moore, ed. 1993b.

Moore, Sally F., ed. 1993b. *Moralizing States and the Ethnography of the Present.* Arlington, VA: American Ethnological Society Monograph Series, no. 5.

Müller-Enbergs, Helmut. 1995. "Warum wird einer IM: Motivation bei der inoffiziellen Mitarbeit mit dem Staatssicherheitsdienst." In Behnke and Fuchs 1995.

Nicholson, Linda, and Steven Seidman, eds. 1995. *Social Postmodernism: Beyond Identity Politics.* Cambridge: Cambridge University Press.

Niethammer, Lutz; Alexander von Plato, and Dorothee Wierling. 1991. *Die volkseigene Erfahrung: Eine Archäologie des Lebens in der Industrieprovinz der DDR.* Berlin: Rowohlt Berlin.

Nordlinger, Eric A. 1981. *On the Autonomy of the Democratic State.* Cambridge: Harvard University Press.

Patterson, Orlando. 1991. *Freedom in the Making of Western Culture.* New York: Basic Books.

Pepper, Stephen C. 1966. *World Hypothesis: A Study in Evidence.* Berkeley: University of California Press.

Perrot, Michelle, and Ann Martin-Fugier. 1991. "The Actors." In Ariès and Duby 1991, vol. 4.

Perrot, Michelle, and Roger-Henri Guerrand. 1991. "Scenes and Places," In Ariès and Duby 1991, vol. 4.

Präsidium der Volkspolizei Berlin, ed. 1985. *Zeittafel zur Geschichte der Volkspolizei Berlin 1945–1961.* East Berlin: Präsidium der Volkspolizei Berlin.

———. 1988. *Zeittafel zur Geschichte der Volkspolizei Berlin 1962–1975.* East Berlin: Präsidium der Volkspolizei Berlin.

Prost, Antoine. 1991 [1987]. "Public and Private Spheres in France." In Ariès and Duby 1991, vol. 5.

Reiner, Robert. 1992 [1985]. *The Politics of the Police.* 2d ed. Toronto: University of Toronto Press.

Rektor der HdMI (Hochschule des Ministerium des Innern, formerly Hochschule der Deutschen Volkspolizei), ed. 1990. Wissenschaftliche Beiträge (2/1990). *Polizeidienst—ein Beruf mit demokratischen Traditionen: Grundzüge eines neuen Traditionsbildes für die Polizei in der DDR.* Berlin: HdMI.

Ricoeur, Paul. 1975. *La métaphore vive.* Paris: Seuil.

———. 1984 [1983]. *Time and Narrative* [Temps et récit]. Vol. 1. Translated by Kathleen McLaughlin and David Pellauer. Chicago: University of Chicago Press.

———. 1991. "Life in Quest of Narrative, and Narrative Identity." In *Narrative and Interpretation,* edited by David Wood. London: Routledge, 1991.

———. 1992 [1990]. *Oneself as Another* [Soi-même comme un autre]. Chicago: University of Chicago Press.

Rogers, Carl. 1995 [1961]. *On Becoming a Person: A Therapist's View of Psychotherapy.* Boston: Houghton Mifflin.

Roesler, Jörg. 1994. "Die Produktionsbrigaden in der Industrie der DDR: Zentrum der Arbeitswelt?" In Kaelble, Kocka, and Zwahr 1994.

Rorty, Richard. 1989. *Contingency, Irony, and Solidarity.* Cambridge: Cambridge University Press.

Rubinstein, Jonathan. 1973. *City Police.* New York: Farrar, Straus, Giroux

Saussure, Ferdinand de. 1959. *Course in General Linguistics.* New York: Philosophical Library.

Said, Edward. 1978. *Orientalism.* New York: Vintage.

———. 1992. *Culture and Imperialism.* New York: Vintage.

Sartre, Jean Paul. 1943. *L'être et le néant: Essai d'ontologie.* Paris: Editions Gallimard.

Scherz, Georg. 1991. *Vereinigung der Polizeibehörden: Herausforderungen bei der Integration zweier Polizeibehörden—aus Berliner Sicht.* Paper presented to the conference, "Leading Police Bureaucracies" (Führung von Polizeibehörden), organized by the German Police Leadership Academy (Polizei-Führungsakademie) Münster, 30 September to 2 October 1991.

———. 1995. "Der Weg der Berliner Polizei vom Stadtjubiläum bis zur Wieder-vereinigung (1987–1992): Eine Dokumentation der Ereignisse." Unpublished manuscript.

Schmid, Carlo. 1979. *Erinnerungen*. Bern: Scherz.

Schmidt, Andreas. 1995. "Gegenstrategien: Über die Möglichkeiten sich zu ver-weigern." In Behnke and Fuchs 1995.

Schütz, Alfred, and Thomas Luckmann. 1979. *Strukturen der Lebenswelt*. Vol. 1. Frankfurt/M: Suhrkamp.

———. 1984. *Strukturen der Lebenswelt*. Vol. 2. Frankfurt/M: Suhrkamp.

Searle, John R. 1969. *Speech Acts*. Cambridge: Cambridge University Press.

Selowski, Harold. 1998. "Die Geschichte der Berliner Schutzmannschaft." In Der Polizeipräsident in Berlin, 1998.

Senator für Inneres, ed. 1986. *Verhalten der Polizeibeamten: PDV 350BR*. Berlin: Der Senator für Inneres.

Sennett, Richard. 1990. *The Conscience of the Eye: The Design and Social Life of Cities*. New York: Norton.

Shweder, Richard A., and Edmund J. Bourne. 1984. "Does the Concept of the Person Vary Cross-Culturally?" In Shweder and LeVine 1984.

Shweder, Richard A., and Robert A. LeVine, eds. 1984. *Culture Theory: Essays on Mind, Self, and Emotion*. Cambridge: Cambridge University Press.

Siebert, Horst. 1992. *Das Wagnis der Einheit: Eine wirtschaftspolitische Thera-pie*. Stuttgart: Deutsche Verlags-Anstalt.

Simmel, Georg. 1983 [1888]. "Die Ausdehnung der Gruppe und die Ausbildung der Individualität." In *Georg Simmel, Schriften zur Soziologie*, edited by Heinz-Jürgen Dahme and Otthein Rammstedt Frankfurt/M: Suhrkamp.

———. 1989 [1902]. *Die Philosophie des Geldes*. Frankfurt/M: Suhrkamp.

Sinn, Gerlinde, and Sinn, Hans-Werner. 1992. *Jumpstart: The Economic Unifi-cation of Germany*. Cambridge: MIT Press.

Skocpol, Theda. 1979. *States and Social Revolutions: A Comparative Analysis of France, Russia, and China*. Cambridge: Cambridge University Press.

———. 1985. *Bringing the State Back In: Strategies of Analysis in Current Re-search*. In Evans, Rueschmeyer, and Skocpol 1985.

———, ed. 1984. *Vision and Method in Historical Sociology*. Cambridge: Cam-bridge University Press.

Smith, David John, ed. 1983. *People and Police in London*. 4 vols. London: Policy Studies Institute.

Soja, Edward W. 1989. *Postmodern Geographies: The Reassertion of Space in Critical Theory*. London: Verso.

Somers, Margaret R. 1994). "The Narrative Constitution of Identity: A Rela-tional and Network Approach." *Theory and Society* 23: 605–49.

SPD (Sozialdemokratische Partei Deutschlands) Grundwertekommission. 1987. "Der Streit der Ideologien und die gemeinsame Sicherheit." Partially reprinted in Diemer and Kuhrt 1994, 220–27.

———. 1989. "Berliner Erklärung zur Deutschlandpolitik." In Diemer and Kuhrt 1994, 236–38.

Steinborn, Norbert, and Hilmar Krüger. 1993. *Die Berliner Polizei 1945–1992: Von der Militärreserve im Kalten Krieg auf dem Weg zur bürgernahen Polizei?* Berlin: Berlin Verlag Arno Spitz.

Stryker, Sheldon. 1992. "Identity Theory." In *Encyclopedia of Sociology*, edited by E. F. Borgatta and M. L. Borgatta. New York: Macmillan.

Suckut, Siegfried. 1994. "Die DDR Blockparteien im Lichte neuer Quellen." In Weber 1994, 99–198.

Taylor, Charles. 1989. *Sources of the Self: The Making of Modern Identity.* Cambridge: Harvard University Press.

———. 1992. *The Ethics of Authenticity.* Cambridge: Harvard University Press.

———. 1994. "The Politics of Recognition." In Gutman 1994.

Taussig, Michael. 1993. *Mimesis and Alterity: A Particular History of the Senses.* London: Routlege.

Todorov, Tzvetan. 1981. *Introduction to Poetics,* translated by Richard Howard. Minneapolis: University of Minnesota Press.

———. 1992 [1982]. *The Conquest of America: The Question of the Other.* New York: HarperPerennial.

Trilling, Lionel. 1972. *Sincerity and Authenticity: The Charles Eliot Norton Lectures, 1969–70.* Cambridge: Harvard University Press.

Turner, Terence. 1991. "We Are Parrots," "Twins Are Birds": Play of Tropes as Operational Structure. In Fernandez 1991b.

Turner, Victor. 1974. *Dramas, Fields, and Metaphors: Symbolic Action in Human Society.* Ithaca, NY: Cornell University Press.

Urry, John. 1995. *Consuming Places.* London: Routledge.

Vaillant, George. 1993. *The Wisdom of the Ego.* Cambridge: Harvard University Press.

Van Maanen, John. 1988. *Tales of the Field: On Writing Ethnography.* Chicago: University of Chicago Press.

Verdery, Katherine. 1996. *What Was Socialism, And What Comes Next?* Princeton: Princeton University Press.

Vico, Giambattista. 1968 [1744]. *The New Science* [Scienza nuova]. Translated by Thomas Goddard Bergin and Max Harold Fisch. Ithaca, NY: Cornell University Press.

Vogel, Hans-Jochen. 1983. "Die bundesstaatliche Ordnung des Grundgesetzes." In Benda, Maihofer, and Vogel 1983, 809–62.

Vollnhals, Clemens. 1994. "Ausführendes Organ der Diktatur des Proletariats: Das Ministerium für Staatssicherheit." In Weber 1994.

Walder, Andrew. 1986. *Communist Neo-Traditionalism: Work and Authority in Chinese Industry.* Berkeley: University of California Press.

Weber, Herrmann. 1991. *Grundriß der Geschichte der DDR 1945–1990.* Hannover: Fackelträger.

———, ed. 1994. *Der SED-Staat: Neues über eine vergangene Diktatur.* München: Olzog.

Weber, Max. 1980 [1922]. *Wirtschaft und Gesellschaft* [Economy and society]. 5th ed. Tübingen: J. C. B. Mohr (Paul Siebeck).

———. 1988a [1920]. *Gesammelte Aufsätze zur Religionssoziologie.* Vol. 1. Tübingen: J. C. B. Mohr (Paul Siebeck).

————. 1988b. "Politik als Beruf." In *Gesammelte Aufsätze zur Politik*. Tübingen: J. C. B. Mohr (Paul Siebeck).

Weigert, Andrew J.; J. Smith Teitge; and Dennis W. Teitge. 1986. *Society and Identity: Toward a Sociological Psychology*. Cambridge: Cambridge University Press.

Weintraub, Karl Joachim. 1978. *The Value of the Individual: Self and Circumstance in Autobiography*. Chicago: University of Chicago Press.

White, Hayden. 1973. *Metahistory: The Historical Imagination in Nineteenth-Century Europe*. Baltimore: Johns Hopkins University Press.

Willis, Paul. 1981. *Learning to Labor: How Working-Class Kids Get Working-Class Jobs*. New York: Columbia University Press.

Wise, Michael. 1998. *Capital Dilemma: Germany's Search for a New Architecture of Democracy*. New York: Princeton Architectural Press.

Wittgenstein, Ludwig. 1984 [1953]. *Philosophische Untersuchungen*. Vol. 1 of *Werkausgabe*. Frankfurt/M: Suhrkamp.

Wollenberger, Vera. 1993. "Eine zweite Vergewaltigung." In *Aktenkundig*, edited by Hans Joachim Schädlich. Reinbek: Rowohlt.

Young, Malcolm. 1991. *An Inside Job: Policing and Police Culture in Britain*. Oxford: Clarendon Press.

Young, Richard A., and Audrey Collin. 1992a. "Constructing Career through Narrative and Context: An Interpretive Perspective." In Young and Collin 1992b.

————, eds. 1992b. *Interpreting Career*. Westport, CT: Praeger.

Zelikow, Philip, and Rice Condoleezza. 1995. *Germany Unified and Europe Transformed: A Study in Statecraft*. Cambridge: Harvard University Press.

Žižek, Slavoj. 1997. *The Plague of Fantasies*. London: Verso.

Zukin, Sharon. 1991. *Landscapes of Power: From Detroit to Disney World*. Berkeley: University of California Press.

ZERV (Zentrale Ermittlungsstelle für Regierungs und Vereinigungskriminalität). 1993. *Jahresbericht*. Berlin: ZERV.

————. 1994. *Jahresbericht*. Berlin: ZERV.

Unpublished Documents

Der Polizeipräsident in Berlin. 1991a. Abteilung Aus- und Fortbildung. *Kurzdarstellung der Aus- und Fortbildungskonzepte in den neuen Bundesländern: hier Berlin*.

————. 1991b. Abteilung Aus- und Fortbildung. *Studienanleitung der Jahreslehrgänge für ehemalige Volkspolizisten zur Verwendung im mittleren und gehobenen Polizeivollzugsdienst*.

MfIA (Ministerium für Innere Angelegenheiten). 1990. *Das Ministerium für Innere Angelegenheiten in der gesellschaftlichen Erneuerung: Bestandsaufnahme und Schlußfolgerungen*. Unpublished schooling material for all offices of the MfIA.

SenInn (Senatsverwaltung für Inneres). 1990a. Referat C. III. *Arbeitsgruppe Um-, Aus- und Fortbildung*. 6 vols.

————. 1990b. Referat III E1. *Vergleich der Studien- und Ausbildungsinhalte für den Erwerb der Befähigung für die einzelnen Laufbahngruppen des Berliner Polizeivollzugsdienstes mit denen der ehemaligen Volkspolizei.* 27 November 1990.

————. 1990c. Referat III E. *Dienstrechtliches und organisatorisches Verfahren der Eingliederung der ehemaligen Dienstkräfte der Volkspolizei in den Polizeivollzugsdienst des Landes Berlin.* 22 December 1990.

————. 1990d. Referat III E. *Hinweise zur Auswertung des Personalfragebogens für die Angehörigen der ehemaligen unteren und mittleren Dienstlaufbahn der Volkspolizei (DVP).* 22 December 1990.

————. 1990e. Referat III E. *Hinweise zur Auswertung des Personalfragebogens für die Angehörigen der ehemaligen höheren Dienstlaufbahn der Volkspolizei (DVP).* 14 December 1990.

————. 1990f. Referat III E2. *Tätigkeiten oder Eigenschaften, die eine Verwendung im höheren Dienst des Landes Berlin in der Regel ausschließen* and *Tätigkeiten oder Eigenschaften, die eine Verwendung im gehobenen Dienst des Landes Berlin in der Regel ausschließen.* November 1990.

————. 1991. *Mitteilungen der Koordinierungs- und Beratungsstelle Nr.1: Zumutbarkeit der Weiterbeschäftigung von Personen, die als offizielle oder inoffizielle Mitarbeiter für das MfS tätig waren.*

————. 1992. *Mitteilungen der Koordinierungs- und Beratungsstelle Nr.2: Prüfung der persönlichen Eignung von Mitarbeitern und Bewerbern aus dem Beitrittsgebiet.*

————. 1994. *Mitteilungen der Koordinierungs- und Beratungsstelle Nr. 3: Dienstrechtliche Beurteilung der Tätigkeit für das MfS.*

INDEX

abortion laws, 95n.8
accession (of GDR to FRG). *See* Basic
  Law: accession by other territories;
  state: annexation by another; unification, German (1990): historical
  process
accession area (name for territory of
  former GDR), 97
action, communicative. *See* performance
Adenauer, Konrad, 106, 326n.4
Afghanistan, 108
agency: acknowledgement of boundaries of, 244; assertion of, 32,
  220–21; attribution in Stasi collaboration, 279, 283; in choosing professions, 86–87, 302; initiative at
  work and, 198–202; in poetics,
  209–10, 220–22; of state, 257
  strategical, 60n.31, 65–66; tacti-
  cal, 60n.31, 65–66. *See also* space,
  writing of
Aida (Verdi), 263
alienation, 11n.13
alliance building. *See* emplotment
Alliance for Germany, 115n.37
Allied powers. *See* France; Great Britain; Soviet Union; United States
allochronization: defined, 146; east-

ern participation in own, 152,
  329; eastern reaction to western,
  150–63; compared with narrative,
  147; western, of east, 148–50,
  325, 330. *See also* dialogue; time
anomie, 11n.13
archival data, 24
Arendt, Hannah, 223n.63, 295
Aristotle, 206, 214n.48, 295
assimilation, western expectation of
  eastern, 59, 162–63, 183, 325–
  26, 329, 344–50
associations, voluntary, 83
attitude-behavior link, 180n.56
authenticity: local, 75; in German history, 102, 183; and identity, modernist and postmodernist theories
  of, 11n.13, 332–33; sincerity and,
  235–36

Babelsberg: borough of Potsdam, 39;
  police station, 39–40
Bachelard, Gaston, 78n.49
Bakhtin, Michael, 42, 81, 291. *See
  also* chronotope; dialogue
Balkans, 83
Baltic seashore, 83
barter exchange, meaning derived
  from, 176